Geographies of Seapower

Geographies of Seapower

Forging Empire in the Andaman and
Nicobar Islands

Callum James O'Connell

Republish
Academic Press

Copyright © Callum James O'Connell, 2025

This work is published by Republish Academic Press

Republish Academic Press is an imprint of Republish LTD, registered in England, company number 15026646, of Cell Block Studios, Portsmouth, Hampshire, PO1 3LJ.

www.republish.uk
info@republish.uk

First published in Portsmouth, UK in 2025.

This book underwent a double-blind peer review process, with one external reviewer. The author also acknowledges the additional support in reviewing provided by:
Dr Matthew Heaslip, Dr Cathryn Pearce, Dr Mathias Seiter, and Dr Ronald Po.

This work is available in multiple formats:

A free, open access (Creative Commons license CC BY-NC 4.0) digital version of this book is available at: www.republish.uk

ePDF ISBN: 978-1-0684943-0-7

Print and ePUB editions are not open access and are not covered by the Creative Commons license. All rights reserved. No part of this book may be reproduced, stored, or transmitted in any form or by any means, electronic or mechanical, without the prior written permission of the publisher, except where permitted by license or law.

Hardback ISBN: 978-1-0684943-1-4
Paperback ISBN: 978-1-0684943-2-1
eBook ISBN: 978-1-0684943-3-8

A catalogue record for this book is available from the British Library.

Cover design: Republish LTD
Editing: Watershed Creative LTD
Typeset: Garper Design
Maps: Catherine Evans

Every effort has been made to trace copyright holders and obtain permission for the use of any third-party material in this book. If any material has been inadvertently included without permission, the publisher will be grateful to correct any omissions and provide proper acknowledgement.

Printed in the United Kingdom by: Print on Demand

Cover images:
Top: Moore, Joseph. The Harbour of Port Cornwallis. Island of Great Andaman with the Fleet Getting Under Weigh for Rangoon. 1824. Watercolour on Paper. © British Library.
Middle Right: Kloss, C. Boden. Nankauri Canoe with Festival Decorations. 1903. Photograph. In The Andamans and Nicobars. Public domain. Colour added by the author.
Bottom Left: Norrie, J. 'Chart of the Andaman and Nicobar Islands, with the Adjacent Continent'. London: Navigation Warehouse and Naval Academy, 1856. Public domain.
Bottom Centre: London Illustrated News. Exploring Barren Island, 1858. Pen and Ink. Public domain. Colour added by the author.
Bottom Right: London Illustrated News. Expedition to the Andaman Islands, 27 March 1858. 1858. Pen and Ink. Public domain. Colour added by the author.

For Carol

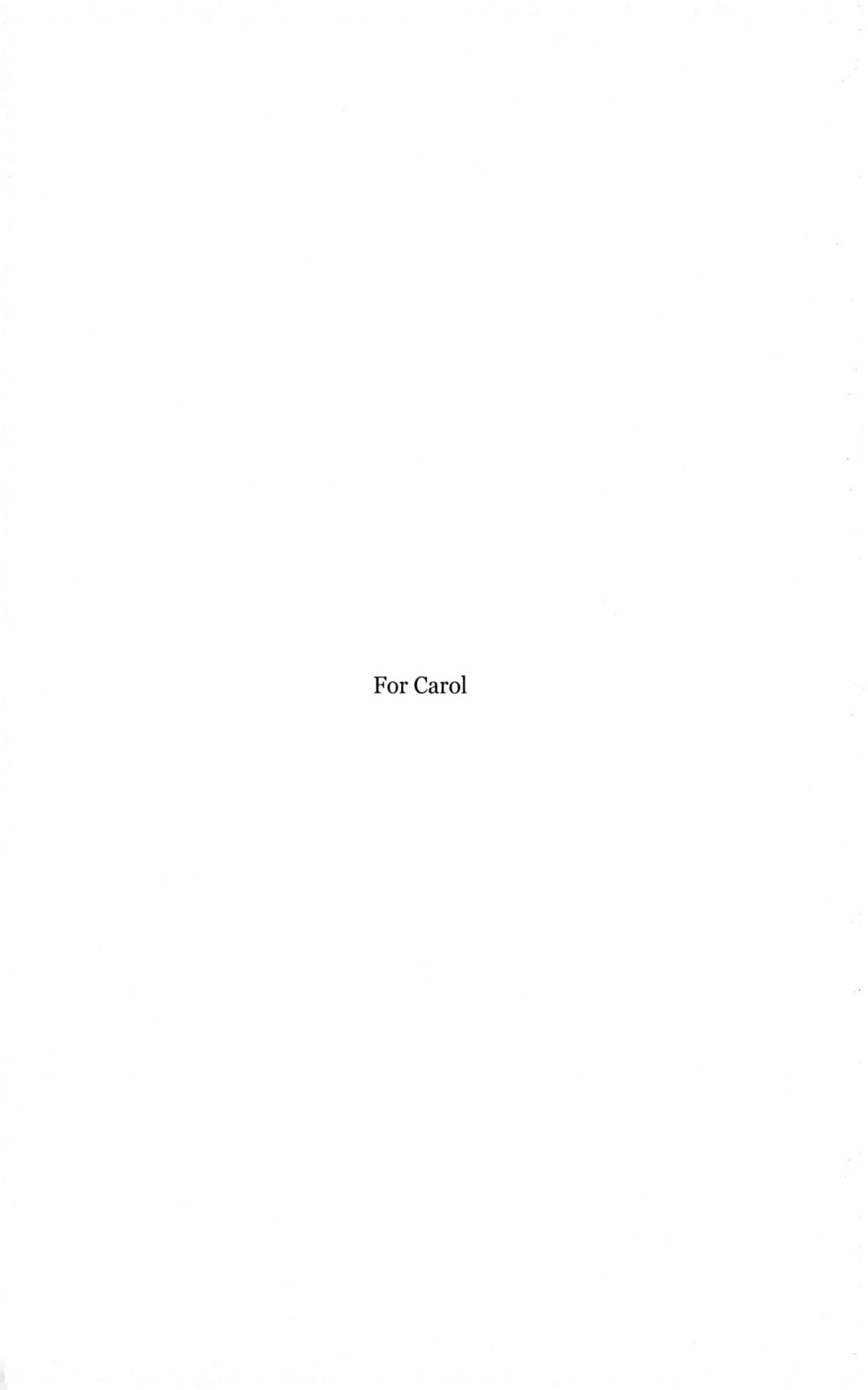

Table of Contents

Introduction
What is Imperial Seapower?   5
Historiography of the Andaman and Nicobar Islands   8
Towards a Refined Understanding of Power at Sea   9

Chapter One: The Bay of Bengal as a British Sea, 1842–1856
SLOC in the Bay of Bengal   18
Disturbances in Pursuit of a *British Sea*   25
Challenges to a *British Sea* – European States   26
Challenges to a *British Sea* – Asian States   28
Savages and Tropicality   31
Who Commands the *British Sea*?   33
Imperial Narratives and Influence on Seapower   38
What next for the *British Sea*?   42

Chapter Two: Island Disturbances and Informal Imperial Defence, 1842–1858
Insecurities in the Imperial Maritime Network   50
Tropical Storms and Weather as an Immobiliser   56
Representation of 'Uncivilised Seas'   60
Colonial Governance and Maritime Security   63
Distant Rebellion Comes Closer   66
Development of an Informal Imperial Defence   69
Colonisation and Imperial Defence   72

Chapter Three: Constructing Geographies: Exploration and Seapower, 1857–1863

Exploration, *Terra Nullius*, and Seapower in the 1850s	79
The Andaman Committee Survey, 1857	84
From the Sea and Into the Field	91
Circulating Knowledge from Calcutta to Kensington	94
Exploration and Imperial Expansion from the Sea	98
Colonisation by Committee	103

Chapter Four: Inscribing Seapower: Hydrography and Networks of Knowledge, 1860–1866

Hydrography in the Bay of Bengal, 1850s to 1860s	111
The East India Company Survey Work, 1789–1795	115
Indian Navy Survey Work, 1860–1866	119
Collecting Data at Sea	125
Circulating the Knowledge	129
Knowledge and Seapower	132
Hydrography and Imperial Authority	136

Chapter Five: Gunboats and Policing: The Little Andaman Campaign, 1867

Gunboats and Policing in the Bay of Bengal in the 1860s	143
Little Andaman Campaign, 1867	147
Gunboats and Other 'Workhorses' of Navies	161
Performing Statehood and Seapower	165

Chapter Six: Blockade, Piracy and Annexation: The Nicobars, 1867–1872

Blockades, Piracy and British Interests in the Bay of Bengal	173
Nicobar Expeditions, 1866-1869	177
From Piracy to Annexation	195
Formation of Andaman and Nicobar Islands	200

Conclusion	203
Acknowledgements	221
Bibliography	223
Notes	253
Index	307

ILLUSTRATIONS

Figure 1: 'Map Illustrating the Great Divisions of British India'. London: W.H. Allen of London, 1871. Public domain.

Figure 2: 'Map of the World Showing the Extent of the British Empire in 1886'. London: The Graphic, 1886. Public domain.

Figure 3: Moore, Joseph. The Harbour of Port Cornwallis. Island of Great Andaman with the Fleet Getting Under Weigh for Rangoon. 1824. Watercolour on Paper. © British Library.

Figure 4: Hullmandel & Walton Lithographers, and Joseph Darvall. 1845. Lithograph. The Wreck on the Andamans Series. Public domain. Colour added by the author (Hardback edition only).

Figure 5: London Illustrated News. The Andamans (The King of Delhi's Prison Island) 27 March 1858. 1858. Pen and Ink. Public domain. Colour added by the author (Hardback edition only).

Figure 6: Author. Photograph of the Cellular Jail, Port Blair. 2023. Photo. © Author.

Figure 7: Author. Abandoned Settlement on Ross Island, Port Blair. 2023. Photo. © Author.

Figure 8: London Illustrated News. Expedition to the Andaman Islands, 27 March 1858. 1858. Pen and Ink. Public domain. Colour added by the author (Hardback edition only).

Figure 9: London Illustrated News. Exploring Barren Island, 1858. Pen and Ink. Public domain. Colour added by the author (Hardback edition only).

Figure 10: Author. Photograph of the Andaman Coastline, Port Blair. 2018. Photo. © Author.

Figure 11: Hydrographic Office. 'Gulf of Bengal, South Andaman I, East Coast, Port Blair'. Old Copy Book, 1861. OCB 514 B1-4. UK Hydrographic Office. Public Domain. Photo by the author.

Figure 12: Colebrooke, Robert. View of Port Cornwallis of the Andaman Islands. 1790. Watercolour on Paper. WD 1476. © British Library.

Figure 13: Weir, Duncan, and Archibald Blair. 'Plan of Port Cornwallis, Great Andaman'. 1800. Misc Charts. C 139. UK Hydrographic Office. Public Domain. Photo by the author.

Figure 14: Norrie, J. 'Chart of the Andaman and Nicobar Islands, with the Adjacent Continent'. London: Navigation Warehouse and Naval Academy, 1856. Public domain

Figure 15: Close up of Chart Title, from: Hydrographic Office. 'Gulf of Bengal, South Andaman I, East Coast, Port Blair'. Old Copy Book, 1861. OCB 514 B1-4. UK Hydrographic Office. Public Domain. Photo by the author.

Figure 16: Close up of Chatham Island Coaling Depot, from: Hydrographic Office. 'Gulf of Bengal, South Andaman I, East Coast, Port Blair'. Old Copy Book, 1861. OCB 514 B1-4. UK Hydrographic Office. Public Domain. Photo by the author.

Figure 17: Author. Photograph From Sea to Shore, Port Blair. 2018. Photo. © Author.

Figure 18: Kloss, C. Boden. Sketch of a Little Andaman Canoe. 1903. Photograph. In The Andamans and Nicobars. Public domain. Colour added by the author.

Figure 19: Wooden screw gun vessel, HMS 'Sylvia. 1866. Photograph. N5395. © National Maritime Museum, Greenwich. Colour added by the author (Hardback edition only).

Figure 20: Kloss, C. Boden. Nankauri Canoe with Festival Decorations. 1903. Photograph. In The Andamans and Nicobars. Public domain. Colour added by the author (Hardback edition only).

Figure 21: Kloss, C. Boden. Inuanga Village, Nankauri Harbour. 1903. Photograph. In The Andamans and Nicobars. Public domain. Colour added by the author (Hardback edition only).

Figure 22: Wooden paddle-wheel sloop, HMS Spiteful. 1873. Photograph. N5395. © National Maritime Museum, Greenwich. Colour added by the author (Hardback edition only).

Figure 23: Port Blair, Andaman Islands, in 1872. 1872. Wood Engraving. Public domain. Colour added by the author (Hardback edition only).

Figure 24: Author. Photograph of Port Blair at Sunset, Port Blair. 2023. Photo. © Author.

Map 1 Bay of Bengal, 1840s–1850s

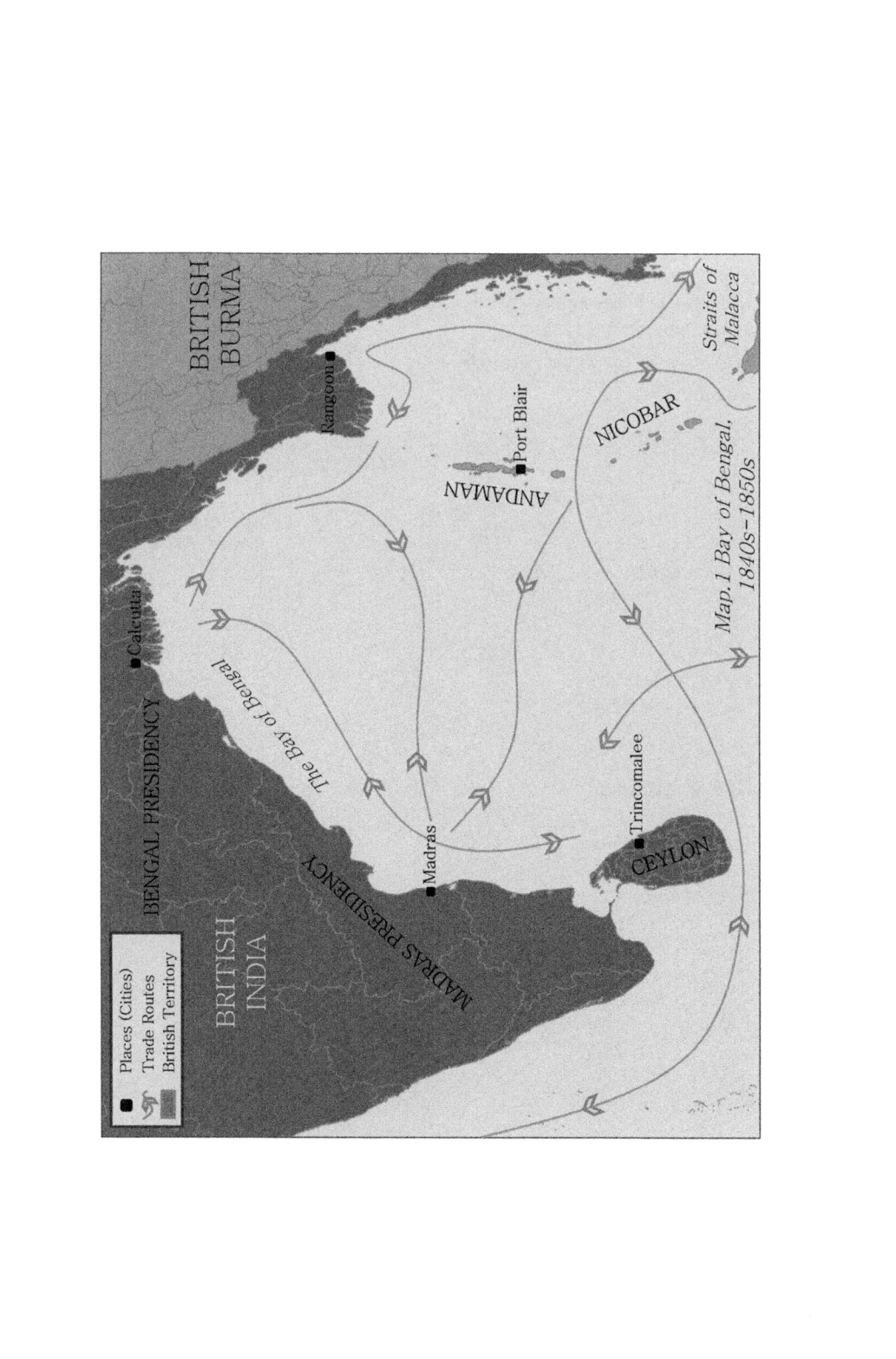

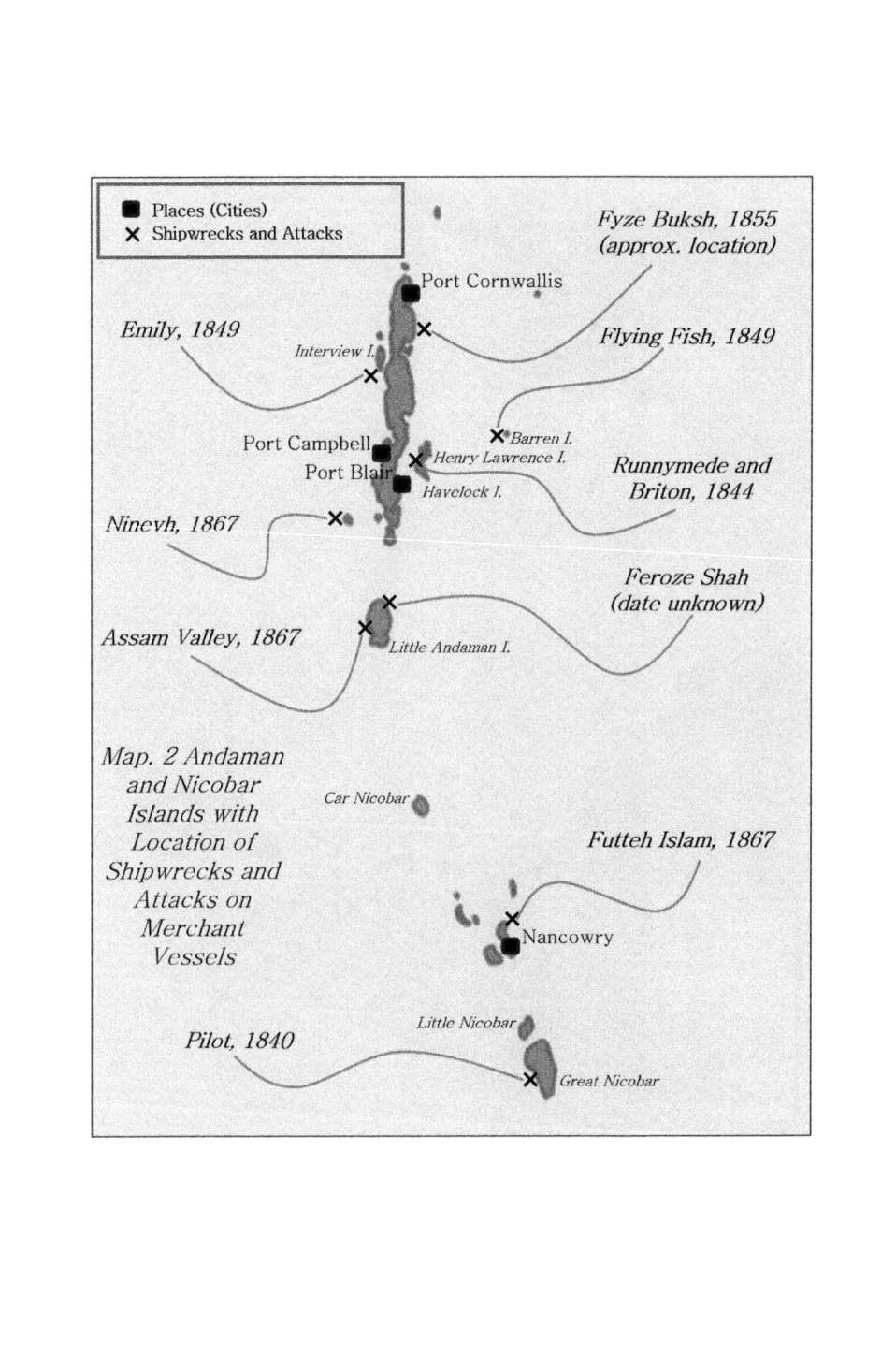

Map. 2 Andaman and Nicobar Islands with Location of Shipwrecks and Attacks on Merchant Vessels

Map. 3 Naval Bases in the 1850s–1860s

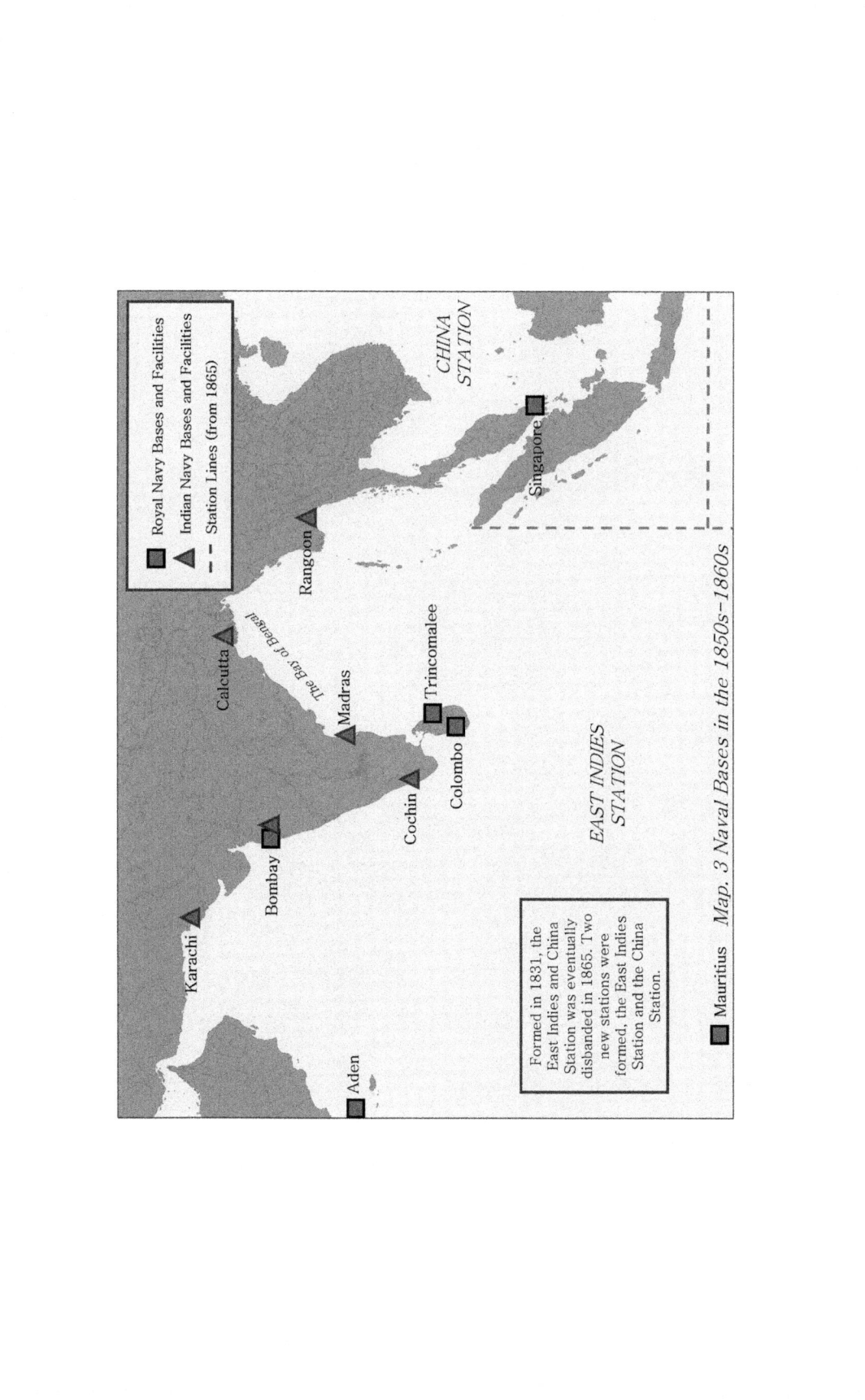

Formed in 1831, the East Indies and China Station was eventually disbanded in 1865. Two new stations were formed, the East Indies Station and the China Station.

INTRODUCTION

In the thick air of the tropics, the Honourable Company Steamer anchored in the deep natural harbour. What seemed an impenetrable jungle hemmed the bay, its dense foliage a barrier to what lay beyond. The crew assembled on the deck of the HCS *Pluto*, setting the shore party – a mix of Indian naval brigadesmen and native infantry – into the workboats to venture ashore. Armed, the shore party rowed into what appeared to be a safe landing space with little reef and light sand. The ground was moist but firm enough for the makeshift flagpole carved from a spare mast. As the shore party formed into ranks, the officer in charge, Captain Henry Man of the Bengal Army, stepped forward with a folded Union Jack in his hands. With some swift rope work and a crisp snap, the flag unfurled, catching the faint breeze that stirred the murky air. The flag ascended the mast slowly, the ropes creaking and saturated with the salt water. A proclamation was read aloud in clear, measured tones, declaring the island now part of British India. For the shore party, the formality of the occasion was dampened by the fecundity of the jungle, mingling with the calls of unseen birds and wildlife which, now, like all on the Islands, came under Crown rule.[1]

This ceremony was a small act in what is now viewed as the grand, relentless march of British maritime control over the Bay of Bengal and the wider Indian Ocean through the 19th century.[2]

It represents the blending of seapower, commercial interests, shifting colonial geographies, and the performative elements of the British imperial state. The ceremony mentioned above is from the annexation of the Andaman Islands on 22 February 1858 in Port Blair.[3] The Andaman Islands, alongside the Nicobar Islands, are the remnants of the Arakan Yoma range in Myanmar (formerly Burma). This range connected to the Indonesian Archipelago before sea levels rose over 25,000 years ago.[4] In the early Victorian era, British government officials considered the Islands strategic for controlling and safeguarding the expansive trade network which crossed the region, being centrally located on the sea trade routes between India and China.

The British permanently maintained a settlement on the Andaman and Nicobar Islands until the Japanese invasion in 1942.[5] This book will, however, focus on the period from 1842 until 1872. The conclusion of the Opium Wars in 1842 saw a dramatic increase in the trade between India and China and, therefore, passing maritime traffic navigating the Andaman and Nicobar waters.[6] This trade was dominated by the East India Company, but included a vast supporting network of British, European, and colonial actors to maintain. As more mariners passed the Islands, they progressively entered the fold of the Empire as a site of perceived savagery, cannibalism, and piracy. These threats to maritime security in the Bay of Bengal required action, including rescue operations, anti-piracy campaigns, and annexations from the Indian Government.[7]

By 1872, the Andaman and Nicobar Islands were annexed and merged under a single Chief Commissioner to administer the Islands, representing a British consolidation of power in the region. 1872 also represents an intriguing juncture in British imperial politics, where Leader of the Opposition Benjamin Disraeli's 'Maintenance of Empire' speech at Crystal Palace in 1872 caught the contemporary zeitgeist towards a more formal treatment of managing the Empire, including its defences.[8] Thus, this period offers an opportunity to view the slow and often informal ways in which imperial seapower forged the expansion of the British Empire in the Bay of Bengal, the challenges to securing imperial trade routes, and how British values and norms were imposed on indigenous communities through naval activity. The use of 'forged' is purposeful. Many of the ways in which British naval actors, including the Royal Navy and East India Company, enforced British rule was violent and sudden.

While the Andaman and Nicobar Islands are the geographical foci, the study of seapower holds the theoretical basis of the ensuing chapters. The study of seapower (or sea power) has traditionally been viewed through the lens of historical patterns, with a focus on controlling the seas in time of war and through state-on-state interactions. Classical seapower scholars, such as Alfred Thayer Mahan and Sir Julian Corbett, who are still prevalent and referenced as foundational texts today, posit that naval power is a neutral and objective instrument of state policy used impartially to achieve political and strategic goals.[9] Power at sea is thus held by the state, and is applied primarily to coerce other states.

Any student of seapower will be well-versed in hearing how Mahanian and Corbettian perspectives will help us understand why navies are vital to a state's security. However, this classical view of seapower neglects how power can manifest below the state and overlooks the role of navies outside of warfighting. The study of great battles, great ships, and great admirals are omnipresent. While these make a fascinating read, they only show one side of the story. Seapower is more than the application of military or commercial control to and from the sea; it also shapes and influences how societies and cultures use and engage the seas. It is an ever-present reality regardless of whether war is approaching or declared.

Put simply, seapower is a form of *power* intended to influence behaviour at *sea*. You may take this as an obvious statement, yet in the study of seapower it is rarely treated with such brevity. This book will instead expand the paradigm in how we look back upon imperial seapower. It will explore the different ways in which power is applied at sea, but also how the sea means different things to different people.

The sea is both a human construction, and a place of distinct physical characteristics. Traditionally in the study of seapower, the physical elements are assessed, from weather and coastlines, fluidity to salinity, and from depths to currents. These elements are often studied in relation to how ships and submarines could operate. A prime example would be how the weather affects sailing ship routes through the 16th to 19th century. These are vitally important to understanding how seapower develops. Nevertheless, there is also a human side to geography which is essential in understanding new perspectives on seapower.

Human geography emphasises the subjective and socially constructed nature of how *space* becomes a *place* of meaning, including the seas. The seas are not just a body of salt water, but a place of communication, a resource, an ecosystem, an economic highway, and a myriad of other interpretations. By combining seapower theory with critical perspectives within contemporary human geography, this interdisciplinary approach provides an opportunity to better understand the cultural, political, and social forces behind the use of navies and imperial control in the Bay of Bengal in the early-to-mid Victorian period.

By showing seapower's geographical antecedents, both physical and human, it enables a deeper understanding of how imperial navies and commerce transformed centuries-old patterns of behaviour in the Bay of Bengal. This includes disrupting the social and cultural norms, and also constructing a new maritime environment that aligned with British imperial expectations.

To speak of geographies of seapower is to recognise that seapower is not simply a projection of power over a neutral, formless sea; it is a practice deeply shaped by spatial, environmental, and human dimensions. It involves the material conditions of the ocean, such as its currents, coasts, islands, and depths. It also includes the human understanding of the seas imposed upon them through mapping, classification, popular culture, and imperial imagination. Seapower emerges from the ability to navigate, control, and assign meaning to maritime space, making it as much a geographical construct as a military or political one.

What is Imperial Seapower?

The Andaman and Nicobar Islands, unlike the Indian mainland, held very little in the realm of exploitable resources in the eyes of the East India Company at the turn of the 19th century. Why then were the Islands considered strategic jewels, essential to British interests? The answer is seapower.

Seapower, or sea power, encompasses a nation's strategic, economic, and military capabilities related to the control and use of the sea. However, there is a slight nuance; sea power is the ability to exert power from and to the sea, whereas *seapower* is a form of power exerted by a state politically and culturally orientated towards the sea.[10] Andrew Lambert defines Britain as a seapower through this book's temporal frame.[11] Hence, the use of *seapower* here.

Seapower signifies a state's ability to project influence, safeguard interests, and maintain security across maritime domains.[12] Historically, seapower has been considered crucial in establishing and maintaining empires, facilitating trade, and asserting dominance.[13] Its components include, but are not limited to, a powerful navy, merchant marine, shipbuilding infrastructure, and strategic naval bases.[14] Seapower is not merely about fleet engagements, for which the popular imagination invokes vast battleships fighting out at sea; it also involves protecting sea lanes, deterring adversaries, and supporting diplomatic efforts through presence and power projection.[15] It reflects a combination of hard power (through naval strength) and soft power (through economic and cultural influence) exerted via maritime space.

The Andaman and Nicobar Islands were located on pivotal shipping routes and were therefore considered essential to British seapower. As seapower means different things to different people, it is worth shaping from the very outset what this book takes as the meaning of *seapower* and why a new approach is needed.

Power is central to seapower. Yet traditionally, the discussion of seapower has taken the 'power' element for granted, treating it as something held by the state and imbued within navies through the application of force. Think gunboats bombarding a city. In a similar vein, power may also be seen as an outcome of naval or commercial power through the lens of hard and/or soft power, such as blockading an economy.[16] While this may be true, there is also a more expansive definition of power prevalent in other disciplines that have integrated postmodernism into their study. Postmodernists view power as decentralised, fluid, and constructed. This contrasts with modern conceptions that often regard power as centralised, hierarchical, and exercised through formal institutions and structures.[17] Postmodernism has expanded the power paradigm, and power has moved beyond the structuralist antecedents, as present in Corbett and Mahan's thinking.

Although there are increasingly critiques of postmodernism as an epistemological framework, there is still value in using elements of the approach to expand the breadth of the study of seapower.[18] Basil Germond's definition of sea power, based on a study of modern to postmodern power, is apt for recognising the breadth of how power can be applied: "an act of power, originating in the sea and one's use of the sea, which consists in influencing other actors' behaviour and creating the necessary conditions for one's own economy to flourish and political system to stabilise and thrive."[19] It is also a very valuable definition as it removes the 'state' as the primary actor. In this instance, the power in seapower is an agency that aims to control or influence behaviour of a variety of different actors to and from the seas, and by a variety of different means. Power can be seen from the muzzle of a cannon, but also the hydrographer's pencil.

The second element of seapower is the *sea*. The sea is a geographical area traditionally associated with a large body of salt water and used interchangeably with oceans.[20] If seapower is fundamentally about control and influence over maritime spaces, where does this control and influence happen? Does it include oceans, seas, channels, chokepoints, littoral and coastal spaces?[21] Without appearing to take the easier option, the answer is all of them. The sea is a geographical construction and means something different to different people. The British saw the seas as a place of commerce and civility, whereas the Andamanese tribes saw it as their home. The same seas, but with very different meaning.

Based on this, I argue for the following definition of imperial seapower: the forms of power applied by imperial naval actors to change the behaviour of an actor or group of actors within a defined geographic space (the sea), over a given period. Each of the following chapters will further explore the different forms of power, the types of imperial naval actor, whose behaviour was intended to change, and in what time frame. It expands upon Germond's work by recognising that while the economy and political system of the British system may have been the driver, there was also an attempt to 'civilise the seas' through seapower. This new approach will demonstrate how the sea was constructed and – in many cases – reconstructed, and finally whose behaviour was intended to change.

The study of seapower *needs* a new approach. Without one, it will remain deterministic in its treatment of both geography and power, and risks oversimplifying complex maritime dynamics that developed through Empire. The intention is not to disprove or remove the likes of Mahan and Corbett, but to show there is a much wider discourse that has value in providing nuanced perspectives of seapower and its role in maintaining empires. This includes improving the understanding of the 'everyday' activities of navies that occur outside warfighting, the sociocultural elements of power at sea, and the complex interactions between geography and seapower that forged imperial space.[22]

Historiography of the Andaman and Nicobar Islands

Having set out the importance of seapower, let's return to the place that scared even the intrepid Sherlock Holmes: "Hum! Hum! What's all this? Moist climate, coral reefs, sharks, Port Blair, convict-barracks... a terror to shipwrecked crews, braining the survivors with their stone-headed clubs, or shooting them poisoned arrows."[23] The Andaman and Nicobar Islands held a contradictory place in the British imperial imagination. The historical narratives of the Islands have often focused on them being a place of 'servitude' as a penal settlement and portraying the indigenous populations as 'savage'.[24] Savagery and servitude narratives continue to permeate not only in academia but also in the contemporary Indian political discourse of the Islands.[25] They were also pivotal nodes for British naval operations and control in the Bay of Bengal.

Historically, the Bay of Bengal was recognised as a critical nexus point connecting the Indian Ocean to the Straits of Malacca and the China Seas in the Victorian period. The 1840s onwards also saw a political nexus during the transition from the East India Company to Crown rule. This period marked a significant shift in British imperial strategy and governance, and the Bay of Bengal, with its strategic location, served as a crucial maritime security hub for controlling trade routes and projecting power across the seas. The decision to colonise the Andaman and Nicobar Islands extended beyond the mere establishment of a penal colony as has been argued before; maritime security and the concern of ensuring British seapower also drove it. This holds considerable contemporary relevance today as China and India increasingly compete over control of vital trade routes in the Indian Ocean, with the Andaman and Nicobar Islands considered the oceanic frontline.[26]

The Andaman and Nicobar Islands already benefit from a rich body of scholarship and source material dominated by postcolonial perspectives, which rightfully look at the racial dimension of the Islands. However, there is increasing scholarship looking at the contemporary strategic value of the Islands for India. Many make the same grandiose statements British officials made in the 18th and 19th centuries, that geography *determines* the Islands' strategic value.[27] The Islands' geographical location has driven policymakers, whether colonial British or contemporary Indian, to determine whether the Islands are strategic. Yet the experience on the ground (inhospitable terrain, the spread of diseases, the difficulty in logistics) does not always match the perception of strategic value.[28]

There is also a fascinating tale upon how the Andaman and Nicobar Islands came to be British sovereign territory at all, which the next chapters will portray. Without seapower, this would not have happened. The East India Company's navy provided the logistics and personnel to explore and chart the Islands, the Royal Navy ensured no other European state could stake a claim, and both navies provided maritime security to protect the fledgling settlement. The Andaman and Nicobar Islands were forged out of British naval power.

Towards a Refined Understanding of Power at Sea

The following chapters will cover everything from cannibalism to cannonballs. They will delve into the economic significance of maritime trade routes in what we now call the Indo-Pacific, the geographical importance of the Islands in strategy and law, how knowledge and science were integral in providing a written form of seapower, and naval operations, including anti-piracy.

Chapter one explores the narratives surrounding the 'British Sea' concept in the Bay of Bengal region. This was a discourse and rhetoric tool used by British strategists and policymakers that claimed the seas as a place of commerce and civility, enthroning British dominance. This chapter assesses the extent to which the notion of a 'British Sea' was a constructed narrative rather than a tangible reality.

Chapter two then delves into the early, informal processes of British imperial defence in the Bay of Bengal through the 1840s and 1850s. It examines the limitations of seapower that prompted the British to establish a settlement on the Andaman Islands, as well as the strategic challenges faced by the British Empire's reliance on naval strength. Drawing on the works of Herbert Richmond and other imperial defence scholars, it explores how the constraints of maintaining a vast maritime empire necessitated the use of island possessions to support and enhance naval operations.[29] Through an analysis of these early defensive strategies, seapower was not based solely upon the might of naval fleets; it was significantly bolstered by the strategic use of islands by the East India Company as logistical hubs, refuelling stations, and surveillance points.

Chapter three investigates the role of seapower in enabling exploration and the transformation of *terra nullius* into British-controlled territories. By applying Alfred Thayer Mahan's geographical components of seapower to the extensive literature on exploration within geography, I will show you how naval power facilitated the discovery, mapping, and subsequent claim of uncharted regions.[30] Coastlines changed to enhance British imperial security. The chapter explores how British expeditions, supported by naval capabilities, were pivotal in redefining vast oceanic spaces into extensions of the British Empire. Seapower constructed statehood and boundaries in the Bay of Bengal, much of which leaves a legacy to this day.

Chapter four delves into the intricate networks of knowledge established through hydrographic activities around the Andaman and Nicobar Islands, examining a form of 'small science' that has often been overlooked in geographical studies. I will examine how detailed mapping and surveying conducted by Indian Navy and Royal Navy officers contributed to an intimate understanding of the Bay of Bengal, which played a critical role in the practical administration and strategic planning of the British Empire. Navies conducted scientific and exploratory functions, which are an essential tool of statecraft and represent knowledge as a form of power.

Chapter five reassesses the role of gunboats in imperial policing, illustrating that the vessels' influence extended beyond technological and armament capabilities. Gunboats had a significant social and cultural dimension of power. Gunboats not only projected hard power through their military presence but also conveyed cultural messages that reinforced imperial dominance. The presence and actions of gunboats were also embedded within broader cultural narratives of civilisation, order, and authority. Gunboats were platforms which shaped interactions between the British Empire and local populations. Studying these interactions offers a more nuanced perspective on the role of naval forces in maintaining and enforcing colonial rule.

Chapter six examines the interplay of piracy, blockades, and race, exploring how these factors led to the annexation of the Nicobar Islands in 1869. I will argue that identity was crucial in these maritime engagements, a dimension often overlooked in traditional seapower studies. It also identifies how racial and cultural identities influenced British naval strategies, including blockades, and regional interactions.[31] The blockade was not just a military tool but a sociocultural tool. Thus, the annexation of the Nicobars is presented not only as a strategic military action but also as a complex process influenced by perceptions of race and identity.

All six chapters of this book share a common theme: a critical reflection on the complex and 'messy' nature of power and the sea. In doing so, the book demonstrates the broader relationship between seapower and the Empire.[32] Seapower is much more than great men, great ships, and great battles. Together, these chapters illustrate that seapower is not just about naval dominance at sea and onto the land, but also cultural hegemony and social control. Imperial seapower influenced sociocultural practices, activities, and behaviours at sea as much as it secured military or commercial dominance. Seapower was used in the Andaman and Nicobar Islands not just as a strategic tool of statecraft to maintain commerce networks, but also a means of forging British values onto this corner of the Bay of Bengal.

CHAPTER ONE

The Bay of Bengal as a British Sea, 1842–1856

In October 1856, a meeting was held in a dimly lit but exquisitely furnished boardroom in Fort William, Calcutta. The President in Council, John Peter Grant, stood tall and resolute as he addressed the room, gazing at fellow civil servants and military men. He spoke of the day's agenda: the Andaman Islands. Pointing to a chart on the wall with a straightened, varnished pointer made from a local banyan tree sapling, he made a sweeping gesture from left to right, highlighting the vast waters stretching from Calcutta to Singapore that represented the territory of the Bengal Presidency. Grant called it a *British Sea*.[33] It was a lifeline for trade and power. He painted a picture of ships sailing unhindered, protected by the might of the Royal Navy and the vigilance of the Indian Navy. He echoed the promise of prosperity through peace.[34]

Pax Britannica, or British Peace, refers to the period of British imperial dominance after the Napoleonic Wars ended in 1815 and up until the start of the First World War in 1914.[35] The British Empire became the global maritime hegemon, and the Royal Navy was unmatched in conventional capabilities, with a vast fleet stationed globally.[36] This naval dominance, it is argued, allowed Britain to ensure the stability of global commerce and expand the Empire, at least until the 1890s when European navies were increasingly viewed as threats.[37] Global historians describe Pax Britannica as a period of relative peace maintained by British economic and naval strength, which was more or less absolute in the Indian Ocean.[38]

However, Pax Britannica is an example of a geopolitical narrative.[39] At its most basic, it is a neat storyline that condenses a complex and vast 100-year period of Britain's imperial activity into a fathomable framework. Although narratives have a place in making geopolitical phenomena accessible, they can oversimplify, reflect biases, and promote misunderstanding. One such narrative was the *British Sea*, a term used by both colonial officers stationed in the region at the time and contemporary scholars to refer to the Bay of Bengal.[40] The Andaman and Nicobar Islands were initially perceived to be of strategic value to Britain's expanding imperial maritime network in the early Victorian period, and thus to the sanctity of the *British Sea* narrative.

The concept of the *British Sea*, or British Lake, reflects the idea that in the 1840s and 1850s, the Bay of Bengal was perceived to be British, both in terms of military control and in expectation of conforming to British values. The narrative was also expanded and used to describe the wider Indian Ocean region by the end of the 19th century.[41] British trade patterns evolved dramatically in the Bay of Bengal during the period between 1842 and 1856, the interlude between the First Opium War (1839–1842) and the Second Opium War (1856–1860). This time frame is critical for understanding the evolving strategic importance of the Bay of Bengal, as the British sea lines of communication (SLOC) expanded significantly in line with the British trade between Chinese and Indian ports, notably opium, tea, silver, and porcelain.[42] Much of this trade would traverse between the Andaman and Nicobar Islands, which were located strategically between the SLOC leaving the Straits of Malacca and into the Bay of Bengal.

Between 1842 and 1856, British trade and commerce transited through the Bay of Bengal in ever greater numbers. It should be noted that much of this trade was previously monopolised by the East India Company. There was, however, a vast network of supporting agents, suppliers, merchants, and intermediaries of various nationalities. The culmination of the Anglo-Burmese war (1852–1853) gave Britain relative stability in the Bay of Bengal from rebellious Asian states and an ability to pursue expanding interests in China.[43] By 1856, the British wished to open Chinese markets further and tested the parameters of the Treaty of Nanjing (1842) by allowing Chinese merchants to register vessels as British in Hong Kong, giving the merchants 'favoured nation status' as defined in the Treaty.[44] Thus, 1856 reflects a turn towards a more aggressive and formal British policy over imperial trade routes, which will be explored in chapter two.

The Bay of Bengal was central to British interests then, but was it a *British Sea*? By deconstructing this narrative, we shall see the challenging realities involved in asserting maritime dominance in a region fraught with piracy, geopolitical rivalries, labyrinthine coastal geographies, and the complexities of colonial administration. It will also show how the Islands were first perceived by British colonial officials as strategic enough to consider colonisation. Stretching from the north of the Bay of Bengal near Burma to the south by Indonesia, the Islands were strategically located along the multiple SLOC that interwove between key imperial trading hubs.

At the time, the Andaman Islands had no permanent European settlement, and the threat of another European state taking sovereignty of the Islands led the Indian Government to pursue some form of settlement on the Andamans in the early 1850s. With that in mind, what were the British perceptions of the Bay of Bengal at the time? What was the role of seapower in forging Empire? The forthcoming narrative exploring the *British Sea* will expand upon the already well-documented political and economic dimensions of British control of this space. It will develop beyond this, to show how the British also expected the Bay of Bengal to conform to British values and ideals of being a 'civilised' sea.[45] Seapower is more than just having a large navy. It is also the ability to change the behaviour of those who live and use the sea towards different ideals and values.

Narrative deconstruction, popularised in critical geopolitics, is a useful tool to demonstrate how narratives have shaped the region's historiography as an imperial space.[46] It helps in critically reflecting on the *British Sea* as a narrative rather than a deterministic description of the Bay of Bengal. Using terms like *British Sea*, or Pax Britannica for that matter, implies a deterministic history and impartial treatment of how seapower contributed to the Empire. By using narrative deconstruction, it is evident that British colonial officials constructed a network of ideals and values based upon how the Bay of Bengal should be and used the *British Sea* as the descriptor. By examining the interplay between these narratives and the realities of naval power at the time, we can better understand the complexities and contradictions inherent in British maritime hegemony.

The *British Sea* is not the only narrative used to explore power at sea, and it is worth exploring the concept of *command of the sea* in the Bay of Bengal. This is to frame the expectations of colonial officials regarding what British military dominance in the region looked like in practice. Sir Julian Corbett, a prominent British naval historian and strategist, published the concept of command of the sea as the ability to control SLOC and deny their use to adversaries in the early 20th century. This was, however, based on his historical analysis of British seapower and its role in protecting imperial trade, which is why it is relevant here.[47] Command of the sea offers a means to frame British naval dominance in the Bay of Bengal but also challenge the determinism of the concept. The *British Sea* was a social construction and so was having *command* of the sea.

Can a state truly have command of the sea? And who has command of the sea, the state's navy or the state itself? These are pertinent questions that will be explored, especially considering the role of the Indian Navy in shaping imperial space.[48] Although John Grainger has comprehensively analysed the collaboration between the Indian Navy and the Royal Navy in this period, his work relies on secondary sources. I will instead integrate primary sources, notably those from the John Charles Mason Collection, to reflect how the Indian Navy contributed to British seapower in the Bay of Bengal between 1842 and 1856 using recently discovered papers.[49]

The first section here will explore British SLOC in the Bay of Bengal and why the Andaman and Nicobar Islands were of frequent interest to the British. The second section delves into Britain's various challenges in maintaining regional dominance and the imperial maritime network. The third section will dissect what is meant by 'British' by exploring the institutions involved in imperial governance and what this means for understanding imperial seapower.

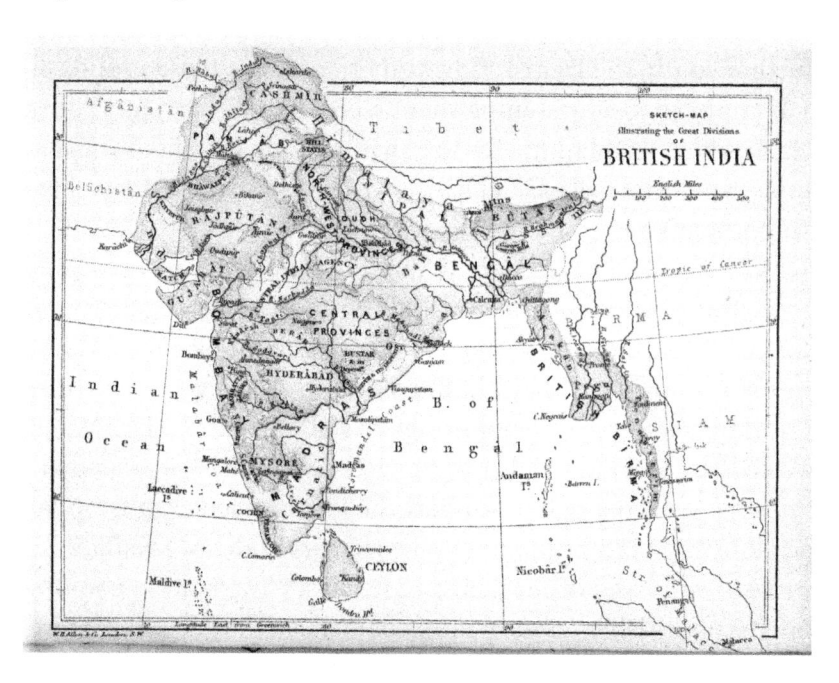

Figure 1: Map of Political Division

SLOC in the Bay of Bengal

The original British colony in the Andaman Islands, established in 1789 by the Government of Bengal, was named Port Cornwallis after the then Governor General of India, Earl Charles Cornwallis, between 1786 and 1793. His brother was Commodore William Cornwallis, the Commander-in-Chief of East Indies Station between 1788 and 1794.[50] The primary purpose of the settlement was to have a port facility that could be protected by a small garrison for use by British naval vessels, thereby ensuring the strategic sailing routes between India and China could be protected.[51] Earl Cornwallis wrote to his brother that the Andamans were of "infinite national importance" due to their locality and would cause significant difficulty for the British if occupied by another state.[52]

Although the British also had interests in the Nicobar Islands further south, the Danish Government claimed these islands on 1 January 1756, christening them New Denmark.[53] The Danish claim added further impetus to a British settlement in the area as trade rapidly increased, and basing for naval vessels and merchant shipping was sought.

While convicts were sent to the settlement between 1789 and 1796, this was to provide cheap labour to clear the vegetation. It was not regarded as a formal penal settlement by either Mouat in his account of the Andamans' history, or by Commodore Cornwallis who instigated the original settlement.[54] Aparna Vaidik also claims that the number of convicts sent to the Andamans was minimal, only enough to support the labour needed to establish a colony, not as a permanent place of servitude for prisoners of British India and other nearby colonies.[55] Evidently, from the origins of British interest in the Andamans in the late 18th century, the strategic naval benefit was the foremost justification for the colonisation of the Islands. Despite its strategic importance, the British colony on the Andaman Islands proved to be commercially unviable and an exceedingly unhealthy place to live. The harsh tropical climate, dense jungle, and prevalence of diseases such as malaria and dysentery made life difficult and dangerous for the settlers.[56]

Ultimately, the colony failed and was abandoned in May 1796 due to the settlers' ill health and unsuitable living conditions.[57] The Bengal Presidency also considered the colony on Prince of Wales Island (now called Penang, Malaysia) more suitable for permanent habitation, including for a penal settlement and abundant harbours.[58] After the evacuation of the settlement in 1796, the British did not rescind their claim on the Andamans, and the Royal Navy and the Bombay Marine (renamed Indian Navy in 1830) vessels frequently sailed close to the Islands to ensure no other European power created a settlement.[59]

In 1824, Port Cornwallis, later known as Port Blair in 1858, became the location for the British fleet rendezvous before the First Burmese War (1824–1826). Both the Royal Navy and Bombay Marine used the large natural harbour and the protection from the weather to organise before sailing to Rangoon.[60] This was what both the Cornwallis brothers intended for the harbour at the turn of the 18th century, and it reflects the perceived value of the Andamans as a safe harbour with strategic access to key hubs in the Bay of Bengal. Chapter two addresses this period in more detail, looking at how the British policed the seas against piracy, conducted rescue operations for shipwrecks, and used the harbour for naval operations.

The Bay of Bengal was, nevertheless, an important space for British maritime communication networks in the 19th century. Britain's mercantile populations and geographical outlooks shifted in the early 19th century with the expansion of worldwide horizons for British society through technology like steamships.[61] The increasing affordability and availability of reliable steam leading up to the 1840s also meant that geographies were changing. Shipping relied less on prevailing winds, and cheaper transportation combined with an insatiable appetite for goods from across the Empire meant more ships at sea.[62] This naturally led to an increased likelihood of British interaction with the Islands located strategically between the Straits Settlements, Burma, and the east coast of India. Ships could travel faster, take heavier loads, and thus larger profits.

The Bay of Bengal played a crucial role in the First Opium War (1839–1842), serving as a critical place of convergence of SLOC for the British Empire's opium and tea trade with China.[63] This vast body of water, linking India and Southeast Asia, was essential for transporting opium from the poppy fields of Bengal to the Chinese market.[64] Also, ships travelling from key ports on India's eastern seaboard, such as Calcutta, Chennai, and Trincomalee, would often sail through the Andaman and Nicobar Islands to reach the Straits of Malacca and on to China or north of the Andaman Islands for Rangoon.[65] The control of this maritime space ensured that the British could enforce their trade interests over European rivals, leverage their naval power for favourable terms with local states, and secure the routes against potential threats from local pirates and other disturbances. The Bay of Bengal was, therefore, a pivotal SLOC not only for commercial gain, but also for maintaining the movement of land and sea military capabilities.

In the early 1840s, the Bay of Bengal was not only of importance to the British, but also other European states and local states.[66] However, calling the Bay of Bengal a *British Sea* is, therefore, a manifestation of the area's importance to both colonial officials between 1842 and 1856 and to contemporary scholars in framing British maritime dominance.[67] There is no exact definition of what constituted a *British Sea* either territorially or in practice. It suggests an 'othering' of one space which aligns with British values and ideals and another space which does not. This flexibility aligns with Ronald Po's description of the Qing maritime model as "overlapping spheres whose boundaries shifted per circumstances of the time".[68] Similarly, the *British Sea* was a fluid concept and changed depending on the circumstances.

By 1842 and with the culmination of the First Opium War, British trade between China and India increased dramatically, as did expectations of Britain's role in civilising foreign nations: "expectations (of opportunities for trade, conversion, and travel) had been inflated by the Treaty of Nanjing."[69] The Treaty of Nanjing was one of a series of imperial acts that opened up trade and access in the region, including the annexation of Burma in January 1853. However, the forced opening of the Chinese markets is considered the most pivotal.[70] The Bay of Bengal was increasingly traversed as SLOC expanded for commerce, religion, and British society travelling.

The Bay of Bengal became a greater route of passage for British maritime communications, which aligns with Corbett's work that views command of the sea through the lens of "issues between nations" and the "destruction of enemy fleets".[71] The *British Sea* concept embodies some elements of the practical application of Corbett's theory in the early Victorian era: the First Opium War, Second Anglo-Burmese War, and Second Opium War were all fought against nations. However, Corbett's work does not acknowledge the role of private navies to a depth adequate to explain the vast force built by the East India Company. The East India Company's private navy, the Indian Navy, was independent of the Royal Navy but integral to British seapower in the region.[72] Between 1842 and 1856, the East India Company's interests heavily overlapped with those of the British state, but they were still distinct.

The Government of India Act of 1833 removed the Company's monopoly on trade in China (the 1813 Act had removed the monopoly over India), effectively making the Company appear as a vast administrative and military body. The legislative power resided in the Governor-General of India, who, as head of the Government of India, was the effective commander of the Indian Navy.[73] The Government of India, therefore, had its own navy that did not come under the command of the Admiralty because of the "fear of the British Government that the expense of governing

India would sink the British budget".[74] The Indian Navy was a significant actor in enabling British seapower in the region, with independence of command from the Royal Navy.

Also, Corbett's analysis does not adequately address the various forms in which naval power is used beyond the realm of state-to-state interactions. The British changed the previous trading patterns, the legal framework over how the seas were used, and the dominant cultural values in the Bay of Bengal to control communications and assert dominance.[75] Many of these elements are not the preserve of the state, such as cultures changing. Naval power asserted new expectations of how the Bay of Bengal was governed and communicated, including how the seas were used. As an example of the limitations of Corbett, he wrote:

> ... the only right we or our enemy can have on the sea is the right of passage; in other words, the only positive value which the high seas have for national life is as a means of communication... by denying an enemy this means of passage we check the movement of his national life at sea.[76]

The quote is telling for two reasons. Firstly, the 'right' of passage was seen as the predominant right; the seas were a place to take and transfer resources and were not primarily seen as a space of cultural exchange. Secondly, using the enemy belies a 'them' and 'other' scenario. You are either British, or you are not. British seapower destroyed enemy fleets and, more importantly, it replaced previously accepted ideals and values of the Bay of Bengal with new British examples.

Concerning the Bay of Bengal as a military space, command of the seas after 1842 meant the ability to patrol and secure maritime routes, safeguard merchant and commercial vessels, and maintain deterrence against piracy and rival powers.[77] The increasing volume of British and colonial shipping passing through the Bay of Bengal required a robust naval presence to ensure the safe passage of goods and to project British power across the region. Although there was a collaboration of efforts between the Royal Navy and the Indian Navy during this period, it was not a cohesive relationship. The Indian Navy "had been undertaking tasks which the Royal Navy felt were beneath it", such as constabulary duties, survey work, anti-piracy operations, and troopship movements.[78] The Royal Navy, on the other hand, focused on a grander vision of "freedom of the seas for trade", which meant being prepared to counter any threats to commerce in the region, notably from both European and Asian navies.[79]

The Indian Navy's primary function, on the other hand, was to protect the East India Company's commercial interests.[80] These activities involved reshaping the maritime practices and cultures of the Bay of Bengal towards those that abided by British expectations of a commerce-centric, civilised sea.[81] Command of the sea is thus the naval element of the *British Sea* narrative, and what I will show you is the sociocultural dimensions that Corbett did not address.

Until the start of the Second Opium War in 1856, the *British Sea* was a narrative evolving as British interests expanded. This expansion was informal and was most often based on commercial needs disrupting local norms and customs: "There was nothing systematic... apart from the general insistence on accepting British norms and behaviour."[82] Nicholas Tarling's work on imperial maritime security in Southeast Asia reflects the British intention to make it the "duty of governments" to provide and encourage a safe environment for the lawful extension of commerce and the safety of British subjects and interests.[83] The *British Sea* can therefore also be seen as a duty of government to maintain.

By the 1850s, the Government of India had an impetus to ensure maritime security for the increasing number of British merchants, traders, and subjects traversing the Bay of Bengal. The failure to do so was one of the core reasons Barry Gough argues that expansion happened in "fits and starts" as the British had to further expand territorially for security and defence.[84] Thus, once again building upon the notion that the *British Sea* was becoming an expectation of government. The Bay of Bengal would, in time, conform to British ideas and values and be a safe place to trade.

The Chinese government's seizure of the *Arrow* in Canton reflects how, by October 1856, the British were testing the Treaty of Nanjing and sincerely desired to expand its parameters with decisive force.[85] It also marked a shift in which Britain more formally approached the management and governance of the Empire.[86] This had ramifications for the Andaman and Nicobar Islands, as we shall see.

The *British Sea* cemented itself as a narrative when colonial officials regularly used it to describe the Bay of Bengal by 1856.[87] This narrative encompasses the idea that the Empire, through its naval power, could maintain control over critical sea lanes, enforce trade policies, and project British values across the Bay of Bengal. It was commerce and civilisation in unity. From 1856, the Royal Navy also "witnessed a gradual trend from strategic dispersal worldwide to concentration in Europe… ultimately home-waters".[88] As noted by N.A.M. Rodger, before 1856 this 'strategic dispersal' was not a formal strategy, meaning the Admiralty dealt with imperial issues ad hoc.[89] 1856 offers a transition point from a more informal expansion of the Empire to one that becomes more of a 'civilising mission' as the century progresses.[90]

The construction of narratives and ideas is central to how humans understand themselves and their actions within distant places, such as visions of tropicality.[91] Alongside an 'orientalist' perspective, how European sailors, imperial officials, and mariners viewed Asian states has received considerable scholarly focus on how it has shaped the Empire.[92] The *British Sea* is another such example, where British naval power and mercantile control over the Indian Ocean through the Victorian era reshaped the space into one with British ideals and values: "manifested in steamships, telegraphs, banks, and other technological transformations… proliferation of consular and colonial courts."[93]

The *British Sea* is also an example of a geographical imagination, which develops from narratives to be a discourse used to construct space specifically: a way of thinking about the world and the interrelationship between cultures, spaces, and differences that make a space a place.[94] This is significant as it expresses the British understanding not only of the Indian Ocean as a geographic region or its physical geography elements, but also of a place with substantial meaning and social construction where "global trade flourished, slavery and piracy were suppressed and liberalism was spread".[95]

Like Pax Britannica, the *British Sea* became a term associated with British maritime supremacy and the superiority of British values, emphasising Britain's ability to exert power globally.[96] It also elevated British values above all others, an aspirational goal for other societies, including European powers, Asian states, and the Andamanese and Nicobarese tribes. The term remade imperial space into one where the British can write the meaning and story. It justifies colonisation by removing past histories and shaping the Bay of Bengal in its image.[97]

Taking this all on board, the *British Sea*, it seems, was a narrative rather than reality. The following section explores the perceived challenges of British control in the Bay of Bengal between 1842 and 1856. These challenges, as defined by the Indian Government, are a valuable means in which to further understand what was meant as a *British Sea*. Describing something as a challenge reflects an obstacle to a goal, and in this case the goal was the pursuit of a *British Sea*. While it could be assumed that the Indian Government and British Government were aligned in this goal, this was not always the case. There were significant complexities in gaining command of the sea, with competing purposes between the Royal Navy and Indian Navy, as we shall see.

Disturbances in Pursuit of a *British Sea*

The *British Sea* was a commonplace discourse within the Government of India in 1856, such as when it was used by the President in Council, John Peter Grant, of the Bengal Civil Service, who used the term to describe the Indian Ocean and the importance to security and British interests.[98] The Commissioner of Arakan, Captain Henry Hopkinson of the Bengal Army, used this term again in 1856 in his persuasive report encouraging the Government of India to settle on the Andamans, stating:

> The Bay of Bengal [is] a *British Sea*, and it is more than ever incumbent upon us to prevent persons not subject to the British Government from setting within the limits.[99]

As we have established, the *British Sea* suggests a place of British economic and military dominance, ensuring secure maritime trade routes and a formidable naval presence to protect their interests against piracy and rival powers. Culturally, it symbolised the British effort to impose their values and control over the region, projecting an image of civilised authority over what they perceived as the untamed and uncivilised local populations.

Although the Andaman Islands had been formally British-claimed territory since 1796, they remained outliers to the steady civilisation and control of imperial oceanic space by the Government of India. Between the First and Second Opium Wars, the Andaman and Nicobar Islands were viewed as a weak point in British dominance in the region. The Islands' sovereignty was threatened by European competitors, while disturbances in regional Asian states absorbed British imperial military resources. More importantly, the Islands also represented a threat to the cultural ideals and values of the *British Sea*. This was from the supposed savagery the Islands represented, a direct challenge to the ordered and civil use of the seas the British sought.

Challenges to a *British Sea* – European States

Like any socially constructed network in flux, the *British Sea* narrative came with expectations that changed over time. In the 1840s, the Government of India in Bengal viewed their responsibility as asserting authority over the region and proving the British ability to dominate the seas. The role of violence in enabling imperial expansion and securing territory is well acknowledged through the first half of the 19th century.[100] The French threat in the home waters in 1840 distracted the Admiralty and left insecurities within strategic thinking about having a dispersed fleet. The First Lord of the Admiralty, the Earl of Minto, writing to the then Prime Minister, Viscount Melbourne, raised concerns about the availability of ships of the line as two were employed in the East Indies and China, respectively.[101] This reflected the competing demands upon seapower to protect the British Isles, the metropole, from continental threats while ensuring there were enough resources to protect the imperial SLOC, enabling trade in the periphery.

While the Admiralty focused on combatting the threat to Britain from continental France in the 1840s, there was also concern about the French intentions in the Bay of Bengal.[102] In the early 1840s, after French missionaries had settled in Car Nicobar, the East Indies Station raised concerns to the Admiralty and the Secretary of the Government of India about the possibility of the French utilising the Nicobar Islands as a place to attack British SLOC.[103] The Government of India responded that they had no "apprehension of the designs of other European nations" and, therefore, no action should be taken.[104] This shows that different British government offices viewed the European threat differently in the Bay of Bengal. With its naval focus, the Admiralty saw the French threat as a global issue. In contrast, the Government of India was regionally focused and mostly interested in trade over any form of conflict which would cost money.[105]

However, by the mid-1850s, the relationship with France had changed. This period saw the British work with the French to pursue joint ventures, including the Crimean War (1853–1856) and the Second Opium Wars (1856–1860). In the case of the Nicobars, colonised by the Danish Crown sporadically since 1756, the British Government and the Foreign Office were keen to avoid any diplomatic consternation over the Islands. After the Treaty of Kiel was signed between Britain and Denmark in 1814, relations remained generally cordial throughout the first half of the 19th century. When the Danish abandoned their colony in Nancowry Harbour in 1848, the Government of India enquired about the possibility of setting up a colony there. However, the Foreign Office told the Indian Government to respect Danish claim.[106] This reflects the consensus among European states at the time regarding territorial claims and sovereignty.

The process of boundary delineation and supporting claims by other European powers, if they were friendly, reflected the territorialisation of space based on "claims on the ideas of geometric cartography".[107] British respect for the Danish Crown's claim to the Nicobars was reciprocated with support for the British claim on the Andamans, legitimising Britain's and other territorial claims in the Indian Ocean. The *British Sea* imagination was enhanced by other European states through a collective re-territorialisation of global islands into the European political framework. So far, no account suggests any European state challenged the British claim to the Andaman Islands since the settlement was abandoned in 1796. Conflicts and skirmishes, whether diplomatic or military on the European continent, would often manifest themselves in the Bay of Bengal via the various European territories in the region.[108] However, the European system of sovereignty was relatively supportive of the British self-narrativising of the Bay of Bengal as a *British Sea*.

Challenges to a *British Sea* – Asian States

Beyond interaction with other European states in the Bay of Bengal, the British confronted multiple littoral Asian states, principalities, and chiefdoms with "naval power as the right arm of a global empire".[109] Both the First Opium Wars (1839–1842) and the Second Opium Wars (1856–1860) showed the extent to which British trade interests would be protected and enforced.[110] By 1856, after the seizure by the Chinese state of the British-flagged vessel *Arrow*, the Royal Navy provided "the sailing ship of the line *Calcutta*, a sailing frigate, three screw sloops, and two paddle steamers" to enforce British interests, alongside Indian Navy vessels.[111]

As the previous section explained, trade with China was integral to the *British Sea* narrative. The connectedness of oceans means that what happened in the South China Sea impacts the Bay of Bengal. The Qing Dynasty represented a challenge to British communication networks in the region through restrictive trade conditions that the British sought to quell with a combination of seapower, diplomatic pressure, and shore landings.[112] This was a pattern which would be repeated across the region.

The British fought another imperial campaign with Burma between 1852 and 1853 over disagreements with the Treaty of Yandabo signed by the East India Company and the Burmese Kingdom in 1826. British trade in Burma increased throughout the 1840s, becoming a major financial hub for merchant shipping in the region.[113] On a more local level, the burgeoning financial sector in Rangoon funded multiple ventures to the Andaman and Nicobar Islands for raw materials. In 1848, Nicholas Tarling records that at least one hundred vessels from Burma visited the Nicobars via the Andamans for commercial products, including coconuts, shells, and timber.[114] This also led to an increase in piracy in the region being reported.

From 1852, a marked shift in tone at the East Indies and China Station noted that "piracy in its worst form is systematically carried on to frightful extent".[115] The consequence was that this undermined the British reputation in the Bay of Bengal, and increased the cost through insurance of getting Chinese goods and labour to Burma for resource mining.[116] The imperial skirmishes all had commerce at the core, and predominantly finding the means to smooth over disturbances to the flow of goods across the Bay of Bengal. With the advent of the Second Anglo-Burmese War (1852–1856), which increased British territorial control over Burma, the Indian Government argued that if a foreign power established itself in the Andamans, it would leave Burma vulnerable to attack and blockade.[117] Like the multiple Opium Wars, the *British Sea* was a network slowly being developed and, more importantly, expanding throughout the 1840s and 1850s. This period saw the slow and steady acquisition of further territory by the British based on economic benefit and security, rather than on a purely territorial or civilising purpose.

So far, the *British Sea* has been discussed within a Western framework of delineation and jurisdiction. Historically, the spaces of the Bay of Bengal, including the Islands, were fluid spaces that allowed seafaring commercial activities to take place over the centuries without regulation or infrastructure by Burmese, Thai, Indonesian, and Malay mariners.[118] Itty Abraham argues that the Andamans represented a "sea of islands" rather than a bounded place, which is indicative of how oceanic space was constructed pre-European formalisation.[119] It is debatable whether British colonial officials actively tried to remove centuries-old traditions in the Andamans; in many cases they were unaware of these traditions and practices. More likely, officials making decisions far away viewed the Islands as *terra nullius*, or nobody's land, and therefore needing formal control. Yet, the *British Sea* epistemology effectively overran previous constructs and produced a formalised and regulated space in the Bay of Bengal in the 1850s.[120]

Figure 2: Map of British Empire

Savages and Tropicality

Alongside the physical threat to British trade and SLOC in the Bay of Bengal, the Islands also undermined British control through the narratives of fear and savagery that shrouded the Islands.[121] The 'unknown' of what lay within the Islands features heavily within public discourse. The colonial officers at Fort William would have only been too aware of the stories of atrocities, including cannibalism and barbarism, which over time became the British geographical imagination of the Islands. What has yet to be assessed is how this impacted strategic decision-making and how it aligns with the *British Sea* narrative. This is central to understanding why the primary reason was for establishing a colony on the Andamans was maritime security. Visions of tropicality and savagery undermined what the British saw as representing their ideals of the Bay of Bengal: a place of free movement, civilised values, and burgeoning trade opportunities.[122] The Islands, at that time, did not fit into the British narrative of the Bay of Bengal in the 1850s. Instead, they were seen as an "impenetrable barrier to the worldwide expansion" of European civilisation.[123]

Discourses around *terra nullius* are intimately intertwined with colonial settlers' representations and beliefs of an empty, uncivilised place.[124] In the case of the Andaman and Nicobar Islands, the local inhabitants and tribes were not formed or integrated into something representing a functioning nation or state. In effect, the view within the imperial offices of the state was that these places would need to be reconstructed within a Westphalian framework, under British rule.[125] Without this, there left an insecurity, a void, upon which the British imagination would crowd with theories of savagery, turpitude, and cannibalism on the Islands. In the mid-19th century, the representation of the tropics featured a contested duality between appearing "pestilential as paradisiacal".[126] There was simultaneously a fascination with the unique, new landscapes coming into the imperial orbit, as much as horror at the proposed savagery within. The Andaman and Nicobar Islands were viewed in this vein.[127]

As the British took more territory and administrative responsibility over the Bay of Bengal region through the 1840s and into the 1850s, having the savagery of the Andamanese and Nicobarese on the doorstep undermined the purity and civility of a British vision of the Bay of Bengal being a *British Sea*. When repeated "outrages committed on defenceless seamen" occurred in the Islands, there was an expectation that measures should be adopted to protect the integrity of what the British saw as their right to traverse and trade in the Indian Ocean.[128] Savagery and tropicality thus undermined Grant and Hopkinson's imagination of the Bay of Bengal as a British space and challenged the legitimacy of the network of British values and ideals being constructed.

By 1856, the concept of the *British Sea* was a prevalent discourse within the Government of India. Despite being under British claim since 1796, the Andaman Islands were considered outliers to the steady civilising influence of British imperial control in the Bay of Bengal. This represented a weak point in the British command of the seas, more so than the perceived challenges from European competitors and Asian states in the vicinity. The strategic significance of the Andaman and Nicobar Islands grew as the British sought to protect their expanding economic interests in Burma and secure critical sea lanes between India and China. The British imperial framework actively sought to transform the fluid, unregulated maritime spaces into a controlled and formalised *British Sea*, overshadowing centuries-old traditions of the indigenous mariners. This transformation was driven by both the need for maritime security and the desire to assert cultural ideals and values, as the British aimed to reshape the Bay of Bengal into a space that reflected their imperial values and interests.

Who Commands the *British Sea*?

Building on this understanding of the *British Sea* we have developed from the previous section, we will now delve into the naval power that underpinned British maritime dominance. This will include how the British sought to achieve command of the sea, a concept central to maintaining their expansive trade networks and asserting imperial authority: "means nothing but the control of maritime communications."[129] The Royal Navy was not, however, the only British seapower force in the region. The Indian Navy was vital in safeguarding critical sea routes.[130]

During the early 1850s, as the settlement of the Andaman Islands became a favoured policy option of the Government of India, the East Indies and China Station (1831–1865) had an operational focus towards anti-slavery on the east coast of Africa, supporting imperial campaigns, and significant anti-piracy operations in the South China Sea to contend with.[131] More widely, the Admiralty already had a full spectrum of obligations globally, with a significant conflict in Europe – the Crimean War – causing a shift in policy towards a more Eurocentric naval force.[132] The Taiping Rebellion also drew naval resources to mainland China through the 1850s in support of British diplomatic and commercial efforts.[133]

Small, isolated disturbances such as those on the Andaman and Nicobar Islands were not a priority for an overstretched force.[134] The gritty reality of policing distant islands such as the Andamans necessitated a unique kind of seapower, which the Royal Navy was not resourced towards nor had an interest in performing. The Royal Navy was much more comfortable with warfighting against conventional fleets, even if it was dragged into localised policing duties.[135]

Imperial literature views the British Empire in India as the 'peak of empire' from the 1850s onwards.[136] However, naval historiography discusses the relative decline of British power and the waning influence of seapower in the latter half of the

19th century.[137] This difference has multiple reasons, but defining what constitutes power is a valuable signifier. Imperial scholars use territory, the formalisation of governance, and commerce as markers of power. Naval scholars instead reflect on the policy, strategy, and fighting efficiency of the Royal Navy as markers of power. Although the continued threat of European navies and support to imperial campaigns provided the Royal Navy with a varied operational portfolio in the Bay of Bengal, it did not have a clear strategic adversary to design the fleet: "relapsed into a state of complacency."[138] The Royal Navy was overstretched in resources and lacked a defining enemy in the 1850s.

The complacency Paul Kennedy discussed is also evident in the changing fortunes of the East Indies and China Station. In 1831, the merging of the East Indies Station with the China Station put the Royal Navy's operations over a significant portion of the world's oceans under one command structure. Conflicts at both extremities of the East Indies and China Station kept the Royal Navy active in the 1850s, including anti-slavery operations on the coast of East Africa, support to imperial campaigns in Burma, and significant counter-piracy activity in China as trade expanded and merchants flooded into the South China Sea.[139] As Barry Gough acknowledges, the East Indies Station also had considerable experience of counter-piracy operations becoming "daily fare" for the Royal Navy in Southeast Asian waters.[140]

The Royal Navy also had a network of naval bases with strategic access to control the communication networks across the Bay of Bengal. The primary naval bases in the area included Colombo, Calcutta, Trincomalee, and Singapore, with auxiliary bases at Sarawak, Rangoon, and Penang.[141] These bases were critical for logistics, repairing, and staging naval operations throughout the region. The concentration of bases along the Indian mainland and into the Straits of Malacca aligns with the important SLOC of the time.

The Straits of Malacca were of immense strategic importance to the Empire. This narrow stretch of water, connecting the Bay of

Bengal with the South China Sea, was one of the world's busiest maritime routes and one of the most profitable.[142] Control over the Bay of Bengal and into the Straits of Malacca ensured the security of British commercial shipping, allowing the free flow of precious commodities such as tea, spices, and opium. The Strait's significance was both economic and military, as it provided a vital chokepoint where naval power could be focused.

In the 1840s and 1850s, the Royal Navy maintained a varied fleet comprising ships of the line, frigates, sloops, brigs, and steam-powered vessels for the vast operational area of the East Indies and China Station.[143] However, the station's composition followed "no conscious design" and was informally constructed around ad hoc needs and available resources.[144] This is why the Royal Navy was unsuitable for tackling piracy and the myriad of other disturbances in the Andaman and Nicobar Islands through the 1850s. It was overstretched with significant priorities elsewhere, had a force orientated towards fleet-conflicts, and had little experience operating against sparsely populated and distributed islands.

The Royal Navy was relatively successful in targeting piracy in the South China Sea and Malaya through negotiations with local states and chiefs, the destruction of vessels, and the increase in the authority of colonial officials to deal with terrestrial matters.[145] However, the smaller tribal structures of the indigenous population of the Andaman and Nicobar Islands proposed a different issue. Rather than the waning influence of seapower, they are more representative of the limits of the Royal Navy's knowledge of island chains at the periphery of the Empire.

The East India Company's navy, the Indian Navy was, in comparison, orientated towards smaller, localised imperial skirmishes.[146] The Indian Navy was previously known as the Bombay Marine before 1830 and had developed in size and scope as the East India Company expanded.[147] By the 1850s, it had a fleet of 60 ships ranging from 1,800-ton steam frigates to gunboats, river steamers, and schooners.[148] While the Royal Navy was the dominant strategic force responsible for enforcing maritime dominance in the Indian Ocean, the Indian Navy, though a commercial entity, played a crucial supporting role in the 1850s by conducting surveys, protecting commercial interests with port guardships, and engaging in anti-piracy operations.[149]

The Indian Navy completed many tasks the Royal Navy thought were beneath it and was even seen as a 'competitor' by the East Indies Station.[150] Many of the officers were exceptionally well-trained and had an intimate knowledge of the region.[151] This quality training, better pay, and access to better lodging ashore often caused friction with their fellow Royal Navy officers in the region.

The Indian Navy also spent the two decades supporting the Royal Navy at various imperial conquests, including: Karachi (1838–1839), Aden (1839), China (1840), New Zealand (1845–1846), Burma (1851) and Persia (1856).[152] All of these were significant operations showcasing a sophistication of seapower which normally is only associated with the navies of state-funded navies. Often overlooked in favour of the Royal Navy's more prominent activities, the Indian Navy was crucial in securing British economic interests and expanding territorial control in the Bay of Bengal.[153]

The East India Company and Indian Navy's success meant that by the end of 1860, there was no significant economic or military power left in the Indian Ocean to challenge Britain's rule or command the seas, leaving Gough to argue the "effectiveness the navy had displayed had been too great".[154] Although the Royal Navy supported imperial campaigns and acted as a deterrent to other European navies, the East India Company was the economic power driving the expansion and consolidation of the Empire through the early 19th century and into the 1850s. The Indian Navy was an essential tool of this expansion.

The Indian Navy's importance to security in the Bay of Bengal cannot be overstated. It conducted many of the constabulary roles in the region, while the Royal Navy could focus on the strategic balance of power and anti-slavery operations.[155] Alongside bases in Calcutta, Cochin, Rangoon, and Penang, the Indian Navy also had access to the network of commercial port facilities for logistics in all major regional trade hubs, giving it considerable mobility and flexibility. This was more comprehensive than the Royal Navy's and a significant operational benefit.[156] While it did collaborate with the East Indies Station, such as during imperial campaigns, there was always rivalry and distinction between the two navies.[157]

Since the 1830s, the Indian Navy no longer protected solely East India Company vessels and had a broader remit to ensure the safe passage of all British merchant ships, including deterring piracy.[158] Furthermore, the Indian Navy's role in conducting surveys and producing nautical charts was vital for the safe navigation of these waters, and it contributed significantly to the Admiralty Hydrographic Office.[159] The Indian Navy was operationally engaged in policing and surveying the Bay of Bengal, and the wider Indian Ocean through the 1840s and 1850s. Much more so, arguably, than the Royal Navy.[160]

The tactical details of the relationship between the Indian Navy and the Royal Navy remain outside the scope, but what is significant is how the Indian Navy contributed to the performance of the *British Sea* narrative. The *British Sea* came with the expectation that the Bay of Bengal would be a place of British naval dominance. As Howard Fuller notes, "the assumption is too easily made that even a great power which still enjoys industrial, maritime and economic primacy cannot fail to yield just the right weapons in just the right way."[161] The Royal Navy was not the sole purveyor of seapower in the region, and thus it should not be assumed this is representative of the "Dark Ages" of the Royal Navy.[162] Instead, the Royal Navy balanced its responsibilities informally with the Indian Navy in the Bay of Bengal to ensure the command of the sea.

In summary, the military aspect of the *British Sea* narrative in the Bay of Bengal during the 1840s and 1850s was underpinned by the combined efforts of the Royal Navy and the Indian Navy. Each force contributed uniquely to British maritime dominance and the imperial maritime network.[163] The Royal Navy focused on ensuring no other state could achieve strategic command of the sea. Meanwhile, the Indian Navy played a crucial role in local operations and skirmishes, conducting surveys, protecting commercial interests, and engaging in anti-piracy activities. By mapping the region and ensuring safe navigation, the Indian Navy also facilitated trade and reinforced British commercial hegemony.[164]

Through engagement in littoral spaces, the Indian Navy imprinted British values and ideals across the Bay of Bengal, as its presence and activities promoted a sense of British order, discipline, and control.[165] The informal division of responsibility between the two navies and how this was decided remains understudied and would make a valuable contribution to understanding the complexities of British seapower in the region. It would further assist the shift away from a nation-state focus of naval power, as embraced by Corbett. Non-state navies, like the Indian Navy, are vital components of seapower.

Imperial Narratives and Influence on Seapower

Indian political commentators often describe the Andaman and Nicobar Islands as being located on the "greatest and most frequented highways of the world".[166] They have also been described as an "unsinkable aircraft carrier" within contemporary Indian security debates.[167] These contemporary narratives are the latest iteration of geopolitical imaginations to describe the Bay of Bengal. Like the *British Sea* discussed in this section, they reflect a particular contemporary view of the strategic environment. This is premised almost entirely on the Islands' locality at the conflux between the Bay of Bengal and the Straits of Malacca. Narratives will always exist, and many will have historical antecedents, albeit with nuances. Deconstructing narratives is, therefore, essential to challenging the biases and assumptions that shape views about geographical spaces and power.

The *British Sea* was a powerful story used to justify and legitimise British imperial ambitions in the Bay of Bengal, reflecting British economic and military dominance and aligning to British ideals and values. As the following chapters progress, this book will show how Britain further shaped and constructed the seas around the Andaman and Nicobar Islands into a British image through colonisation, exploration, surveying, and naval operations. Reading on, you will find that by 1872 there is a strong case that the British finally did manage to turn the Bay of Bengal into a *British Sea*.

As Tamson Pietsch notes, in framing the Bay of Bengal and surrounding maritime regions as a *British Sea*, British colonial officials provided an informal framework that guided naval and colonial policies.[168] It emphasises the need for control over critical maritime spaces to ensure the Empire's security and prosperity. Understanding this concept as a narrative helps uncover British imperialism's ideological underpinnings and move away from a sense of determinism that suggests British power was almost absolute in the region. The Empire was not a formal enterprise between the 1840s and 1850s; it was ad hoc in development and utilitarian in scope.[169] The Andaman and Nicobar Islands were of interest as they reflected a need at the time, rather than a long-term ambition.

Seapower is also deeply intertwined with the *British Sea* narrative. During the 1840s and 1850s, the purpose of seapower was viewed as the application of military might by nations to control the means of communication.[170] However, there is also an element of crafting a story of British dominance and civilisation within seapower. The application of imperial seapower is both influenced by, and influences, the *British Sea* narrative. The narrative helped frame the Bay of Bengal as a British space, thus promoting an image of control and order imposed by British naval forces. The comments from Hopkinson and Grant outlined previously highlighted an expectation of British maritime dominance, which influenced and shaped the Indian

Government's decision-making to look at how seapower could be applied to maintain this dominance.[171] The power of such narratives lies in their ability to shape perceptions, influence policies, and legitimise actions.[172] The application of seapower is thus influenced by the *British Sea* narrative, which shaped colonial officials' expectations of the maritime environment.

Seapower also influences the development of the *British Sea* narrative and how it is recorded in contemporary scholarship. The *British Sea* narrative in the Bay of Bengal has long acknowledged the importance of naval dominance, primarily ensured by the Royal Navy.[173] The Royal Navy's role in this period was to secure maritime trade routes, deter rival powers, and maintain command of the sea, thereby guaranteeing British economic and strategic interests in the region. It was strategic in scope. The Royal Navy's presence through the East Indies and China Station was to act as a deterrent to other European and Asian states and apply force where needed.[174] The dominance of the Royal Navy seapower in the Indian Ocean during this period, unmatched by any other nation, is considered a key driver for the *British Sea*. Seapower influences the *British Sea* narrative by providing the means by which no other nation can compete: "it is difficult to see that a serious challenge could be mounted."[175] There is no *British Sea* without command of the sea.

As previously discussed, the Indian Navy played a crucial role in policing, surveying, and conducting constabulary duties. While the Royal Navy was the strategic force, the Indian Navy undertook the gritty, tactical needs of imperial policing that ensured the Bay of Bengal followed British legal structures, ideals, and values.[176] Through these activities, the Indian Navy instilled a sense of order and discipline that aligned with British colonial policies. This imposition of values was part of a broader effort to reshape the Bay of Bengal into a civilised space that conformed to British expectations and standards. If the command of the sea is the control of communications, then the Indian Navy controls communications including the everyday activity conducted in the littoral spaces of the *British Sea*.

The Andaman and Nicobar Islands were vitally important to the *British Sea* narrative due to their strategic location. Situated along the critical SLOC between India and China, these islands were considered crucial for maintaining control over the Bay of Bengal by the Indian Government. This strategic significance only grew as British interests in Burma and China expanded. The Islands' location made them a potential base for any rival power looking to disrupt British dominance, thus making their control essential to the Bay of Bengal becoming a *British Sea*.

However, the Islands were also seen through a lens of tropicality and were often perceived as uncivilised spaces that needed to be brought under British control. Discourses around *terra nullius* are intimately intertwined with colonial settlers' representations and beliefs of an empty, uncivilised place. The Andaman and Nicobar Islands were both a strategic place of interest, and a manifestation of the 'other' regarding the values of a *British Sea*.[177]

Figure 3: Fleet Rendevous

What next for the *British Sea*?

The *British Sea* narrative that developed between 1842 and 1856 in the Bay of Bengal reflects a complex interplay of the economic, military, and cultural dimensions of British imperialism. The narrative served to justify and reinforce British administrative and military expansion, representing the Bay of Bengal as a space that should, by rights, conform to British values and standards in the eyes of the colonial officials. The strategic significance of the Andaman and Nicobar Islands, located along the expanding SLOC, became increasingly pertinent and led to British interest in establishing a colony on the Andaman Islands, which chapter two will address. While the Royal Navy played a pivotal role in ensuring that no other state could achieve strategic command of the sea, the Indian Navy's local operations were crucial in reshaping maritime practices and enforcing British ideals at the tactical level. Thus, British imperial seapower was multifaceted, having a military dimension and a sociocultural impact in the Bay of Bengal.

The Indian Government's efforts to transform the Bay of Bengal into a regulated and controlled space illustrate the broader imperial objective of integrating the region into an economic, political, and military framework aligned with British interests. However, using a *British Sea* to explain the region simplifies and obscures the complexities and contradictions inherent in British maritime hegemony. Taking a nuanced examination upon the roles played by the Royal Navy and the Indian Navy in gaining command of the seas reveals the diverse and sometimes competing objectives within British seapower. British naval power in the region was split between a strategically focused Royal Navy that patrolled the SLOC, deterred European adversaries, and supported large imperial campaigns against local states. On the other hand, the Indian Navy conducted port security, anti-piracy operations, support to large and small imperial campaigns, and extensive survey work. It was much more intimately involved in the day-to-day seafaring life of the Bay of Bengal.

It is essential to deconstruct the narratives of seapower in order to understand the nuances of power at sea. By doing so, you can reveal the underlying ideologies and biases that shaped how maritime power was perceived and practised in the Bay of Bengal. Narratives like the *British Sea* streamline the complex realities of imperial seapower, often presenting a deterministic and sanitised view of history that can overlook the contested nature of power. Arguably, the British never had absolute power in the region during this period, as the *British Sea* narrative infers. The Indian Navy, and the Indian Government for that matter, perceived the Bay of Bengal differently from the Royal Navy in terms of how seapower should be applied.

It is also time to challenge further Corbett's command of the sea concept by recognising the roles of non-state actors and the sociocultural dimensions of maritime communications. Corbett's theory primarily addresses the strategic and military aspects of seapower, focusing on controlling SLOC and destroying enemy fleets. I hope you will agree with me that such a narrow view overlooks the complex realities of seapower, including the role of private navies like the Indian Navy and how British ideals and values were imposed upon sea spaces. Seapower is not just about large battleships and charismatic admirals!

The next chapter will build upon the concept of the *British Sea* by shifting focus to the Andaman and Nicobar Islands, examining how they were a disruptive space within the British maritime framework. The Islands' perceived lawlessness, repeated instances of piracy, and acts of violence against shipwrecked mariners challenged the *British Sea's* underlying values and ideals.

CHAPTER TWO

Island Disturbances and Informal Imperial Defence, 1842–1858

On 20 June 1844, two East India Company troopships, the *Briton* and the *Runnymede*, found themselves in the depths of a cyclone near the Andaman Islands. The dark, tumultuous waves crashed against their hulls with relentless force. The ships carried the 80th Regiment of the Foot and their families from Sydney to, it was hoped, Calcutta. Captain Alexander Hall of the *Briton* and Captain William Clement Doutty of the *Runnymede*, unaware of each other's ship's presence in the visceral moment, watched helplessly as the storm drove their vessels toward the treacherous shores of John Lawrence Island. The winds howled like a banshee, tearing at the sails and shattering the long, disturbed silence of the night. The ships groaned under the strain, timbers creaking. Petty officers shouted orders; their voices barely audible over the cacophony of the cyclone. Soon, land was struck. The island loomed before the shipwrecked parties as dawn broke, a foreboding mass of dense jungle and rocky outcrops.

    This narrative is based on the book *Wreck on the Andamans* by William Darvall, published in London a year after the event in 1845.[178] The *Briton*, the *Runnymede*, and the British soldiers with their families had been shipwrecked on one of the islands of the Andaman archipelago. This was, however, not an isolated incident. Between 1842 and 1858, many of acts of piracy, shipwrecks, and unpredictable weather caused disturbances to the flow of trade through the Andaman and Nicobar Islands.

Since the culmination of the First Opium War in 1842 and the Treaty of Nanjing, British traders and merchants had increasingly been crossing the Bay of Bengal, taking goods and materials between India, China, and the various commercial hubs in the region.[179] The Andaman and Nicobar Islands were centrally located in these SLOC. As passing traffic increased, so did the Islands' engagement with the British imperial maritime network.

Anyaa Anim-Adoo describes Britain's imperial maritime network as the military and commercial routes between ports that "improved communications and bolstered commerce" at sea.[180] By the 1840s, the Andaman and Nicobar Islands were in the middle of a significant imperial maritime network, but were increasingly seen as a disturbance. A friction to the flow of commerce and civility across the Bay of Bengal.

Chapter one discussed the Bay of Bengal as a *British Sea*, a place of British military, economic, and cultural dominance. Here, I will build upon this foundation but instead look at maritime disturbances in the local waters around the Andaman and Nicobar Islands. It means taking island-level analysis, to complement the ocean approach of the last chapter. Island studies is an interdisciplinary field that examines islands as unique sociocultural, political, and ecological spaces.[181] Focusing on an island perspective rather than an oceanic one can help us understand the localised and specific disruptions the Andaman and Nicobar Islands posed to Britain's imperial maritime network. It is a small shift in our geographic vision, but helps us see seapower differently.

In 1858, the Indian Government took possession of the Andaman Islands once more. It was a strategic decision by the Indian Government to return to the Andaman Islands, in part to re-establish a permanent settlement in what is now known as Port Blair. Multiple factors influenced the decision in 1858. This included piracy, violent acts committed on shipwrecked parties by the 'natives', and the volatile weather in the Bay of Bengal.

These disturbances challenged the notion that the Bay of Bengal was a civilised space of peace and British dominion.

The decision to colonise the Andaman Islands in 1858 was, in part, to restore a sense of order to the littoral spaces around the Islands. It was not, as the current consensus of postcolonial scholarship suggests, purely based on the need for a penal settlement after the India Mutiny of 1857.[182] Across the British Empire, the reliance on the seas meant it was necessary to maintain command of the seas against all obstacles. As with much of British colonial policymaking of the period, it was a response to events rather than a concerted, planned affair.

Alongside the want to reduce piracy and attacks, the Royal Navy was also supportive of the plans to establish a presence on the Islands. It was considered an ideal base in which to defend this corner of the Bay of Bengal, and part of the wider imperial defence network. Herbert Richmond defines imperial defence as the strategic and coordinated efforts to protect and maintain the security of the Empire by sea:

> The Empire being a scattered body of islands, whose only communication with the outer world and with each other is by sea, it is essential that the route by sea shall be as secure for the movements of commerce or troops as it was that the Roads of Rome should be safe for legions.[183]

Andrew Lambert also notes that imperial defence developed out of a post-Crimean War (1853–1856) environment with a new balance of power emerging between European states.[184] Others argue that formal imperial defence policies emerged later in the 1860s with the need to secure coaling stations and the publication of the House of Commons Select Committee on Colonial Defence report (1861).[185] While it is clear that a more formal imperial defence strategy developed over the following few decades after the Crimean War, the Indian Government had an informal policy of defending imperial possessions through the 1840s and 1850s. This is earlier than most contemporary scholars suggest.

John Grainger identified the informal but "systematic" means by which seapower was used in the Bay of Bengal. This informal system was based on protecting and expanding communication routes through a reactive territorial or political expansion. I will enhance Grainger's argument by reflecting on how the Indian Government used the Indian Navy and Royal Navy for differing purposes to secure communications at sea. The Andaman and Nicobar Islands were also indicative of islands being seen as places of both disturbances and potential strategic advantage.[186]

The Indian Rebellion of 1857, previously known as the Indian Mutiny, happened during the discussions on the Islands occurring in Calcutta. This event changed the dynamics of the decision-making process, as we shall see.[187] The Government of India Act 1858 triggered the comprehensive transfer of power from the East India Company to the British Crown, which included the transfer of the Indian Navy to the Royal Navy. This transfer of power and its implications for British seapower had a profound impact on the future of British imperial seapower.

So far, the Andamanese are only discussed as an immobiliser to British ambitions. This is not, by any stretch, to remove the Andamanese's agency. It is instead a reflection that the Andamanese society is predominantly oral-based, leaving no archival sources, and the major anthropological studies only began in the 1860s after a permanent British settlement was established.[188] The focus here is on the justifications of why the Indian Government colonised the Andamans; this requires a concentration on the British officials' mentality and physicality towards the Islands. Equally, the voices of the Indian Rebellion of 1857 are not included, as other scholars have addressed this issue.[189]

While the focus may appear to linger solely on the Andaman Islands in 1858 throughout this chapter, the Nicobar Islands are inherently intertwined and have a shared historiography.[190] As Nidhi Mahajan noted, studying islands requires a "multi-sited, archipelagic" understanding of the fluidity of interaction between spaces.[191] The Nicobars are an essential place for understanding why the British colonised the Andamans for acts of piracy on the Islands and their geographical vicinity to the Andamans. They were, however, nominally a Danish territory since 1754.[192] Chapter six addresses the eventual annexation of the Nicobar Islands in 1869, but to British colonial officials through the 1840s and 1850s, the disturbances were arising from both the Andaman and Nicobar Islands.

Overall, what you will read next explains the reasoning behind the Indian Government's decision to colonise the Andaman Islands in 1858 in a new light. Previous accounts of this decision have focused on the eventual penal colony set up on the Islands. While the archival sources note that the Indian Government was intending to use Port Blair as a penal colony, they also state the imperative of securing maritime security. This decision was based, in part, on quelling the maritime disturbances caused to the British imperial maritime network between 1842 and 1858. The Indian Government, with support from the British Government, sought to restore order and assert control over the littoral spaces of the Bay of Bengal.

Figure 4: Wreck on Andamans

Insecurities in the Imperial Maritime Network

The Andaman and Nicobar Islands have a long history of piracy, sharing common historiographies with other Southeast Asian islands that have offered a safe haven for those seeking a space away from regulated commerce and, more importantly, access to readily available resources.[193] Contemporary literature on piracy has focused on the Horn of Africa and naval coalition efforts to remove the threat.[194] However, during the 1840s and 1850s, there was not an official definition or terminology for piracy.[195] The East Indies and China Station submitted a report to the Government of India in 1852 about piratical activity in the Nicobars. It does not, however, define piracy but uses the term to explain any act that emanated away from norms of practice or damaged British interests.[196] This included direct violent action against vessels, attacks on shipwrecked crews, or stealing from ships and coastal zones.[197]

This broad definition inevitably led to conflict with local mariners. Sometimes what were deemed piratical acts could just be centuries-old practices. This includes Malay fishermen collecting sea slugs and edible nests on the Nicobar Islands.[198] Piracy was a catch-all term for criminality at sea or behaviours that went against British notions of good practice at sea.

The Government of India formally recorded the first piracy case in the Nicobars in December 1840. HMS *Cruiser*, commanded by Captain Henry Giffard RN, found a boat drifting in the Andaman Sea from the whaler *Pilot* of London. The surviving crew reported that "the natives of one of the Nicobars" had murdered the captain and taken possession of the ship in Ho-Ho harbour as the whaler was collecting refreshments.[199] As a response, HMS *Cruiser* returned to Ho-Ho on the Southern Nicobar Islands and burnt around 70 huts, destroyed canoes, and damaged cultivated land.[200] The extent to which Captain Giffard acted upon standard operating practices or his own volition is unclear. However, it reflects a norm within imperial policing of providing overwhelming force to disturbances caused against British interests.[201] Nicholas Tarling argues that this event could have triggered future piracy in the Nicobars, partly as an act of revenge by the inhabitants after damage to their villages.[202] Chapter six will explore this legacy in more detail. If this was the case, it is indicative of piracy starting through necessity. A contemporary example would be how overfishing in the waters of Somalia caused piracy to flourish since 2007, as traditional economies are upended as resources are diverted.[203]

Upon hearing of the incident, the East Indies and China Station also sent HMS *Childers*. Under the command of Captain Edward Halstead RN in July 1841, with the steamer *Ganges* in support, the *Childers* went in search of more information about the acts of piracy "and the feelings and habits" of the inhabitants.[204] However, this was complicated by the Danish claim on the Nicobars. The Government of India and the Foreign Office viewed Denmark as the sovereign power that should tackle piracy on the Islands.[205] Although Captain Halstead continued the survey, finding evidence of multiple shipwrecks, no further action was taken against the inhabitants, and the report was shared with the Danish Governor of Sesampore for action.[206] Irrelevant to how much the British wanted to solve the potential immobility of maritime traffic, they did not have jurisdiction in the Nicobars.

After the *Pilot* incident, there were numerous accounts of further attacks on the Nicobar Islands, including in 1845 on the ship *Mary*.[207] The sheer volume and breadth of the Islands made it difficult to get accurate intelligence. Then, all the Government of India could recommend was:

> ... these circumstances should be made publicly known and that all commanders of trading vessels... be recommended to employ, during their stay, a portion of their crew as an aimed watch.[208]

The futility of this advice can be seen in the continuation of piracy in the Nicobars. The lack of British action in securing the seas for merchants was causing consternation in Calcutta, particularly from the Bengal Chamber of Commerce and the merchant community.[209]

The Marine Department was the body of the Indian Government responsible for overseeing maritime operations, including the management of the Indian Navy.[210] It also was responsible for ensuring the safety of trade networks and frequently liaised with the Royal Navy, through the East Indies and China Station.[211] It eventually proposed having two vessels sent to the Nicobars for surveying work and targeting piracy. Notably the Andaman Islands were also included.

The inclusion of the Andaman Islands recognises the shared geography with the Nicobars, but also a lack of understanding. At this time, the Indian Government had a very basic knowledge of the tribal structures and assumed the indigenous populations in the Andaman and Nicobar Islands were one and the same.[212]

Eventually, the Royal Navy sent two vessels, which indicates the incident's importance. The Royal Navy predominantly focused on strategic issues that affected the trade fluidity or a threat from a nation, whereas the Indian Navy focused on anti-piracy and riverine operations.[213] Notable too are the type of vessels sent. These were HMS *Spiteful,* a new wood paddle sloop, and HMS *Fox*, a fifth-rate ship of the line.[214] Under the command of Commodore Sir Henry Blackmore RN from the Straits Settlement, the ships set sail from Singapore in January 1845.[215] The sending of two powerful Royal Navy ships and a commodore underlines the importance felt in 1845 about the danger of British ships being attacked. The attacks challenged the sanctity of the *British Sea* and the security of the imperial maritime network.

Spiteful and *Fox* carried out survey work and intelligence gathering over a few weeks. However, the ships' crew could not conduct any action against the suspected pirates due to the Danish claim on the Nicobars and concern from the Foreign Office about potential diplomatic repercussions if naval force was to be applied in Danish overseas territory.[216] Commodore Blackmore's actions and the response from the Royal Navy were indicative of the belief that brute force was the primary means by which to suppress piracy.[217] A combination of destroying pirate strongholds, regular surveying and patrols, and using warships as potential decoys to lure the pirates out was the tactical means to achieve this.[218] While this may have worked in the Malay Archipelago previously, the effectiveness of this approach in dispersed and sparsely populated islands like the Andamans or Nicobars was limited.[219]

The type of sporadic, opportunistic piracy that occurred on the Islands was a unique challenge for both the Royal Navy and the Indian Navy. Many of the tactics used to tackle piracy in Malaya, such as negotiating with local states, destroying craft, and understanding the cause (often conflict with other states), would not work in the Andamans.[220] The Islands' geography meant multiple ships would need to be on constant patrol to monitor the 500 miles north to south and the 572 islands. The tribal structures of the Andamanese and Nicobarese were also not understood in detail until the anthropology work of Maurice Vidal Portman in 1891.[221] Therefore, attempts to negotiate were unsuccessful due to the communication barrier.

Even if there was successful communication between naval personnel and the indigenous populations, the tribes lived on different islands and were not a cohesive society in a Westphalian sense. The tribes did not function as a conventional state, making large-scale peace settlement impossible with a treaty of some form, as was the case in Malaysia.[222] Captain Henry Hopkinson, the Commissioner of Arakan, made this argument in 1856, noting that, in his view, only a permanent settlement on the Islands would provide a platform to fully tackle the scourge of piracy.[223]

The argument from Hopkinson in 1856 reflects the perceived inability of naval power alone to bring security and control to the seas around the Andamans. The *Spiteful* and the *Fox's* attempts reflected what was and was not possible with naval power. Piracy, therefore, became a political and terrestrial issue. The Indian Government agreed to the requirement of a permanent settlement on the Andamans.[224] Unlike today, in the mid-19th century taking over territory for security was considered just, acceptable, and preferable to instability in trading routes.[225] It was a tried and tested means of bringing the desired form of stability.[226]

The Andaman and Nicobar Islands undermined the sanctity of the British imagination for the Bay of Bengal; the savagery at the edge of a civilised ocean caused friction. The acts of piracy and attacks on shipwrecked crews, which will be discussed next, caused enough friction in maritime mobility to warrant a naval response. Friction limited commerce. Commerce, the lifeblood of the Empire, could be physically stopped, and the maritime community became psychologically agitated by the fear of the Islands.[227]

The acts of piracy from the Islands through the 1840s and into the 1850s undermined this notion of British superiority. It showed an inability to discipline those on the fringes that challenged the Empire's expansion.[228] If Britain could not protect mariners, including British vessels and subjects, from acts of barbarity and piracy then did the British have command of the sea?

Through numerical advantage and technological development, the Royal Navy ensured the command of the sea in the conventional sense against other navies and major foreign littoral conflicts.[229] However, the Indian Navy was primarily involved in smaller campaigns and anti-piracy operations in the Bay of Bengal. Why was it not steaming to the Andaman and Nicobar Islands at the first sign of piracy? As a commercial entity, the Indian Government was in vast debt by the 1840s and would minimise naval operations as much as it could.[230] The question was about prioritisation. The Islands remained a barrier to British shipping's ability to move safely, but at this juncture, the threat was not considered severe enough to warrant intervention into the 1850s. The Royal Navy and Indian Navy, at the time, did not have adequate ship numbers, financial support, or knowledge of the Andaman and Nicobar Islands tribal structures to tackle piracy effectively. It was technologically complex gunboats versus wooden canoes of Malabar teak, and the canoes were outmanoeuvring the opponent.

While some attacks happened at sea in the littoral spaces around the Islands, other attacks occurred on shipwrecked vessels. Even during the 1850s, the coastal areas around the Andaman and Nicobar Islands were either only primitively surveyed or uncharted.[231] Shipwrecking was a very real prospect for mariners caught in bad weather with nothing but a loose sketch of a coastline to navigate from. There is a vibrant literature which addresses the sociocultural implications of shipwrecks within imperial and coastal British contexts.[232] The isolated location of the Islands meant information about a shipwreck could take days to be received by the Indian Government. By that point, even the arrival of a British warship was too late to protect the crew or save the vessel.

Such an example happened in 1849, when Captain George Brooke RN of the HMS *Proserpine* was sent to the Andamans after reports that the barques *Emily* and *Flying Fish* were shipwrecked. The reports were received from members of the merchant community who had saved survivors that had been collected by passing merchant vessels. They reportedly saw the vessels shipwrecked from a distance, and the survivors suggested the inhabitants' murdered other members of the crew that sought safety on the shore.[233] In 1852, the HCS *Tenasserim* was also sent to the Nicobars after additional vessels, including an unnamed English barque, were reported in the media to have been attacked. An armed party from the ship's company of the *Tenasserim* went ashore to check for further survivors but found none. Although they did find evidence of multiple other shipwrecks and belongings, the Islands were increasingly seen as a dangerous and mysterious place.[234] A place where the unfortunate would disappear.

Gunboats such as the *Proserpine* and *Tenasserim* were effective platforms when concentrated firepower and force were needed. However, in the Islands, they offered little capability against the tribes, which were transitory and would often escape into the depths of the jungle at the sight of a naval ship.[235] There was also no assessment of what might be causing the local tribes to attack the trapped mariners beyond a judgement of savagery. It was not until studies by Maurice Vidal Portman, an Indian naval officer, in the 1890s that attempts were made to understand why the Andamanese and Nicobarese would have attacked shipwrecked crews.[236] Portman's assessment was that the Andamanese and Nicobarese believed they were protecting their homes from invaders.[237] Nevertheless, through the 1840s and into the 1850s, the Andaman and Nicobar Islands began entering the British popular imagination as a place to be feared.

Figure 5: Andaman Shipwreck

Tropical Storms and Weather as an Immobiliser

It was not, however, just piracy or shipwrecks which could cause immobility to ships around the Islands. The Bay of Bengal is a region prone to powerful tropical storms and cyclones, and these could have a devastating impact on ships caught at sea, as noted by Henry Piddington in his analysis of the storm in 1844:

> ... that a defeat from the elements may be as disastrous as one from the enemy, and by the failure of succours, involve even farther losses, I shall not I trust be thought over earnest when I urge again on every man the intense importance of this science to Englishmen, above all other nations of the globe.[238]

Piddington was a former English sea captain who published prolifically in the 1830s and 1840s on topics ranging from geology to meteorology. Notably, he coined the term cyclone.[239] As a seaman and scientist, he believed that the British could overcome the elements through scientific methods, as shown in his quote above. At the time, however, the weather was seen as a threat to the imperial maritime network.

Vipul Singh described how being at the mercy of the elements at a time when modern science was gradually suggesting nature could be controlled brought environmental anxiety to the British psyche in places like the Bay of Bengal.[240] Although science was advancing rapidly in this era, new navigation technologies were often inaccurate at sea or would often be expensive.[241]

One of the most significant events that featured heavily in both imperial and domestic British press was the 1844 shipwreck of the *Runnymede* and *Briton*, a combination of bad weather and shipwrecking. The shipwreck led to the publication of a book in Britain by Joseph Darvall, which the shipowners commissioned.[242] Although sceptics argued that the book dramatised the event to ensure the insurance money was paid, it nevertheless ensured the story entered the British public's imagination.

After a storm in 1844, the *Runnymede* and *Briton* shipwrecked on the same island in the Andaman archipelago, John Lawrence Island. The fact that there were many survivors meant that accounts could be circulated and shared with the public in detail for the first time. It captured the public's imagination through tales of grit and encounters with 'savages' and 'cannibals'.

The quote from Piddington mentioned previously referred to the same storm in 1844. The quote takes on new meaning when understanding the implications of the *Runnymede* and *Briton* incident. The passengers included three companies of Her Majesty's 80th Regiment of the Foot, and detachments from 10th and 50th Regiments of the Foot.[243] Combined with their families and the ships' crew, this was over 400 British people. The loss of the ships could have been a greater disaster for the British imperial state than in a battle with a grievous enemy. The weather could have had disastrous consequences on communications at sea and the integrity of the Indian Government.

A significant recovery operation involving multiple vessels was undertaken. In a similar way to the recovery of HMS *Thetis* in 1830, the shipwrecks of the *Runnymede* and *Briton* represent how the imperial maritime network of "power and knowledge was momentarily broken".[244] It visibly expressed the vulnerability of British mariners around the Andaman Islands in a stark, almost fairy-tale manner. It differed from the narratives of the romantic maritime tradition associated with steamship travel in the 19th century that characterised the development of the *British Sea* imagination.[245] It was not an example of steam-powered leviathans forging through the sea, but brittle hulls vulnerable to nature and unknown 'savages'.

Although there was no loss of life reported, there was a perceptible feeling of environmental anxiety for British mariners in the region. Through providence, the crew, soldiers, and families on board the *Briton* and *Runnymede* survived through pluck and luck. Over the coming decade, the environmental anxiety developed into a palpable sense for action. This was aimed at the Indian Government. The shipwreck incident is, again, like piracy, notable for showing that the *British Sea* narrative could easily be undermined by factors outside of the Government of India's control.

Yet, as a regulating power, they were expected to be able to offer mitigation, such as providing sanctuary for ships caught by monsoon storms and finding ways to quell attacks by the inhabitants of the Islands. There were a multitude of successful voyages in and around the Islands between 1840 and 1858, yet the emotional impact and fear from unsuccessful journeys ultimately triggered action. By 1857, the combination of environmental and piratical anxiety had become a "disgrace to the British government", according to Commissioner of Tavoy John Colpoys Haughton. This was, he argued, due to the inability to ensure safe passage for shipping in the waters around the Andamans.[246]

The Andaman and Nicobar Islands entered the British geographical understanding as a place of fear. This was reinforced by acts of piracy, unpredictable weather and cyclones, and the perceived savagery of the indigenous population through the 1840s and early 1850s. Imperial history is slowly acknowledging the role of public opinion, identity, and the media in assessing how the Empire developed.[247] The value of looking at public discourse and media coverage of the Islands from the 1840s until the resettlement in 1858 is that it provides further evidence upon how the colonial government and merchant community saw the *British Sea* and what this meant to them.

Public fears were influential in the halls of Fort William. The decision to resettle the Andamans was seen as an imperative, as noted in 1858 by Haughton, the Commissioner of Tavoy. The negative perception of British government policy towards maritime security was impacting the movement of commerce in the Bay of Bengal.[248] The story of the *Runnymede* and *Briton* featured in all major national and regional newspapers in Britain and major newspapers in British territories, including the *Bengal Gazette*.

Public opinion was one side of the voices requesting change. The views of colonial officers were also important, as they saw governance in the maritime as key to the sustainable growth of

British trade and governance. Both voices contributed to the Indian Government's eventual decision to colonise the Andamans.

Representation of 'Uncivilised Seas'

The Standard first reported on the Islands on 20 September 1841, noting the occurrence of an "atrocious murder and daring piracy" after a ship sought sanctuary in Nancowry Harbour.[249] This set the tone and narrative for reporting on the Islands over the next decade. It is indicative of how British newspapers commonly reported on shipwrecks and attacks by the inhabitants across the Empire.[250] By 1852, the reporting reached fever pitch. The *Liverpool Mercury,* reporting on another incident in Nancowry Harbour, portrayed how the natives killed a European mother and "hacked a child to pieces".[251] The *London Daily News* similarly reported on the incident, noting that a ship from Calcutta with English passengers had been attacked, and then the "savages sank [the ship]".[252]

Such emotive language, evoking fear and challenging moral values within the readership, threatened the perceived superiority of British civilisation and values. Although similar tropes were applied to shipwrecks in British communities, there was also an element of orientalism to those written about the Andaman and Nicobar Islands.[253] This further fuelled the narrative of an uncivilised space and somewhere which attacked British culture through acts of savagery. This was reported from London to Liverpool, both key British maritime hubs.

The incident involving the *Runnymede* and *Briton* was also widely reported in the other British papers, with the *Glasgow Herald* writing:

> ... but for the resolute defence of our men who were set on watch, there is little doubt every one of them would have been massacred... Three of the 80th were shot while searching for shells along the beach.[254]

The use of 'our' provides a sense of collective ownership to the British readers, and the idea that 'every one of them' would have been massacred was sensationalist. Many imperial conflicts had been started on less. The fact that British soldiers were shot by the Andamanese also portrayed a sense of weakness and threat to Britishness. When describing the fate of the *Briton*, the *York Herald* begs the reader to imagine what would have happened to the "311 soldiers, 34 women, and 51 children".[255]

Again, themes of savagery presented the Islands as a space of vulnerability for Britons. It was a place where the state could not protect them; only British pluck saved the day. Meanwhile, the British readership was still reading reports and tales of Britain's imperial strength and prowess, so stories such as these challenged and played on vulnerabilities in the British imagination.

Although similar themes of savagery and barbarity were portrayed in imperial newspapers, including the *Bengal Gazette*, there was a slight nuance. The Islands represented a physical barrier to trade, as much as they did a cultural barrier to the civilisation of the Indian Ocean. The coverage in the *Bengal Gazette* of the 1852 acts of piracy notes that while horrendous, there was also a need for the British mariners and traders to "feel" secure and safe in the Andaman and Nicobar Islands.[256] While this does not speak for the entirety of imperial newspaper reporting, it does represent the critical theme coherent with other papers published in the territory of British India. Acts of piracy and maritime disturbance were considered to undermine the Bay of Bengal as a space of trading. Less on the culture, and more on the commerce.

Developing from this commercial theme, trade bodies, including the Calcutta Chamber of Commerce (Bengal Chamber of Commerce from 1853), had long written prominently as pressure groups since 1841. The trade bodies attempted to ensure the protection of maritime mobility in the Bay of Bengal, ensuring it was a top priority for the Indian Government.[257] The Calcutta Chamber of Commerce, representing corporations and industries with interests in Eastern India, recognised the Andaman and Nicobar Islands' strategic location: "directly in the track of vessels bound for the straits."[258] The Islands were considered to be located in a pivotal juncture within the imperial maritime network.

The *British Sea* narrative for the Chamber meant the safe movement of goods to market by sea, which throughout the 1840s and into the 1850s was undermined by activity in the littoral of the Andaman and Nicobar Islands. Newspaper accounts of attacked mariners only added to dissatisfaction among the trading community.[259] It also shows the difference between a British readership interested in tales and stories of tropicality, and a trading community within the region that wanted actionable information and marine intelligence.

While newspaper public discourse is helpful for understanding the wider narratives and how the Islands were represented to different audiences, it has inherent biases. It does not always correlate precisely with what the public or decision-makers actively believed or acted upon.[260] This can somewhat be alleviated by looking at the opinion of geographically privileged individuals, such as those colonial officials and merchants in the region who have a lived experience about how the Islands orientated around their work.[261]

The term *accidental imperialist* or *absent-minded imperialist* has recently gained traction within the study of Empire.[262] It reflects that many British officials and traders, although believing in the superiority of British civilisation, were often trying to improve their situations or improve trade rather than a systemic belief in expansionism.[263] The expansion of the imperial territory was sporadic, particularly in the 1840s and 1850s, and primarily based on commercial needs.[264] It was not a grand, relentless march of state ambition.

One example is Captain Crisp, a British merchant from Moulmein, who tried to lobby Fort William in 1836 to colonise the Nicobars.[265] As mentioned previously, the British Government respected the Danish claim and rejected Captain Crisp's even after the incident about French interests. Captain Crisp continued to trade in the region, making frequent voyages between Moulmein, the Andamans, and the Nicobars throughout the 1840s.[266] By 1849, he had stretched to new lengths to ensure British sovereignty over the Nicobars, as a report by the Marine Department notes:

> On the removal of the Danish Establishment from the Nicobars, the chiefs of the Island of Nicobar hoisted the British flag, and expected through Mr Crisp, a merchant of Moulmein, their wish to be under the British Government, but we approve you having declined to recognise this.[267]

Although once again unsuccessful, Captain Crisp's effort shows that an ambitious individual's activity would reach the discussion of the Court of Directors and the Indian Government. Crisp's assertion that you cannot control piracy in the area with settlement in the Nicobars was ultimately correct, as chapter six will discuss.

Colonial Governance and Maritime Security

The increased awareness of piracy in the Andamans changed the dynamics of the Government of India's response, although the concern was clearly orientated towards British shipping and subjects. For example, when a Burmese junk collecting coconuts in the Andamans was attacked by pirates in 1851, with some of the crew murdered, the response from the Government of India was "no reply needed".[268] By 1853, it was clear that the nature of the British claim on the Andamans meant there was considerably more flexibility in scope to act. Most significantly, there was also sovereign responsibility to act, as noted by the Marine Department in 1853.[269] In 1852, the East Indies and China Station also collated reports and proposed recommendations to combat piracy in the Nicobars, using the Andamans as a base.[270] There was a belief that naval power, in the form of gunboats with "withering shell-fire", could demoralise the pirates and enable safe mobility.[271]

The limited distinction between acts of piracy in the Andamans and the Nicobars showed that the Government of India viewed the

Islands as a collective chain rather than distinct territories with separate geographies.[272] What distinguished them was simply the sovereign claims between different European states. The dilemma was complicated by the suggestion from the East Indies and China Station that the pirates were Chinese. The inability to distinguish between the inhabitants and foreign pirates shows a lack of local knowledge and, in many ways, a failure to understand piracy on the Islands. While both the Royal Navy and Indian Navy had the experience of targeting organised pirates in the Malay Archipelago and destroying their ships and support networks, it was much more challenging to do the same to the inhabitants of the Islands who were using wooden canoes which could easily be hidden on land.[273]

By 1855, seven other vessels were reported to have been attacked in the Nicobar Islands over two years.[274] What finally triggered the Government of India to act was the murder of three seamen from the brig *Fyze Buksh* in the Andaman Islands.[275] This received considerable media attention in Britain and imperial reporting, noting that as a former British settlement, there must be a resolve to combat the issue.[276]

Options discussed by the Government of India included permanently stationing a commodore with a gunboat crewed by Malays and based in the Andamans as a deterrent.[277] Although successful elsewhere, this approach was deemed unsuitable due to the size and breadth of the Islands. It would not be a suitable deterrent for inhabitants, who had so far shown no interest or fear of Western technology.[278] Again, this reflects the growing belief that naval power alone would not be able to secure the seas around the Andaman and Nicobar Islands. There was clearly a lack of local knowledge.

The recommendation for a commodore to be permanently stationed in the Andamans came from the Governor of Singapore. It was not the Government of India who rejected the idea however, it was deemed resource-intensive and excessive by the Admiralty.[279] This shows the divide between the various organisations responsible for ensuring imperial security, with various governorships proposing different solutions to Fort William.

Captain Henry Hopkinson, the Commissioner of Arakan, recommended in 1856 that a permanent settlement would be feasible in scope and cost. Hopkinson saw that any sunk cost now would be better than the broader impact on trade decreasing in the region. Viscount Canning, Governor-General of India, initially opposed the idea thinking of the potential for bad press if another colony in the Andamans had to be abandoned again in disgrace.[280]

Captain Hopkinson is regarded as the first official to formally suggest the idea of a penal colony in 1856.[281] His account also emphasises the strategic value of the Andamans from a naval perspective:

> That many vessels have been wrecked on the Andaman Islands, and many shipwrecked mariners destroyed by the savage inhabitants are facts of notoriety... harbour, or harbours of refuge at a convenient part of one or more of these islands should conduce to the security of traffic, and to the general interests of humanity.[282]

Savagery, harbours of refuge, and trade insecurity; these all represented challenges to the *British Sea* by the 1850s. In the eyes of the Indian Government, the expected ideals and values of the *British Sea* were being undermined in the littoral of the Andaman and Nicobar Islands. Hopkinson's account was based on his experience leading a littoral trading region in Burma and the difficulties he faced as Commissioner of an area with responsibility for enforcing local security. Security was central to maintaining support for British governance over imperial subjects. Often, stability was inexplicably the primary reason Britain initially gave the new colonies for being subject to their rule.[283]

Hopkinson's report was submitted to Canning in February 1856. It was widely read and influential in the Government of India's shift towards acquiring the Andamans rather than requesting further naval patrols.[284] It also shows once more that maritime security concerns were at the forefront of the decision to colonise the Andamans. Canning eventually approved a survey to gather additional information on the suitability of a settlement on the Andaman Islands.[285] In March 1857 Indian Navy vessels were being prepared to start surveying the coast of the Andamans in preparation for a new settlement.[286]

The advent of the Indian Mutiny in 1857, however, significantly impacted the state of security in the Bay of Bengal.

Distant Rebellion Comes Closer

The Indian Rebellion of 1857 has been written about extensively by imperial historians, particularly on how the governance of India shifted.[287] The sepoys and the political protestors that rose against British rule in India have significant agency in the decision to settle on the Andaman Islands, and this is well recorded in the historiography of the Islands.[288] What has not received much attention is how the Rebellion on the Indian subcontinent disrupted Britain's network and plans to settle in the Andamans, and how this influenced the shift in the Indian Government's narrative about the purpose of the settlement in the Islands.

For the Royal Navy and the Indian Navy, the Indian Rebellion led to a traditional Pax Britannica role of imperial policing.[289] Naval brigades supported operations in the littorals, with the ships HMS *Shannon* and HMS *Pearl* from Hong Kong and Singapore respectively, sent to the eastern coast of India to Calcutta in 1857.[290] Both ships provided fire support and delivered Naval Brigades to assist British forces on the mainland, with HMS *Shannon's* ships company notably supporting the Relief of Lucknow.[291] The speed in which the Royal Navy reacted was considered impressive by the Indian Government, and the efficiency with which it applied hard power from the sea was considered a success.[292] When this response is compared to the acts of piracy in the Islands, which had been stretching for well over a decade, it reflects how the Andaman and Nicobar Islands were low on the Indian Government's priority order.

The Rebellion created two significant outcomes that shaped the future history of the Islands. Firstly, the Government of India Act 1858, which shifted sovereignty from the East India Company to the British Crown. The Act of 1858 established Crown rule, which included sovereignty over all of British India, from Baluchistan to Singapore.[293] This entailed increased responsibility for British subjects in India, including those trading from ports with vessels that transversed the Andaman Seas.[294] Secondly, there was an immediate demand to find a penal settlement for the multitude of political prisoners that emanated from the Mutiny.[295] The search was on for somewhere distant and practical for a penal settlement for Indian prisoners.

Also of note, the Admiralty now had the Indian Navy under its command, thus also the responsibilities previously covered by them.[296] This shift had substantial implications for imperial defence in the Bay of Bengal.

Although there was a major shift in ruling British India, the work of the Indian Navy continued swiftly on. The survey work on the Andaman Islands first proposed in early 1857 was temporarily postponed for a few months until the situation on the subcontinent was deemed to have stabilised, and it began again in November 1857. The Indian Government and the Indian Navy agreed upon a proposal to survey the Andamans, and a vessel and team were to be sent to the Islands to investigate a suitable site for a settlement.[297] In contradiction to the recommendations of the East Indies and China Station, the political apparatus in Fort William, whether based on experience or evidence of naval vessels' inability to control the situation, saw permanent basing as the only viable option for achieving maritime security.

Viscount Canning and the Council of India eventually approved the colonisation of the Andaman Islands on 15 January 1858. The Union Jack rose above Port Blair (renamed Port

Cornwallis) on 22 February 1858.[298] This decision was made after an expedition to the Islands between November 1857 and January 1858, which is the focus of chapter three. The initial orders were sent to Captain Henry Man, Bengal Army. At the time, he was serving as the Superintendent of Convicts in Moulmein, and his orders were to:

> … establish a penal settlement on the Andamans, for the reception, in the first instance, of convicts sentenced to imprisonment, and to transportation, for the crimes of muting and rebellion and for other offences connected therewith.[299]

Significantly, there is no mention of maritime security, tackling piracy, finding a sanctuary for shipping or any other oceanic reference. Although this reflects the nature of the orders, which were tactical and focused on his responsibility, the inference from contemporary historians is to take this in its purest form and argue the colonisation of the Andamans was to create a place of servitude. This is, however, insufficient as an explanation alone.

Over a decade of maritime disturbances in the littoral spaces around the Andaman and Nicobar Islands caused an 'environmental anxiety' and a challenge to British supremacy at sea. This anxiety was considered at senior levels of the Indian Government through the 1850s, and in 1856, Canning approved a survey expedition to the Andamans to find a place for a settlement that could be used as a bastion to protect British shipping. It was only during and into the aftermath of the Indian Rebellion that the penal settlement became the foci of British imperial interest in the Andamans. Imperial delivery was sporadic and focused on the priority of the day.

By 1858, with further reports of piracy inbound, the official response from the Government of India was "no remarks required" indicating that creating a permanent settlement would, in their view, eventually deter and remove the piratical threat through having a permanent naval presence on the Islands.[300] Chapter six will explore how piracy was eventually eradicated from the

Islands, as it took another ten years to remove the scourge. What is significant by 1858 is that the Indian Government believed that a permanent colony was necessary to tackle piracy and bring security. Naval power in the form of gunboats, for all their firepower and agility, were considered unsuitable.

Development of an Informal Imperial Defence

The Andaman and Nicobar Islands undermined the sanctity of the ideals and values of how the British saw the Bay of Bengal. The Islands represented a place of savagery at the edge of a civilised ocean, which caused friction to identities.

The acts of piracy and attacks on shipwrecked crews also caused further friction in maritime mobility in the Bay of Bengal. The lifeblood of the Empire, as it was perceived by the merchant community, could be physically stopped and also psychologically agitated through the fear of the Islands. The acts of piracy undermined the belief of British superiority, both culturally and in governance. There was an inability to discipline those on the fringes that challenged the Empire's expansion.[301] The Islands were a barrier to British commerce and the maritime communities' ability to move at will, and safely, via the seas in the Bay of Bengal.

Although there was no formal strategy for imperial defence in the Bay of Bengal through the 1840s and 1850s, the Indian Government actively sought a means to control it strategically and protect the imperial maritime networks that traversed the seas.[302] The informal imperial defence strategy of the Indian Government before 1858 largely revolved around addressing maritime insecurities through ad hoc measures, responding to crises rather than a proactive or cohesive policy.[303] The Andaman and Nicobar Islands played a significant role in this defence network due to their strategic location in the Bay of Bengal, with an increasing number of vessels sailing in and around the littoral spaces of the Islands.

The Islands were also seen as points of disruption, mainly because of acts of piracy, shipwrecks, and hostile interactions with the indigenous populations. Evidently, this undermined the belief that the Bay of Bengal represented a *British Sea* in the eyes of the British maritime community and colonial officials due to these disturbances. The Indian Government's efforts to control these disturbances were reactive and often limited due to the increasing debt caused by governing India.[304] Where possible, the Indian Government relied on the Royal Navy's sporadic patrols and the Indian Navy's presence in trade hubs to quell disturbances.[305]

John Charles Mason was the Marine Secretary to the Indian Government from 1837 until retiring in 1857. The Indian Government eventually persuaded him to retain his position in 1858, and he was highly influential in reorganising the Marine Department's purpose and design under the new Indian Government apparatus.[306] Mason characterised the division of labour between the Royal Navy and the Indian Navy as ineffective.[307] The Royal Navy, stretched thin with global commitments, focused on major strategic concerns and needed more resources to have a constant presence in smaller, regional trade hubs. This can be seen in the Royal Navy's inability to maintain a continuous presence in the Andaman and Nicobar Islands beyond cursory surveys.

The Royal Navy's involvement regionally was primarily reactive, engaging after significant incidents of piracy or localised attacks had already occurred. This left gaps in the maritime security network that, according to Mason, the Indian Government struggled to fill.[308] It reflected the limits of an informal approach to imperial defence between the 1840s and 1850s. It also demonstrates that there was an approach to imperial defence, however ineffective, before the 1856 starting point that contemporary scholarship associates with imperial defence.[309] Officials in the Admiralty and Marine Department saw a delineation of tasking to provide security. It was a gentleman's agreement, rather than formal government policy.

After the transfer of control from the East India Company to the British Crown in November 1858, the Indian Navy's responsibilities shifted significantly, leading to its rebranding as the Bombay and Bengal Marine.[310] This was based on Mason's recommendation that a separate navy was no longer needed as it was a duplication of effort. There was also significant pressure from the Admiralty, which did not "like the idea of a competitor".[311] This transition under the Admiralty brought a more structured approach to imperial defence in the Bay of Bengal. Still, it was not a formal strategy for maritime security in the Indian Ocean, but Mason's work began delineating responsibility between the navies. A formal policy was developing beyond a gentleman's agreement.

The Bengal and Bombay Marine, now under the direct command of the Admiralty, was tasked with lower-level responsibilities, including riverine gunboats, port security, and troopship movements.[312] Its major warships were sold at auction, but it kept a force of smaller gunboats, auxiliary vessels, and river steamers.[313] Although 1863 is considered 'the end' of the Indian Navy up until significant reformation before the Second World War, the Bengal and Bombay Marine nevertheless maintained an essential role in British seapower in the region. It acted as a supporting force for the Royal Navy in the Bay of Bengal, conducting many duties the Royal Navy would have traditionally fulfilled in other colonial territories in the 1850s and 1860s.[314]

Although imperial defence and the application of seapower were to evolve significantly after 1858, the Andaman and Nicobar Islands remained disruptive to the British imperial maritime network. The transformation of the Indian Navy and the consolidation of naval resources under the Admiralty would take many years.[315] The idea of the Bay of Bengal as a completely secure British maritime space was still more of an aspiration than a reality, as acts of piracy and attacks were still occurring on the Andaman and Nicobar Islands.[316]

The Indian Government's administrative changes were vast, although they were more of an evolution than a revolution.

The Government still functioned as the primary means of ruling the Bay of Bengal region, and soon attention returned to the Andaman Islands.[317] Again, the Indian Government did not develop a formal imperial defence strategy after 1858 but continued a reactive stance that often included annexing ports, islands, and territories along key SLOC.[318] It was nevertheless planned and followed a consistent pattern of action. This included Mauritius in 1810, Singapore in 1819, Hong Kong in 1842, and Sarawak in 1842.[319] The Andaman Islands follow this trend of colonising islands to form the security spine of the imperial maritime network.

Figure 6: Cellular Jail

Colonisation and Imperial Defence

The British decision to colonise the Andamans in 1858 was, in part, for maritime security purposes. It was not just to establish a penal settlement as the consensus in postcolonial literature suggests. The Government of India debated establishing a penal settlement in 1858, which became the prime focus after the Rebellion on the Indian subcontinent. This is what has been recorded in the tactical orders given to colonial officials, but does not reflect the wider discussions in Fort William over the preceding two decades. The fact that acts of piracy were increasing in the Islands, along with the continuing barbarity against shipwrecked crews, meant that throughout the 1840s and 1850s, Britain's economic interests in the Bay of Bengal were being undermined. The Islands challenged the belief within British maritime and colonial circles that the Bay of Bengal was a controlled, civilised space. The Andaman Islands were thus colonised in 1858 to ensure maritime security and 'civilise' the sea, alongside the need for a penal settlement.

The disturbances caused by the Islands were not merely strategic challenges to British trade in the region but were deeply rooted in the complex interactions between the local environments, indigenous populations, and the British colonial apparatus. A combination of acts of piracy, attacks on shipwrecked crews, and volatile weather patterns made the Andaman and Nicobar Islands a place of fear within the imperial maritime networks. These geographies of fear, or environmental anxiety as Singh describes it, led to a decision by the Indian Government to survey the Islands in 1856 to gauge the suitability of a settlement that could bring order to the littoral spaces around the Islands.[320]

Although the 1857 Indian Rebellion initially halted this survey work, it nevertheless reflects that the eventual decision to colonise the Andaman Islands in 1858 was partly due to maritime security concerns. There was an expectation that the Indian Government would solve this disturbance. The failures of both the Royal Navy and the Indian Navy to effectively secure these waters through patrols exposed the limitations of British naval power in this period. It was perceived that only a permanent settlement would suffice to stop the disturbances.

However, establishing a permanent settlement on island spaces, like the Andaman Islands, was common in this period. It represented the informal means of imperial defence in the Bay of Bengal, focusing on reactive action and imperial acquisitions to quell repeated problems.[321] The strategic importance of the Andaman and Nicobar Islands to the British imperial maritime networks lies in their position along crucial SLOC in the Bay of Bengal. While there was not a formal defence strategy, there was clearly collaboration and agreement between the Admiralty and the Marine Department on how best to defend British territories. This was happening prior to 1856, when many scholars argue that imperial defence originated.

A reactive use of naval power and territorial acquisition drove the informal means of securing the defence of the British Empire. The state as the primary actor of imperial defence, as proposed by Herbert Richmond, is also not as clear-cut as previously thought. The East India Company, through the political vehicle of the Indian Government, managed the defence of imperial possessions in the region up until 1858 in many ways. While the East India Company was a quasi-state, it still represented a commercial corporation with its navy. This is the first step in widening the scope of imperial defence, which suggests that 1856 was the earliest point at which the British began practising imperial defence.[322] This is clear in the relationship between the Royal Navy's East Indies and China Station and the Indian Navy, which had differing mission responsibilities in this period. The Government of India Act of 1858 changed the organisational delineation between the forces, reflecting an attempt to improve and create a more formal defence of British interests in the Bay of Bengal. There was already a foundation upon which to build to enact this change.

CHAPTER THREE

Constructing Geographies: Exploration and Seapower, 1857–1863

The Andaman Committee arrived at Port Cornwallis in the Andaman Islands in November 1857, stepping off the HCS *Pluto* after a four-day voyage from Calcutta. They were greeted by the remnants of an old British colony, abandoned over fifty years before. The carcasses of wooden bungalows lingered. The verdant forest encroached on the crumbling structures; vines twisted through shattered windows. The air was thick with humidity and the calls of unseen birds. A sense of foreboding marred the tropical beauty, the untouched wilderness seeming both majestic and menacing. Dr Frederic Mouat and his second-in-command, Lieutenant James Arnold of the Indian Navy, discussed the mission: to determine if this faraway place could serve as a penal settlement. They assessed the natural harbour, the freshwater streams, and the rich soil, noting both the potential for agriculture and the challenges of disease. Alongside the rest of their party, Mouat and Arnold would spend the coming days exploring this uncharted archipelago.

After the expedition, the Andaman Committee would go on to present a report to the Indian Government, which eventually led to the colonisation of the Andaman Islands for a second time on 22 February 1858.[323] Previously, chapters one and two explored how piracy, shipwrecks, and volatile weather in the Bay of Bengal in the 1840s and 1850s ignited the Indian Government to re-engage with the Andaman and Nicobar Islands. The maritime disturbances disrupted the British attempts to control the seas, both militarily and socially. The Indian Rebellion (1857–1858), however, shifted the priority to finding a penal settlement.[324] Here we will explore the Andaman Committee's expedition to the Andaman Islands, from the origins of the expedition in Calcutta through 1856, and up to the publication of Mouat's book in London in 1863.[325] By analysing the expedition from its roots to publication, it will become apparent how the Indian Government effectively reconstructed maritime space through knowledge production. Constructing maritime space is a unique form of power, and one which should be included as a form of seapower.

Seapower has often treated geography as fixed and determined. It was the chart upon which seapower happens. To see this determinism, you only need to look at Alfred Thayer Mahan's outlook on geography, treating it simply as the "principal conditions affecting sea power".[326] Geography was more than just the 'conditions' in which seapower occurs: geography shapes and is shaped by seapower. Geography is not simply a "great highway", but another dimension in which seapower changes and influences.[327]

The Andaman Committee is also a fascinating event that demonstrates the role of navies in supporting smaller imperial expeditions. There is a rich historiography on the role of the Royal Navy in supporting large, state-funded expeditions with a focus on scientific discovery.[328] The sailing of HMS *Beagle* with Charles Darwin or the voyage of HMS *Endeavour* with Captain James Cook RN are both well known. Smaller expeditions, such as the Andaman Committee supported by the Indian Navy, have been overlooked, but they offer insight into the 'everyday' activity of navies supporting imperial governments.

The Indian Navy was a supporting agent in imperial exploration. The recent study of exploration has evolved, moving beyond uncritical narratives of heroic explorers to examining the intricate contexts that shaped geographical knowledge.[329] Scholars such as David Livingstone, David Arnold, Charles Withers, and

Felix Driver have highlighted how the production of geographical knowledge was a complex, negotiated process involving collection, surveying, mapping, and archiving.[330] These processes happen in the comfort of the city and far away out in the field.

Exploration was instrumental in constructing the British geographical imagination of the world; an imagination being how individuals and societies perceive spatial relationships, places, and environments.[331] Expeditions, such as the Andaman Committee, created knowledge that changed the Indian Government's geographical imagination of the Andaman Islands and influenced the decision-making process and the application of naval power.

Understanding the British imagination of the Andaman and Nicobar Islands, alongside the role of seapower in enabling exploration, provides a nuanced understanding of how navies supported imperial territorial acquisition. As discussed in chapters one and two, the Indian Navy continued to be an integral element of British seapower in the region after the Government of India Act 1858. The Indian Navy was already an established knowledge-producer since its inception, but after 1858, it became increasingly focused on survey work. It disseminated geographical knowledge through exploration and surveys across the Bay of Bengal until the transformation of the force in 1863.[332]

Exploration, such as the Andaman expedition, was often based on *terra nullius* principles. The concept of *terra nullius*, meaning 'land belonging to no one', was a European legal and ideological classification used to appropriate territories.[333] Despite being inhabited by indigenous populations, the Indian Government used this notion to legitimise British claims and reshape the Andaman Islands into the British legal, political, and cultural framework. We will explore how such geographic constructs were integral to the imperial project, facilitating the transformation of these lands into British territories.

By exploring how geographies of the sea were fluid and constructed, we can challenge the determinism of Mahan's elements of seapower. As conceptualised by Mahan, seapower operates within a deterministic ontology of geography as a physical spatial zone, within which nations can act and identify through borders. This was a common framework for contemporary strategists and geographers of the early 20th century, such as Halford Mackinder and Vaughan Cornish.[334]

Whereas Mackinder's and Cornish's theoretical underpinnings have undergone a critical reflection, Mahan's has not.[335] Mahan's work has often been critiqued, but this has been more for historical accuracy, the consistency of his arguments, or how impactful he has been.[336] Instead, I will directly challenge the epistemology of Mahan's use of geography through his 'Elements of Sea Power', notably: geographical position, physical confirmation, and extent of territory.[337] These are not all fixed and determined. Through seapower, the British constantly changed the Empire's position, coastlines, and extent of territory through expansion. Geographies are constantly being constructed and reconstructed.

Figure 7: Abandoned Settlement

Exploration, *Terra Nullius*, and Seapower in the 1850s

The spatial turn in the humanities and social sciences has developed our understanding of what exploration involved and produced. It is no longer the hagiographic portraits of its 'great men'.[338] Instead, we can see the multiple contexts that shape and forge geographical theories, discourses, and practices.[339] David Livingstone traces the origins and evolution of geography as a fluid practice rather than a fixed activity.[340] Arnold, Withers, and Driver have also challenged the factual certainty with which early geographers represented geographical knowledge during imperial expeditions.[341] Rather than a factual reality, it was based on their social situation: "in a material and imaginative space."[342] The production of geographical knowledge about coastlines and islands was as much about the method as the author's identity.

Often attributed to explorers and scientists, producing geographical knowledge by the 1850s was a negotiated process involving collecting, surveying, mapping, and archiving.[343] This happened both in the metropolis and in the field. This process made imperial space, literally and figuratively. It filled charts and maps with data and information but also brought tales and stories of places beyond Britain's shores to the British public.[344]

Notable among the data collectors and storytellers of the Empire were the 'scientific servicemen'. These were geographically privileged and disciplined military men employed by the imperial government.[345] The men – and they were almost always men through the 1850s – held considerable credibility. They were known for their professionalism with technology (such as instruments). Through their official employment, they would also travel long distances undertaking study.[346] Scientific servicemen also had a privileged position in representing the imperial government. This gave credibility and authority on behalf of the Crown or Company, and also access to vast resources such a modern ships and weaponry.[347] As Kenneth Morgan argues, access to state resources was one of the prime reasons Joseph

Banks maintained such an intimate connection with associates at the Admiralty, via the Navy Board, particularly during his participation in the exploration of Australia.[348] Indian Navy personnel, such as Lieutenant Heathcote, were exceptionally well-trained and had privileged access across the imperial maritime network in the Bay of Bengal.

Driver acknowledges the Royal Navy's integral role in "extending the reach of British power and knowledge" during the 19th century.[349] However what is less known is how other British naval actors, such as the Indian Navy, also supported imperial expeditions. Through the 1840s and the 1850s, the Indian Navy supported imperial expeditions with logistical support, including the expedition to Oman and the east coast of Arabia (1835), survey expeditions in Mesopotamia (1841), boundary surveys between Persia and Turkey (1844), and a vast political expedition into Burma (1855).[350] This was alongside a constant and routine surveying of all the major harbours, ports, and SLOC across the Bay of Bengal.[351]

Equally, while the Royal Navy's role in supporting large, grand voyages of exploration is well documented, from books to television documentaries, its role in small-scale exploration remains under-researched, as is the knowledge it produced that supported military efficiency.[352] The Royal Navy and the Indian Navy were both important actors in producing and circulating geographical knowledge through exploration, that supported both the political and military aspirations of the imperial state.

Both the Indian Navy and Royal Navy supported imperial knowledge networks, which are systems of interconnected individuals, institutions, and information that produce, distribute, and circulate knowledge within a particular field.[353] Solari and Livingstone have shown the value of studying the processes and circulation of geographical knowledge that contributed to 16th-century Spanish maritime networks through the Casa de la Contratacion and *Relaciones Geograficas Map of Tabasco*.[354]

Knowledge of the seas was a vital form of power held by the British imperial state, that it could use to expand commerce, control colonies, and spread British civility.

Previous studies on the Royal Navy and expeditions have been centred on the specific publications, datasets, or charts from the expeditions.[355] Instead, what you will read next looks at the Andaman Committee expedition as a network. It will cover the planning stages through to the publication and dissemination of knowledge in imperial capitals. This knowledge, communicated through charts and reports, was vital in the decision-making process of the imperial state, and enabled it to wield power across oceans.[356]

Mahan also considered imperial knowledge networks essential for navies to exploit the "natural conditions" and secure command of the sea.[357] It is noteworthy that of the six principles affecting seapower identified by Mahan, all have reference to geographical study: three are spatial (geographical position, physical conformation, and extent of territory), and three are cultural and geopolitical (number of population, character of people, and character of government).[358] However, Mahan treats these elements as fixed and determined. For imperial states such as Britain, in reality these elements were fluid and ever-changing. Through the 1840s and 1850s, the Indian Government reshaped the elements of seapower through territorial acquisition and treaties – expeditions and exploration constructed new geographies.[359]

The linkages between imperial knowledge creation and territorial acquisition were not new in the 1850s. Since the Age of Enlightenment (17th and 18th centuries), there had been a consensus based on the Baconian principles of empiricism that geographical knowledge was attained through observation and experimentation, arriving at a more rational and logical account of how the world functions.[360] Contemporary scholarship has framed empiricism within a constructivist idea of geographical knowledge, which develops from Thomas Kuhn's work.[361] Steven Shapin then applied these principles to science.[362] The premise is that knowledge is part of society and, therefore, a social creation. What constitutes geographical knowledge inevitably changes with society. Knowledge, in this framework, is a social construction.

However, applying a constructivist framework to knowledge creation in the 1850s only goes so far in explaining how exploration creates knowledge. There is social knowledge based on human inference and a scientific knowledge based on data collection.[363] An example of social knowledge would be how the Andaman Committee choose names such as 'Port Blair' rather than using the names used by the indigenous Andamanese to delineate spatial areas. This is a form of social knowledge derived from social awareness, cultural norms, and collective experiences, whereas scientific knowledge is based on systematic observation, experimentation, and empirical evidence.

As Paul Boghossian argues, there is still mutually agreed, rationally based, and scientifically derived data on, say, how deep the water is. The depths on the chart are helpful as there is a consensus about what they mean internationally. Various mariners can use charts for safe travel at sea. Regardless of the difference between the types of knowledge, colonial territories such as the Andaman and Nicobar Islands were socially constructed based on Western values and expectations.[364] Scientific knowledge was used to reinforce claims, make it easier to manage and exploit colonies' resources, while also expanding knowledge.

With the Andamans, a European ideal of 'tropicality' was central to the Islands' place in the British geographical imagination. It was considered a place of verdant nature with an uncivilised populace. As chapter two explored, this was an imagination held by the British sailors and officers who operated around the Islands.[365] While scholarship often recognises the inherent visions and ideas held by institutions, we often do not look at personal interpretations of the young sailors and mariners who experience exploration.[366] What you will read next is based on the diaries, ships' logs, and the travel writings of British mariners to complement the institutional level of inscription, such as charts, to get a more comprehensive overview of the networks of knowledge from exploration.[367]

Nevertheless, understanding institutions' role in the Andaman Committee's knowledge network is still essential. The Royal Society, Royal Geographical Society, and Bombay Geographical Society are all examples of institutions that either instigated knowledge collection in the Andamans, managed the collection process through guidance, analysed the collected material, or eventually published the work.[368] These institutions also gave members status, particularly the Royal Society, which was a place for a 'distinguished' gentleman of science.[369] Institutions act as networks or assemblages of diverse elements, including people and structures. These elements also include non-human actors like technologies, objects, and even ideas or concepts.[370]

By 1857 and the founding of the Andaman Committee by the Indian Government, the construction of imperial space was a complex process shaped by ideals, discourses, and practices. These were rooted in both social and scientific knowledge. The 'scientific serviceman' concept reflected the role of geographically privileged military men, who extended British power and knowledge through their professionalism and access to state resources. How the Indian Navy, alongside the Royal Navy, played a crucial role in supporting the expedition to the Andaman Islands will be explored next.

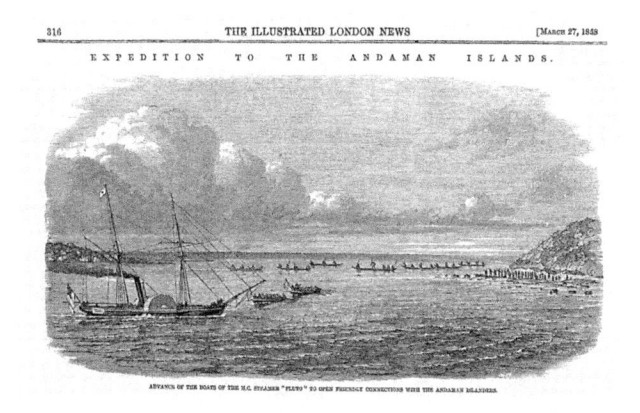

Figure 8: Expedition to Andamans

The Andaman Committee Survey, 1857

The Government of India initially considered surveying the Islands in 1852.[371] No resources were allocated at the time as it was not deemed a priority while the Second Anglo-Burmese War (1852–1853) was taking place. By 1857, the Indian Navy's resources continued to be stretched, this time by the Indian Rebellion.[372] However, an expedition and survey of the Andamans was prioritised due to the significant maritime traffic "between Madras and Pegu at the time".[373] As we saw in chapter two, the Andamans were colonised not just to house a penal settlement; maritime trade routes needed to be protected. The Indian Government saw the work of the Committee as essential to ensure the security and sanctity of the imperial maritime network.

The Indian Government formed the Andaman Committee on 20 November 1857, with the instruction of establishing a suitable site for a colony. It consisted of Dr Frederic John Mouat (President of the Committee, Bengal Army), Lieutenant James Arnold Heathcote (Indian Navy), and Dr George Playfair (Bengal Army).[374] There was a retinue of supporting staff, including the ship's companies, native infantry, and other attendees which are unfortunately not recorded.

The survey work and corresponding report completed by the Committee not only charted the archipelago's intricate human and physical geography but also generated a wealth of strategic knowledge that was relayed back to the Marine Department of the Indian Government.[375] It also formed the basis of the Indian Navy's following survey work of 1861, which you can read about in the next chapter.

The Andaman Committee was not a new or novel concept. A rich scholarship explores the role of British and European expeditions in surveying and collecting knowledge on the suitability of places to establish colonies and settlements.[376] The recognition that geographical knowledge is socially constructed links aptly to the idea that an empire was a force of progress.[377]

This period witnessed a concerted effort to map Europe's colonial possessions, to 'fill in' the blank spaces on the map for the pursuit of science.

Still, the pursuit of expansionism of empires cannot be disentangled from the pursuit of economic and trade advantages.[378] Developing out of the Foucault tradition, critical scholars have challenged the immutability of geographical knowledge such as charts, maps, historical information, and country descriptions produced by the various institutions of the Empire. This includes government organisations like the India Office, Foreign Office, War Office, and Admiralty.[379] Maps and charts are rich with representations of power and should not be treated as impartial reflections of geography or the "physical conformation" of a coastline.[380] Most British map projections, including the Mercator, have Britain in the centre of the world. Is Britain truly in the middle of the world? Geographically the world is not flat, so maps and charts are simply interpretations of the world in 2D. Therefore, they contain many hidden biases and agendas, alongside methodical data which accurately places the world into navigable format.

Returning to the Committee, the significance of the exploration extended beyond cartographic achievements; it encapsulates the British Empire's broader maritime ambitions and its unyielding quest for security in the Bay of Bengal. It was another attempt to forge a *British Sea*. By meticulously mapping the Andaman Islands, the British effectively transformed obscure landmasses into critical assets, bolstering their naval and commercial capabilities by turning *terra nullius* into British-authenticated data points that other European powers would recognise.

The map or chart acts as evidence of sovereignty and a navigation tool. The East India Company previously colonised the Andaman Islands in 1789, although the settlement failed and was abandoned in 1796. From the outset of the expedition, the Indian Government saw the Committee as a means to reassert sovereignty over the Islands.[381] Over the 58 years that had passed, much of the previous knowledge of the Islands was warranted as credible within one era, due to the methods of data collection and who collected the data.[382] Credibility was not about being a good scientist alone.

For British naval officers, often the legitimacy came from rank and a technologically advanced skillset, including the use of empiricism and instruments: "The legitimacy of new knowledge was to be made in the civility and good order of collective production."[383] Individual exploits by members of the Royal Navy, such as Captain Cook's voyages, have focused on the advanced skills of naval personnel.[384] The Indian Navy has yet to be viewed in the same light, even though the officers were exceptionally well-trained and, in many instances, had a better "maritime proficiency" than other British naval actors in the region.[385]

In the 1850s, Indian Navy officers were trained and competent in conducting observations, peer review, and disseminating geographical knowledge.[386] There is, however, a sociology of geographical knowledge; the social forces of truth, trust, and credibility are needed for any knowledge to count as authoritative and legitimate.[387]

The extent of legitimacy relied on a combination of gender, social background, race, and professionalism. These traits were often identified with being the ideal "gentleman" in Western societies.[388] Steven Shapin acknowledges that the reliability of a particular piece of testimony had to be made at a distance, and therefore the characteristics of who were deemed most 'trustworthy' in society were taken to be what was needed.[389]

The need to trust at a distance made the selection of the Committee members essential. The account below from Maurice Vidal Portman's collection of letters between the Indian Government and the Andaman Committee justifies the decisions:

> Dr. Mouat will be President of the Committee, and in general charge of the expedition. His attention will be more particularly given to matters connected with the enquiry, with which his

duties as Inspector of Jails in Bengal have made him familiar. The medical and scientific duties of the expedition will devolve upon Dr. Playfair. And those connected with the survey of the coast and the harbour, will be attended to by Lieutenant Heathcote. Lieutenant Heathcote will understand that a minute or detailed survey is not required; it will be sufficient to ascertain the general features of the channels or anchorages.[390]

Mouat made an interesting choice as the Committee's president, having a strong medical background as a surgeon for the Indian Medical Services. A rigorous and trusted member of society, Health was also considered key to ensuring a sustainable colony after the 1795 experience.[391] As a noted prison reformer who had recently taken up the position of Inspector of Jails in the Lower Provinces, he could advise on the suitability for a penal settlement.[392] Mouat, therefore, represented a reliable, gentlemanly figure of science.

More important to the study of seapower is the addition of Heathcote. His presence represents not just the integral nature of surveying to the whole endeavour but also that he was the interlocutor between the foremost enablers of the logistics of the survey work: the Indian Navy.[393] Heathcote was the primary means by which the Indian Government, via the Indian Navy, received information and updates about the three-month expedition.[394] The Indian Navy was the only means of communication between the Andaman Islands and the Indian Government in Calcutta. There was no telegraph on the Islands for another 30 years, and no ships stopped there for fear of savagery and cannibalism.

Heathcote was also the epitome of a scientific serviceman, even though Indian naval officers are often overlooked in contemporary historiographies.[395] Heathcote simultaneously conducted survey work and liaised with the other Indian Navy vessels in the area and the broader chain of command.

A much wider group of individuals, from mariners to local guides, would have been involved in supporting the expedition.[396]

However, in Mouat's published account of the expedition and the official correspondence between the Committee and the Indian Government, there is no record of additional augmentees unfortunately.

During the 1850s, Indian naval officers were increasingly engaged with the production of scientific knowledge: "connection with science and its growing visibility in society... the opportunity to obtain scientific credentials and thereby advance socially."[397] Indian naval officers, like their Royal Navy counterparts, would have had a basic understanding of the scientific method and on how to conduct survey work, but this was often treated as "other duties".[398]

Although there is no evidence in the correspondence between the Andaman Committee and the Indian Government regarding what equipment, instruments or specific surveying techniques were taken by the expedition, the Admiralty previously published its *Manual of Scientific Enquiry: Prepared for the Use of Her Majesty's Navy and Adapted for Travellers in General* in 1849, as part of a collaboration with John Murray, which provides oversight of the methodology at the time.[399] This was shared widely through the Indian Navy, so it is highly likely to have been used, or at least known about. As Erika Behrisch acknowledges, the *Manual of Scientific Enquiry* was not a revolutionary text but reflected the popular methodological trends of the time. Its contents would have been well known by naval officers of the time.[400]

The assumption cannot be made, however, that the Committee had the most technologically advanced equipment. As Simon Schaffer notes, the distance from the technological 'centre of gravity' in London meant that the Indian Government often had to pay exorbitant costs to get fragile equipment from Britain, with no guarantee it would survive the journey: "troubles of the instrument trade and long-range commerce in the exact sciences."[401]

Concurrently, as the Andaman Committee was undertaking work in the field, 'armchair geographers' were conducting sedentary research and collation in Calcutta.[402] Armchair geographers are those who produce geographical knowledge from primary sources created by others and secondary sources. They were not active in the 'field' collecting data but had more of a cohering function. Previous surveys of the Andaman Islands, such as the survey work by Alexander Dalrymple in the late 18th century, were collated by the Marine Department, the administrative body in command of the Indian Navy.[403] According to Felix Driver, this was to maximise the data available to provide credible decision-making: "provided a vastly greater bank of field data... transforming speculative assumptions about the way the world ought to be instead of the way the world actually was."[404]

Of the many armchair geographers studied, most are those who supported land exploration.[405] Rob Iliffe and Azadeh Achbari have instead analysed the networks surrounding the accumulation and dissemination of knowledge that enabled the British imperial maritime network.[406] Both identify the pivotal role of British naval actors in providing ships and "commanders" to support voyages of discovery; the key term here is 'support'.[407] Yet navies are consigned simply to being contributing actors in support of civilian institutions, like the Royal Society. That is an underestimation of the role navies performed. In 1857, the Marine Department was collating, producing, and analysing material that would complement the report published by the Andaman Committee to ensure a combination of primary and secondary data. This reflects more than a supporting function.

The Marine Department also provided the ships and supplies to transport the Committee to the Andaman Islands. The HCS *Pluto* (steam frigate), took the Committee and provisions from Moulmein to the Andamans for a four-day voyage, arriving on 8 December.[408] The HCS *Semiramis* (steam-frigate), commanded by Captain David Campbell of the Indian Navy, soon followed to support with supplies, convicts for labour, and security in the form of an officer and 20 European seamen.[409] Between 1855 and 1863, most survey work by the Royal Navy was conducted in hired vessels due to the drain on resources from the Crimean War.[410] The Indian Navy's expedition to the Andaman Islands in 1857 again reflects its importance to British seapower where the Royal Navy is warfighting a peer-adversary. It provided maritime logistical support where an overstretched Royal Navy could not.

The ships also did more than just transport the Committee from Moulmein to the Andaman Islands. Richard Sorrenson's reappraisal on the purpose of ships in science explored how ships performed as a transport, scientific instrument, and a place of belonging for the sailors on board.[411] As a place of science, Indian Navy vessels had a long history of being leaders in the production of survey work.[412] The former hydrographer to the East India Company, Alexander Dalrymple, established the Admiralty Hydrographic Office in 1795. Since then, the Marine Department and the Admiralty had been strong collaborators and would share material to benefit commerce and naval power.[413]

In 1855, as the discussion to settle on the Andamans resumed, the Admiralty sent 50 charts to the Marine Department covering the coastline of the Islands, including those produced by Lt Archibald Blair, Bombay Marine (see chapter four).[414] In 1857, Heathcote had access to a plethora of Admiralty charts as he prepared to conduct survey work around Port Cornwallis.[415] These charts would have acted as a base point for surveying and assisted in the expedition's navigation. The British's effective knowledge of the seas was a significant advantage in the Bay of Bengal, which had the "world's most strategic shipping lanes, and through the medium of maps, the Royal Navy believed it could exercise dominion".[416] Here was an example of mutual benefit in sharing information that traversed London to Calcutta, and into the Bay of Bengal.

The Andaman Committee received specific orders from the Indian Government before they set sail towards the end of November 1857. The Committee was to proceed and collect information about the Andaman Islands' geographical, climatic, and environmental conditions and revised coastal dates to assess their suitability for establishing a settlement.[417] The Indian Government defined the Indian Navy's role as providing logistical support, maritime surveillance, protection, and transportation for the Committee. Heathcote was the official point of contact. Although there was the possibility of using civilian vessels for the expedition, this was deemed inadequate based on the time and importance of the expedition.[418] Fundamentally, the Indian Navy was the only means to get the knowledge, resources, firepower, and logistics to enable the expedition.

Figure 9: Exploring Barren Island

From the Sea and Into the Field

Mouat published a book and delivered a lecture to the Royal Geographical Society in 1862. This provided a narrative of his experience of the Andaman Committee's expedition. Mouat's book is flourished with intriguing insights into flora and fauna, adventurous tales of the civility of the indigenous population, and a history of the Andamans. He also clearly portrays how he sees the role of the Andaman Committee as the logical next phase of the Andamans' history.[419]

Upon the Committee's arrival in the Andamans in 1857, they immediately began a comprehensive survey of the area to evaluate its suitability for settlement. It began in Port Cornwallis, which was previously regarded by Archibald Blair, an East India Company surveyor in the 1790s, as the most suitable spot for a settlement. Port Cornwallis was renamed Port Blair by the Committee in memory of the accuracy of Blair's charting, which you will read about in the next chapter.[420]

The Committee also explored various other locations across the Andaman Islands over the course of the following months. However, Port Blair was identified as the most suitable location due to its strategic position and natural harbour.[421] As they explored, the Committee's activities included assessing the terrain, climate, soil quality, and the availability of fresh water and other natural resources. All are essential elements for a sustainable settlement.[422] The Committee also explored the potential for agriculture and the feasibility of constructing secure facilities for housing prisoners. They evaluated the local flora and fauna and considered the presence of indigenous tribes and their potential interaction with a colony.[423] This detailed investigation was crucial in getting the evidence needed to inform government decision-making at reach.

A large quantity of data was collated in the report, which shows how the supporting party to the Committee had a wide skillset: "specialization made it difficult if not impossible for a single individual to keep up with, much less make significant contributions in, multiple fields."[424] The Committee aimed to thoroughly understand the entire archipelago's geography, resources, and potential challenges to establish a settlement on the Islands.

It was, however, a political endeavour in purpose rather than one based on the pure pursuit of knowledge alone. Claims of sovereignty were enhanced by accurate knowledge of places branded *terra nullius*, like the Andaman Islands.[425] In many ways, this goes against the very essence of the Baconian method. The Committee collected and surveyed to support an already pre-established perspective: a colony was required on the Andamans. It reflects the challenge of using the notion of a 'scientific serviceman'. In many ways, science as a practice was used as a methodological veil to justify imperial expansion.

One can argue whether the Andaman Committee of 1857 were true scientists or patrons of Empire, or both. They nevertheless collected a diverse range of knowledge about the Andaman Islands, inscribed in various formats. Geographical data was stored in logbooks, hydrography narratives, sketch maps, and notes of the Islands, including their topography, coastal lines, and inland features.[426] Heathcote and the crew on board the *Semiramis* conducted the coastal survey work, essential for assessing safe navigational routes. As was common practice, climate and environmental conditions, such as weather patterns, were also recorded in ships' logs for analysis by public scientists and other government departments, like the Admiralty Hydrographic Office.[427]

Mouat also heavily noted interactions with the indigenous populations, including their customs, ethnographic descriptions, language notes, and observations of social structures. This becomes a significant feature of his post-expedition book, and sketches of the Andamanese were the most prominent feature in his book.[428] Mouat's narrative is heavily placed within "European ideas about the tropics" and uses savage imagery to describe the indigenous populations, which was the norm at the time.[429] Postcolonial scholars have intensively researched Mouat and the Andaman Committee's engagement with and interaction with the Andamanese during this expedition, showing how this reinforced a 'savage' imagination.[430]

While Mouat made many sketches of the Andamanese bodies, he only loosely discussed the impact of the expedition on British bodies. The health of the British surveyors while conducting their duties was impacted by the heat and lack of fresh water.[431] The Indian Navy was instructed to take the Committee and supporting parties to sea to improve health. This reflected a vulnerability that, for understandable reasons, is not often addressed in narratives of exploration.[432]

Surveying and exploring took its toll on the body. Alongside a general deterioration of health caused by the environmental situation in the Andamans, there was also the ever-present danger of accidents at sea and engagement with the indigenous inhabitants. Heathcote was one of a number of the party who received a wound from arrows fired by the Andamanese.

Circulating Knowledge from Calcutta to Kensington

After months in the field, the Committee produced vast quantities of data inscribed in written reports, maps, charts, sketches, and logs. This data was eventually compiled into a comprehensive report that Mouat presented to the Indian Government.[433] Written records allowed the work to be easily transported and referenced while retaining the authority and legitimacy of their content. However, physical copies alone were not enough to add legitimacy, and Mouat immediately met the Viceroy of India, Lord Charles Canning, in Calcutta upon arrival to brief on his report. Such was the expected importance of the survey work.[434] Authority was as much about personal relationships as it was rigorous scientific work.

After the Andaman Committee arrived back in Calcutta, the most significant result of the survey was the sight of an Andamanese islander nicknamed 'Jack'. Jack was captured and brought back on board the *Pluto*. According to Mouat, he was "examined and cross-examined" by Lady Charlotte Canning but otherwise bathed in conversations of the "romantic" voyage in clubs to other Britishers.[435] This also expresses the divide between what is now perceived as hard science and where imperial exploration edges in the novelty. Jack soon became ill with cholera within a few months, so was returned to Port Blair, where there is no further record of him. He was also Arthur Conan Doyle's inspiration for a character Tonga in *The Sign of Four*.

Mouat, as President of the Committee, formally submitted his report on 1 January 1858 to the Home Department of the Government of India (a copy is recorded in Portman's text), alongside Heathcote's chart work.[436] The primary audience and commissioning agency for the Andaman Committee's reports was the Indian Government, which meant the report focused on the essentials for settlement: access, water, habitability, and safety. The extent to which the reports and survey work were reviewed by officials responsible for Calcutta's colonial governance is unknown. Still, the Indian Government considered them of a reputable and worthy standard to send to the Royal Geographical Society and the Admiralty.[437]

Mouat also ensured printed copies were distributed across key departments in Calcutta, including the Home Department, Marine Department, and Military Department.[438] Specific copies were sent to the Indian Navy and Bengal Army, respectively, recognising the military utility of the work.[439] Mouat eventually published a book and lectured at the Royal Geographical Society on his findings, reflecting the intriguing grey zone between science and imperial conquest.[440]

Although Moat's methodology was scientifically grounded, the outcome was inevitable; the Andaman Islands' geography was rewritten. The Andaman Committee became minor celebrities for their actions. Christine Macleod argues this is the mythologisation of imperial science that merges science with a militaristic national identity.[441]

The Andaman Committee's work provided the relevant evidence to recolonise the Andamans, with the raising of the British flag in a small ceremony by Captain Henry Man, Bengal Army, on 22 February 1858.[442] Mouat was intimately involved throughout, as he was informed when the formal bill was passed by the Indian Government confirming British intentions to colonise the Islands by the Secretary.[443] That is less than two months from the publication of the Andaman Committee's report to Indian Navy vessels sailing the Bay of Bengal with settlers to Port Blair to establish a colony.[444]

The speed of annexation reflects that the findings of the Andaman Committee were expected, and also the priority of finding a place outside of India to place political prisoners.[445] As a comparison, it took over two years to decide to even send the expedition. The political decision to establish a colony in the Andamans referenced the Committee's recommendations and findings throughout. After the decision, the Viceroy wrote to Mouat indicating the report's importance to the decision-making process.[446] This marked a significant moment in the colonial history of the Andaman Islands, as Britain re-established colonial rule, and is representative of what Clayton argues to be the creation of imperial space through the scientific method.[447]

The comprehensive maritime knowledge provided by the Committee about the geography, coastlines, harbours, and other aspects of the Andamans was also distributed to the Marine Office and Admiralty.[448] British imperial institutions converged on an agreed pathway to colonise the Islands. That is not to say all shared the view; only a record of agreed actions by the Indian Government is available. However, the actions of the constituent parts of the Indian Government, the Indian Navy, and the Home Department all aligned.

A consensus developed and a formal ceremony was commissioned to mark the colonisation of the Andamans. The government justified and set up the settlement in Port Blair by utilising the assessments of the geography, climate, natural resources, and ethnographic descriptions outlined in the Committee's findings. As Ben-Dror argues, surveying and cartography rewrite space and create new historical narratives in favour of the rewriter.[449] As such, the Committee's work must be seen in the light of imperial expansion more so than as a scientific expedition.

The report and survey work provided the evidence needed to justify re-settlement by filling in the "blanks" of understanding and creating data that made the decision appear rational through the scientific method.[450] Therefore, the Andamans' suitability as a settlement becomes widely accepted within a community based on data. Once the Indian Government accepted and implemented the Committee's recommendations, the intricate details, the extensive surveys, and the decision-making processes that resulted from the report were sent to the archive. The Andamans formally became "bounded" through cartographic representations as a British place from 1858 onwards.[451]

Almost immediately, the focus shifted to the administration and operation of the colony in Port Blair. The Indian Navy prepared multiple vessels, including the *Dalhousie*, *Tubal Cain*, and *Sesostris*, with supplies, officials, and convicts to Port Blair.[452] The Committee's report on the nuanced understanding of the local geography, environment, and indigenous societies faded into the background. The focus shifted from science to administration. The reports served their purpose and seamlessly integrated into the broader narrative of colonial administration as founded on scientific endeavour.

While the report itself was targeted towards the political apparatus, the Andaman Committee's work was also shared widely in geographical circles. Mouat presented his findings to the Royal Geographical Society as a paper and lecture in 1862.[453] He also published a successful monograph in 1863.[454] Like the Royal Society, the Royal Geographical Society was a key platform for discussing geographical discoveries, colonial administration strategies, and the "rigorous testing of geographical hypothesis".[455]

In presenting to the Society, Mouat and his work would have been peer-reviewed and gained greater legitimacy within the imperial establishment as it was authenticated and integrated into the knowledge base even further.[456] Knowledge travelled across the Empire while retaining legitimacy due to the method, the individuals, and institutional networks.[457] The relevance to this book is that Mouat's description of the Andamans focused on the indigenous populations, further enhancing the 'savage' imagery of the Andamans entrenching within the British psyche in the late Victorian era. Again, the role of the Andaman Islands within the British imperial maritime network was largely ignored, although he did emphasise the significance of the Indian Navy as an enabler. Ultimately, savagery sells better than seapower!

After completing their work with the Andaman Committee, the members were reassigned back to their respective areas of British colonial administration. Exploration was not, however, all glamorous. As Glyn Williams writes, the effect of the "miseries of seasickness and the frequent spells of longing for home" takes its toll.[458] Mouat was sent back to Britain with a sickness certificate by the Bengal Army at his request.[459] For Heathcote, although his involvement with the Committee would have added to his understanding of colonial governance, his request to become the Superintendent of the Penal Settlement was eventually rejected in 1859, although it is unclear why.[460] It shows that the transformation of the Indian Navy after the Government of India Act 1858 meant Indian naval officers saw an opportunity for career progression not just at sea, but as core officials of colonial administration.[461]

Exploration and Imperial Expansion from the Sea

Throughout 1858, significant changes to the Indian Government occurred as it transitioned from Company to Crown rule.[462] Following the merger of the Indian Navy as a subordinate organisation to the Royal Navy in 1858, the newly consolidated naval force continued to undertake significant surveying work, primarily focused on maritime and coastal areas of strategic importance from the Persian Gulf to the Bay of Bengal.[463] This work included charting sea routes, mapping coastlines, and conducting hydrographic surveys, which chapter four will discuss.

The work of the Andaman Committee bought value to the navies. Heathcote's survey work became the data point for charts used by the Admiralty and the Indian Navy when sailing around the Andamans. This work not only contributed to the safety and efficiency of naval operations but also had broader implications for commerce and wider imperial security. Safe passage was essential for troop movements conducted by the Indian Navy, mainly to Hong Kong and Singapore.[464]

The work of the Andaman Committee also underscores the intrinsic link between surveying, expeditions, and seapower. The Committee's findings show how knowledge was an essential, though often overlooked, element of seapower. The detailed geographical and environmental surveys conducted by the Committee were crucial in establishing the Andaman Islands as a strategic port in the imperial maritime network. Indian naval vessels, such as the *Fire Queen*, an iron paddle vessel, were simultaneously conducting survey work and what we know as constabulary duties.[465] While stationed in Port Blair in 1860, in the early days of the settlement, it completed extensive survey work of the Islands and protected the settlement from indigenous attacks.[466] The flexibility of naval vessels means they could simultaneously be places of science and firepower.

Expeditions and the production of knowledge were intertwined with military might. At this point, Indian naval officers were also heavily engaged in lobbying for additional survey work as they recognised its strategic importance, such as the papers published by the Bombay Geographical Society in 1860 on both the Andamans' and the Bay of Bengal's role in the security of British imperial networks.[467] Lieutenant Alfred Dundas Taylor and Lieutenant Thomas Morris Philbrick of the Indian Navy saw how increased knowledge, through the scientific method, would enhance British seapower. Increased knowledge provided an advantage to both British commercial and military shipping through improved navigation. The Indian naval officers saw beyond the military advantage of increased knowledge and how the seas were also a means for the British political and societal advantage.

This understanding of the importance of the seas "across the spectrum of national life" is what Andrew Lambert defines as a true seapower.[468] The Indian Navy, through knowledge, contributed to British seapower in the Bay of Bengal at the operational and tactical levels. It also shows how the Indian naval officers saw a means to shape the geographical position, the physical conformation, and the extent of territory of the British Empire in the Bay of Bengal to be as advantageous as possible for control of communications here.

The Indian Government thus reshaped and constructed new geographies in the Bay of Bengal after the Andaman Committee expedition. This led to territorial acquisition, changing coastlines. As chapter two showed, the Indian Government believed combining the Andaman Islands into Britain's imperial maritime network would enhance security. The expedition thus provided a means to formalise the acquisition of the Andaman Islands, and also provide evidence of the British claim.

In constructing new geographies, the Indian Government effectively turned ambiguous or contested spaces around the Andamans into demarcated zones of control and influence. The renaming of places, like Port Blair, and the creation of detailed navigational charts facilitated the imposition of British legal and administrative frameworks.[469] It was a form of ownership through the power to name.

Equally, names like Barren Island inferred emptiness and discomfort. The publication of an accurate chart with British names was a representative way of reinforcing claims of sovereignty over the Andamans.[470] If seapower is regarded as the capacity of a nation to control maritime communications through naval supremacy, then the Andaman Committee expedition reflects this control at a sociocultural level by changing geographies.[471] Seapower enabled the Indian Government to construct the Bay of Bengal as a British space, with the Committee providing the reports, charts, and data that reinforced the claim the Andamans were British sovereign territory. The Andamans were not unique either; this process was repeated across the Bay of Bengal through the 18th and 19th centuries.[472]

The dissemination of the Andaman Committee's outputs also exhibits the deep interconnection between science, seapower, and the British state in the 1850s. It also, simultaneously, shows the disconnection. The involvement of organisations like the Royal Geographical Society in fostering scientific exploration and knowledge dissemination strengthened imperial governance.[473] It provided an 'impartial' and peer-reviewed means to legitimise territorial acquisition. After being presented in the lecture rooms of the Society's Regent Street address, the Committee's findings became accepted knowledge within British society.[474] This process was essential for turning knowledge produced thousands of miles away into something credible and immutable.

Beyond recognition of the logistical support, the Indian Navy's role in transport, protection, and data collection is not mentioned in Mouat's account to the Royal Geographical Society. This represents the dislocation. The role of navies in British imperial expeditions was multifaceted. The Royal Navy served as the instrument of strategic maritime power, enabling the unhindered movement of expeditions from potential aggressors, such as European and Asian states. At the same time, the Indian Navy facilitated scientific exploration through logistical support to surveys and expeditions, as well as scientific advancements in navigation, cartography, and environmental understanding of the Bay of Bengal.[475]

Nevertheless, as seen in the case of Mouat, British audiences were sold a narrative of exploration that highlighted the extremes, and not the day-to-day experience.[476] To the British public, sea voyages were seen as mundane compared to the sublime tropicality of places such as the Andaman Islands, which were new to the British imagination.[477] Much of the Committee's work was mundane and monotonous, and the expectation of 'glory' back in Britain encouraged an aggrandised view of how this time was represented in written form.[478] A gentle period of reflection while sailing does not sell, and stories of cannibalism do.[479]

Hence, Mouat's narrative often exaggerates savagery. Jeffrey Auerbach suggests the boredom of the "... daily routine of eating, watch, muster, and reading" for those travelling by sea has meant that the role of navies has been overlooked in the everyday activity of imperial administration.[480] In the case of Mouat, the Indian naval vessels are overlooked as the mundane part of the journey. As a consequence of this, the broader role of the Indian Navy in the success of the expedition is also overlooked in historical record.[481]

The Indian Navy was vital to the expedition's success. Heathcote's survey work, which formed the basis for Admiralty charts, underscored the essential role of geographical knowledge in seapower, ensuring safe passage for troop movements and reinforcing British maritime dominance.[482] Although the initial survey work was not as detailed as you would expect from a Hydrographic Office chart, it was enough to transform ambiguous imperial spaces into British spheres of control, facilitating the imposition of British legal and administrative frameworks.[483] This construction of new geographies of the Andaman Islands, enabled by seapower, reinforced the British claim over the Islands. It demonstrates how territorial acquisition was formalised through naval-enabled expeditions.

Figure 10: Andaman Coastline

Colonisation by Committee

The Andaman Committee expedition of 1857–1858 marks the first formal British intervention into the interior of the Andaman Islands for over 50 years. From the very outset, the mission given to the Committee by the Indian Government was to devise and craft the knowledge needed to establish a suitable site for a penal colony. It was, however, still an expedition routed in seapower; through a penal colony, the British sought a permanent presence in this strategic location in the Bay of Bengal.

The Committee, consisting of Bengal civil servants, Bengal Army soldiers, and mariners from the Indian Navy, embarked on a detailed exploration of the Andaman Islands. Using scientific methodologies, they collected a variety of geographical knowledge, including coastlines, terrain, climate, soil quality, availability of fresh water, and flora and fauna.[484] Alongside, Mouat recorded interactions with indigenous populations. The comprehensive data collection culminated in a report sent to the Viceroy of India in March 1858 that provided the evidence needed for the re-colonisation of the Andaman Islands.

The Indian Navy was critical in enabling and supporting smaller imperial endeavours that are often overlooked in favour of grander, scientific voyages of discovery in the literature. Unlike the more extensively studied Royal Navy, the Indian Navy's contributions to imperial acquisition and knowledge networks have been overlooked. The Indian Navy was indispensable for the Andaman Committee, providing logistical support, transportation, and protection.

The Indian Navy was also unique in being a British naval actor with state funding through the partially nationalised East India Company, but independent of the Admiralty. It was, up until 1858, under a separate command structure. The expedition identified the Indian Navy's maritime proficiency in conducting research and navigating the complex marine environment of the Bay of Bengal, which it gained through over a century of institutional knowledge of operating in the area. This proficiency was the envy of colleagues in the Royal Navy and was a contributing reason to the disbanding of the Indian Navy in 1863.[485]

The Indian Navy's support for the expedition was multifaceted. From a mobility perspective, the Indian Navy provided the necessary steam gunboats, such as the *Pluto* and *Semiramis*, and ensured the safety of the Committee members. This protection was crucial in an era where the threat of piracy and indigenous attacks was ever-present on the Andamans, as chapter two explored. The Andamans were known as a place of savagery and cannibalism in the British geographical imagination.[486] Additionally, the Indian Navy's extensive expertise in hydrographic surveying was instrumental in rapidly charting the Andamanese littoral spaces over a short period of time. This was essential for establishing a sustainable settlement and the increasing maritime traffic in the region diverting through the Islands along vital British SLOC.

The Indian Navy's involvement corroborates its capability to perform scientific and military functions simultaneously, reinforcing its importance in the broader context of British imperial seapower in the Bay of Bengal through the 1850s. It also shows the various means in which power can be applied by naval vessels. Knowledge, and the ability to produce it, is a form of power.

For the Indian Government, the Indian Navy was the only actor capable of supporting the Andaman Committee expedition. The Royal Navy, focused on strategic maritime dominance and threats from national actors, was overstretched, particularly following the Crimean War. Equally, civilian merchant marine lacked the necessary protection and authority to undertake such a mission; although British flagged, civilian vessels did not represent a formal British government office, such as the Indian Government. The Indian Navy, with its local expertise, government authority, and firepower was uniquely suited to navigate the challenges of the Andaman Islands. It enabled the Committee to create the knowledge which would reconstruct the geographies of the Andaman Islands into a British framework.

Reconstructing the geographies of the Andaman Islands also enhanced British seapower. By critically reflecting on the geographic elements of Mahan's principles of seapower, the Andaman Committee expedition illustrates how geographical knowledge was used to reshape Britain's geographical position, physical conformation, and extent of territory in the Bay of Bengal. The expedition's findings challenge Mahan's deterministic view of geography as a set of physical conditions upon which naval power is applied. Geographies can change, and naval power enables geographies to change. The Indian Government, through the expedition, reshaped the maritime space of the Bay of Bengal by producing new geographical knowledge that served imperial objectives, notably territorial acquisition. Geography is not fixed spatially or temporally; it is fluid and socially influenced.

Seapower was essential to rewriting the Andaman Islands' geographies towards a British ideal. The Indian Government used the Andaman Committee expedition to rewrite maritime space using scientific methods, changing the sociocultural dimensions of the island towards a British ideal.[487] The renaming of Port Blair in 1857 was a symbolic example. There was no reflection on the indigenous name of the harbour, and the Committee chose the name after a notable hydrographer of the Indian Navy, who had surveyed the harbour in the 1790s.

Similarly, by conducting detailed surveys and producing authoritative charts, the expedition turned the ambiguous territories of the Andaman Islands into a defined space of British control. With accurate knowledge came improved navigation and increased trade.[488] The renaming of places and the creation of nautical charts facilitated the imposition of British legal and administrative frameworks onto the Andamans.

Seapower was the means to assert authority, not through gunboats, but through advanced knowledge. Through the production and dissemination of geographical knowledge, navies played a crucial role in colonial expansion, more so than the literature currently reflects. The Andaman Committee expedition exemplifies how naval forces were instruments of military power but also agents of scientific and geographical inquiry. The knowledge produced with the support of the Indian Navy during the expedition was vital for the strategic decision of the Indian Government to colonise the Andamans.

The Andaman Committee expedition of 1857–1858 highlights the essential role of navies in supporting small imperial expeditions, demonstrating the everyday activities that sustained and expanded British imperial influence. The Indian Navy's involvement in logistics, protection, and scientific surveying was crucial to constructing imperial geographies. Seapower can shape and redefine geographical spaces through knowledge production, challenging traditional views within seapower studies that treat geography as a static backdrop for naval activity. The next chapter will develop upon the themes of knowledge and navies, and analyse how the Indian Navy collated, collected, and circulated knowledge through hydrography to support British imperial ambitions further.

CHAPTER FOUR

Inscribing Seapower: Hydrography and Networks of Knowledge, 1860–1866

The HMINS *Clyde* rocked faintly in the calm waters around Havelock Island, northeast of Port Blair. It was an hour past dawn. The seas around the Andaman Islands were at their most docile. Midshipman William Marshall, Indian Navy, stood on the deck, pencil in hand, writing down the depths as the crew shouted out measurements. The sun beat down, casting a golden sheen on the water, and the air was thick with the scent of the viridescent shoreline. "Eight fathoms!" a sailor called out, his voice steady and robust. Marshall noted it down, glancing up occasionally to align the ship's position to his chart. Each measurement, each shout, brought a clearer picture of the seabed. For all the pleasure of science, it was a monotonous and repetitive task.

While it may now be a pleasant experience to sail the two-hour journey from Port Blair to Havelock Island, navigating easily between shoals and reefs with ease, this was far from the reality for early Victorian mariners. Until the advent of accurate charts from extensive survey work, it was a perilous journey that could easily end up with a fractured hull and a sinking ship.[489] Historians of empires have long recognised that accurate maritime knowledge was essential for expansionist European imperial powers to project power and ensure safe navigation along expanding trade routes.[490] However, the focus has been on the role of civilian bodies and institutions in producing knowledge, and the military networks have been understudied, according to Jordan Goodman.[491]

Some works address specific elements of the military's involvement in imperial knowledge, such as the role of institutions like the Admiralty Hydrographic Office.[492] There are also studies into the role of military men, such as 'scientific servicemen', and how these individuals have contributed towards our understanding of the world through 'big science'.[493] Big science refers to the extensive, exceptionally well-funded scientific voyages of discovery, such as Commodore George Anson's or Captain James Cook's circumnavigations of the world.[494]

I will take a different approach and look at another example of 'small-science', such as in chapter three. In this case, I will focus on the survey work occurring in littoral spaces across the British Empire, often by individual ships as a form of 'everyday' activity.[495] By 'everyday', this refers to how surveying was part of the normal duties for Indian naval vessels at the time and would have been seen as regular activity.

Small science, such as survey work, provided essential geographical data that enhanced imperial governance by supporting precise navigation into ports, enforcing territorial claims, and regional planning. There are many types of knowledge which navies produce, from health to intelligence, but geographical knowledge was deeply intertwined with imperial control.[496] Chapter three addressed the role of navies in supporting small imperial expeditions, including surveying as a contributing method, to understand how imperial space was made. Here I will instead focus on how hydrography was a form of power in itself. Hydrography would bring clarity to geographies and, through inscription on charts, become a record of British control.

I will use a similar approach to John Law and Amara Solari by treating surveying as a network, from planning to circulation.[497] Law's and Solari's network of analysis of Spanish and Portuguese maritime centres of calculation reflected how knowledge was a form of power over sea spaces. As noted by Vice Admiral John

Edgell RN, a former hydrographer of the Royal Navy: "surveying is inseparable from that of discovery and exploration; these in turn depended upon a thirst for knowledge and the quest for trade."[498] Creating an accurate and detailed knowledge of maritime spaces represents a symbol of being a seapower, just as much as having a 68-pounder muzzle-loading smoothbore gun on the *Clyde* was.[499]

To understand the role of navies in small science, I will explore the survey work started in 1860 by the Indian Navy and undertaken around the Andaman Islands after the Indian Government's recolonisation. Once again I will look at the process as a network, from field to chart, which includes the publication of the 1861 Hydrographic Office Chart *Gulf of Bengal, South Andaman I, East Coast, Port Blair*.[500] Even after being published in chart form and made publicly available by the Hydrographic Office in 1863, variations to this specific chart were added until 1866 after the Trigonometry Survey of India, and this development will be addressed.

The 1861 chart of Port Blair was not, however, a stand-alone piece of survey work. It used data from two previous surveys of the Andaman Islands, one by Lieutenant Archibald Blair of the Bombay Marine in 1789 and the other by the Andaman Committee in 1857–1858.

An additional purpose of looking at the network of surveying around the Andamans in the 1850s and 1860s is to challenge Ken Booth's listings of the function of navies as being policing, diplomatic, or military functions.[501] This narrow delineation misses the vital role of navies in contributing knowledge that enables statehood. The Royal Navy and Indian Navy have a long history of knowledge experts who used science to enhance warfighting and found institutions to promote imperial prosperity. This includes Alexander Dalrymple and the Hydrographic Office, Vice Admiral Robert Fitzroy and the Meteorological Office, and Sir John Franklin and Sir Francis Beaufort, founders of the Royal Geographical Society.

Recent work by Erika Behrisch and Sara Caputo has begun recognising the role of the Admiralty as a place of science and knowledge. However, Behrisch does not address how this knowledge was used for "purposes of military might", which I will do here.[502] Although Micheal Barritt's work accounts for the importance of hydrography to warfare, the temporal focus is the Napoleonic Wars. It also does not account for the changes in hydrography brought by steam power.[503]

Knowledge production was a significant function of British naval actors in support of imperial governments, and it remains vital to contemporary operations in the 21st century.[504] *Knowledge* should feature as one of the 'four' functions of navies, expanding Booth's trinity. Knowledge was a form of power that enabled the British to militarily and economically dominate the Bay of Bengal through the period known as Pax Britannica.

The first section of this chapter will contextualise surveying in the Bay of Bengal in the 1850s. The next section will look at the *Gulf of Bengal, South Andaman I, East Coast, Port Blair* chart published by the Admiralty from 1861 until 1866, including the reasons for any changes in this period. The final section will reflect on the implications of surveying as a practice on seapower.

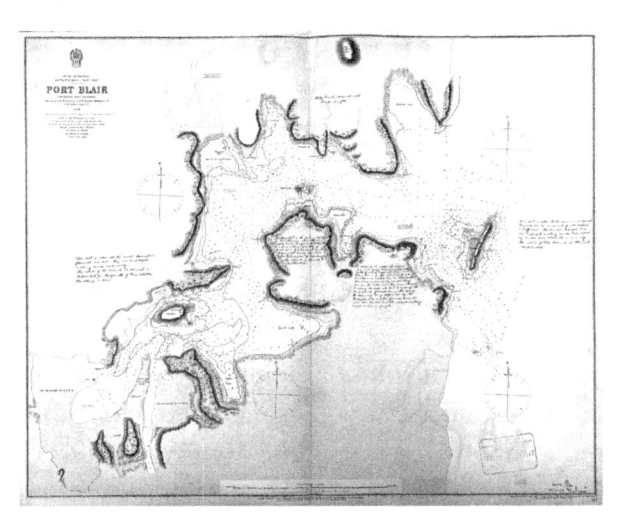

Figure 11: Port Blair

Hydrography in the Bay of Bengal, 1850s to 1860s

Hydrography is a multifaceted body of knowledge, but its essence is based on geographical thought. Geography, both in terms of its practices and the knowledge it produces, changed dramatically throughout the Victorian era, as chapter three expressed.[505] Geographical knowledge is recognised to consist of a set of related practices: surveying, geometry, cartography, travel writing, botany, hydrography, and historical description, among others.[506] A surveyor on board a British naval ship would have had a comprehensive ability to conduct some, if not all, of the practices listed previously through training and the use of guides.[507]

These practices also overlap. Surveying occurs terrestrially or at sea. In its maritime sense, it was the science of determining positions of points and the distances and angles between them to produce a chart.[508] Hydrography is the broader practice that included both the science of measuring, describing the physical features of bodies of water, and the adjacent land for the purpose of navigation.[509] For clarity, the process of data collection is defined as surveying, whereas the knowledge produced was a form of hydrography. This is based on the definitions used by the Hydrographic Office in the 1850s.[510] This is also a key difference between chapter three and four; chapter three addressed the data collection (surveying) as part of a wider endeavour, whereas this chapter addresses the networks of knowledge (hydrography).

Hydrography had both practical and philosophical implications for British society which we will explore, but fundamentally its accumulation was driven largely by the demands of trade and territorial conquest.[511] The spatial turn in the social sciences has since challenged the rudimentary nature in which geographical knowledge, like hydrography, was considered an immobile outcome of empire, by recognising the "indelible mark left by different social and cultural milieux".[512] Geographical knowledge, therefore, means different things, to different people, in different places.

At the same time as the spatial turn in history and geography, sociologists of science Bruno Latour and Stephen Woolgar pioneered the idea that to understand the making of scientific knowledge, it was necessary to see how it was made and to map the entirety of the network.[513] While the chart by the Indian Navy reflects a particular world view applied to a 2D inscription, the process of producing the chart and the circulation of the end product is even more enlightening. Survey work, as Latour noted, often emerged out of state-directed navigation projects and expeditions to unchartered places that were premised on expanding knowledge or for the sheer human endeavour.[514] It is generally accepted that the state benefitted most from exploration, including the notion that accurate hydrographic knowledge was an essential element of a successful maritime-centric state.[515] Knowledge of the sea, particularly hydrography, was vital for the enactment of power at sea in this period.[516]

Throughout the 1850s, the Indian Government had a relatively comprehensive hydrographic understanding of littoral spaces and major SLOC of the Bay of Bengal, except around the deep-sea spaces and the Andaman and Nicobar Islands.[517] In consequence, the Andaman Committee of 1858 was commissioned in part to conduct survey work. The Indian Government wanted accurate knowledge to ensure the safety of shipping, enforce the territorial claim, and provide a superior understanding of the operating environment for British military actors.[518]

To get accurate knowledge, you needed accurate instruments. Jordan Goodman argues there needs to be a re-alignment to the 'hardware' of imperial knowledge, from ships to compasses.[519] Richard Sorrenson's reappraisal on the purpose of ships in science explored how ships performed as a transport, scientific instrument, and a place of belonging for the sailors on board, as well as the significance of who commissioned it.[520] There has since been a rich literature on ships and the production of knowledge and geography more widely.[521] Doug MacDougall's study into the voyage of HMS *Challenger* reflects how and why Royal Navy ships were organised specifically for the purpose of grand voyages of discovery, but there is little reference to the everyday scientific work undertaken by naval vessels.[522]

Whether for hydrography, coastal survey (coastline mapping), botanical or ethnographic study, much of the scientific work the Royal Navy or Indian Navy conducted was in addition to other duties.[523] It was part of everyday life on board. In fact, unlike *Challenger*, many Indian naval vessels conducted surveying alongside constabulary duties while protecting Port Blair, as we shall see.

While surveying the Andaman Islands, the Indian Navy would have used a variety of texts and means of inscription. More recently, scholarship has focused on the objects in which knowledge was either collected or published, including logbooks, technical works like the Admiralty narratives, the watercolours which complemented many charts, and the 'Manual of Scientific Inquiry'.[524] While these objects have meaning contained in their inscription, their physical form enabled them to be present on salty decks and long voyages without perishing, such as John Herschel's 1886 *Manual of Scientific Inquiry*.[525] We often take these things for granted, but part of the success of the manuals was to have the right information, that was understandable, but also portable. These manuals provided a standardised format, which meant the data collected by surveyors in the Andaman Islands was understandable and useable to analysts and draughtsman thousands of miles away in urban centres of calculation like the Hydrographic Office.

To run a vast empire across thousands of miles, you need a plethora of different forms of knowledge. For the Indian Government, the utility of knowledge was based on how it supported administration, maintained power, or enforced control after the transition from Company to Crown rule.[526] It was not the wider pursuit of human advancement which was the reasoning behind the Royal Society, as an example.[527] While it is true that both the Indian Government and the Admiralty are knowledge institutions, they will instead be classified as 'oligopticons' as they have a limited, controlled view of proceedings focused on effective governance or the application of seapower in support of governance: "Britain's maritime power rested on, and reproduced, practices and principles of statehood, science and communication."[528]

The Admiralty Hydrographic Office, however, represents a centre of calculation: an institution where information is gathered, processed, and used to make decisions or exert influence.[529] There is limited research about centres of calculation for British naval activity in the mid-19th century onwards, as identified by Felix Driver.[530] The role of the Admiralty's Hydrographic Office in the early 1860s was a place where geographical knowledge was legitimised and shared for military endeavour. The Hydrographic Office was established in 1795 by the former Hydrographer to the East Indian Company, Alexander Dalrymple.[531] There is a significant body of literature which has explored the role of the Office in Britain's mastery of the seas in the late Victorian era.[532] This literature, however, looks at the Hydrographic Office independently rather than as part of a wider network including organisations like the Indian Navy.

Figure 12: View of Port Cornwallis

The Hydrographic Office was an effective centre of calculation that enabled British seapower in the Bay of Bengal, and beyond. Centres of calculation collated knowledge, both past and present. This includes past surveys, such as the work conducted by Lt Archibald Blair, Bombay Marine. His surveying was considered of such gravitas that the Andaman Committee named Port Blair in his honour.

The East India Company Survey Work, 1789–1795

The surveying completed by Lt Archibald Blair, a surveyor for the East India Company's Bombay Marine, formed the foundation of the understanding of the Andaman Islands for the next 50 years through the reports and charts it produced.[533] Aboard the HCS *Ranger* and HCS *Viper* over three years, Blair's work became the dataset that was used in support of the Andaman Committee to survey the Islands in 1857. It was also the first point of reference for the 1861 coastal survey work.[534] While Charles Rathbone Low also argues that Blair's data was so comprehensive "the Supreme Government was induced to establish a penal settlement", chapter one has established this was not the case and in fact the harbours and naval utility were the driving reason.[535] Nevertheless, Blair's survey became the standard of knowledge on the Andamans; it was accepted and used without the need to challenge its conception.

The Indian Government and the Commander-in-Chief of East Indies, Commodore Edward Vernon RN, saw the Andamans as "the most proper rendezvous port, ready for any occasion" in 1779.[536] The Andamans were, however, not the only area of interest to the Royal Navy and Indian Government at the time. There was also some interest on whether to establish a settlement at the Nicobar Islands by the Indian Government in 1785, which was eventually rejected due to Danish interest and claims.[537]

Alexander Dalrymple, before he transferred from his role of Hydrographer to the East India Company to the Admiralty into the same position, collated a series of charts from various sources covering the Islands in 1790.[538] These assisted the first formal settlement, which began in 1789.[539] These discussions between Vernon and the Indian Government represent a way of turning bureaucracy and science into constructing geographical knowledge to match the British imagination: "assumptions about the way the world ought to be into accurate knowledge of the way the world actually was."[540]

In practice, navigation was more of an art than science in the 1790s, relying on the use of stars and sextants. Therefore, any charts available were extremely valuable.[541] The voyage to the Andamans by Blair would have largely been based on the charts Dalrymple had collected, including mariners' tales from ports and historical fables.[542] There are only limited accounts of how the East India Company managed survey work in the late 18th century, with much of the focus on where surveys were conducted rather than the process.[543] The historiography of surveying becomes more comprehensive once the Hydrographic Office was established under Dalrymple, and the various manuals were published and distributed.[544]

Erika Behrisch's study does, however, provide an account of surveying practices for the latter half of the 19th century.[545] Based on this, we can infer that the survey work conducted by Blair was comprehensive and numerous. However, he was not the only participant in this survey network. He had the use of members of the relevant ship's company. What we do know is that Blair was accompanied by Lieutenant Robert Hyde Colebrooke of the Bengal Engineers.[546] Colebrooke was notable for his artistic ability and produced watercolour sketches of Port Blair.[547] Colebrooke was an active scholar, publishing in the *Journal of the Asiatic Society of Bengal* and attuned to the scientific method, making him an ideal collaborator to support Blair.[548]

Over the three-year period in which Blair and Colebrooke surveyed, they significantly enhanced the geographical and navigational understanding of this strategically located archipelago. The surveys produced detailed maps and charts, delineating the intricate coastline, underwater hazards, and potential anchorage sites vital for safe navigation and future maritime expeditions.[549] This information was crucial for the British naval and commercial interests in the region, particularly in controlling the sea routes and enhancing trade by ensuring mariners had the proper knowledge and no longer relied on "written memoirs to guide a captain step-by-step through a journey".[550] Surveying created order in the maritime spaces, and the Andaman and Nicobar Islands were no exception.

Blair and Colebrooke's maps and charts can be considered immutable mobiles, information that can be transported across time and space without significantly altering their structure or meaning.[551] However, as Jordan Branch notes, while they may be authoritative in the data they represent, such as coastline or depth, they are not impartial: "Mapping gave sovereign statehood its territorially exclusive character." This early mapping exercise by Blair and his fellow mariners forms a central tenet of the British claim to the Andamans, as does the naming process.[552]

It is also notable that copies of Blair's original charts can be found in the archives of the Royal Navy, the Hydrographic Office (now UKHO), and the Indian Government.[553] These surveys contributed to the broader British imperial objectives of exploration and territorial acquisition and hence archived in three major repositories of the British imperial state. By gaining a thorough knowledge of the Andamans, the East India Company laid the groundwork for future colonisation and military use of the Islands by bringing them into the imperial maritime network.

Additionally, the survey work facilitated the collection of weather and climate data, data on health, and natural history information.[554] In collecting this vast swathe of data, recent critical studies within historical geography and history have acknowledged that behind all 'great men' was a series of people that had significant agency in the success (or failure) of voyages of discovery and exploration: "... the guides, translators, hosts, labourers and a myriad of other "local"... assisted and facilitated European[s]."[555] This perspective is symbolic of re-assessing the production of geographical knowledge to uncover the subaltern or marginalised figures involved in these networks.[556]

Peter Martin's work on Arctic maritime exploration recognises that indigenous knowledge was assimilated into the reports of European mariners in the early 20th century, and the credits for this were often ignored once published.[557] There is no mention of indigenous support in this knowledge production network. However, Portman identified communication with the Andamanese in and around Port Cornwallis during the survey work, and based on previous subaltern work, there was a likelihood of some form of knowledge transfer engagement.[558]

The colonial gaze also framed the survey work, reflecting the surveyor's internal biases.[559] Constructivist interpretations of knowledge separate physical geographical data from ethnographic when assessing imperial knowledge.[560] Certain data, like depth and tide, are very different from assessments of the intellect of the indigenous tribe, which are founded only on observation and not based on data collection through instrumentation. Hence, using the scientific method provides an immutability to the charts, weather accounts, health reports, details on the flora/fauna, and accounts of the indigenous population. This allowed a reader in London, Paris, or Amsterdam to interpret and understand the data.

The charts, reports, paintings, and other data were eventually collated and archived by the East India Company in Fort William, Bengal. In many respects, these reports were the first accounts of these islands to be treated as 'authoritative', primarily due to the scientific method and position of men like Blair and Colebrooke, authoritative and respectable agents of Empire. The settlement in Port Cornwallis, called Port Blair from 1858 onwards, became untenable due to the deteriorating health of the British settlers.[561] Colonial administrators used the final reports published by both Blair and Colebrooke in the 1850s to assist in the resettlement of the Islands. Surveying by the Bengal Marine in the 1790s, supported by other British imperial actors, provided the British with a textual claim for continued sovereignty over the Islands that could be used as proof for the intervening 50 years. Once again, knowledge is a vital component of seapower. It provided a means for territorial acquisition.

Figure 13: Port Cornwallis

Indian Navy Survey Work, 1860-1866

The Indian Navy's 1861 survey of the Andaman Islands coastline was primarily intended to provide accurate and comprehensive charting of the Islands and their vicinity.[562] The Indian Government commissioned it after the decision to approve the new settlement based in Port Blair.[563] This was crucial for the safe transit of commercial shipping and military vessels across important SLOC that crossed the Bay of Bengal, an essential tenet of the *British Sea* narrative.[564] It also offers an opportunity to expand upon Behrisch's noted shortfall in the literature, which is how surveying links to "purposes of military might".[565]

Accurate hydrographical knowledge was a form of military might that enables seapower. British seapower was effective worldwide as it had precise geographical and environmental information, which was essential for strategic planning, navigation, and effective deployment of military forces.[566]

In the early days of the settlement, the Marine Department of the Indian Government noted the danger of passage around the Andaman Islands in February 1860.[567] Reports of ships lost at sea while sailing towards Port Blair in October 1860 provided an example of the danger.[568]

The solution from the Port Blair administration was to request an increase in survey work conducted by the Indian Navy around the Islands for three reasons.[569] Firstly, there was a pressing need for accurate and reliable charts for navigation and ensuring safe passage for ships. Secondly, it was vital for the performance of British sovereignty over the Islands. Rewriting and renaming the Islands along British names and being the 'supreme' holder of knowledge over the Islands represented core aspects of expressing imperial sovereignty and control.[570]

Finally, by 1860, survey work was essential to ensure the correct laying of undersea cables between India and outstations like Port Blair.[571] This was a stated priority of the Indian Government by 1861 and reflected how the Port Blair settlement was slowly, but formally, entering the British imperial maritime network.[572] Seapower is regarded as the control of communications at sea, and accurate hydrographical knowledge enhanced Britain's ability to ensure the safety and protection of this communication.

The Marine Department granted the request to the Port Blair administration, and in 1861, a dedicated survey ship was sent to Port Blair.[573] The ship's company of the *Clyde* were to conduct a comprehensive survey across the breadth of the Andamans and down to the Nicobars. For reasons of scope, I will focus on the chart produced for Port Blair.[574] Although we will treat this survey as a new network, it was not a fresh endeavour. Since the 1858 India Act, the Indian Navy was subordinate to the Royal Navy. It was slowly being transformed from a force with large gunboats and a significant regional naval power to one with coastal and auxiliary functions.[575]

The Indian Navy did, however, retain its surveying responsibilities. The force became responsible for survey work within the territorial control of the Indian Government.[576] An arrangement between the Secretary of State for India and the Admiralty in March 1861 meant the "whole of the marine-survey, chart, and hydrographic business... undertaken by the Hydrographer".[577] Now, the Indian Navy had a formal and direct relationship with the Admiralty Hydrographic Office for the first time.

While the Indian Navy and Admiralty collaborated with surveying before the early 1860s, this was friendly rather than a command-based relationship. The Hydrographic Office holds a collection of mixed foreign charts and coastal drawings of the Andaman and Nicobar Islands before 1861 from Indian naval sources.[578] On the other hand, the Hydrographic Office also holds a collection of Remarks Books from Royal Navy vessels, but not Indian naval vessels.[579] The books recorded the observations of a ship while sailing, including: "directions for sailing into and out of ports, marks for anchoring, potential wooding and watering, local provisions and refreshments, fortifications, and the value and size of local shipping and trade."[580] The Indian Navy shared knowledge with the Hydrographic Office, but it did not have a formal requirement to hand over Remarks Books, for example.

Behrisch notes that the Hydrographic Office would have consulted every faculty and evidence base available to produce the charts.[581] This is particularly true of the precedent set under Rear Admiral Sir Francis Beaufort (Hydrographer of the Navy, 1829–1855), who encouraged standardised data recording methods and turned the Hydrography Office into a centre of calculation in Whitehall, London.[582] This knowledge was stored and archived in London, and the surveyors in India would not have had direct physical access to this wealth of material. The surveyor focused on data collection without the need for strategic oversight of the entire process.

What was the urgency for new charts of Port Blair? Soon after the report by the Andaman Committee reached Calcutta in March 1858, additional vessels were sent to Port Blair with the resources needed to build and protect the colony.[583] HMINS *Sesostris* was initially assigned as the guardship to protect the first settlement in Port Blair in 1859 but was called away for duty elsewhere.[584] HMINS *Clive* was sent to provide additional security with a contingent of forces for shore protection.[585] The storeship *Tubal Cain* was sent with stores and convicts for labour.[586] These vessels would also take measurements and record data as they were sailing to and from Port Blair. However, this contribution had more to do with correcting mistakes or things missed on the charts rather than a comprehensive data collection for a chart.[587] With more and more government vessels sailing into Port Blair, comprehensive charts were needed.

Soon, a regular transit service between Port Blair and Calcutta started, with the *Fire Queen* frequently sailing backwards and forwards to the two ports from February 1861.[588] The settlement was undergoing rapid development and transformation, and the Indian Navy was at the heart of efforts; it was a logistical lifeline, protection agent, and knowledge producer.[589] Navies are inherently flexible. The Indian Navy was slowly being transformed, but it could still conduct duties for which the Royal Navy did not have the resources or did not want to do.[590]

The 1860–1861 survey work was a more systematic and thorough endeavour than the more informal data collected by the *Sesostris*, *Clive*, and *Tubal Cain*. The new work was intended to provide a detailed understanding of the Andamans' coastline and coastal topography. It was to be conducted by the Indian Navy on the HMINS *Clyde*, despatched in early 1860 with orders to comprehensively survey the area.[591] The *Clyde* was a 300-ton,

80hp screw gunboat and was one of the more heavily armed steamships of Her Majesty's Indian Navy.[592]

As William Hasty and Kimberly Peters note, ships are overlooked but integral actors in the maritime space, and there was a particular reason for choosing the *Clyde*.[593] Low, in his account of the survey work of the Indian Navy, records that:

> In the years 1860, Mr Midshipman W. Marshall, of the 'Clyde' gunboat, then stationed at the Andaman Islands, surveyed, unassisted, Port Blair, Middle Straits, and the Cocos Islands. The chart of the former has been published by the Admiralty, and the two latter were lithographed in India. Owing to the savage character of the Andamaners, the surveys were executed in boats fully manned and armed, with outposts stationed in the jungle to prevent surprises.[594]

As the *Clyde* was one of the most heavily armed vessels of the Indian Navy, it reflects how the Indian Navy wanted a ship that could sail independently for the long, arduous, and monotonous hours of survey work away from the relative safety of the settlement in Port Blair while being able to protect itself. Although the Andamanese were not a state threat, the use of a gunboat is representative of Victorian-era naval policing.[595] Even after the Port Blair settlement was established, the colonial administrators remained insecure about the threats across the Islands.

Alongside its armament, the *Clyde* also had a shallow draft to navigate closer to shorelines. In the places that the *Clyde* could not reach, such as reefs, the ship's company would have instead used the on-board rowboat. The combination of a shallow draft and rowboat made the *Clyde* ideal for detailed coastal surveying. It was adapted to littoral waters and with firepower to protect itself.

With its experienced navigators and surveyors in the Bay of Bengal, the Indian Navy was well-equipped to undertake this challenging task. These navigators and surveyors could chart the intricate coastline of foreign lands and still be prepared to use naval force; they were the embodiment of the scientific serviceman, as described by Randolph Cock.[596]

The Indian Navy was also finding a new role within the Indian Government at this point. Since 1859, John Charles Mason, Marine Secretary to the East India Company and now Secretary of the Marine and Transport Department, had pushed for the Indian Navy to be focused on trade and transport rather than warfighting.[597] Surveying, thus, fell under this banner. This restructuring in purpose allowed for better coordination and planning of surveying missions. The Indian Navy undertook more ambitious and extensive surveying projects.[598] This can be seen visually in the detailed chart of Port Blair in 1861, which includes depths, water sources, and the location of settlements, compared to Blair's chart, which features a very basic coastline.

Whereas Lieutenant James Arnold Heathcote of the Indian Navy survey 1858 focused on access to and from settlement locations, the 1860 survey was a much more comprehensive study. The 1860 survey had military and commercial utility. The result was intended to support the publication of a new Admiralty chart of the area.[599]

Although there would have been other commercially available charts, such as the 1856 chart of the Andaman Islands by the hydrographer J.W. Norrie, the Admiralty versions were becoming standardised and considered reliable sources.[600] The Admiralty charts also contained all the basic information a naval or merchant captain would need. The military utility of accurate charting of Port Blair was part of what Davey argues was the "next generation of naval operations".[601] This was because steam ships were not dependent on the winds, and could sail new routes and closer to shore without risks. The increased mobility of steamships allowed access to locations without the weather being in favour.[602] Therefore, the Admiralty Chart reflects the symbiosis of naval power and maritime knowledge in the imperial administration. Admiralty charts were a tool of navigation and power projection.[603]

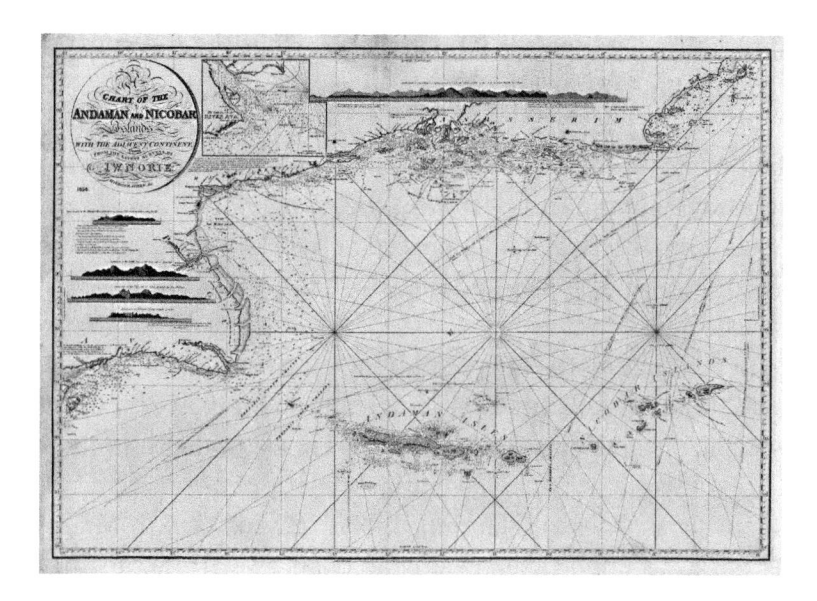

Figure 14: Norrie Chart

Collecting Data at Sea

Lieutenant William Burnie Dickson and Mr W. Marshall Midshipman, of the Indian Navy, oversaw the 1860 surveying mission. Katherine Anderson's work on hydrography, although based on the 1830s, provides a valuable framework for what data the surveyors would have been looking for.[604] The Andrew David Collection at the UKHO also provides an overview of the content of the sailing directions produced at the time.[605]

Firstly, they would concentrate on surveying, which involved: charting the seabed, measuring water depths, identifying navigational hazards like rocks, wrecks, and uncharted islands, and anything that could impede safe navigation.[606] Secondly, they would have collected data on the coastline, including topographical surveying, to create accurate coastal maps, identify landmarks, and understand the coastal terrain through geographical measurements.[607] Thirdly, they would have engaged in meteorological observations and recorded weather patterns and oceanographic data such as tides, currents, and water temperatures, which are vital for understanding the maritime environment.[608]

The Remarks Books also show the wider observations taken by naval officers. They would assess natural resources, anchorage spots, and potential locations suitable for naval vessels. Once collated and analysed at the Hydrographic Office, this comprehensive methodology would provide valuable data to create a chart.

In conducting the survey, the Indian naval officers adhered to the standard maritime surveying methodologies of the time: systematic coastal traversal, using lead lines for depth sounding and sextants for celestial navigation to determine positions, and charting coastlines and landmarks by triangulation.[609] Much of this work was undertaken in smaller boats away from the *Clyde*:

> From this base, surveying officers headed out in smaller boats armed with notebooks, sextants, chronometer, compass and sounding line.[610]

However, this is where the surveyors were most vulnerable to attacks from the indigenous population. There were frequent interactions between the Indian naval vessels and the indigenous populations. Often, these were not violent encounters, but mutual suspicion from the Indian naval officers meant that the crews were taken away from surveying into defensive positions back on board the *Clyde*.[611] In the early 1860s, the Andaman Islands were still perceived as a place of savagery within the British geographical imagination, as discussed in chapter two. During the survey, the *Clyde* was also sent to interdict a Malay vessel suspiciously close to Port Blair.[612] Again, this reflects the tension between surveying being a primary duty for the mission, but secondary to the broader use of navies as platforms to exert hard power.[613]

The surveyors onboard the *Clyde* used a range of nautical and surveying equipment typical of the era, including sextants and compasses for navigation, lead lines for depth sounding, chronometers for determining longitude, and telescopes for sighting landmarks.[614] Observations were meticulously recorded, often in logbooks or survey sheets.[615] They would have sketched the coastline to record topographical features, integrating these sketches with numerical data to create comprehensive charts.[616]

All the findings would be carefully noted in a clear and organised manner, using the period's standard nautical terms and measurement units.[617] This meticulous approach ensured that the data would be coherent and interpretable by other naval officers and, more importantly, by the Hydrographic Office in London. The significance of a consistent methodology is that distance does not detract from geographical familiarity, whether it is the same nautical language or charting conventions. This allowed charts to be drawn at a distance by the six naval assistants and five draughtsmen in London from data collected 5,677 miles away.[618]

Although Dickson and Marshall's original data is not available in the records of the Indian Government or the Hydrographic Office archives, officers "were more often collectors of raw data than interpreters of it".[619] Certain Indian naval officers, such as Lieutenants Thomas Philbrick and Alfred Taylor, were active in the academic community in 1860.[620] However, many naval officers conducted their duty and completed the data collection as requested rather than proactively. Dickson and Marshall sent the data through the chain of command without keeping copies or presenting it to learned organisations like the Bombay Geographical Society, making the original data hard to trace.[621] Some scientific servicemen were more 'scientific'; others were naval officers foremost.

The fact that we do not have Dickson's or Marshall's original reports is disappointing from the perspective of academic interest. Still, it does not impede the assessment of the network. This is because the standardisation and formalisation of instruction undertaken by the Hydrographic Office over the preceding 50 years up to the 1860s meant there was a clear precedent of what happened to the data.[622]

Upon completing the survey, the surveyors would have undertaken several post-survey procedures to get their work ready for transit via ship back to Britain, as telecommunication was still in its infancy.[623] They would compile and organise all the gathered data, including sketches, depth readings, and navigational notes, in line with established procedures enhanced by Beaufort's time as Hydrographer of the Navy.[624] This data would then be sent back to the Admiralty's Hydrographic Office via the well-established marine transportation network centred around the Marine Department in Calcutta.[625] These communication networks were essential for maintaining and expanding the Empire's navigational efficiency and security, alongside representing a form of long-distance control.[626]

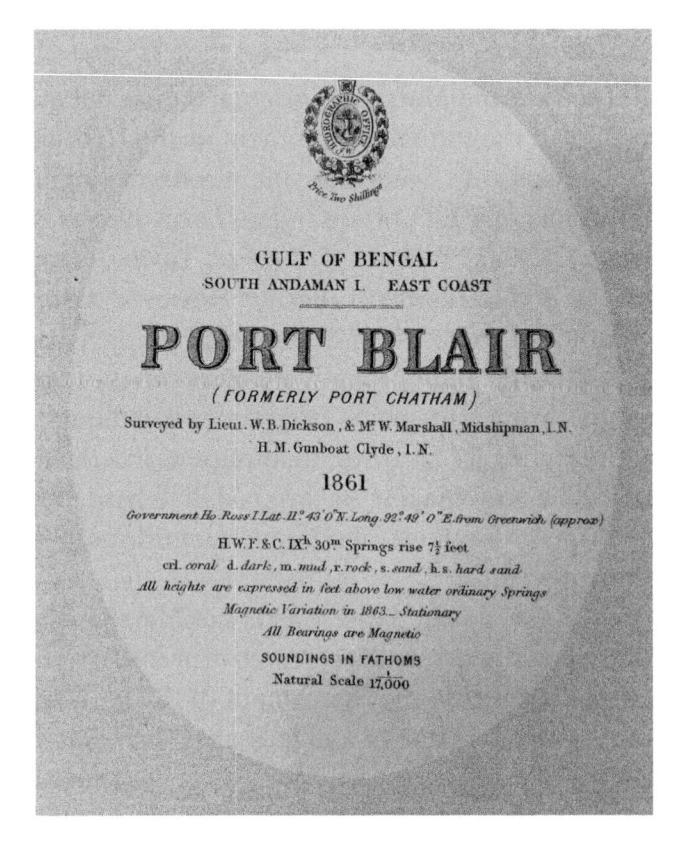

Figure 15: Chart Title

Circulating the Knowledge

The Hydrographic Office acted as a vibrant imperial centre of calculation. It was the receiving destination for Dickson and Marshall's survey work. At the Hydrographic Office, the data would undergo rigorous analysis, verification, and integration into the existing body of navigational knowledge. The Hydrographic Office, then under Rear Admiral John Washington (Hydrographer of the Navy 1855–1863), had not yet taken full ownership of the East India Company's records at India House.[627] However, the Hydrographic Office had a strong collaborative relationship with the East India Company, so information was likely shared.[628]

At the Hydrographic Office, six naval assistants (analysts in today's lexicon) and draughtsman processed the data and drew up the charts.[629] This division of labour expresses a significant enterprise-level efficiency. It allowed for the expertise of the surveying officers in the field who were competent in mathematics and the scientific method, like Dickson, who could convey first-hand knowledge of the surveyed areas to cartographic experts in Britain. Once in Britain, the naval assistants had access to better resources and tools for chart-making and did not have the distraction of everyday life at sea to contend with.

The Hydrographic Office was an example where those in the field (naval officers) and those who could be described as 'armchair' geographers (naval assistants) collaborated effectively.[630] As Azadeh Achbari argues, this efficient and productive network has been overlooked for the competitive and discourse-led scientific endeavours of professional scientists.[631] The Royal Navy and Indian Navy were stalwarts of the imperial knowledge scene and, to a much greater extent than simply providing funding or logistics for other scientific endeavours, which is a prevailing narrative among some in maritime history.[632] Although the Indian Navy and Royal Navy were primarily fighting forces in this period, they contributed significantly to the imperial knowledge base.

As a reputable organisation, the Hydrographic Office was expected to be meticulous in its analysis and keep up with the latest scientific developments.[633] The Hydrographic Office was a "metropolitan authority" in that sense.[634] This institutional reputation and use of the scientific method were crucial in creating a trustworthy product whose integrity was not disputed. The complex, multifaceted data and experiences collected by the Indian Navy would be distilled into a neat, user-friendly format: the nautical chart. Once published as a chart, it obscures the intricate processes, judgements, and uncertainties of the original survey work. Thus, with all its complexities and nuances, the original survey work becomes a 'black box' – a taken-for-granted, reliable entity for maritime navigation.

Regardless of the quality, the Admiralty never enforced their use in the merchant community. This is because it did not want to be liable for any incidents that occurred with their use.[635] However, once published, the 1861 chart of Port Blair became an authoritative tool used by mariners. It was relied upon for accuracy without the user understanding or questioning the underlying survey methodologies or data. It also reflects the significant power of the Hydrographic Office. Like Law's assessment of Portuguese 16th-century maritime control, the Admiralty held substantial power to take data from a source thousands of miles away and turn it into a trusted and reputable product without sharing this data.[636] Being a seapower means creating knowledge at distances, and then applying that knowledge.

Completed in 1861, the final chart, *Gulf of Bengal, South Andaman I, East Coast, Port Blair*, was published and made publicly available in 1863 by J.D. Potter for the Admiralty. It encapsulated a wealth of knowledge; it detailed the coastline's contours, providing precise information on the shape and features of the littoral spaces within the harbour at Port Blair. The chart was a comprehensive representation of both the maritime and terrestrial aspects of Port Blair for the mariner and a symbol of

British colonial possession through representation; both examples of what Ryan describes as the 'cartographic eye'.[637]

More importantly, the chart represented British seapower. The knowledge network used to produce the map involved both the Royal Navy and Indian Navy. It also encompassed over 60 years of corporate and maritime knowledge and defined the extent of British control in the Bay of Bengal. No other government or navy in the region had that form of knowledge of the Andaman Islands. It was an example of seapower by inscription.

Surveying continued in the Andaman Islands after the work of the *Clyde* was completed by 1861. The Indian Navy was soon to be renamed once more as the Bombay Marine on 30 April 1863.[638] At this juncture, the Royal Navy took over the surveying in the Andaman and Nicobar Islands from 1863 until 1866.[639] This was not a formal survey but the everyday small science that navies contributed to the imperial knowledge bank as sands shifted and settlements spread.[640] Surveying assisted in maintaining the British claim of the Andamans, and by 1863, the Indian Government was using the charts created by the 1861 survey work to demarcate the British territorial claim.[641] These charts were published and disseminated for use by the Navy and merchant mariners, significantly improving the safety of commercial navigation. Incidents of shipwrecks decreased dramatically after 1861, according to the Port Blair administration in 1871.[642]

Completing a survey also led to a continuous cycle of improvement. Notice to Mariners would soon be published in newspapers and a printed publication monthly to enhance the reliability of the chart of Port Blair in 1863.[643] Additionally, the Trigonometry Survey of India improved its accuracy in 1866. After that, there were no significant additions to the chart, hence the temporal focus of this chapter. The 1861 chart was still being published before a new survey was conducted and the Hydrographic Office published a new chart in 1888.[644]

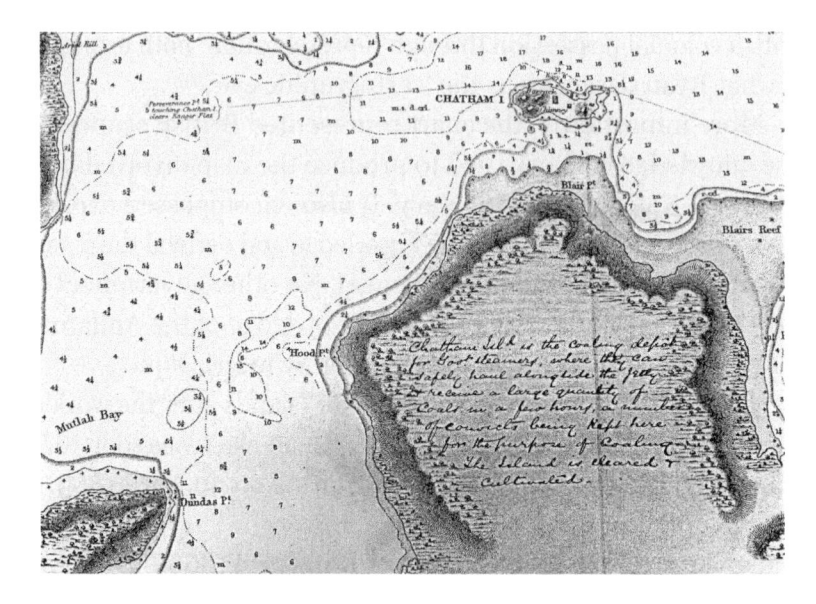

Figure 16: Close Up Chatham

Knowledge and Seapower

There was a pivotal difference in the foundations of the 1860 survey work and previous surveys by the East India Company in the late 18th century. Blair's survey was primarily exploratory and foundational, focusing on charting unexplored territories for the first time, turning 'blank' spaces on charts into useable representations. His work was driven by the immediate expectations of colonial expansion and settlement, emphasising basic navigational safety and territorial assessment.

By contrast, the Indian Navy survey in 1861 reflected a more systematic, scientific, and detailed approach. Surveying had improved dramatically in this period, but there was also a broader awareness of how hydrography enhanced seapower. Better knowledge equated to more effective use of ships, whether for shorter and safer commercial transit or for military posturing.[645] Hence, while Blair's work marked the initial phase of exploration, Dickson and Marshall's survey represented a phase of consolidation, precise management, and utilisation of the seas around the Andaman Islands.

The Indian Navy's survey work was meticulous and labour-intensive.[646] More importantly, the end product, *Gulf of Bengal, South Andaman I, East Coast, Port Blair Admiralty Chart*, is available over 160 years later to view and hold. Whether or not the depths are still accurate is debatable. It is, however, a recognisable inscription of Port Blair, one of which will still point out all the key features a mariner may need today. This is a testament to the immutability and mobility of the chart, as well as the role of naval actors in conducting the small science that enabled imperial control. Work by the Indian Navy, like the Royal Navy, was a crucial component of maritime exploration and imperialism, providing vital information that facilitated naval supremacy and commercial expansion of the British Empire.[647] The 1861 chart was eventually replaced by a new Admiralty chart in 1888 based on new survey work commissioned across the Indian Ocean.[648]

While the *Port Blair* chart lasted over 25 years in service, the Indian Navy, as a warfighting force did not. From 1858, the Indian Navy's role developed rapidly into what is now classed as a coastal security force as it transitioned into a subordinate unit of the Royal Navy. Nevertheless, it remained a significant part of Britain's seapower, with a fleet of ships and well-trained personnel.[649] The Indian Navy's survey of the Andaman Islands in 1861 demonstrated its significant role in British imperial strategic initiatives, which had both scientific and imperial ambitions.

The Indian Navy's survey work was scientific in nature, involving systematic and precise methodologies to chart the Islands' geography, hydrography, and other relevant maritime data. This scientific approach was essential for producing accurate nautical charts and understanding the natural environment, which was critical for safe navigation and effective maritime management. On the other hand, the survey was undeniably an extension of imperial objectives. The detailed charting and understanding of the

Andamans were integral to the British projection of sovereignty. British names equal British territory.

Thus, the Indian Navy's survey in 1861 represents a confluence of scientific inquiry and imperialist strategy. This is symbolised in the re-tasking of the *Clyde* itself, which went from surveying in early 1861 to being sent to the Persian Gulf to conduct patrol operations in 1862.[650] While Booth acknowledges the ability of a ship to retask to new operations, the flexibility in the skill of naval personnel to rapidly shift tasks is often overlooked.[651] What makes a good warfighter does not always make a good scientist.

There is sociology to producing knowledge; the social forces of truth, trust, and credibility influence whether hydrography is considered accurate or not. The conduct in which the knowledge was collated, collected, and circulated changes whether the end product is authoritative.[652] The extent of legitimacy relied on a combination of gender, social background, race and professionalism, traits often identified with being the ideal "gentleman" in Western societies.[653] Indian naval officers were considered disciplined and men of science, and had authority to create geographies through data.[654] Surveying as a practice created new hydrographical knowledge and, thus, new understandings of the seas.

The Indian Navy's role in enabling 'small science' through surveying the Andaman Islands between 1858 and 1863, and the Royal Navy after that, challenges Ken Booth's triumvirate of functions of navies. Knowledge is vital to seapower. James Davey describes the virtuous cycle of improvement that enhanced British seapower:

> Officers on station dedicated time to hydrographical pursuits, circulating the data to their peers and to the Hydrographical Office. The existence of a centralised hydrographical institution meant that such information was retained, compiled and used to make increasingly accurate charts, which in turn assisted the next generation of naval operations. This was British sea power, the conjunction of administrative and operational expertise, at its most effective.[655]

Knowledge is a form of power. Hydrography is, then, a form of power. Davey notes above that hydrography is another means of controlling maritime spaces, a more nuanced form of power. The detailed surveys and charts produced by the Indian Navy for Port Blair were not just tools for navigation but also instruments of imperial control.[656] By scientifically mapping littoral spaces, the Indian Navy could provide the knowledge needed to assert British sovereignty, monitor maritime routes, and ensure the security of its commercial interests. The role of navies and 'small science', both producer and publisher, is not acknowledged in Booth's work. It is neither a diplomatic function nor policing function.[657]

Hydrography is vital to imperial seapower and gave the British naval actors an advantage over adversaries. Therefore, knowledge production should be considered a core function of navies, alongside warfighting, diplomacy, and constabulary duties. Without knowledge, the other functions cannot operate.

Studying the role of navies in supporting 'small science' also illustrates the Admiralty Hydrographic Office as a vital imperial centre of calculation. The Hydrographic Office epitomised a knowledge organisation, systematically gathering data from various surveys, verifying and integrating data from the field, and turning it into comprehensive nautical charts through analysis. These charts were distributed throughout the British naval and commercial fleets, standardising navigational knowledge. The Hydrographic Office ensured the continued reliability of charts by providing Notice to Mariners of any urgent changes, and cohering survey work through management.

The Hydrographic Office served as a pivotal hub where raw data was transformed into strategic information, exemplifying the process of converting empirical observations into accepted knowledge.[658] Again, this reflects how seapower is enhanced through knowledge. Seapower also constructs geographical space. The systematic organisation and dissemination of geographical data was essential for maintaining naval supremacy and effective imperial governance, and the Hydrographic Office was at the heart of this. A naval bombardment was only possible with accurate hydrographical and geographical knowledge.

Hydrography and Imperial Authority

The Indian Navy's survey work in the Andaman Islands in 1860, culminated in the 1861 Hydrographic Office's *Gulf of Bengal, South Andaman I, East Coast, Port Blair*, which was updated until 1866 with minor edits. In producing this chart, it demonstrates the significant role of navies in contributing to 'small science' and reinforcing imperial control. This survey work provided hydrographical knowledge that enabled precise navigation across vital imperial SLOC in the Bay of Bengal, enforced territorial claims, and supported the development of the newly established Port Blair settlement.

Unlike the grand voyages of scientific discovery, small science was an everyday activity for the Indian Navy and the Royal Navy. It integrated practical and systematic methodologies to develop detailed hydrographic knowledge that was created at reach and processed thousands of miles away. The meticulous and labour-intensive efforts of officers like Lieutenant William Burnie Dickson and Midshipman William Marshall of the Indian Navy ensured that accurate nautical charts were produced, enhancing the safety of maritime operations and supporting British commercial and military interests in the Bay of Bengal.

The Admiralty Hydrographic Office was also an imperial centre of calculation, systematically transforming raw data from surveys into comprehensive and reliable nautical charts. These charts standardised navigational knowledge across the British naval and commercial fleets, enabling effective maritime communications and imperial governance. By turning empirical observations into accepted knowledge, the Hydrographic Office exemplified how seapower is both a consumer and producer of geographical knowledge. Knowledge is essential for maintaining naval supremacy. The study of navies in supporting small science thus reveals the intricate relationship between knowledge production, seapower, and imperial control. It challenges the traditional views on the functions of navies as predominantly based around warfighting, policing, and diplomacy.[659]

The Indian Navy was a vital seapower agent in the Bay of Bengal up until 1863, particularly through surveying and having a deep institutional knowledge of the operating environment in the Bay of Bengal. Hence, I hope you will agree that we must expand upon Ken Booth's rigid categorisation of naval functions. Knowledge production and circulation was, and is, a major function of navies. Booth's triumvirate of policing, diplomatic, and military functions does not acknowledge the plethora of tasks navies have and continue to do, such as surveying. Survey missions were critical for making accurate geographical knowledge, which enabled the control of imperial governments over communication routes by ensuring safe navigation, asserting territorial claims, and facilitating strategic planning. This nuanced view emphasises that navies' contributions to imperial power go beyond conventional military, policing, or diplomatic roles.

Challenging Booth's framework is essential for a deeper understanding of imperial seapower. The production and dissemination of hydrographic knowledge was fundamental to maintaining British naval supremacy and effective imperial control. Understanding the Hydrographic Office as a 'centre of calculation' identifies the intricate processes that enabled the construction of imperial spaces from afar. By converting field data into authoritative charts and navigational tools, the Hydrographic Office played a pivotal role in shaping the geographical imagination and administrative reach of the British Empire. This centralisation and standardisation of knowledge ensured that British maritime operations were conducted with high accuracy and reliability, thereby enhancing the overall efficiency of the imperial maritime network. The ability to produce hydrographical knowledge at reach is, also, a form of power at sea in itself. It demonstrated the power of the British imperial state to forge new geographies based on British imperial interests.

The ability of the Hydrographic Office to systematically gather, verify, and integrate data from various surveys allowed it to produce standardised nautical charts and navigational information thousands of miles away from the actual survey sites. This process transformed raw empirical data collected in remote locations like the Andaman Islands into coherent, reliable knowledge that could be easily circulated and utilised across the British Empire. The creation and dissemination of this standardised knowledge facilitated safe navigation and efficient maritime operations and reinforced British imperial control over distant territories. It gave British mariners a knowledge advantage, whether for warfighting or commerce.

Overall, the extensive survey work from 1858 until 1861 reflects the gradual incorporation of the Andaman Islands into the broader imperial maritime network, both militarily and socioculturally. The surveys and subsequent charts produced by the Indian Navy turned what was considered a 'savage' place into one that was controlled and ordered according to British values and ideals. After the publication of the Admiralty chart of Port Blair, which was part of a series of other charts from the same survey project, incidents of shipwrecking reduced dramatically.[660] This provided one element of stability to the *British Sea*, but piracy and attacks from the indigenous population still had to be overcome, which will be the focus of chapters five and six. By 1866, the Andaman and Nicobar Islands were still causing disturbances to Britain's attempts to secure, stabilise, and, in their eyes, civilise the Bay of Bengal.

CHAPTER FIVE

Gunboats and Policing: The Little Andaman Campaign, 1867

The *Assam Valley* was anchored off the coast of Little Andaman. The captain, seeking provisions and water for his forthcoming journey across the Bay of Bengal, sent a shore party to the island. He joined at the last moment, wanting to stretch his legs on shore. To feel the soft sand over salty decks made a welcome change. Recollecting, he realised he had not felt land beneath his feet since leaving Rangoon weeks before.

The shore party soon moved among the palms on the fringes of the white beach, collecting coconuts, and searching for a fresh stream. The humid air was thick with the scent of salt and green leaves. Suddenly, silence. The captain stared around him. From the jungle to the beach, the crew were surrounded. He had heard rumours from other mariners, but this was the first time he had seen the Onge tribe of Little Andaman. From the deck of the *Assam Valley*, the remaining crew watched in horror as the captain and seven men were dragged into the dense undergrowth, their cries swallowed by the jungle. The *Assam Valley's* master, unable to help his captain and men on shore, sought help the only way he could: he set sail for home, Rangoon.

This historical narrative portrays the moment a shore party from a European-crewed merchant vessel was attacked on Little Andaman on 21 March 1867, based on contemporary accounts.[661] This event led to the Indian Government sending gunboats of the Royal Navy and the Bombay Marine to Little Andaman, part of the Andaman Islands.[662]

Sending a gunboat was seen as a symbol of power that would leave an enemy quaking with fear. James Cable's book on 'gunboat diplomacy', and Antony Preston and John Major's reference work on gunboats and Victorian seapower have significantly shaped the historiography of gunboats and empires along these lines.[663] Gunboats were seen as formidable instruments of imperial technological dominance, emblematic of superior naval power.

Though compact and ostensibly less imposing than larger warships, gunboats leveraged mobility and powerful armaments to project power across vast and often inaccessible territories, facilitating rapid and flexible responses to colonial disturbances. Gunboats were therefore vital to imperial policing at sea. Hard power has frequently been the primary lens through which gunboats have been explored in imperial campaigns like the Second Anglo-Burmese War (1852–1853), the Second Opium Wars (1856–1860), and the Anglo-Japanese War (1863–1864).[664] These campaigns all occurred while the Andaman and Nicobar Islands were gradually becoming part of the British imperial state, and all feature gunboats as bastions of British might and the 'workhorses' of power at sea.

The campaigns in Burma, Canton, and Kagoshima in the 1850s to the 1860s were all against state actors. In contrast to these significant endeavours, how effective were gunboats against non-state actors, such as the indigenous population of Little Andaman? Between April and May 1867, the Royal Navy and Bombay Marine conducted various naval operations around Little Andaman, which was located approximately 75 miles south of Port Blair. These operations were intended to target the perpetrators of an attack on the *Assam Valley*, a merchant vessel. The ship had stopped in a bay off Little Andaman on 21 March 1867 to collect coconuts, sending a crew party ashore. Upon arrival, the party was attacked and taken hostage. The remaining crew sailed to Rangoon and reported the attack to the Government of India. The contemporary

Gunboats and Policing: The Little Andaman Campaign, 1867

British accounts describe the incident emotively as a massacre, a bloodbath, and murder most foul.[665]

Upon hearing the news, the Indian Government requested both the Royal Navy and Bengal Marine to send gunboats to Little Andaman, to defeat and deter the inhabitants from future attacks. These, however, were unsuccessful. After various small naval patrols and interdictions by gunboats failed, the Little Andaman Campaign was commissioned in May 1867. The campaign is sometimes referred to as an expedition, but I will use the Little Andaman Campaign to align with the official British military record.[666] This campaign involved the Indian Navy transporting three British Army infantry companies to Little Andaman as a "show of force" and a means of "projecting physical military power".[667]

While bringing firepower to foreign shores was invaluable in specific scenarios, such as in the Crimean War (1853–1856), gunboats were not the only 'workhorses' of imperial security.[668] Other auxiliary vessels, from troop transports to port protection steamers, provided a means to exert imperial seapower in local sea spaces.[669] Imperial policing involved more than gunboats. Both gunboats and auxiliary vessels could be used to project and reinforce imperial authority through symbolic displays of strength and mobility. The use of the term 'symbolic' is purposeful, as there is a performative element to seapower, which you shall soon see.

In addition, it is essential to go beyond hard power as the main vector through which force is applied in imperial policing. Another form of power is that of mobility. Mobility is vital to seapower, and imperial policing is no different. The mobility of naval power has often been studied one-dimensionally and linearly, focusing on getting from A to B.[670] However mobilities studies, a school of thought within geography, illustrates how military mobility influences and is influenced by political and cultural drivers.[671] Gunboats and auxiliary vessels of the Royal Navy and Bengal Marine were also mobile symbols of British ideals and values.

Simultaneously, the ships were projecting military might but also performing control.

What does it mean to perform control? In the case of the naval operations of Little Andaman, it was essential for the Indian Government to be *seen* doing something to respond to the attacks. Gunboats and naval auxiliary vessels are mobile platforms of statehood, and the presence of these vessels can evoke a variety of emotion. The Indian Government hoped to instil fear in the Little Andamanese, but with the same actions reassure the British merchant community that security was restored. Imperial policing was, in part, a performance intended to present maritime space as aligned with the legal structures, economic networks, and ideals of civilisation held by the British.

The performance of imperial policing was just as important as the "smashing blow" gunboats provided.[672] The violence associated with gunboat operations, and the stories of daring raids and bombardments, has made it a prominent area of study within naval history.[673] I will instead focus on the primary reports from officers and men who participated in the Little Andaman Campaign of 1867, and accounts of the deliberations within the Indian Government that commissioned the campaign. This is in order to show the limitations of using gunboats and naval gunfire on indigenous tribes, how other types of vessels in the Bombay Marine fleet supported imperial policing, and the performance of power that facilitated the British Empire's ability to assert and maintain authority over distant territories in the Bay of Bengal.

No accounts of the Little Andaman population's experience of the campaign exist; detailed anthropology work was not conducted for another 20 years.[674] However, this chapter uses other works from historical geography and imperial history to recognise agency and incorporate indigenous perspectives.

Figure 17: From Sea to Shore

Gunboats and Policing in the Bay of Bengal in the 1860s

In the 1860s, as steam power gradually augmented sail as the primary means of propulsion, gunboats were increasingly operating within the Bay of Bengal.[675] The Bombay Marine and the Royal Navy both operated steam platforms in the region.[676] This period also saw the Indian Government seek to further solidify its presence and authority in the Bay of Bengal after the transition from Company to Crown rule, including within newly established colonies such as Port Blair.[677] Port Blair represented a strategic foothold in the critical SLOC between the 'Treaty' ports in China and British India.[678]

Gunboats were useful for two reasons: the application of quick gunfire support against local and external threats to 'quell disturbances', and as symbols of British naval prowess and technological advancement.[679] These small, agile vessels were instrumental in extending the reach of colonial administration from isolated island settlements like Port Blair. They enabled the British to patrol extensive coastal areas, project power into islands and bays at reach, and enforce control over territory and people.

Gunboats form part of the broader imperial policy of using smaller vessels to ensure and maintain dominance in key strategic outposts.[680] In many ways, gunboats could be considered the workhorses of the Empire, the backbone of imperial defence, which is often overlooked by the "much-studied battle fleet".[681] John Beeler even classifies the Royal Navy as split between a battlefleet to protect the homeland and gunboats to protect the Empire.[682] Gunboats were cheaper, required less crew, and could be used in littoral waters. They were a useful means to increase the mass of a navy rapidly.

On the other hand, Bombay Marine ships were usually augmented with naval brigadesmen and Indian Army soldiers: "mobile units with their powerful self-contained landing forces."[683] This mix of personnel from the Bombay Marine and local colonial land forces represented a nexus of experienced seafarers and those with regional knowledge. This was critical in navigating the challenging local terrain and waters, as well as more nuanced issues such as dealing with the complexities of, say, the Andamans' complex tribal networks.

In contrast to the well-organised and technologically advanced gunboat crews, the primary 'enemy force' near the Andaman Islands was not another European naval power as predicted by the Admiralty in 1858, but indigenous tribes. The tribes, without a consistent means of communication with the British settlers, were often misunderstood and misrepresented as hostile and savage, presenting a different kind of challenge to those of state or organised actors. For example, the Battle of Aberdeen was fought between naval brigadesmen and the Andamanese tribes on 14 May 1859 in Port Blair. This included the gunboat *Charlotte* opening fire on the Andamanese armed with "iron-headed arrows".[684]

The Little Andamanese were not equipped with modern Western weaponry or naval capabilities (beyond wooden war canoes) but relied on an intimate knowledge of their dense island terrain to defend themselves.[685] Unlike the Borneo pirates between 1840 and 1849, the Little Andamanese did not attack or steal from vessels at sea. They only appeared to attack passing ships if the crew came ashore. This was, in all regards, a defensive measure.[686]

This stark contrast in weaponry highlighted the asymmetry typical of colonial encounters, where European powers employed advanced technology and formal military tactics against indigenous populations whose resistance strategies were limited in comparison.[687] That is not to say the indigenous population were ineffective; a growing body of literature seeks to rebalance this narrative by showing how many indigenous populations were more skilled and quality operators against imperial forces.[688] Instead, it reflects that the Little Andamanese were not a strategic threat but became a "repeated problem in the same area" to the British.[689]

The Little Andamanese made no effort to challenge Britain's sovereign claim over the Andaman Islands, conduct anything that resembled offensive action, or even commit acts of piracy. The pursuit of seapower is by its very nature a pursuit of dominance in some respect. It was also not always 'fleet versus fleet' or 'peer versus peer' scenarios.

Through the 1860s, the Royal Navy, the Bombay Marine, and the Indian Government were increasingly collaborating over maritime security and imperial policing. The Royal Navy station structure became the primary conduit for collaborating and delegating tasking. The mid-Victorian Navy was split between large ironclad battleships for homeland defence and as symbols for 'deterrence', and a multiplicity of tiny gunboats outside European waters.[690] In 1867, the East Indies Station was a force of nine gunboats split between Bombay and Calcutta.[691] When the China Station was divided from the East Indies two years previously, in 1865, 24 of the fighting ships (35 in total, including auxiliaries) were sent to China, leaving nine vessels stationed in the Indian Ocean area. This reflects the priorities of the time, and the belief that the Indian Ocean was relatively benign and free from peer-adversary threats.[692]

The East Indies Station was responsible for overseeing all naval operations in the area, ranging from protecting commercial shipping lanes to conducting anti-piracy patrols. It was also tasked with supporting colonial administrative objectives, and had the Bombay Marine as a subsidiary force. The Bombay Marine contributed significant regional expertise and manpower to this relationship. With a modest fleet of small steam gunboats for port security, troopships, and support vessels, it acted as a crucial auxiliary force that understood the local maritime environment and cultural landscape.[693]

Through this collaborative network of naval and governmental entities, the British Empire attempted to manage its colonial assets and respond to internal and external threats. The overall aim was to uphold its maritime dominance in the strategically crucial waters of the Indian Ocean, particularly with the increasing trade with China since the culmination of Second Opium War.[694] This collaboration was orchestrated under the strategic oversight of the Admiralty in London, which dealt with the Indian Government through the Secretary to the Indian Government for strategic concerns and East Indies Station for operational matters.

This period also saw the growth of the political leadership of the establishment in Port Blair, with an Assistant Superintendent to be filled by either an Indian Army or Indian Navy officer.[695] Imperial seapower was a complex mesh of activity and jurisdiction. The Royal Navy was one such actor, reflecting the interconnected nature of military and civilian governance in sustaining the Empire's expansive and often contentious frontier regions through seapower. The Bombay Marine was an agent of British seapower, even if the historiography is only now catching up with this fact.[696]

Little Andaman Campaign, 1867

On 21 March 1867, the crew of the *Assam Valley*, a European-owned merchant vessel, were attacked on the shore of Little Andaman. The crew that went ashore were taken into the jungle and eventually died, either immediately or within a few months.[697] This was not the first time a ship had been attacked while landing on Little Andaman. Maurice Vidal Portman argues that the attacks by the Onge (a tribal group of the Andamans) were intended to protect their territory rather than be offensive acts or thefts.[698] Combined with additional wrecks that occurred at sea, including the *Ninevh* on North Sentinel and *Ferozeshah* on South Brother Island, the Indian Government was required to respond through pressure from the merchant community.[699] The attacks increased the costs of shipping in the region, as insurance increased and crew wages increased to account for the additional risk.

Although there is little record of the *Assam Valley*, it had a European crew and a small steam engine complemented by a sail.[700] It was indicative of the many merchant vessels that plied the Andaman Sea trading between British Burma, the Straits Settlements, and various trade hubs in the Bay of Bengal.[701] The Onge attacked the crew once they got ashore, and it was suspected that they were all eventually murdered and tortured.[702] The attack on this vessel showed the Port Blair administration's limits in maintaining control over the Islands claimed since 1858. It demonstrated the precarious security situation in the outer islands of the Andaman Islands, where there was no permanent British presence, and the constant threat posed by indigenous groups resistant or unaware of British rule.

This event was profoundly significant for the credibility of the colony at Port Blair. It exposed the need for a more substantial, consistent naval presence to protect vital shipping routes.[703] In short, it could be perceived as undermining the British sovereignty of the Islands if another group, the Onge, were seen to be able to attack merchants without any repercussions from the British.

The attack on the crew of the *Assam Valley* also held significant implications for the prestige of the Indian Government in the Bay of Bengal, primarily because it was a British-owned vessel manned by a European crew. This attack went beyond local violence; it struck at the perceived stability and supremacy of Britain's economic interests in the region. The vessel was integral to maintaining the flow of goods and resources, vital to the economic fabric of the Empire's trade network throughout the Indian Ocean. Most importantly, the survivability of disparate outposts like Port Blair depended on the cheap flow of goods by sea, which was now being challenged.

Furthermore, such an incident could undermine international perceptions of Britain's ability to protect its assets and ensure the safety of its trade routes. The economic ramifications were immediate, raising concerns among merchants and insurers and potentially increasing the costs associated with shipping and trade due to heightened security risks. Lieutenant-Colonel Barret Ford, Superintendent of Port Blair, noted in his communication with the captain of HMIMS *Arracan*, Commander Henry Barrow of the Indian Navy, on 15 May 1867 that resolving the threat from Little Andaman was urgent to maintain mariner morale and trade movement.[704] The attack threatened the local colonial order and had broader economic consequences, impacting Britain's standing in the Bay of Bengal and its Asian economic interests.

This made the swift and effective response by the British naval forces a matter of both strategic security and economic necessity. The incident precipitated a naval campaign to Little Andaman aimed at subduing the local resistance and fortifying the perceived security of the trade routes crossing this part of the sea.[705]

When the *Assam Valley* was initially reported missing in Rangoon, HMS *Sylvia*, a Cormorant Class gunboat from the China Station, was dispatched to investigate the circumstances surrounding its disappearance, search for any survivors, and provide a deterrent for any future 'crimes'.[706] The *Sylvia*, which was in the Straits of Malacca at the time of the request, liaised

Gunboats and Policing: The Little Andaman Campaign, 1867

with both the British Commissioner of Burma and the Admiralty throughout.[707] Upon arrival at the last known location of the *Assam Valley*, *Sylvia* thoroughly searched the area but found no trace of the crew. The ship's captain, Commander Edward Brooker, took drawings of the huts and fired warning shots into the jungle.[708]

In hindsight, it is easy to question the effectiveness of firing warning shots into a vast jungle. However, this was standard practice at the time and part of the performance of seapower to deter and scare.[709] Whether a target was hit or not was inconsequential. The intended effect was to express the firepower available and symbolise what could happen. Another performative element was to give hope to any of the *Assam Valley's* crew if they were still alive.

Ultimately, *Sylvia* would find no survivors. This absence of survivors underscored the severity of the situation and the potential dangers posed by the indigenous populations to British mariners who strayed into the bays of Little Andaman. The failure to locate survivors also deepened the mystery surrounding the crew's fate from the *Assam Valley* and added to the collective fear of mariners who traversed the Andaman Seas.

The experience of the *Sylvia* also served as a stark reminder of the operational challenges faced by the Royal Navy and other naval actors in maintaining security and exerting control over the Empire's vast, and often treacherous, maritime frontiers. Ian Hernon argues that as the disparate and isolated indigenous populations were not integrated into the imperial structure, they were an unknown and unpredictable threat.[710] The case of Little Andaman embodies that assessment, as the crew of the *Sylvia*, according to the ship's reports, viewed the Little Andamanese through a lens of savagery.

HMS *Sylvia* did not find evidence of the crew, either alive or dead, and nor did it have the resources for a campaign into the jungle. Brooker thus sent a warning to any forthcoming naval responders:

> I would venture to remark that some little acquaintance with native cunning in all parts of the world emboldens me to hope that any further search after the missing party will be conducted with that prudence and caution which the advantages that natives have in bush fighting over Europeans, coupled with the well-known implacability of the Andamanese… particularly as the natives of these islands have additional advantages in the impenetrable nature of the jungle which so closely fringes a dangerous and rocky coast.[711]

This led to a reassessment of the security measures and strategies employed in the region. It prompted a more aggressive stance in the subsequent military and naval actions to ensure the safety and stability of the colony at Port Blair and its surrounding waters.[712]

The jungle was considered too dense for a gunboat to be effective, and the nature of the asymmetric threat of the Onge was not something the East Indies Station had considerable experience in dealing with in the Indian Ocean.[713] Little Andaman was seen as an unforgiving, uncontrolled place by the Royal Navy crew. Calling the Onge "cunning" was also a disingenuous reflection and clear orientalism by Brooker.

In response to the escalating security concerns highlighted by the attack on the crew of the *Assam Valley*, the Indian Government's Military Department made a request to the Bombay Marine for a naval campaign to the Andaman Islands.[714] This call for intervention underscores the unique logistical challenges faced by the British administration in such remote territories, and how the Bombay Marine still had an integral role in the imperial security system. Albeit, this was more of a tactical-level importance compared to the early 1850s.[715] The Bombay Marine was solicited for this task because it represented the most feasible means of rapidly and effectively projecting British military force to the Islands through a campaign into the interior "to prevent future outrage".[716] Although able to augment soldiers, Royal Navy gunboats from the East Indies Station were not orientated for these operations.

After *Sylvia's* visit, the next ship on the scene was the Port Blair gunboat, HMIMS *Kwan Tung,* of the Bombay Marine.[717] The gunboat was also sent to find the crew, visiting where the surviving crew members last reported to have seen their fellows. The *Kwan Tung* was also unable to find any traces of the crew, and once again left firing shots into the jungle as a warning.

A formal request from the Indian Government's Military Department to the Marine Department was sent after this further attempt. Permission was swiftly granted for HMIMS *Arracan*, a paddle steamer troopship with space for 500 troops operated by the Bombay Marine, to be sent to Little Andaman.[718] This was a significant escalation in resource.

Based on the intelligence gathered by *Sylvia*, the Indian Government planned a campaign to address the security concerns on Little Andaman.[719] The Superintendent of Port Blair, Lieutenant-Colonel Barret Ford of the Bengal Army, was crucial in coordinating support for this mission. His cooperation underlines how local colonial governance structures and Royal Navy intelligence combined together to influence the direction of the ensuing naval campaign.[720]

Ford also provided intelligence and local knowledge to the Little Andaman Campaign. This area had remained largely unexplored and, consequently, there was minimal levers of active control or understanding of the geographies.[721] The crew of the *Arracan*, typically based in Calcutta, lacked familiarity with the terrain and the local population, thus posing a significant risk to safe operations.

Little Andaman was strewn with unknown threats. However, Ford provided troops stationed in Port Blair with experience in similar environments to support the Bombay Marine: 24th (the 2nd Warwickshire) Regiment of Foot.[722] This is notable for two reasons: the Regiment had fought in the Indian Rebellion of 1857 and had considerable experience fighting in multiple imperial campaigns. It was also a British regiment, not a British-led Bengal Army contingent.[723] This represents the campaign's significance to the Indian Government, sending a prized, experienced force.

The decision to explore Little Andaman also had a strategic dimension, as it was aimed at showing security through presence and the perception of control over all parts of the archipelago. This was alongside gaining clarity on what happened on Little Andaman and reducing the likelihood of future attacks. The involvement of *Arracan* and the support offered by the Superintendent highlighted a coordinated approach between naval and colonial administration resources, ensuring that the campaign was not only a way to inflict retribution but also a crucial step towards the Andamans' comprehensive territorial and security management.

The use of a troopship also demonstrates the limits of gunboats as platforms for imperial policing. In this case, naval transports with expeditionary troops were considered necessary to counter threats on Little Andaman. The geographical isolation meant that a significant number of troops needed to be protected, provisioned, and put ashore.[724] Gunboats had firepower through guns, but the *Arracan* brought the ability to transport troops effectively. The Bombay Marine's troopship naval power came from its mobility over its armament.

The Superintendent of Port Blair gave two specific objectives for the *Arracan* campaign: first, to gather definitive information about the fate of the ship and its crew, and second, to administer punitive measures against those responsible for the attacks.[725] The mission's objectives could be summarised as intelligence and retribution. Gathering accurate intelligence was critical for understanding the specifics of the incident and informing future security measures on the Islands. In doing this, it was hoped that British authority would be enforced and future acts of aggression deterred by demonstrating the consequences of such actions to the Little Andamanese.

This approach was typical of imperial policing in the era, often combining a 'mobile show of force' to maintain control over occupied territories as a "preferred and cheaper weapon" to having a permanent presence.[726] The campaign objectives emphasise the challenges faced by the British Empire in managing remote corners of colonies, when resources were constrained. Resistance could often be sporadic and unpredictable, necessitating mobile platforms of power to maintain order and uphold the semblance of imperial control.

Imperial policing was not an impartial act. Antony Preston and John Major suggest that gunboats and policing "should be judged by the standards of the age", but often these standards are only partially acknowledged in naval history.[727] There is a complex interplay of colonial power and racial perceptions that underline the use of gunboats and auxiliary vessels. James Cable's analysis on gunboat diplomacy treats gunboats as mere instruments of statecraft, designed to project power and enforce compliance in distant territories: "advantageous to British interests or that policy... to achieve such ends."[728] However, this perspective overlooks the deeper ideological and cultural dimensions embedded in such military actions.

British perceptions of savagery and racial superiority profoundly influenced the punitive campaign against the Onge. The *Arracan*, as a mobile platform of power, not only carried soldiers but also prevailing racial ideologies that categorised the indigenous population as primitive and in need of 'control' or 'punishment'. In HMS *Sylvia's* initial intelligence also, the crew can clearly be seen to profile the Onge as savages lacking civility.[729] Gunboats are mobile platforms of hard power, the flash and bang of naval forces. They are also mobile platforms of prejudices and beliefs, which shape how that hard power is applied. The actions of the Bombay Marine in Little Andaman were entwined with the propagation of racial hierarchies and the justification of imperial policing through the lens of a 'civilisational' discourse.

The response to the attack on the *Assam Valley* also illustrates the collaborative, yet hierarchical, nature of British colonial military operations in the Bay of Bengal. While the initial request for support originated from the Indian Government under the premise of the Chief Commissioner of Burma, it was the Commander-in-Chief East Indies Station, Commodore Charles Hillyar RN, who had overall command of the Bombay Marine and facilitated the campaign.[730] This division of responsibilities reflects the integrated but distinct roles within the colonial governance framework, where civil authorities identified threats and first attempted to use the resources available (such as the *Kwan Tung*) before requesting additional support and advice through the Royal Navy station structure.[731]

Little Andaman Canoe.

Figure 18: Andaman Canoe

The deployment of the *Arracan* and the involvement of the 24th (the 2nd Warwickshire) Regiment of Foot underscores the vital role of auxiliary vessels in supporting colonial military operations through mobility. The troopship was crucial in this context. It was not only a means of transport but a secure base of operations that the soldiers could be launched from and to which they could retreat, if necessary, under the protection of the vessel.

The *Arracan* provided a flexible platform that allowed the military to project power directly onto the island, access remote areas quickly, and maintain a lifeline to naval support and security.

Additionally, *Arracan's* ability to patrol nearby waters ensured the area remained secure while the troops were on land, deterring potential threats from the indigenous population or other adversarial forces during the operation. While *Arracan* itself was built without naval guns, the 24th (the 2nd Warwickshire) Regiment of Foot and naval brigadesmen could use the ship as a firing platform with any weaponry bought on the campaign.[732]

While the deployment of the *Arracan* on the campaign to Little Andaman provided logistical support and a secure base, its effectiveness as a tool of imperial policing and conflict resolution, especially against the indigenous population, is debatable. Traditional displays of naval power to coerce adversaries into compliance, such as using gunboats as a threat, are often ineffective against non-state actors unfamiliar with or indifferent to such displays.[733]

There is no archival evidence recording the perspective of the indigenous tribes on Little Andaman through the campaign. With their unique cultural contexts and lack of a formal experience of maritime power, it is almost impossible to gauge how the *Arracan* campaign was perceived from this angle. Although ethnographic studies could assist, these were not conducted until the 1890s.[734] Hence, it is necessary to rely on what is available in the wider postcolonial literature.

On the other hand, the sailors, soldiers, and naval brigadesmen's experiences are recorded in detail. The accounts from these military men clearly show how they perceived the Onge as cannibals and savages.[735] When the contingent went ashore in search of the seven missing crew members of the *Assam Valley*, the grim discovery of a skull and decomposing bodies only reinforced this perception of savagery and brutality within the soldiers and sailors.[736]

The Bombay Marine crew and Indian Army soldiers had a psychological and physical detachment to an isolated and barely explored area such as Little Andaman, which limited their understanding and interaction with local dynamics. Quickly, this could lead to misjudgements in handling confrontations. This limitation in knowledge presents a broader issue of both the application and effectiveness of imperial policing methods, like gunboats or brigadesmen ashore, in scenarios involving non-state actors (if effectiveness is gauged as an action achieving an intended change in behaviour). Conventional power displays did not translate into expected political leverage or conflict resolution as was the case with Malay pirates, where the threat of force could lead to diplomatic agreement.[737] Upon taking over the China Station, Vice Admiral Henry Keppel RN noted the frustration and difficulty of dealing with local 'pirates' in the Nicobar Islands who seemed unaffected by threats of conflict.[738] These pirates were, in fact, the indigenous population.

While naval vessels provide essential support, the actual execution of the Little Andaman Campaign relied heavily on ground forces, landing ashore and entering thick, tropical forests. The 24th (the 2nd Warwickshire) Regiment of Foot and the Bombay Marine naval brigadesmen represent the hard power in this instance. Lieutenant William Much, Officer Commanding 2nd Battalion and the detachment, provided a comprehensive report of the landing, with a short entry below:

> ... firing on the Natives who were not visible to us. About 300 yards on we came across the bodies of 4 men, the heads of whom, mere skulls in appearance, protrude from the ground, the rest of the bodies being partially covered with sand... my whole attention being on the critical position in which we were placed, from the want of ammunition.[739]

The reports from Lieutenant Much and Commander Barrow of the Indian Navy (captain of the *Arracan*) focus on the campaign primarily through the landing ashore. They express the difficulty of landing troops, the uncertainty of what they faced, and displays of bravery. They both report that the Onge fired arrows at the British troops as they landed, and returned volleys of fire.

What Much and Barrow do not mention is that while the campaign found the presumed bodies of four European seamen, they also left many Onge dead. The evidence account from Petty Officer A.W. Wilson (naval brigadesman) is the only mention of any Andamanese killed, reflecting either a perception of limited importance or a want not to discuss the deaths:

> I also found the bodies of 4 Europeans buried in a line close together, with their feet towards the sea, the bodies were lying at full length, there was no flesh on sculls, nor yet hairs. The bodies were in a decomposed state and the stench stifling. One was wrapped in a canvas coat, as used by sailors, in pretty good order, I did not remove and I could not say by whom the bodies had been buried. The number of Andamanese killed I positively say, as counted by me, was 57.[740]

Similarly, neither Much nor Barrow conclude whether the campaign was a success. Beyond finding the bodies, which could not be confirmed as the mariners of the *Assam Valley* due to the state of the decomposition, it is difficult to argue whether the campaign had the expected effect of deterring future attacks, especially when the soldiers and naval brigadesmen themselves were attacked throughout the campaign.

Yet, this was not how the imperial administration portrayed the campaign. It was represented as a successful endeavour, with the brave actions of the 2nd Battalion detachment earning one officer and four soldiers the Victoria Cross.[741] It was embellished as to become part of imperial folklore. Although the campaign was marked by the inability to find those responsible for the attack on the *Assam Valley,* it presented a nuanced outcome for the British authorities. The fact that a military operation was conducted, coupled with the awarding of Victoria Crosses to members of the 24th (the 2nd Warwickshire) Regiment of Foot, supported the narrative of British military omnipotence in the region. I am not challenging whether the medals were justified, but more that having military awards provided a means of recording the success to a public audience.

The campaign eventually served a dual purpose for the Indian Government. First, it conveyed a strong message of resolve and capability to the marine community, demonstrating the willingness and readiness of British forces to respond to threats. Second, the public recognition of acts of bravery and the narrative of success built around the Victoria Crosses helped construct a perception of restored security and order. This was crucial for maintaining the confidence among the colonial maritime community. It was also essential for a colony like the Port Blair administration, which was not self-sufficient and required most goods to be imported. The presentation of success reinforced the semblance of control and effectiveness of authority the British held over the wider Andaman Islands chain. In essence, it showed the British had the mobility of power to enforce ideals, values, and political control across all islands in the Andaman chain.

After the Bombay Marine operation concluded, the responsibility for maintaining security reverted to the authorities at Port Blair. While the Bombay Marine's smaller gunboat, like the *Kwan Tung*, returned to local security and patrol duties, the China Station and the East Indies Station continued planning and delivering on tackling piracy in the region.[742] By the late 1860s, the Royal Navy's gunboats increasingly became involved in counter-piracy activity around the Bay of Bengal and South China Sea (see chapter six).

Ultimately, the Indian Government did not conduct further operations in Little Andaman after the campaign. Instead, it instructed mariners not to call at Little Andaman and told the Superintendent of Port Blair that any such attacks must be responded to immediately.[743] If power at sea is defined as the ability to change the behaviour of a group of actors, then in this instance British seapower only changed the behaviour of other

British mariners. The perception that security was restored provided a sense of safety to the British merchant community, and sailing near the Islands continued. There is no credible evidence to suggest the behaviour of the Onge changed.

The Little Andaman Campaign is a unique case study. Only a few places in 1867, in an increasingly globalised world, still had isolated tribal populations located in the middle of crucial imperial SLOC. Nevertheless, the limited effectiveness of *Sylvia's* and *Kwan Tung's* early intervention show how gunboats were not omnipotent platforms of imperial power. The Onge could evade the small shore parties, and the threat of naval gunfire was also limited in effect on Little Andaman compared to that of a city with significant infrastructure that could be damaged, such as in Rangoon in 1852.[744] While it may be a unique geography, the methods of imperial policing were representative of standards of the time.

There is also a performative element to imperial policing in the Little Andaman Campaign. Gunboats and auxiliary vessels are a visceral and technological symbol of seapower. The visible presence of such a vessel acts as a psychological tool to change behaviour, but it is not always the enemy's behaviour. With the Little Andaman Campaign, the very fact a campaign was undertaken provided a sense of security which meant the British merchant community in the Bay of Bengal began using the waters around the Islands again. The behaviour change was within the imperial seapower state. This performative element helped construct and sustain the belief in imperial dominance in the Bay of Bengal. Yet it did not need to be a gunboat; any British naval vessel had a presence and authority. The key is the mobility of power, both of guns and ideas.

Naval mobility allowed the British to adapt quickly to emerging threats, maintaining a sense of omnipresent security at sea. In reality, this was as much a constructed belief as it was one truly founded upon operational capability. In the case of Little

Andaman, security was enhanced mainly through ideas and beliefs. The British had performed power but had not changed anything on the ground or found the perpetrators. After the campaign, the Superintendent of Port Blair issued a notice to mariners to avoid landing on Little Andaman because of the danger.[745] The danger remained, but it would be circumvented and mitigated.

Still, there was a physical element to the security around Little Andaman: permanent naval presence. It was reinforced through the visible and rapid deployment of gunboats and other vessels to disturbances. Being seen to act was just as important as the act in this instance. These vessels embodied the British Empire's commitment to protect its interests and enforce its laws, irrespective of the actual threat level. The limited effectiveness of the gunboats in combat roles against non-state actors, such as the Onge population in canoes, was secondary.

Figure 19: HMS Sylvia

Gunboats and Other 'Workhorses' of Navies

Gunboats have emerged as potent symbols of imperial strength and authority, embodying the British Empire's ability to enforce its will and maintain order across its vast territories. Scholars such as Beeler, Gough, and Lambert split the Royal Navy fleet structure between battleships orientated towards protecting the homeland and as a deterrent, and a larger mass of gunboat vessels outside European waters for policing, or what is now classed as constabulary duties.[746] However, this symbolic delineation often overshadowed the effectiveness of gunboats in specific military tasks. In conflicts with non-state actors, traditional forms of naval power were augmented with auxiliary forces such as the Bombay Marine. The Little Andaman Campaign is therefore representative of the limits of gunboats in bringing military effect to isolated islands with an indigenous population. It is also representative of how auxiliary naval vessels can support imperial policing through amphibious landings.

Nevertheless, the presence of gunboats in colonial waters did serve as a visual reminder of the Empire's technological superiority and global reach.[747] This perception was strategically cultivated to instil a sense of British control to the maritime community in the Bay of Bengal, to deter potential rebellion, and reassure allies and trade partners of the Empire's stability and strength. Even in situations where their practical impact was limited, such as with the *Sylvia* and *Kwan Tung*, gunboats reinforced the narrative of an all-powerful British Empire, capable of projecting power swiftly and decisively anywhere along its extensive maritime frontiers.

Thus, the value of gunboats extended well beyond their immediate military capabilities; their value to imperial policy was the mobility of power through the ideals and values they reinforced. In this case, the ideals and values were British authority in the region. With the Little Andaman incident, the fact that a technologically advanced ship *could* be sent to act on the perceived insecurity was crucial, whether it was a gunboat or an auxiliary ship. It was about the belief that something was being done, and naval power was present.

The Little Andaman incident also demonstrates that gunboats played a crucial role in building confidence among colonial administrators and local colonial populations alike. They were not just visual reminders, but they held a significant performative value that often a troopship could not muster. Gunboats were not just physical tools of the Empire but also powerful symbols of its enduring authority and confidence. They embodied strength through reassurance. It is, however, not just the armament of gunboats that is integral to their value but the mobility of power they represent.

The *Sylvia* and *Kwan Tung* were small yet robust, providing a physical manifestation of the British Empire's ability to operate independently across diverse and often hostile environments, such as Little Andaman. These gunboats had the flexibility to navigate shallow, narrow waterways between islands. They also had relative autonomy in logistics and command that made them ideal for projecting power in regions where more sizeable naval assets, such as ironclads, could not operate as effectively. The focus on gunboats, although understandable, has led to an oversight of the broader auxiliary forces used in imperial policing, such as the eventual need for a larger troopship, the *Arracan*, to operate in Little Andaman.

While gunboats were a pertinent choice for 'gunboat diplomacy' against state actors, there was a limitation in bringing to the fore a heavily armoured ship against disparate tribal groups. Instead, what is needed is the ability to bring seapower ashore through troop transportation. The Little Andaman Campaign was not an isolated example of this; the campaigns in Borneo (1840–1849), Cocos-Keeling Islands (1857), and various incidents in Malaya are all indicative of operations to quell disturbances, where gunboats were augmented with auxiliary forces.[748] Gunboats were not the supreme or sole platform for imperial policing.

Gunboats and auxiliary vessels served as mobile platforms of British sovereignty, values, and ideals. They projected military power and transported British cultural and political beliefs to distant shores. This mobility of ideas enabled the British Empire to extend its influence far beyond territorial centres of gravity, such as Port Blair, to disparate islands stretching across the Bay of Bengal. This was by embedding Western ideologies and governance practices into these diverse cultural landscapes, enforced by naval power. The treatment of indigenous tribes in the Little Andaman incident exemplified this process. Interactions with naval forces were largely reactionary, driven by the immediate needs of colonial security rather than any concerted effort to understand local customs or societal structures.

Imperial policing is often explored through the technological and strategic drivers, which has meant the ways in which British seapower impacted indigenous communities has been overlooked in past studies. The fact that 57 Onge were killed during the campaign, and this does not make it into the reports of either commanding officer, is telling. It reflects a common theme of a 'white' priority in Victorian imperial policing.[749] This power imbalance reflected a broader imperial attitude of dominance and control over indigenous populations, where the primary aim was to quell any resistance and establish order quickly, and not to foster mutual understanding. In this way, gunboats and auxiliary vessels were enforcers of British military might and bearers of its cultural hegemony.

The disappearance of seven crew members from the *Assam Valley* elicited a senior-level response from the Indian Government. It was coordinated through the Commissioner of British Burma, which belies how a seemingly minor attack on non-British subjects was perceived as a significant threat to the broader security and stability of British colonial interests in the Bay of Bengal. The Indian Government's decision to manage the crisis through such a senior diplomatic figure illustrates the critical importance placed on maintaining secure and stable maritime routes, not only for the impact on commerce but also for the political symbolism of control and protection provided under British governance.

Maritime security was intricately linked to the overall integrity and authority of the British Empire. The need for a proactive and coordinated response to the *Assam Valley* attack indicates the premium placed on ensuring maritime security. It also reflects one of the nuances in institutional power identified by Bruno Latour, that the focus is often "too much in 'being' and not enough in 'having' [power]".[750] *Being* in power refers to the actuality of holding a position of authority, whereas *having* power refers to the possession of influence or capability to affect the outcomes and behaviours of others. The key for the Indian Government in the *Assam Valley* attack was to be seen as *having* authority, even if it was just *being* in power.

The Little Andaman incident can be summarised as a disruption to the maritime order and the belief in the *British Sea* as discussed in chapter one. The campaign was an attempt to restore stability. Both gunboats and auxiliary vessels played a crucial role in maintaining imperial security around Port Blair, serving as a versatile and mobile force capable of projecting British naval power across the Andaman archipelago. Their presence bolstered the British Empire's ability to patrol waters, deter potential threats, and respond swiftly to incidents, thereby upholding the authority and stability deemed necessary for colonial governance.

However, the effectiveness of these gunboats was notably limited when dealing with non-state actors. Local indigenous populations like the Onge had unconventional tactics and a deep understanding of the local terrain, which often nullified the technological advantages of naval power. The tribes' sporadic attacks posed significant challenges to gunboats, which, despite their operational capabilities, sometimes struggled to achieve decisive outcomes against such adversaries. Sometimes, bringing seapower ashore was the only solution.

Performing Statehood and Seapower

The Little Andaman Campaign demonstrates the complexities and limitations of using gunboats for imperial policing, particularly against non-state actors. The attack of the *Assam Valley* in March 1867 showed the precariousness of British control over remote territories and the informal way in which the imperial security network spread to 'Westernise' previously uncontrolled maritime spaces. The military response by the Royal Navy and Bombay Marine around Little Andaman between April and May 1867 showcased the limits of gunboats, but also the mobility and versatility of auxiliary vessels in projecting power. Gunboats were not the only 'workhorses' of the Empire. Auxiliary naval vessels such as guardships, troopships, and support vessels also contributed to imperial seapower.

Gunboats and auxiliary vessels provided rapid and flexible responses to colonial disturbances, and projecting power was as much about the mobility and performance of military presence as it was about actual combat capabilities. The performative element of seapower is often overlooked. Here, it was emblematically represented by the operations of HMS *Sylvia* from the China Station, which was rapidly deployed to the scene of the attack on the *Assam Valley*. Such responses were not just about search and rescue or punitive actions against indigenous tribes; they were demonstrations of the capability to project power swiftly and effectively to the farthest reaches of the Empire. This strategic mobility facilitated the enforcement of the imperial rule and demonstrated British sovereignty over vast maritime and territorial expanses. Thus, gunboats and naval auxiliary vessels epitomised the extension of British authority, embodying the Empire's ability to connect disparate geographies under the control of the British Empire through imperial policing.

The Little Andaman incident also shows the limitations of using gunboats against non-peer adversaries like indigenous populations living in isolated communities. This is where the conventional metrics of naval power do not necessarily translate into effective control or conflict resolution. As instruments of a powerful state, gunboats are indeed formidable against peer forces or state structures. The efficacy of gunboats diminishes when deployed against non-state actors with complex social and geographical landscapes that are not conducive to traditional naval engagements. This mismatch, as represented by the need for the *Arracan* troopship to be deployed to Little Andaman, demonstrated the role of auxiliary colonial forces like the Bombay Marine in supporting British overseas imperial policing. Thus, the narrative of gunboats as unilaterally powerful tools must be developed to recognise the role of a wider assortment of vessels.

Finally, gunboats and imperial policing activities at sea need to be viewed through the lens of mobility. Historically, seapower has often been portrayed as an impartial and effective tool of empire, crucial for maintaining control and facilitating expansion. However, the nuanced realities of naval operations like the Little Andaman Campaign show that seapower is not just a tool for 'fleet versus fleet', but a tool of control over populations. Through the mobility of power naval vessels enable, distant islands can come under the authority of a British imperial state. Seapower empowers some actors and disempowers others. Such a revaluation deepens our understanding of the historical relationship between seapower and the Empire.

After the Little Andaman Campaign, there were no reported attacks in the Andaman Islands in the forthcoming years. Whether that is down to the deterrence effect of the campaign, or the fact that Little Andaman was closed off through a Notice to Mariners is debatable. However, further incidents of maritime violence occurred in the Nicobar Islands through the 1860s, perpetrated instead by a Nicobarese tribe in Nancowry Harbour. Unlike the beach attack by the Onge, this event occurred at sea. It was classified as piracy and warranted a very different response by the British, including a larger campaign involving two Royal Navy warships. The next chapter explores the final stages in Britain's forging of the sparsely populated island chains in the Bay of Bengal into a *British Sea*. It will tell the story of how piracy led to the British annexing the Nicobar Islands, creating a political union that lasts until this day.

CHAPTER SIX

Blockade, Piracy and Annexation: The Nicobars, 1867–1872

Following the attack on the *Assam Valley* on Little Andaman, the focus of the British administration swiftly pivoted 200 miles south to the Nicobar Islands. In June 1867, a battered ship arrived in Penang.[751] The *Futteh Islam,* a British-owned merchant brig, had been attacked while harbouring in Nancowry Harbour. The captain of the *Futteh Islam* had hoped to trade with the Nicobarese as he eased into the harbour. The local Nicobarese Chief and around 30 men approached the ship in canoes, at first peacefully, and they were permitted onto the deck of the *Futteh Islam*. A sudden and vicious attack ensued.

Out of a total ship's company of 24, only three survived. The surviving seaman had hidden under some mats during the ambush and managed to return the ship to the Straits Settlement to inform the authorities about the act of 'piracy'. Almost immediately, the Indian Government requested the Royal Navy's East Indies Station to blockade the Nicobars to quell the disturbance and eradicate piracy from the Islands. Was this really an act of piracy? Why was a blockade needed? The response by the British imperial state tells us much about seapower.

Despite the Indian Government's request, a blockade was not implemented. This was due to a lack of available vessels to maintain a blockade and questions regarding the efficacy of such an approach. However, the Royal Navy dispatched HMS *Wasp* and HMS *Satellite* to conduct anti-piracy operations, which, in effect, resulted in an escalation of violence and involved directly attacking the Nicobarese. In this chapter, you will read about the intricacies of how naval power was used to control movement in littoral seas. I will examine the interaction between different aspects of the British imperial state, the challenges of operating against 'pirates' on isolated island groups, the appropriateness of this label, and the ultimate limits of seapower that paved the way for British colonisation of the Nicobars between 1868 and 1869. By 1872, the Nicobar Islands were formally placed under the administration of the Chief Commissioner in Port Blair, which effectively turned the Bay of Bengal, finally, into a *British Sea*.

To understand the intricacies of imperial seapower, I will expand upon Stephen Roskill's and Geoffrey Till's definition of a blockade, by examining official government correspondence, naval logs, and contemporary letters to understand the sociocultural dimensions of a blockade.[752] Roskill defines a blockade as a strategic operation to prevent maritime traffic from entering or leaving enemy ports or coastlines, essentially cutting off the enemy's supply lines and communication. A blockade exerts economic pressure and limits the enemy's operational capabilities by controlling the sea routes. Although other prominent scholars have analysed blockades, Roskill's work is grounded in the naval history of the Empire, including the period of this book.[753]

Till offers a slightly different perspective, highlighting the blockade's broader geopolitical implications. He reflects on the importance of a blockade as more than an economic or military manoeuvre, but also as a tool of psychological and political warfare that can influence diplomacy and public opinion. Roskill and Till both portray blockades through the lens of strategic necessity and focus solely on fleet-to-fleet interactions.[754]

Imperial British forces often used blockade as a complementary measure alongside campaigns ashore in what Brooks describes as a "pattern of escalation".[755] This includes the blockade of the Pearl River (1839), the blockade of Rangoon (1852), and the bombardment of Kagoshima (1862), which had all started as a blockade.[756] A blockade was often used as part of an escalatory approach, it could quickly morph into a bombardment or expedition, or de-escalate into a demonstration of power.[757] It is part of a spectrum of naval force used to control movement at sea.

While both Roskill's and Till's approaches have significant merits, this state-centric definition overlooks how imperial powers used blockades and escalatory measures to shape the sociocultural dimensions of littoral maritime spaces. In the case of the Nicobar Islands, the Indian Government perceived naval force as a means to control how indigenous populations communicated by the seas. The blockade, as an example, was intended to shape the use and values of littoral spaces. These measures were not neutral, dispassionate measures of maritime control, but targeted actions to change centuries-old patterns of behaviours in the Bay of Bengal.

Once the Royal Navy deemed a blockade to be too resource-intensive, it instead launched a small military expedition to the Nicobar Islands in 1867. This included destroying the Nicobarese's fleet of 70ft war canoes, damaging villages and infrastructure, and threatening further retribution. In essence, this achieved what the Indian Government sought from a blockade: limiting Nicobarese access to the sea, changing behaviours towards a British ideal – "accepting British norms of behaviour."[758]

Alongside this, the eventual skirmishes between Royal Navy forces and the Nicobarese represent another example of cultural misunderstanding embedded in imperial naval activity, as emphasised in the previous chapter. Were the Nicobarese savage pirates, as the contemporary naval ports suggested? In fact, the classification of the Nicobarese as 'pirates' reflects more on the identity and values of the British than it does on the activities of the Nicobarese. At the time, European ideal of 'tropicality' was central to the Nicobars' place in the British geographical imagination. It was seen as a place of verdant nature with an uncivilised populace.

In the 19th century, the British Government's definition of piracy was somewhat nebulous. It lacked the precise legal framework today under the United Nations Convention on the Law of the Sea (UNCLOS).[759] Piracy was broadly understood as acts of robbery, violence, or depredation committed at sea by private individuals without state authorisation, primarily targeting merchant vessels for personal gain.[760] This pragmatic but vague definition could be applied to those who went against the *British Sea* principles you saw first in chapter one.

Consequently, the Royal Navy often dealt with piracy in the Bay of Bengal through naval patrols, punitive expeditions, and treaties with local rulers, adapting its approach depending on the incident.[761] The first section here will contextualise the settlement of Port Blair and the administrative relationship with the Nicobars, especially in light of the Little Andaman Campaign in 1867. This event fostered an air of instability and justified a perceived need for aggressive measures in the eyes of colonial administrators. This provides a foundation to then understand why the British saw naval force as the only viable means to respond to the act of piracy in Nancowry Harbour.

Figure 20: War Canoe

Blockades, Piracy and British Interests in the Bay of Bengal

The concept of a naval blockade, as defined by Stephen Roskill, can be either naval or economic/commercial in target and restricts enemy activity either entirely to base locations (close type) or from a distance with some movement allowed (open type): "always instituted with the object of destroying, or at least immobilising, the main enemy fleet."[762] The Paris Declaration Respecting Maritime Law, signed on 16 April 1856, significantly impacted the delivery of naval blockades. To be legal, a blockade must have been declared in advance and maintained by a competent force to be legally recognised.[763] This treaty shifted blockades towards more regulation and formalised maritime practices, reducing the likelihood of indiscriminate or unjust blockades after the Crimean War in 1856. As you shall see, the need for a near-permanent presence was one of the reasons Commodore Charles Farrell Hillyar, Commander-in-Chief of the East Indies Station, argued against implementing a blockade of the Nicobars when formally asked by the Indian Government in 1867.[764]

Before 1856 and the signing of the Paris Declaration, blockades were a combination of localised actions, including limiting the movement of civilians in littoral spaces and fleet-to-fleet actions limiting the movement of warships and trade.[765] The Royal Navy had experience conducting localised and strategic Indo-Pacific blockades.[766] For the East Indies and China Station (1831–1865), its operational experience with blockades revolved around smaller, fluid imperial campaigns. This included the blockade of Rangoon in April 1852. This was not, however, a model of best practice in how to conduct a blockade: "The Governor of Rangoon sent a saucy message to the blockading squadron... as he was tired of watching them swing at anchor, making mysterious signals."[767]

Nicholas Tarling also identifies multiple examples of Royal Navy blockade-like activity in Malaysia, where attempts to counter piracy fit the definition of a blockade. These activities has the intention of restricting the "capacity to use the sea", and were a blockade in all but name.[768] Similar arguments could be made of the broader efforts to counter piracy, such as how naval vessels were being used to restrict movement and access over confined littoral areas.[769] The represents the difficulty in defining what was and was not a blockade before the formal definition in 1856.

Although it can sometimes appear unclear when a blockade was a blockade, there was a common thread of using naval power to effectively change the behaviour of a community or group in how they used the seas. This aligns with one of the recommendations presented to the Secretary of State for India in 1868. The recommendation from Captain Arthur Kinloch, Bengal Army, suggested the threat from indigenous tribes in the periphery of Port Blair's territory could only be curtailed by naval power.[770] Although the term 'blockade' was not used, Kinloch recommended the periodic isolation of a particular area, such as a stretch of coastline, to prevent the entry and exit of goods and people as a deterrent for any aggression.

The British use of blockade-like measures in response to threats against merchant shipping in the Bay of Bengal from supposed acts of piracy was a common occurrence. It again demonstrates that the stability and security of British merchant routes were a paramount concern, not merely for economic reasons but also as a continued display of British maritime dominance in the region. This dominance brought trust, and trust encouraged merchants to traverse the seas. When piracy, or activities labelled as such, threatened this stability it triggered a substantial response from the imperial government to maintain uninterrupted trade and showcase the Empire's capability to protect its interests.[771] This was the case with the attack on the crew of the *Futteh Islam*.

Any instability around the Nicobar Islands directly impacted vital elements of the British Empire's economic infrastructure in the Bay of Bengal, notably the merchant shipping routes that facilitated the lucrative trade between India and China.[772] These routes were vital arteries for the flow of goods such as opium, textiles, and later tea, which were foundational to the economic interdependence of the British colonial markets.[773] British merchant vessels traversing these waters transported goods and also carried the economic lifeline of isolated colonies like Port Blair, which were yet to be self-sufficient.

The threat of piracy, whether real or exaggerated, posed a significant risk not only to the physical safety of these goods and crews. It also challenged British governance and the state's economic stability and reputation. In this light, the role of the Royal Navy was to use "force to maintain the status quo" and safeguard these vital economic interests against any impact from piracy.[774] Like the incident discussed in the previous chapter, the fact that the *Futteh Islam* was a British trading vessel meant that once attacked, the merchant community expected a British response to reassure them.

The Nicobarese tribes, thus labelled as pirates by the Indian Government, were cast within a narrative that depicted piracy as an uncivilised and barbaric act in the contemporary discourse of the 1860s.[775] As noted, in 1867 the Superintendent of Port Blair advised mariners not to land or go ashore at any of the outlining islands that comprised the Andaman and Nicobar Chain.[776] However, the *Futteh Islam* was attacked at sea. The ship may have been at anchor, but the Nicobarese used canoes to get to the vessel. This simple difference in how the ship was attacked dramatically changed the paradigm. It was now an act of piracy.

There is no clear evidence to suggest a motive for attacking the crew. Captain Norman Bedingfield RN, of HMS *Wasp*, suspected other traders in Nancowry Harbour could have paid or encouraged the Nicobarese to attack in exchange for sharing the contents of *Futteh Islam's* money chest.[777] The British did not, however, explore this claim and the official government record put the motive down as an example of savage, piratical behaviour.

After the attack, the Indian Government saw that the threat was coming from the sea, in large war canoes. The portrayal of 'pirates' was a useful trope for the colonial powers. It provided a justification for a naval operation to deter piracy but also test the imposition of control over indigenous populations deemed unruly or lawless.[778] In the 1840s and 1850s, piracy was not merely a criminal activity; it was often represented as an inherent characteristic of 'othered' societies. Authorities used piracy to rationalise their civilising missions, military interventions, or a crackdown on unwanted behaviours at sea.[779] For the Nicobarese, this branding as pirates also aligned with the British pretext to extend their control over the Nicobar Islands by being seen to eradicate piracy and instil law and order, whether through blockade or other means.[780]

Categorisation of piracy served multiple imperial purposes: it reinforced the racial and cultural superiority presumed by colonial ideologies, justified the expansion of military and administrative reach, and ultimately facilitated the control of SLOC. The label of piracy was a powerful tool in the imperial narrative, used to delegitimise indigenous maritime practices that conflicted with colonial commercial and strategic interests. However, defining the Nicobarese as pirates was "neither straightforward nor consistent" in its designation.[781] Seapower scholars often treat the 'enemy' as fixed and predominantly focus on state actors.[782] In this case, it was an indigenous population. The narrative of pirates, in this instance, has a clear tone of orientalism.

In the comings days after the report of the *Futteh Islam* reached Penang, the Indian Government requested a blockade be implemented around the wider Nicobars.[783] The blockade was intended to restrict access to an area of the sea for a period, in this case, from Nancowry Harbour. The Royal Navy's East Indies Station had responsibility for this stretch of water. The station was concurrently engaged in extensive anti-slavery operations around East Africa, which strained its resources and divided its focus.[784]

Since 1865, the station was significantly restructured, with the East Indies and China Stations separating into the East

Indies Station and China Station, respectively.[785] This meant that although the formal boundary between the stations was the Malacca Strait, there was inevitably an overlap and an element of burden sharing where appropriate.[786] The Andaman and Nicobar Islands were on the periphery of both stations. This was both a geographical periphery and mission periphery.

The Commander-in-Chief of the East Indies station was a commodore, and the Commander-in-Chief of the China Station was a Rear Admiral. This meant that with the geographical ambiguity, decisions were often raised to the China Station until the Nicobars were formally placed under the control of the Indian Government in 1868. During the early 1860s, the East Indies Station conducted anti-slavery operations from East Africa.[787] This was a key pillar of British foreign policy, and Zanzibar was an epicentre of the slave trade until it was abolished in 1873.[788] Around 2,000 miles from Calcutta in the port of Singapore, the incoming Commander-in-Chief of the China Station, Vice Admiral Henry Keppel, had a very different operational focus. He stated that the eradication of piracy was to be the primary focus of the station during his tenure.[789]

This period also saw an increase in legal changes in the maritime domain. The Paris Declaration Respecting Maritime Law of 1856 significantly impacted the practice of blockades. It mandated that blockades must be declared and maintained by a competent force to be legally recognised. This treaty led to more regulated maritime practices, reducing indiscriminate blockades post-Crimean War that were previously frequent occurrences in imperial campaigns. This new declaration made it difficult for the East Indies Station to respond to the request from the Indian Government to blockade Nancowry Harbour in 1867, as you will see.

Nicobar Expeditions, 1866-1869

Although the exact date of the attack on the British brig *Futteh Islam* is unknown, the ship set sail from Penang in August 1866 on its way to Yangon (now Rangoon).[790] It was British-owned but crewed by Burmese and 'native' mariners and seamen.[791] On route, the *Futteh Islam* stopped off in Nancowry Harbour, where the Nicobarese greeted the ship at sea, offering goods to trade and barter. This informal trading relationship was not new and had become the norm for Burmese, Chinese and local mariners and seamen since the 1830s.[792] Without a state presence in the Nicobar Islands, there were no taxes or customs, meaning goods could be acquired from the Nicobarese through bartering, particularly metals, in exchange for coconuts and exquisite shells. This could make a quick profit for the mariners and seamen selling back in Rangoon, Penang or Singapore.[793]

Very few secondary sources exist on the relationship between traders and the Nicobarese before 1872, when the Nicobars would eventually come under the Port Blair administration. Hence, the reflections you will now read come from a selection of primary sources, including the accounts of the three survivors of the attack and other traders interviewed by the Royal Navy in Nancowry Harbour. They are, therefore, not comprehensive, but at least reflect the British institutional understanding of trade in the Nicobars at the time. The British understanding was that although the Nicobarese were self-sufficient, they relied on the 'barter trade' with passing merchants for metals and other goods.[794] This is important to note. The belief that the Nicobarese needed trade meant the British thought restricting access at sea would lead to a behaviour change.

At the time, the Nicobar Islands were a Danish colony, where, despite the claim, Denmark neither maintained a permanent presence nor made regular visits.[795] This lack of state oversight created a perceived European power vacuum. It also contributed to the Islands' reputation within maritime circles as a hazardous, dangerous area. This backdrop set the stage for heightened British concerns about the security of maritime traffic meandering via the Andaman Islands down south to the Nicobars, especially given the proximity to the SLOC leaving the Straits of Malacca onto India. The consensus formed towards a naval response, which was considered necessary to repair faith after the attack on the *Futteh Islam*.[796]

The dissemination of information about the attack on the *Futteh Islam* played a critical role in the subsequent response. The reports of the attack, and the dramatic circumstances surrounding it, initially reached Penang in January 1867. This was through the crew who had managed to survive the attack by hiding from the Nicobarese.[797] After taking control of the vessel, they navigated back to Penang, bringing first-hand accounts of the violence they had witnessed, which the Lieutenant Governor of Penang recorded for posterity.[798] There was, as yet, no indication of what triggered the attack:

> There seems to have been no provocation on the part of the crew of the brig and this is probably one of the many native vessels that have been plundered by these scoundrels, the others scuttled afterwards.[799]

This information was corroborated by the accounts of Sheik Daood and Sheik Sultan, who were traders that regularly engaged with the Nicobarese. The *Wasp* took their reports when it visited Nancowry on 28 June 1867.[800] The record of the attack given by the sheiks appeared sudden and brutal. Twenty-one crew members were killed on the deck of the *Futteh Islam* with bow and arrows, knives and clubs.

It also took the three remaining crew members of the *Futteh Islam* many months to reach a British administrative centre. Having left Penang in August 1866, the crew eventually returned to Penang again in January 1867. There is no account of when the attack took place, or what the vessel was doing in that period. What it does indicate is the difficulty of sailing a brig with only three crew members. Even with the advent of steam technology and increased maritime traffic in the area, it could still take months to transit the waters, depending on the winds, the competence of the crew, and the serviceability of the vessel.[801]

This illustrates why the Secretary of State for India wanted a naval response, such as a blockade, as a reassurance measure and to understand the activity in the Nicobars.[802]

Penang was a significant port and a hub of British activity in the Straits Settlement. Once the survivors had reached the port, the issue was raised directly to the Lieutenant-Governor, Sir Archibald Edward Harbord Anson. Anson requested support from the Royal Navy via the Senior Officer in the Straits of Malacca, on board HMS *Pearl*. Commodore Hillyar, C-in-C of the East Indies Station, offered to support and sent HMS *Wasp* to undertake reconnaissance within Nancowry Harbour in April 1867.[803] Hillyar initially supported the option to blockade and limit the ability of the Nicobarese to commit acts of piracy and barter trade. Although he maintained that the option depended on the outcome of the *Wasp's* expedition.

> The necessity of this blockade will depend, as I think your Excellency will agree with me, on the reports that I may receive on this subject from Captain Bedingfield, of Her Majesty's Ship Wasp, and whether any steps have been taken by that Officer and the Governor of the Straits Settlements to settle this matter.[804]

This reflects Hillyar's attempt to gather evidence on the issue first to gauge whether a blockade was warranted or whether another form of action may be more appropriate.

The issue was also brought to the attention of the senior levels of the Indian Government.[805] It was also compounded by sensational claims that "white women" were held hostage on the island.[806] This struck a nerve within the imperial maritime network. The Indian Government considered that a robust response was necessary to address the perceived lawlessness and brutality of the pirates in the Nicobar Islands. As Barry Gough argues, whether this had a military effect or was performative in nature, the key was to ensure that the maritime community believed in the Royal Navy's ability to uphold security.[807]

Figure 21: Nancowry Village

The attack on the *Futteh Islam* enhanced the already dangerous reputation of the Nicobars, and the Government of India requested a gunboat to blockade the Islands to avoid any future acts of piracy.[808] The Government of India favoured a blockade to 'isolate' the threat and prevent pirates from accessing the seas where British and European ships may venture.[809] Both the Government of India and Commodore Hillyar had received description of events that focused heavily on how the attack happened at sea. Logically, the belief was that the response should naturally limit movement in sea spaces.

The ambiguous nature of the attack represents what Lakshmi Subramanian argues was a manifestation of the colonial states' inability to see piracy in its truest form, which takes place in "different littoral zones that had far-reaching linkages with the hinterland".[810] Although there was some recognition that contact must be made with the indigenous population to communicate and seek a resolution, the focus on isolating the pirates underscored the necessity perceived by the British to intervene more decisively than in the Little Andaman Incident.[811] The focus was, evidently, on securing maritime routes through segregating the supposed troublesome Nicobarese pirates.

Alongside suppressing any threats to navigation, it is clear the Indian Government saw this incident as reflective of a need to leverage and justify expanding their influence and control over the Nicobar Islands.[812] Diplomatic efforts began almost immediately in London to gauge how the Danish Government would respond.

The Indian Government formally requested support for a blockade from the Commodore of the East Indies Station, Hillyar, highlighting its desire to "isolate" pirates' access to the seas and bring the seas around the Islands under the control of Britain's imperial maritime security umbrella.[813] Note that it was the seas, not the land, that the British wanted to secure at this point. The reasons for requesting a blockade over an expedition, such as with the Little Andaman Campaign in chapter five, were twofold. As the attack took place at sea, it seemed reasonable to assume a maritime response would halt the activity of the pirates. Also, a blockade would put British naval assets in the region, showing a permanent presence as a reassurance measure to the merchant community.

However, Hillyar privately responded to the Viceroy that he could not ensure that a blockade would be full or binding with the resources available at the East Indies Station.[814] Although the Paris Declaration Respecting Maritime Law of 1856 is not mentioned by name, the language used by Hillyar was almost identical, which could reflect his reference to this recently signed treaty. Regardless of the reference, the naval recommendation was that a blockade would not be suitable. It underscored the limitations of naval assets available for colonial tasks.

Consequently, Hillyar expressed his ability to spare only one ship for any duties around Nancowry Harbour, which was HMS *Wasp*.[815] Despite these constraints, the decision to allocate limited naval resources to the Nicobar blockade demonstrates the balancing act that the British naval forces had to perform, often making compromises to maintain security and order across the

Empire's vast and diverse territories. It also reflects the hierarchy of responsibilities of the East Indies Station at the time, with the East African slave trade being an operational priority over potential localised attacks from pirates in the Bay of Bengal.

Hillyar's initial reluctance to divert resources to the Nicobars was not only due to the ongoing commitments in Africa but also because of the inherent uncertainty about the actual threat level posed by the situation in the area. The Military Department of the government in Burma, although supporting a blockade, acknowledged that there was a lack of precise intelligence about the extent of the pirate threat. It questioned whether this was an isolated or reoccurring occurrence.[816] This lack of certainty for action by the government offices based in Calcutta and Rangoon contrasts with the situation in the Straits Settlements, where authorities had both the first-hand accounts of the *Futteh Islam* attack. The China Station, with ships in the Straits Settlements, had recently been actively involved in combating piracy in Malaya, developing a more routine and systematic approach to such threats.[817]

This internal institutional divergence shows the difficulty in getting accurate intelligence. It explains why the true nature of the threat could not be fully articulated, and why a blockade made sense when decision-making was taken at a considerable distance. The arrival of Commodore Leopold Heath RN as the new Commander-in-Chief of the East Indies Station in July 1867 did not change the East Indies Station's approach to a blockade. Heath's stance instead promoted a more aggressive approach to dealing with the littoral activity of the Nicobarese by targeting the infrastructure on shore.[818] In practice, this meant burning canoes and villages.

Before proceeding, it is also worth expanding on the distinction between the incidents at Little Andaman, which had taken place in May 1867, and the attack on the *Futteh Islam*. The former occurred ashore involving confrontations on land, while the latter was a maritime attack, executed while a vessel was at anchor in Nancowry

Harbour. Although it may seem minor, the difference between an attack at sea and an attack on the shore is significant. To the Indian Government, it characterised the perceived maritime confidence of the Nicobarese and represented a challenge to British control and navigation at sea.[819] Terrestrially, the Nicobars were not deemed significant and had little to offer, but the Islands' position along the SLOC was vital to Britain's maritime trade.[820]

The only reports of the attack were those of the surviving members of the *Futteh Islam*, and with little further evidence, the bias swung heavily towards representations of barbarity. It portrayed the pirates as capable and fearless. In hindsight, it is easy to perceive a blockade as overblown, but to a colonial administrator, the threat would have seemed genuine, and the safety of merchant shipping was paramount. Heath's suggestion of targeting the Nicobarese war canoes also recognised the need to limit the Nicobarese's ability to engage in such acts at sea.[821]

In June 1867, HMS *Wasp,* under the command of Captain Norman Bedingfield RN, reconnoitred the site of the *Futteh Islam* attack.[822] During this mission, the crew of the *Wasp* found traces suggesting that European women were kept as prisoners, an alarming find that significantly escalated the urgency of the situation. The incident moved from one of maritime trade disturbances into the sociocultural realm. It was a case of the civilised being held hostage by the uncivilised.

Consequently, the *Wasp* returned to Penang, from which a pressing request was made for additional support from the Lieutenant Governor of the Straits Settlements.[823] However, a significant reshuffle of the Straits Settlement meant the incident was perceived as low priority at the time. It was in the process of being merged under the Colonial Office. The *Wasp* went to Singapore to await permission to return to Nancowry to help release the prisoners and punish the pirates.[824] The reconnaissance by HMS *Wasp* provided the clarity needed and set the stage for further intervention. The *Wasp's* findings were corroborated by evidence from the Port Blair guardship *Kwan Tung*, which also briefly visited Nancowry Harbour after the *Wasp*.[825]

On 22 July 1867, under the instruction of the newly appointed Commodore Leopold Heath, the *Wasp* returned to the Nicobar Islands alongside HMS *Satellite* (a wood screw corvette) under the command of Captain William Henry Edye RN, to conduct an anti-piracy operation ashore.[826] This marked a significant escalation in the British naval response.[827] An attempt to blockade had escalated into an expedition ashore.

The *Satellite* also had soldiers from the Madras Native Infantry on board to support the shore operation. The addition of native infantry reflected Heath's proactive stance on tackling the infrastructure of piracy first, before judging the need for a blockade after this action. A blockade was still a policy option, depending on what the ships found.

Upon arrival, the crews from *Wasp* and *Satellite* attempted to diplomatically engage with the Nicobarese tribe, aiming to resolve the situation without further violence.[828] However, negotiations faltered through the inability to understand the Nicobarese language. The shore party then resorted to burning the 70ft war canoes identified as the ones used in the attack on the *Futteh Islam*, alongside any other vessel that could be used for 'piratical purposes'.[829] It is unclear how the shore party identified the vessels, as there was no translator to engage with the Nicobarese.

The canoes were a vital part of Nicobarese life, used for fishing and moving around the various communities. The captain of the *Wasp* and *Satellite* would have also known this, as this fact was reported to the captain of HMS *Sylvia* before sailing, who identified the significance of canoes to everyday life and mobility.[830] This act was not only punitive but also symbolic, aiming to dismantle the very means by which the Nicobarese could pose a threat at sea and as a deterrent for any future acts. Although there are no studies of Nicobarese canoes in this period, if a comparison is made to other indigenous populations, then replacing the canoes would have taken significant resources and several weeks to months to build, depending on the size. It would have also limited the ability of the Nicobarese to fish, which was a key part of their diet.[831] Destroying the canoes would have impacted the Nicobarese for a significant period, and this impact stretched beyond piracy and into the means of subsistence of the tribes.

The deployment of the Madras Native Infantry on board the *Satellite* also signifies a deepening of the operational complexity undertaken on the Nicobars. It symbolises the gravity with which the British treated the alleged acts of piracy and kidnapping, necessitating resources from multiple different departments of the imperial state. The Madras Native Infantry, alongside the ship's company of *Wasp* and *Satellite,* advanced into the Nicobarese villages, where they found that the inhabitants had pre-emptively abandoned their homes, possibly anticipating retaliatory action.[832] This abandonment, however, did not prevent the discovery of multiple European items within the vacated villages, including European clothes, diaries, and tools from various ships:

> Three or four merchant vessels have been captured within as many years, their crews murdered, and the women on board reserved for a worse fate.[833]

This was tangible evidence that lent credence to the reports of attacks stretching beyond just the *Futteh Islam* on European shipping and the looting of their goods.[834]

The findings of the shore party, as detailed in Bedingfield's reports, also included the capture of a few Nicobarese men. Interrogations of these captives revealed a grim picture: all the Europeans involved, except for a young girl, had been murdered.[835] This testimony not only confirmed the suspicions of the Indian Government but also highlighted how the *Futteh Islam* was not an isolated incident. The Nicobarese had, it appears, also targeted other merchant vessels in Nancowry Harbour over the last decade. In the eyes of the British, these revelations further justified the escalated military response and pondered how, without a permanent European presence on the Islands, security could be preserved.[836]

Due to resource constraints, HMS *Wasp* and HMS *Satellite* were subsequently ordered to return to Trincomalee, signalling that a permanent blockade of the Nicobar Islands was not feasible at that time, nor was it considered required based on the threat level from Heath's perspective.[837] This decision partly underscores the logistical challenges faced by the Royal Navy in maintaining sustained operations across vast regions, but more significantly, the differences in perspective across imperial governments. The imperial state comprised multiple organisations, both civilian and military, with different portfolios and responsibilities. Geographically, the closest governance hub was Port Blair, but the closest major naval base was Singapore. The Indian Government was still requesting a blockade, and the issue was soon raised to a more senior naval officer in the region, Vice Admiral Henry Keppel RN, Commander-in-Chief of the China Station.[838]

Keppel's entry into negotiations with the Indian Government indicates the continuing significance of the incident and the increasing strategic value attributed to the Nicobars by the government in India.[839] The Islands were a potential site of violence if mariners happened to venture into Nancowry. As the Nicobars are close to the busy transit routes via the Straits of Malacca, there was no guarantee that a ship would not stop at the Islands for commercial gain, or to escape from monsoon weather. There were however insufficient resources in the East Indies for a temporary blockade, and the landings by Royal Navy vessels had only found traces of European prisoners. A growing consensus emerged that a permanent British presence in the Nicobars was necessary, which is what Keppel was promoting.[840]

Keppel sent HMS *Perseus*, a wood screw sloop from the China Station, to investigate one last time before he committed to some form of naval presence, whether that be a blockade or a permanent settlement.[841] This shift in strategy reflected the ongoing difficulty faced by the Indian Government in accurately assessing and responding to the threat on isolated and uncontrolled islands in the Bay of Bengal, even after the colonisation of the Andamans in 1858. The nature of piracy, with its inherent mobility, posed a particular challenge. Even after the punitive action of burning the canoes, there remained substantial uncertainty about whether such measures had effectively neutralised the threat or temporarily disrupted it. You could only judge that effectiveness by being *present* and observing in Nancowry, or waiting for another report of murder most foul.

The decision to consider a permanent presence on the Nicobars was increasingly discussed through the late stages of 1867. The discussion revolved around establishing a sustained security apparatus to monitor, deter, and quickly react to future threats affecting mariners around the Nicobar Islands. This was the perspective of the Superintendent of Port Blair and the overarching Military Department in Burma, who both recommended a permanent presence on the Nicobars if a blockade was not implemented.[842]

The geographical spread of the Nicobars, and the ability to find and engage with the Nicobarese, made conventional naval policing methods ineffective. Thus, establishing a permanent base represented a pivot towards a more persistent regional security posture. Nevertheless, the fundamental justification behind the permanent presence was a wish to control *how* and *why* the Nicobarese used the sea, just like the original justification for a blockade.

In hindsight, it would be easy to say the initial approach of the Indian Government and the Royal Navy towards conducting a blockade around the Nicobar Islands revealed a fundamental overestimation and mischaracterisation of the Nicobarese as pirates. Rather than being understood in their sociocultural context, the Nicobarese were primarily viewed as an obstacle to British maritime security objectives and disrupting the maritime order. In lieu, they became categorised as pirates.[843] This limited perception ultimately influenced the decisions to apply naval force, as the tribes were treated predominantly as a hindrance rather than stakeholders whose cooperation might be secured through more nuanced engagement strategies.[844]

The outwardly aggressive objective, to isolate and contain through force, framed any contact with the Nicobarese. The interactions were coercive or confrontational rather than diplomatic or cooperative due to the British imagination of the Nicobars. The eventual perceived need for a more permanent presence also underscores the inability of overwhelming force against isolated communities to be effective, as you read in chapter five. The type of naval power applied to the Nicobarese, just as in the case of Little Andaman, failed to create a more sustained and informed interaction with the indigenous population. Force was, in the eyes of the colonial officials, the only measure which would work. If that failed, establish a colony.

HMS *Perseus*, a screw sloop from the China Station, arrived in the Nicobar Islands on 22 December 1867. It continued the efforts initiated by HMS *Wasp* by landing a party ashore.[845] However, for the Nicobarese, who abandoned their villages again upon the arrival of the British, evasion was their only means of countering the naval forces. Unfortunately, no texts on the Nicobarese exist to understand their behaviour. The first anthropological studies were not until the early 1870s when the British created a settlement on the Islands.[846] However, in the naval reports of 1867, the Nicobarese did not use guns or swords; their only weaponry was bows, arrows, and clubs. In many ways, the fact that the Nicobarese evaded the British rather than fight reflects that the 'savagery' label would be much more appropriate for the behaviour of the Royal Navy personnel.

Evasion tactics made it exceedingly difficult to exert control and curb piracy in such a remote region, as there was no means to communicate with the Nicobarese. The mobility and intimate geographical knowledge of the Nicobarese allowed them to effectively evade direct confrontations with British forces, who lacked the expertise or resources to venture deep into the jungle terrain. The repeated abandonment of villages not only demonstrates the Nicobarese's resistance tactic but also reflects the broader challenge of targeting and engaging with indigenous tribes who wish to resist foreign domination and control. This scenario illustrates the limitations of imperial naval power in culturally unfamiliar, geographically challenging environments against non-state actors.

By the close of December 1867, the discussion had moved rapidly from blockade to a complete annexation of the Nicobar Islands at the upper echelons of British imperial governance. According to Colonel Henry Man of the Bengal Army, only a permanent settlement in Nancowry would ensure no more attacks were made in the future.[847] Also the Viceroy of India, the Secretary of State for India, and representatives from the Marine Department grappled with the logistical and administrative challenges posed by incorporating these remote islands into the governance framework.[848] The primary issue was determining the most suitable administrative centre for the Nicobar Islands. The Straits Settlements were deemed unsuitable due to their limited resources and existing administrative burdens.[849]

Pressure from the Indian Government, notably Colonel Henry Man, advocated for the administration to be incorporated into India.[850] He specifically suggested that the Islands be managed from the Port Blair station on the nearby Andaman Islands.[851] This arrangement was seen as more pragmatic. It leveraged Port Blair's established colonial infrastructure (including maritime assets) and relative proximity, facilitating more effective governance and oversight over the Nicobar Islands to reduce piracy. It was also convenient for Man; as a captain, he raised the flag in the colonisation ceremony discussed in chapter two, and he would eventually become the next superintendent of Port Blair in 1869.[852] This is not to suggest that Man's interest here was purely guided by promotion. There is no evidence to suggest that. Instead, it reflects the informal way imperial officers gained positions through knowledge and happenstance. Man understood the Andaman Islands well, which was considered 'close enough' to the Nicobars to make him a subject matter expert.[853]

Figure 22: HMS Spiteful

Establishing British control over the Nicobar Islands took another year following the *Wasp*, *Satellite* and *Perseus* interventions. The centre of activity shifted to London and Europe. Negotiations with Denmark were necessary due to the Nicobars' legal status as a Danish colony, albeit without a permanent presence, and this lack of European oversight continued to cause concern to the Military Department in Burma.[854] The outcome of diplomatic discussion with Denmark was announced in January 1869: Denmark had formally approved British annexation.[855]

The annexation of the Nicobar Islands reinforced British seapower in the region. It ultimately secured the SLOC for one group (merchants of British and European goods) against the freedom of using the sea of another (the Nicobarese). It gave the

Port Blair administration the ability to influence the behaviour of the Nicobarese at sea, even down to sociocultural practices such as how they traded and the ceremonial use of war canoes.

By March 1869, Heath was instructed to send a British warship to take possession of the Nicobars.[856] Thus, the East Indies Station dispatched HMS *Spiteful* (a wood paddle sloop).[857] It had a definitive mandate from the Government of India to assert control over the Islands:

> I, Arthur Morell, a Commander in Her Britannic Majesty's Naval Service, and now Commanding Her Majesty's Ship-of-war Spiteful, having received instructions thereto from Commodore Sir Leopold Heath, K.o.B., Commanding Her Majesty's Naval Forces in the Indian Seas, acting on the requisition of the Earl of Mayo, Viceroy and Governor General of India, do now on this the day of... in the name and on behalf of the Indian Government of Her Majesty the Queen of Great Britain and Ireland, take possession of this island of Nancowry, together with all others commonly known as the Nicobar Islands, that is to say, the island of Car-Nicobar and Great Nicobar with those lying between them including Tillanchong, and in token thereof I now hoist the flag of Great Britain, proclaiming to all concerned the supremacy of Her Most Gracious Majesty, declaring the said islands to be subject to Her Majesty's Indian Government, and calling upon the inhabitants of the said islands to submit themselves to Her Majesty's laws as administered by the Government of India.[858]

The proclamation is important in listing all relevant offices of the state. This shift from maritime policing to territorial acquisition was marked symbolically and performatively when the crew of the *Spiteful* raised the Union Jack on 27 March 1869 in Nancowry Harbour, signalling the formal assertion of British sovereignty.[859]

The settlement at the Nicobars would now come under the administration of the Andaman Islands, the first formal relationship between the Andaman and Nicobar Islands that continues to exist today.[860] Through a proclamation and a few sentences, the British claimed space as their own incorporating the Nicobar Islands under British imperial authority.

The crew of HMS *Spiteful* also undertook practical measures such as clearing jungle areas and preparing the ground for a more permanent presence.[861] Colonel Man, now promoted to Superintendent of the Andamans, soon arrived and began the concerted efforts to establish a settlement. His arrival effectively marked the transition from a naval operation to one now grounded in territoriality through colonial administration.[862] The action taken in the Nicobars expresses the limits of British naval forces to patrol and assert complete control over distant, sparsely inhabited island chains in the Bay of Bengal. It required the British to establish a settlement to administer regions deemed crucial for maritime security. In doing so in Nancowry Harbour, it consolidated British imperial control over an island chain previously known as a place of ambiguity and sporadic engagement at the periphery of the Empire.[863]

After annexation, the responsibility for the security of the Nicobars shifted to the Superintendent of Port Blair.[864] Nevertheless, the Royal Navy's previous deployments to the Nicobars illustrate its pivotal function in enforcing imperial policy, projecting power away from colonial hubs, and securing trade routes deemed essential for the Empire's economic vitality when out of reach of terrestrial control. This, inevitably, continued in some form, and the relationship centred around the East Indies Station remained core.[865] The Madras Native Infantry or even the Bombay Marine, for example, did not have the resources to conduct operations at what were considered distant island chains.[866]

More importantly, the Royal Navy played a crucial role in asserting and securing British sovereignty over the Nicobar Islands, emphasising the interplay between seapower and national sovereignty beyond mere military engagement. It was performative as much as a conventional military force. The deployment of HMS

Perseus to the Nicobars was a ceremonial assertion of imperial dominion: a performance of power.[867]

Upon arrival, *Perseus'* crew was tasked with raising the British flag, reading a proclamation of sovereignty, and firing a 'Royal Salute' of 21 guns by order of the Indian Government.[868] According to international law, the occupation must be continuous for an annexation to be recognised as legitimate and lasting.[869] Consequently, *Perseus'* presence was not merely symbolic but also a legal necessity to maintain uninterrupted British authority until it could be relieved by another vessel from Port Blair.[870] This use of naval power to perform sovereignty underscores how integral maritime forces were in enacting and maintaining national claims, particularly in remote or contested territories like the Nicobars.

The crew of the British gunboats also performed 'Britishness'; that is the imprinting of British values and customs in distant imperial spaces.[871] The Royal Navy's treatment of the Nicobarese during this period embodies 'othering' and orientalism.[872] The Nicobarese were construed not as unique societies with rich histories and cultures but as problems to be managed or obstacles to be removed. They were simply 'pirates' in the British imagination.[873] This perspective is reflective of a broader imperial attitude that often reduced non-European peoples to stereotypes or threats within the colonial narrative.[874] This approach enabled easier justification for harsh measures taken in the name of security and order under the guise of civilising missions. This is evident in the reports from both the *Wasp* and *Perseus*, and how the Indian Government recorded the event for posterity.[875]

However, these actions were consistent with the norms of the day, driven by the prevailing ideologies and operational doctrines of European colonial powers.[876] This does not excuse the practices; it simply places them within a historical context.

After the annexation of the Nicobar Islands in 1869, the Indian Government consolidated communications and administration in the Bay of Bengal over the next three years.[877] Recognising the utility of the Andaman Islands, the Indian Government established an important telegraph cable station here that acted as a hub for communications across the Bay of Bengal and down to Australia.[878] Firstly, this aimed to integrate islands into the broader imperial communication network. Succinct communication to the administrative capital in Calcutta was vital for disseminating policy and governance.[879] Secondly, this undersea cable also offered a cost-effective solution for linking British imperial capitals across Southeast Asia to Australia, as it was significantly cheaper than terrestrial or maritime mail alternatives.[880]

Alongside these advancements in communications, there was a concerted effort to solidify administrative control. In 1872, Port Blair was formally designated as the centre of administration for the Andaman and Nicobar Islands, governed by a Chief Commissioner.[881] This centralised authority and enhanced governance in the centre of the Bay of Bengal. By 1872, the British imperial administration had effectively removed the threat of piracy, 'civilised' the Andaman and Nicobar Islands through settlement, established greater control over the SLOC in the Bay of Bengal, and had no effective maritime adversary in the region. The Bay of Bengal had become a *British Sea* in representation and practice.

From Piracy to Annexation

The definition of piracy, the attempted blockade, and naval involvement in the claim of sovereignty over the Nicobars reveal deeper insights into the often-overlooked dimensions of imperial seapower. Blockades traditionally have been framed as strategies to cut off an enemy's supplies and communications within a war context, as Stephen Roskill and Geoffrey Till have argued. However, the Nicobar scenario illustrates that blockades were also viewed as instruments of imperial policy aimed at asserting control over contested maritime spaces and indigenous populations through segregation and the control of space.[882]

Imperial naval actions were about performing authority, securing economic routes, and ensuring behaviours at sea matched British expectations. This can be seen in how the commanders of the *Wasp*, *Perseus* and military colonial officers all used vocabularies such as *isolate*, *limit*, and *control* when describing the intended consequences of their actions towards the Nicobarese. The Royal Navy was a tool of social and cultural quarantining, even if this may have been an unintended consequence of naval action.

The stark contrast between the Nicobarese war canoes and the Royal Navy's steam gunboats encapsulates the profound imbalance of seapower and the asymmetrical relationship between the Nicobarese and the British actors. The war canoes, traditional and wooden structured, represented a form of seapower deeply rooted in local customs and geographic familiarity, optimised for shallow waters and quick, small-scale operations against other war canoes.[883] In contrast, the Royal Navy's steam gunboats embodied industrial military technology, equipped with advanced navigation systems, powerful engines, and heavy armaments.[884] The Royal Navy's ships represent brute force, whereas the Nicobarese canoes were geographically tailored to the environment. Recent literature has examined indigenous canoes and reflected on the effectiveness of the boats.[885] This includes the ability to evade Western militaries, as the Nicobarese did.

British steam-powered gunboats were not merely tools of warfare but instruments of imperial control. They were designed to project power, enforce dominance, and suppress any local resistance with overwhelming force.[886] Although there was no direct engagement between gunboats and canoes on the waters around the Nicobar Islands, the naval commanders sought to destroy the canoes to limit the Nicobarese's capability and access to the seas. It vividly illustrates the broader colonial encounter: a confrontation between indigenous peoples whose tactics and tools were deeply intertwined with their historical and environmental context, but no match for European colonisers' 'superior' technology.[887]

This imbalance fundamentally shaped the interactions, outcomes, and historical narratives of the encounter between the Royal Navy and the Nicobarese in 1867. There has since been no reflection in academic literature on whether the Nicobarese truly were pirates.[888] As Lakshmi Subramanian argues in the context of the west coast of India, pirates were often simply "tribes of differing status, of a space for refuge and asylum to disposed coastal groups who were akin to stateless people".[889] Although I will not argue either way, the designation of piracy is most significant in how it shaped imperial policy.[890] The ability to designate a population as 'pirates' was a form of power in itself. According to Bruno Latour, this is an example of an act which gave the British the ability to select an identity for the Nicobarese and to assign their meaning: "deprived of its conditions."[891] The British had the power to assign identities of communities in maritime spaces.

The portrayal of the Nicobarese tribes as pirates catalysed a significant naval response from the British, illustrating the critical role that perceptions and labels play in shaping naval interventions. This designation of the Nicobarese as maritime threats, specifically as pirates by the Indian Government, emphasised a different scale and nature of response compared to the Little Andaman incident, where the threat was defined as shore-based. The distinction between maritime and terrestrial threats was crucial; the mobility and unpredictability associated with pirates in Nancowry Harbour directly challenged the safety, security, and, most importantly, the mobility of international maritime routes, demanding an immediate and robust naval response.[892] The Little Andaman threat could be contained, whereas the threat from the Nicobars could not.

The Little Andaman Campaign restored the faith in security, and the threat was considered to no longer imperil the imperial maritime network.[893] Through recommendations not to land on the Islands and regular patrols, the Superintendent of Port Blair saw the threat as manageable.[894] In contrast, the attack on the decks of the *Futteh Islam* represented an attack on British implied sovereignty. It is unclear whether the *Futteh Islam* was flying a British flag, but it was British-owned. A British-owned vessel in the 1860s would have been seen as a floating space of British territory, even if its legal definition did not apply as such.[895] It held symbolic Britishness.

There was a marked difference in how the state responded, depending on whether the incident happened ashore or a few metres past the surf into the harbour area. The British prioritised threats according to their perceived impact on vital interests, particularly trade routes, making a threat at sea supposedly more severe. By framing the Nicobarese as pirates, the British provided a blueprint to justify more aggressive and visible military actions in the Nicobars. This was to neutralise what they presented as a clear and present danger to maritime security.[896] Thus, the British reinforced their control over the region, eventually leading to annexation.

In March 1869, Viceroy Lord Mayo once again noted that 'piracy' in the vicinity of the Nicobar Islands in 1867 significantly disrupted the perceived fluidity and security of British maritime trade routes.[897] This senior government figure's portrayal of the incidents as piracy heightened perceptions of vulnerability among merchant vessels traversing these critical waterways, posing a direct threat to the British economic interests in the Bay of Bengal. The vulnerability of these maritime assets compelled the Indian Government to perceive these acts not merely as isolated criminal behaviours but as long-term threats that required immediate and decisive action.

Whether it was a blockade, landing party ashore, or the eventual annexation of the Islands, the justification for all these naval actions was to isolate and limit access to the sea of the Nicobarese tribes in Nancowry Harbour.[898] The response,

Blockade, Piracy and Annexation: The Nicobars, 1867-1872

therefore, was not just about countering piracy but ensuring the uninterrupted flow of trade that underpinned the British Empire's economy and authority. This was to the detriment of freedom of movement of the Nicobarese, and their centuries-old patterns of behaviour.

Figure 23: Port Blair 1872

The cooperation between the East Indies Station and the China Station during the Nicobar Islands crisis also exemplified the interconnectedness of British naval operations across different regions. It also shows the resource constraints and differing station priorities, the intricate details of which are out of the scope of this book but should be addressed in the future. The anti-slave trade operations in Africa, a major focus for the East Indies Station during this period, significantly drained resources that were perceived to be needed by the Indian Government in the Indian Ocean. The prioritised resource allocation for suppressing the East African slave trade meant that the East Indies Station had limited availability of ships and personnel to enforce a sustained blockade around the Nicobar Islands. The inability to conduct a robust blockade around the Nicobars meant resources from the China Station were needed, which had a nuanced institutional response to piracy gained from experience in Malaya and China.[899]

The annexation of the Nicobar Islands underscores a fundamental truth about seapower: it was about the ability to influence and control the actions of actors in a geographic space, and not just states. The Indian Government saw seapower as a means to control behaviours of indigenous populations in the Nicobar Islands.

Formation of Andaman and Nicobar Islands

The attempted blockade and ensuing naval action in the Nicobars in 1867 demonstrate the necessity for a critical reflection within seapower studies, particularly in reassessing the scope and justification behind the use of naval power on indigenous populations. The indigenous populations of Nancowry soon faced significant disruptions to their way of life to fit the British expectations. As such, seapower studies must evolve to incorporate these critical perspectives, understanding blockades and other military actions as more than just fleet-to-fleet actions. Incorporating these considerations will lead to a more nuanced and comprehensive understanding of seapower and its consequences during the late Victorian era.

The attack on the *Futteh Islam*, and the consequential response by the British imperial state, also presents the limitations of naval power in achieving absolute control over expansive maritime regions like the Bay of Bengal. The Royal Navy's struggle to maintain a sustained presence and enforce order around the Nicobar Islands underscores the logistical and strategic challenges inherent in policing such vast areas through intermittent naval operations alone. Although a blockade was not enacted, the East Indies and China Station both sent vessels to effectively cut off the ability of the Nicobarese to use the seas by destroying canoes and shore infrastructure. Whether or not this was successful is debatable, although there were no reports of piracy again during the tenure of the establishment of the settlement in Nancowry Harbour, which was until 1888.[900] Although this could represent an end to piracy, it is more likely that with a permanent settlement on the Nicobars, the definition of piracy was no longer used to apply to the Nicobarese as they were better understood as users of the sea.

Compared to the treatment of the tribal population on Little Andaman, the branding of the Nicobarese as 'pirates' signifies a form of orientalism. The term 'pirate' carried with it connotations of lawlessness and barbarism that aligned with orientalist stereotypes of the tribal groups across the Andaman and Nicobars.[901] These stereotypes depicted these groups as fundamentally disorderly and needing Western intervention. This designation served a strategic purpose by simplifying complex sociocultural realities into a binary of 'civilised versus uncivilised', thereby making the case for British governance seem natural and inevitable.

After various naval actions, the Royal Navy was still intimately involved in the forging of the Empire. The eventual annexation was performed by raising the Union Jack, a 21-gun salute and a proclamation read by the Captain of HMS

Spiteful on 22 March 1869 in Nancowry Harbour. The presence of *Spiteful* not only performed statehood but also served as a visible symbol of imperial authority, which was crucial for both legal reasons and as a perceived deterrent to the Nicobarese. These elements are a performance and symbolise an established way of asserting a claim. Once again, the Indian Government used the colonisation of islands to bring a British form of 'stability' to littoral waters. By 1872 and the consolidation of power by the Indian Government, the Bay of Bengal was a *British Sea*. There were no disturbances in the coming decades from piracy, or attacks on shipwrecked crews, and Port Blair and Nancowry Harbour offered sanctuary during monsoon storms.

Overall, the incident in the Nicobar Islands in 1867 illustrated how the attempted blockade, landings, or operations around the Islands served fundamentally as a restriction on the use of space by the indigenous population. This challenges the traditional format of a 'fleet versus fleet' paradigm used by naval scholars, which I argue requires expanding.[902] The intention of naval action was to exclude certain civilian groups from accessing maritime routes and resources, justified by the 'security' needs of the dominant power, which, in this case, was the British imperial state. It is essential to understand not just the operational implications of naval action but also *whose* behaviour is intended to change and *why*. This approach encourages a deeper consideration of the social, cultural, and political manifestations of seapower.

CONCLUSION

Theory is not most people's cup of tea. When you can be reading about explosive exploits of mariners through the ages, why spend time reading about the way in which scholars organise and evaluate seapower? Theory is, however, essential. It is the framework within which we explore, record, and tell the stories of navies and seapower.

There is a strong and universally accepted selection of foundational texts from classical scholars such as Alfred Thayer Mahan, Julian Corbett, Raoul Castex, and Sergey Gorshkov, among others, who laid the groundwork for understanding seapower and maritime strategy.[903] These works emphasise statecraft, the importance of sea control, and the influence of naval power on global politics. Mahan and Corbett, in particular, remain influential as a theoretical basis in explaining contemporary seapower to this day.[904] Both have featured in the chapters you have just read for that very reason.

However, this field has not undergone a significant critical reflection on the classical scholars and theorists, who were writing in the first half of the 20th century and from a European perspective. There remains a lingering deterministic treatment of geography and a preponderance of seeing navies as neutral, if not positive, actors of empires and the state.[905] There is a focus on the military aspects of seapower from a technologist and technical perspective rather than addressing the sociocultural dimensions.[906] Equally, isolated moments of fleet-to-fleet action precede the everyday experience and reality, and the overall narrative follows a linear tract that suggests there was a clear rise and fall of British dominance.[907]

Most importantly, too many naval historians have focused on what could be simplified as great men, great battles, and great ships.[908] This book has not been a call to dismiss these works, which are all valuable, rigorous in execution, and have a rightful place in the historiography. Instead, what I have tried to share is a more nuanced way to reflect upon seapower, to challenge the various assumptions and understand the preconceptions held within the field.

Seapower is also fundamentally a geographical concept. It enabled the construction of new imperial geographies. By the 1850s, most British people, including geographically privileged men like naval officers, would have hardly known about the Andaman and Nicobar Islands, bar potentially as a reference point on a chart.[909] It took an expedition to the Andaman Islands in 1858 before a comprehensive account of their characteristics was published in Britain.[910] It took another five more years of survey work before accurate Andaman and Nicobar Islands charts were produced by the Admiralty Hydrographic Office.[911] Knowledge networks arose around the Islands, and geography was written (or rewritten) through exploration and survey work. This knowledge was then transported back to London via Calcutta and shared within coffee houses and learned societies like the Royal Geographical Society in the metropole.

The Indian Government commissioned the voyage to the Andaman Islands in 1858 to fundamentally reshape the national coastline in the Bay of Bengal to deter other European navies. This followed a long history of the British acquiring island territories as a way to enhance seapower, whether for docks, fuel storage, commercial reasons, or great power politics.[912] The Indian Navy was essential in supporting this exploration, showing the multitude of roles navies performed in the Empire beyond warfighting. The mobilities of navies, alongside their firepower, meant they were ideal platforms for expedition parties to travel long distances into scarcely ventured places such as the Andaman and Nicobar Islands.[913]

Seapower also rewrites sea spaces through the practices of surveying and hydrography.[914] The Royal Navy and hydrography have often been studied as scientific endeavours involving the measurement and description of physical marine features, which enable the force to operate at reach and navigate confidently.[915] Hydrography therefore plays a crucial role in the political, social, and cultural construction of maritime spaces. After the survey work was completed and the chart printed, the Andaman and Nicobar Islands were no longer recorded in either the indigenous or in other European languages. The harbours, bays, reefs, and inlets had the English language imposed upon them and were recorded for prosperity as such in charts. Also, hydrographers effectively transform unknown or contested waters into navigable and controlled territories.[916] This process is inherently political and has sociocultural ramifications.

Various military operations were conducted on the Andaman and Nicobar Islands in the late 1860s. However, the traditional metrics of armament and firepower as symbols of imperial strength were only one of the means of enacting power. It was not the 68-pounder muzzle-loaded gun on the deck of the steam gunboats patrolling the waters of the Andaman and Nicobar Islands which changed geographies alone, but the beliefs of the British serviceman. The crews brought with them ideals of civility and civilisation, which shaped the way in which the armament was used, and the scenarios in which it was not used, during imperial campaigns.

The Royal Navy's role in major imperial skirmishes between 1842 and 1872, including the Opium Wars (1839–1842 and 1856–1860), the Anglo-Burmese War (1852–1853), the Persian Wars (1856–1857), the Indian Rebellion (1857–1858), and the

Anglo-Japanese War (1863–1864) is well documented.[917] However, the Royal Navy's role in smaller imperial campaigns remained understudied. Although you have read about the Little Andaman Campaign and the Nicobar expeditions here, these represent only two actions. Much more work will be needed to explore the plethora of naval actions in localised conflicts.

The Indian Navy, under its various guises, contributed significantly to British seapower. The Indian Navy was initially formed in 1612 as the militarised naval arm of the British East India Company.[918] It went through a multitude of name changes, often reflecting a flux of responsibilities and roles notably switching between both combatant and non-combatant: Honourable East India Company's Marine (1612–1686), Bombay Marine (1686–1830), Indian Navy (1830–1863), Bombay and Bengal Marine (1863–1877), Her Majesty's Indian Marine (1877–1892), Royal Indian Marine (1892–1934), and finally Royal Indian Navy (1934 onwards).[919]

Previous studies on the Indian Navy were written centuries apart, and also from a majority British histographical perspective.[920] Kalesh Mohanan's recent publication complements the contemporary post-independence history of the Indian Navy, but only briefly engages with its pre-World War Two history.[921] British seapower was much more than the Royal Navy alone, and this book has demonstrated that the Indian Navy was much more integral to British maritime power than previously acknowledged. The Indian Navy was essential for enabling Empire to expand into the Andaman and Nicobar Islands.

From Marco Polo to Arthur Conan Doyle, European travellers and writers have perpetuated tales of savagery and servitude on the Andaman and Nicobar Islands[922] These narratives, rooted in British encounters with the indigenous populations from the 19th century and the penal colony, have been critically dissected by postcolonial scholars over the past two decades. However, this book has demonstrated the Islands' strategic importance to British ambitions in the region, showing how their acquisition and control were integral to British naval operations and imperial defence. The Islands should be acknowledged for their role in the *security* of the Empire, as much as for savagery and servitude.

Figure 24: Port Blair at Sunset

In the mid-19th century, the Andaman and Nicobar Islands represented more than just an island chain on a chart; they were a contested space, testing the limits of British imperial power and ambitions in the Bay of Bengal. This book has examined the transformation of the Andaman and Nicobar Islands from 1842 to 1872, a period marked by increased British commerce, trade, and maritime traffic following the First Opium War. The Islands had a long history and infamy for their perceived savagery and cannibalism in the British and European public imagination, and early encounters with mariners reinforced this perspective. Accounts of attacks from pirates and hostile indigenous populations reinforced this representation within the British press and the decision-making apparatus of the Indian Government.

These dangers posed a significant challenge to the British aim of dominating the Bay of Bengal and, in the 1850s, the expectation the Bay would be a *British Sea*. However, the British gradually extended their control through systematic efforts in surveying, mapping, naval patrols, and eventually establishing a penal colony in 1858. By 1872, the Islands were firmly under British rule, and piracy and attacks on merchant shipping markedly decreased. This confirmed the transformation of the Andaman and Nicobar Islands into a civilised and controlled place within the British imperial gaze. The *British Sea* was, according to the Indian Government, a reality.

The purpose of this book was to use the Andaman and Nicobar Islands between 1842 and 1872 as a nexus to demonstrate the value of taking a critical approach to imperial seapower, and how this could be achieved. The emphasis is on *value*. Critical reflections have occurred in all major humanities and social sciences disciplines, but not within the realms of seapower studies with vigour. Partly, this is due to the navies being prohibitively expensive and only within the reach of nation-states, but also the humanities and social sciences lack of engagement with militaries. Hence, although the Andaman and Nicobar Islands act as a geographical thread, I have engaged with a breadth of seapower concepts to show how we can think differently about power in the maritime.

Seapower influenced, and was influenced by, the beliefs and expectations of maritime space held by the British imperial government. This is apparent when you look at the development of the *British Sea* narrative from 1842 to 1856 in the Bay of Bengal. In deconstructing the narrative, it revealed the underlying ideologies and biases that shaped British perceptions and practices of maritime power in the region. The narrative was used to reinforce British imperial expansion by portraying the Bay of Bengal as inherently suited to, and in need of, British control.

The imperial government saw British maritime dominance as a means to impart British ideals of 'civility' and 'order' over the Andaman and Nicobar Islands. Imperial seapower was more than military and commercial might at sea. There was also a social and cultural dimension to power. Seapower is as much about beliefs and expectations of how maritime space should be, as it is about having the fleets and ships to physically sail the seas and enforce that control.

In deconstructing the British Sea narrative, it is also clear how the eventual British decision to colonise the Andaman Islands in 1858 was driven by maritime security. It was more than just the need for a penal settlement post-Indian Rebellion (1857–1858), as contemporary postcolonial scholarship argues. The impact of increasing piracy and attacks on shipwrecked crews challenged the Bay of Bengal as being a 'civilised' and ordered space in the eyes of the imperial administration. These disturbances challenged the perception of British control over the Bay of Bengal, undermining the *British Sea* narrative.

Despite efforts by the Royal Navy and the Indian Navy, naval patrols and minor interventions proved insufficient to secure the waters, revealing the limitations of imperial seapower in addressing threats on sparsely populated island chains without a permanent European settlement. Consequently, colonising the Andaman Islands was seen as the only effective means to ensure maritime security and protect British economic interests.

The settlement on the Andaman Islands was also part of the imperial defence network. With a focus on states as the formal actor, contemporary imperial defence scholarship has neglected the role of the East India Company and its political body, the Indian Government, in protecting the Empire. Colonising small islands, like the Andamans, was part of a broader, reactive strategy of the Indian Government since the 1840s to maintain control over crucial SLOC in the Bay of Bengal.

Colonisation was not an isolated process. It was deeply intertwined with small expeditions, exploration, and knowledge production. The Andaman Committee expedition of 1857–1858 was one such example. It marked the first formal British intervention into the interior of the Andaman Islands since 1796. The Committee's mission from the Indian Government was to establish a penal colony and secure a permanent British presence in the Bay of Bengal. The Indian Navy was pivotal in enabling imperial expeditions, providing essential logistical support, transportation, and protection for the Committee amidst threats of piracy and indigenous attacks. The Indian Navy's expertise of operating in the Bay of Bengal, based on over two centuries of corporate knowledge, enabled a rapid and detailed expedition within Andamanese littoral spaces. From logistical support to protection, navies provided the means and expertise to colonise distant territories.

Colonising the Andaman Islands in 1858 effectively reshaped the geographies of the Bay of Bengal towards one which enhanced British seapower. The Indian Navy's and Royal Navy's survey work in the Andaman Islands between 1858 and 1861 highlights how 'small science', such as hydrography, was a means to reinforce British imperial control. By providing detailed and accurate hydrographic knowledge, the Indian Navy ensured safe navigation across vital imperial SLOC, supported the development of Port Blair as a new settlement, and enforced territorial claims. The Admiralty Hydrographic Office was a vital imperial centre of calculation. It transformed raw data into standardised, reliable nautical charts that facilitated efficient maritime operations and extended British imperial reach.

By assessing the networks of knowledge emanating through hydrographic work in the Andamans, we should reconsider what the primary functions of navies are, moving beyond warfighting, diplomacy, and constabulary duties. The ability to organise survey work in Calcutta, conduct data collection in the field in Port Blair, analyse the data in London, and disseminate charts globally to mariners represents a form of seapower which is just as vital as effective gunnery. Knowledge is both an output and input to seapower; it should, therefore, be recognised as a core function of imperial navies.

That does not, however, detract from seapower being a means to apply violence. The Little Andaman incident of 1867 was indicative of the application of seapower to quell disturbances using gunboats, challenging traditional views of gunboats as mere practical tools of empire. The incident demonstrates the limits of the gunboats in imperial policing, the performative power of seapower, and the mobility of British ideas and values. Other vessels, such as auxiliary and troopships, could be just as effective in projecting British authority and ideals across vast distances. The collaboration between the Royal Navy, the Bombay Marine, and the Indian Government exemplified the informal yet critical network of imperial security that had still not yet become a formal 'imperial defence strategy'. Gunboats and other vessels used for imperial policing were more than instruments of military might; they were also platforms for disseminating British ideals and values. It was a means of shaping maritime spaces and reinforcing imperial control by changing the behaviour of indigenous populations living on the fringes of Empire.

Alongside imperial policing, blockades and anti-piracy operations in imperial contexts, such as the Nicobar Islands in 1867, demonstrate how seapower goes beyond hard power and into the sociocultural domain. Seapower is not solely about fleet-to-fleet engagements but also about controlling and excluding the use of maritime spaces to certain actors. The attempt to blockade the Nicobars and label the Nicobarese as pirates exhibited how the Indian Government enforced 'accepted behaviours and norms' through seapower. It directly challenges Stephen Roskill's and Geoffrey Till's fleet and state-centric focus by illustrating how blockades and naval action are complex social and cultural interventions rather than mere military manoeuvres alone.[923] The impact of navies goes beyond the fleet and state, and to truly understand the implications of seapower, one must also consider how seapower changes social and cultural behaviours.

Seapower is about controlling geographical spaces through a multifaceted wielding of different forms of power. This is a different treatment of seapower than the current consensus within naval history and international relations, which is state-centric and often treats geography as a passive background. It challenges the sometimes linear and deterministic perspectives of geography, as seen in the work of Julian Corbett (command of the sea), Herbert Richmond (imperial defence), Alfred Thayer Mahan (elements of seapower), Ken Booth (functions of seapower), Antony Preston and John Major (gunboats), and Stephen Roskill (blockade and naval action). This book has shown that to understand what imperial seapower constituted, it is necessary to move beyond the state-centric and deterministic antecedents in the study of seapower. It is not, however, a revolutionary new approach that rewrites all that has been written before. I simply propose that we look at how seapower shapes social and cultural interactions at sea, not just political and military.

Seapower is also fundamentally geographical. As a concept, geographers have left the study of it to naval historians and international relations theorists. By integrating seapower into the broader discourse of geography, I hope that I have displayed the value of looking at naval and maritime activity through geographical lenses such as geopolitics, mobilities, and historical geography. Seapower is about how power is applied and experienced in sea spaces. It is not merely a military strategy but a spatial practice that shapes and is shaped by geographical landscapes and imaginations.

Although the temporal scope of this book stopped on the advent of the Andaman and Nicobar Islands becoming administratively joined under a Chief Commissioner in 1872, the Islands' serpentine relationship with seapower continued.

Between 1872 and the start of the First World War in 1914, the Islands increasingly became perceived as a strategic bastion vital for the defence of the British Empire in the Bay of Bengal by the Admiralty.[924] In 1876, the Indian Government requested a 'man-o-war' be sent to Port Blair every few months to show the significance of the British colony to any would-be aggressor.[925] The performance of statehood through seapower continued, reflecting the continued importance of the Islands to the British imperial maritime network through the 1870s and into the 1880s.

By 1886, the Colonial Defence Committee instigated a global study into the effectiveness of defence across the Empire, including the role of Port Blair.[926] However, extensive research by the Royal Engineers revealed significant shortcomings in Port Blair's defences, identifying them as a potential vulnerability rather than a robust defensive outpost.[927] The report's findings align with many of the themes discussed in this book, such as perceived strategic value versus the reality of maintaining a British presence on the Islands. Ultimately, the Indian Government requested that resources be spent on "more significant" ports rather than the Andaman Islands.[928] It nevertheless illustrates that, by the 1890s, the Andaman and Nicobar Islands were increasingly seen through a lens of military utility over the penal settlement, reinforcing the argument in this book about the maritime dimensions of the colonisation of the Andaman Islands.[929]

Between the 1880s and 1918, the Andaman and Nicobar Islands continued to play a vital role in British imperial defence, and additional study in this space would provide a nuanced contribution to the contemporary seapower literature of this period.[930] An example is Britain's reliance on the Japanese Navy for security east of Suez during the First World War.[931] The Andaman and Nicobar Islands were used as ports for Japanese ships during the war, and a critical study of this would offer a new perspective on Anglo-Japanese naval cooperation prior to the Second World War.[932]

Although the Andaman and Nicobar Islands were not a major naval base during the First World War, the Islands still participated in imperial defence by acting instead as a base for meteorological and intelligence collection stations.[933] The Islands provided "an assurance of the security of the Bay and was symbolic of British control over the eastern part of the Indian Ocean".[934] Assessing the role of imperial island possessions, such as the Andaman and Nicobar Islands, during the First World War would increase awareness of whether imperial defence was successful, the extent to which there was a strategy, and how imperial seapower manifested to protect the SLOC in the region.[935] It would also demonstrate the role of the Bengal and Bombay Marine in the event of war, how the Royal Navy and Japanese Navy collaborated to combat German commerce raiding in the Indian Ocean, and whether Port Blair was used as an operational base, among others.

A critical reflection on seapower would also offer an opportunity to view the 'violent peace' (1919–1939) between the First and Second World Wars differently. Naval history's temptation towards grand narratives and linear perspectives on the historiography of the Royal Navy marks the post-First World War as the start of the decline, the "Ebbing Tide" and the beginning of the "Lean Days".[936] Seapower is much more diverse and multifaceted than these sweeping statements suggest. Within the Indian Ocean context, the 'violent peace' period led to increased discussions at the Admiralty about the extent to which Dominion navies should have operational independence or be unified into an 'imperial navy' encompassing all parts of the Empire.[937]

The threat also shifted in the Bay of Bengal, and Japan was seen as an emerging adversary by the 1930s.[938] Much of the strategy to stop a Japanese advance into the Indian Ocean was based around the bastion of Singapore, with the rest of the Indian Ocean considered secure as long as the Straits of Malacca were held.[939] The Andaman and Nicobar Islands, at the opposite end of the Straits of Malacca to Singapore, were considered strategic by the Admiralty to this defence. In 1939, they ensured shell fishing was banned as this was considered a cover for Japanese naval intelligence gathering.[940] The Andaman and Nicobar Islands thus offer an opportunity to explore the Anglo-Japanese pre-war relationship in the Indian Ocean, whether as a place of cultural exchange or competition. The methodology of this book also provides the means to challenge the deterministic view of geography, such as 'Fortress Singapore', and the extent to which narratives enhanced the belief of the invincibility of British power in the region.

The Second World War in the Indian Ocean is well documented, with comprehensive accounts from Andrew Boyd and Charles Stephenson on the Royal Navy covering 1935–1944.[941] Additional accounts cover the activities of the Imperial Japanese Navy, analysis of submarine warfare in the region, the Japanese sinking of HMS *Prince of Wales* and HMS *Repulse*, and the surrender of Singapore.[942] However, the Andaman and Nicobar Islands rarely feature in this literature, even though they were the only part of British India invaded by the Japanese in 1942 (Burma was an independent colony as of 1937).[943]

In 1945, a major Allied task force was established to retake the Islands at the behest of Admiral Lord Louis Mountbatten.[944] The Andaman Islands were also a place of British special operations activity throughout the war, including Operation Baldhead.[945] Understanding how the Andaman and Nicobar Islands formed part of British war planning, and latterly, how the amphibious operations were conducted, can provide an insight into whether the Andaman Islands are an 'unsinkable aircraft carrier' and what this means for India's contemporary defence strategies.[946]

After the Second World War, the context for post-war British strategy focused on the need to reorientate the wartime economy back to peacetime purposes and engage with imperial possessions through trade.[947] However, very rapidly, this British-centric approach to defence and commerce unravelled.[948] The Andaman and Nicobar Islands eventually became part of the Republic of India in 1950, much to the protestation of the Pakistan and Burmese governments and many among the British defence community, all noting the strategic value of the Islands.

Notably, from a naval perspective, the most influential proponent of possession ceding to India was the then Viceroy of India, Lord Louis Mountbatten, who already had an intimate knowledge of the Islands from his time as Supreme Allied Commander of the Southeast Asia Theatre.[949] Once again, it is an example of Britain negotiating and constructing maritime space in the Andaman and Nicobar Islands.

Overall, I hope this book has provided you with the foundations to develop your own critical reflection on imperial seapower, and also to provide a greater understanding on what indeed constitutes power at sea. Seapower extends beyond military and commercial might and includes the ability to assert values, reshape spaces towards ideals, and construct new knowledge.

There is a pressing need to understand how seapower functioned as a critical element of imperial governance and defence, extending beyond major battles and fleet movements to include the everyday activities that ensured maritime efficiency and territorial control. The call from Matthew Heaslip below, made about the wealth of issues currently affecting maritime spaces, from climate change to resource depletion, identifies the challenge:

> The challenge looking ahead to the rest of the 21st century seems to be how best to coordinate the process of ensuring that in another century, historians will be able to report significant successes in navigating a prosperous, healthier, less polluted, and safer path.[950]

Great men, great battles, and great ships are not the solution to combatting climate change, overfishing, or cable cutting in the 21st century. Nor, as this book has shown, were men, battles, and ship the means to bring stability to the maritime environment of the Bay of Bengal in the 19th century.

The study of seapower needs to move beyond classical, deterministic underpinnings to understand the past better and, more importantly, find solutions for the future. A more nuanced understanding of historical seapower can, in turn, be used as a platform to understand the issues facing the oceans today.

While imperial seapower was used to control communications and enhance the security of trade routes, future seapower can assist in controlling the effects of climate change or enhance food security, as a couple of such examples.[951]

Seapower can, and should, be a constructive force for good as this century develops.

If you found value in this book and would like to engage more deeply with its themes and findings, scan the QR code below to access supplementary materials, including a FREE Electronic Version of the book.

Scanning the QR code will take you to the Republish app.

Once you have scanned the code and created an account on the app, search 'Callum James O'Connell' or 'Geographies of Seapower' in the discovery bar.

Here you will be able to 'Follow' Callum and get access to a wealth of additional material.

You will be able to learn more about Callum's research background, ask him questions directly in the messenger function, and engage with an ever-expanding library of work discussed in the book. This includes:

- Free open access ePDF of the book.
- Additional commentary and reflections on the book.
- Video interviews and recorded lectures.
- Announcements of new resources, including online courses.

Scan the code and search for Callum O'Connell or 'Geographies of Seapower' now!

Powered by:

Republish

Republish

Republish is on a mission to reimagine academic publishing.

Publishing represents a journey and not a one-off process. It is not just a single book or journal article. Knowledge and ideas are continuous, and they evolve. We blend the values of traditional academia and the continuous development of software technologies, providing a dedicated online space for academics and organisations to build a profile based on their professional identity and personal brand, which evolve with them. Once you have effortlessly built your profile on our platform, you can use our tools to build a community of followers, publish in new ways, and earn revenue through a subscription tool.

We encourage the exploration of different methods, enabling research to reach new and wider audiences. Publishing should be faster, reward should be fairer and factual integrity should be maintained.

Search www.republish.uk or email info@republish.uk to learn more.

Republish Academic Press

Republish Academic Press is an imprint of Republish.

The purpose of Republish Academic Press is to enable recent PhD graduates the ability to publish their thesis as a peer-reviewed book *fast* and receive a fair revenue to *kickstart* their careers.

A book is the pinnacle of rigorous research and original thinking, and original thinkers should be recognised. We believe "thesis to book" neatly represents the start of an academic journey but certainly does not end there. We provide our authors with the tools to transform their research from a thesis to a book and beyond.

Sign up with us, and we'll help you reach new audiences. Our packages include book publishing (hardback, softback, e-versions), marketing and social media support, multimedia formats, and to be part of the best community in academia!

Search www.republish.uk or email info@republish.uk to learn more.

ACKNOWLEDGEMENTS

This book has its origins in my doctoral research, and I remain deeply indebted to those who supported and shaped its development along the way. First and foremost, I wish to express my deepest gratitude to my supervisors. Dr. Matthew Heaslip has been an unwavering pillar of support, offering both intellectual provocation and exceptional guidance. His challenges and insights have substantially enriched the intellectual dimensions of this book. Dr. Cathryn Pearce has been equally encouraging, providing invaluable perspective and steadfast support throughout the journey. I am also grateful to Professor James Ryan, Professor Alessio Patalano, and Dr Richard Schofield for their early contributions, which helped shape the direction and foundations of this project.

A special note of thanks goes to Professor Kevin Rowlands, whose practical guidance and wise counsel have been essential, not only in supporting my research, but also in demonstrating the enduring relevance and impact of seapower.

My thanks go to the dedicated archival staff I have had the pleasure of working with, particularly at the National Archives of India, the UK Hydrographic Office, and the Naval Historical Branch, whose assistance was critical in accessing key materials. I am also grateful to the Society of Nautical Research for the

Anderson Fund grant which enabled me to access previously unseen archival material.

Turning a thesis into a book is no simple endeavour. This was made even more difficult when an 'April Fools' joke turned into the challenge of publishing this book within a month. Nevertheless, we did it! I would like to express my sincere appreciation to the editorial and design teams at Republish Academic Press for their professionalism, support, and commitment to nurturing early-career scholarship. From peer-review to proofreading, each stage bought new insights which has made me very proud of the result.

On a personal note, I am profoundly grateful to my partner, Catherine Evans, for her enduring patience and support. In particular, her polite toleration of my ever-growing collection of books on naval history, geography, and empire. I recognise that, for some, Victorian naval power may not be seen as ideal holiday reading. Thank you also to Niall O'Connell and Adam Mew for supporting me through the challenging months as I balanced starting a new business with them and completing my PhD. Thank you also to Ben Smail for joining me to the Andaman Islands, especially as you thought it was a beach holiday before I sprung my research topic on you! I also extend a heartfelt thanks to my parents and grandparents, whose support, understanding, and quiet encouragement have carried me through every stage of this process.

Finally, to all those who contributed in ways great and small, even if not named here, my sincere thanks.

BIBLIOGRAPHY

This book focuses on how the British and Indian Governments perceived and applied seapower in and around the Andaman and Nicobar Islands between 1842 and 1872. Hence, the India Office Records at both the British Library (London) and The National Archives of India (New Delhi) provided the official government record and a significant proportion of the primary material. The Admiralty collections at the National Archives were also relied upon heavily as the official record of the Royal Navy in the era.

However, the official record provides only one account; it neglects diverse perspectives from actors outside the government, and it overlooks the 'everyday' activities that contribute to seapower. To overcome this, multiple specialist archives were visited, including: the Hydrographic Office Archive (Taunton), the Naval Historical Branch (Portsmouth), Tower Hamlets Archive (London), the John Rylands Research Institute and Library (Manchester), Liddell Hart Centre for Military Archives (London), the Royal Geographical Society Library (London), among others listed in the bibliography.

The most significant challenge with the archival research for this book was finding sources that either come from, or acknowledge, an indigenous perspective. The Andamanese and Nicobarese were an oral society, and it was not until anthropological studies by British colonial officials in the 1860s and 1870s that accounts began to emerge of the indigenous population. Even then, these accounts are laced with an 'orientalist' perspective and do not offer a comprehensive source to understand the perspective of the Andamanese and Nicobarese on British seapower. However, where possible, this book has incorporated work from other indigenous studies to enable some form of acknowledgement of wider perspectives.

Primary Sources

Archival Primary Sources:
The National Archives of India, New Delhi
Public Records
- Foreign Department
- Home Department
- Military Department

British Library, London
India Office Records (IOR)
- IOR C: Council of India
- IOR E: East India Company General Correspondence
- IOR G: East India Company Factory Records
- IOR H: Home Miscellaneous
- IOR L: Mil Military Department
- IOR L: PJ Public and Judicial Department
- IOR L: PS Political and Secret Department Papers
- IOR V: Official Publications
- European Manuscripts (MSS)

General Reference Collection

John Rylands Research Institute and Library, Manchester
John Charles Mason Collection of East India Company Papers
Indian Navy List

Liddell Hart Centre for Military Archives, London
General Sir Ian Standish Monteith Hamilton Papers

Museum of Freemasonry, London
Rev William Alexander Ayton Collection

National Maritime Museum, Greenwich
William Cornwallis Letters and Papers

***Naval Historical Branch*, Portsmouth**
Pamphlets and Manuscripts
Navy Lists

***Royal Geographical Society*, London**
Richard Carnac Temple Papers
Monographs

***Royal Archives*, Windsor**
Melbourne Papers

***The National Archives*, Kew**
Admiralty
- ADM 101: Office of the Director General of the Medical Department of the Navy and predecessors: Medical Journals
- ADM 125: China Station: Correspondence
- ADM 127: Indies Station: Correspondence
- ADM 352: Hydrographic Department and Original Surveys

War Office
- WO 98: Correspondence and Papers Concerning the Victoria Cross
- WO 334: Army Medical Department: Returns and Reports

Tower Hamlets Archive
Papers of John Charles Mason (1798-1881) mainly to the East India Company's Interests in Poplar

***UK Hydrographic Office Archives*, Taunton**
Andrew David Collection
Old Copy Books
Miscellaneous Charts
Miscellaneous Papers (Remarks Books)

***University of Southampton Archives*, Southampton**
Mountbatten Papers

Online Primary Sources:

House of Commons Parliamentary Papers
Survey Reports and Papers, Defence Committee

Qatar National Library
India Office Records and Private Papers

Published Primary Sources:

Colebrooke, Robert. 'On the Andaman Islands'. In Transactions of the Society Instituted in Bengal for Inquiring into the History and Antiquities, the Arts, Sciences and Literature of Asia in 1799. Calcutta: Asiatic Society of Bengal, 1799.

Darvall, Joseph. The Wreck on the Andamans. London: Pelham Richardson, 1845.

Dawson, Llewellyn. Memoirs of Hydrography. Part II. Eastbourne: The Imperial Library, 1885

Dougherty, Rev. John Anderson. The East Indies Station: The Cruise of H.M.S 'Garnet'. Malta: Muscat Printing Office, 1890.

Herschel, John. Manual of Scientific Inquiry. Prepared for the Use of Officers in Her Majesty's Navy. 5th ed. London: Eyre and Spottiswode, 1886.

Low, Charles Rathbone. History of the Indian Navy (1613-1863). Vol. 1. 2 vols. Delhi: Manas Publications, 1877.

———. History of the Indian Navy (1613-1863), Vol.II. London: Richard Bentley & Son, 1877.

Moat, Frederick. Adventures and Researches Among The Andaman Islanders. London: Hurst and Blackett, 1863.

Piddington, Henry. Twelfth Memoir with Reference to Storms in India. Calcutta: Journal of the Asiatic Society of Bengal, 1840.

Portman, Maurice Vidal. A History of Our Relations with the Andamanese, Vol.I. Calcutta: Office of the Superintendent of Government Printing, 1899.

Portman, Maurice Vidal. A History of Our Relations with the Andamanese, Vol.II. Calcutta: Office of the Superintendent of Government Printing, 1899.

Tizard, Thomas. *Chronological List of the Officers Conducting British Maritime Discoveries and Surveys*. London: H.M. Stationary Office, 1900.

Woodhouse, Capt. A. T. A Voice from Port Blair: By an Officer. Bombay: Education Society's Press, 1872.

Newspapers and Periodicals:

Bengal Gazette
Daily News
Glasgow Herald
Liverpool Mercury
The Standard
York Herald

Secondary Sources

Abraham, Itty. 'India's Unsinkable Aircraft Carrier'. *Economic and Political Weekly* 50, no. 39 (2015): 10–13.

———. 'The Andamans as a "Sea of Islands": Reconnecting Old Geographies through Poaching'. *Inter-Asia Cultural Studies* 19, no. 1 (2018): 2–20.

Bibliography

Achbari, A. 'Building Networks for Science: Conflict and Cooperation in Nineteenth-Century Global Marine Studies'. *Isis* 106, no. 2 (2015): 257–82. https://doi.org/10.1086/682020.

Adam, Barbara. *Theorizing Culture: An Interdisciplinary Critique After Postmodernism.* New York: Routledge, 2019.

Adler, Antony. 'The Ship as Laboratory: Making Space for Field Science at Sea'. *Journal of the History of Biology* 47, no. 3 (2014): 333–62. https://doi.org/10.1007/s10739-013-9367-7.

Agnew, John, and David Livingstone, eds. *The SAGE Handbook of Geographical Knowledge.* London: SAGE, 2011.

Akerman, James R., ed. *The Imperial Map: Cartography and the Mastery of Empire.* Chicago: University of Chicago Press, 2009.

Alpers, Edward A. 'On Becoming a British Lake: Piracy, Slaving, and British Imperialism in the Indian Ocean during the First Half of the Nineteenth Century'. In *Indian Ocean Slavery in the Age of Abolition*, edited by Robert W. Harms, Bernard K. Freamon, and David W. Blight, 45–58. New Haven: Yale University Press, 2013.

———. *The Indian Ocean in World History.* Oxford: Oxford University Press, 2014.

Amirell, Stefan. *Piracy in World History.* Amsterdam: Amsterdam University Press, 2022.

Amrith, Sunil S. *Crossing the Bay of Bengal: The Furies of Nature and the Fortunes of Migrants.* Cambridge: Harvard University Press, 2013.

Anderson, C. 'Writing Indigenous Women's Lives in the Bay of Bengal: Cultures of Empire in the Andaman Islands, 1789-1906'. *Journal of Social History* 45, no. 2 (2011): 480–96. https://doi.org/10.1093/jsh/shr054.

Anderson, Clare. 'Colonization, Kidnap and Confinement in the Andamans Penal Colony, 1771–1864'. *Journal of Historical Geography* 37, no. 1 (2011): 68–81. https://doi.org/10.1016/j.jhg.2010.07.001.

———. *Subaltern Lives: Biographies of Colonialism in the Indian Ocean World, 1790-1920.* Cambridge: Cambridge University Press, 2012.

———. 'The Age of Revolution in the Indian Ocean, Bay of Bengal and South China Sea: A Maritime Perspective'. In *Mutiny and Maritime Radicalism in the Age of Revolution: A Global Survey*, edited by Clare Anderson, Niklas Frykman, Lex Heerma van Voss, and Marcus Rediker, 1–19. Cambridge: University of Cambridge Press, 2013.

———. 'The Andaman Islands Penal Colony: Race, Class, Criminality, and the British Empire'. *International Review of Social History* 63, no. S26 (2018): 25–43. https://doi.org/10.1017/S0020859018000202.

———. *The Indian Uprising of 1857-8: Prisons, Prisoners, and Rebellion.* London: Anthem Press, 2007.

Anderson, Clare, Madhumita Mazumdar, and Vishvajit Pandya. *New Histories of the Andaman Islands Landscape, Place and Identity in the Bay of Bengal, 1790-2012.* Cambridge: Cambridge University Press, 2018.

Anderson, Katharine. 'The Hydrographer's Narrative: Writing Global Knowledge in the 1830s'. *Journal of Historical Geography* 63 (2019): 48–60. https://doi.org/10.1016/j.jhg.2018.09.002.

Anim-Addo, Anyaa. 'Steaming between the Islands: Nineteenth-Century Maritime Networks and the Caribbean Archipelago'. *Island Studies Journal* 8, no. 1 (2013): 25–38. https://doi.org/10.24043/isj.274.

Anim-Addo, Anyaa, William Hasty, and Kimberley Peters, eds. *The Mobilities of Ships*. London: Routledge, 2017.

Armitage, David, Alison Bashford, and Sujit Sivasundaram. *Oceanic Histories*. Cambridge: University of Cambridge Press, 2017. https://doi.org/10.1017/9781108399722.

Armston-Sheret, Edward. 'Diversifying the Historical Geography of Exploration: Subaltern Body Work on British-Led Expeditions c.1850–1914'. *Journal of Historical Geography* 80 (2023): 58–68. https://doi.org/10.1016/j.jhg.2023.02.004.

Armstrong, Benjamin, and A Mahan. *21st Century Mahan: Sound Military Conclusions for the Modern Era*. Annapolis: Naval Institute Press, 2013.

Arnold, David. '"Illusory Riches": Representations of the Tropical World, 1840-1950'. *Singapore Journal of Tropical Geography* 21, no. 1 (2000): 6–18. https://doi.org/10.1111/1467-9493.00060.

———. *The Tropics and the Travelling Gaze: India, Landscape, and Science 1800-1856*. Seattle: University of Washington Press, 2006.

Auerbach, Jeffrey A. *Imperial Boredom: Monotony and the British Empire*. Oxford: Oxford University Press, 2018.

Baldacchino, Godfrey. 'Islands, Island Studies, Island Studies Journal'. *Island Studies Journal* 1, no. 1 (2006): 3–18. https://doi.org/10.24043/isj.185.

Ballantyne, Tony, and Antoinette Burton. *Empires and the Reach of the Global, 1870-1945*. Cambridge: Harvard University Press, 2012.

Bandopadhyay, P. C., and A. Carter. 'Introduction to the Geography and Geomorphology of the Andaman–Nicobar Islands'. *Geological Society, London, Memoirs* 47, no. 1 (2017): 9–18. https://doi.org/10.1144/M47.2.

Barritt, Michael. *Nelson's Pathfinders: A Forgotten Story in the Triumph of British Sea Power*. New Haven: Yale University Press, 2024.

Barrow, Ian J, *The East India Company, 1600-1858: A Short History with Documents*. Indianapolis: Hackett Publishing Company, Inc, 2017.

Beeler, John. 'Steam, Strategy and Schurman: Imperial Defence in the Post-Crimean Era, 1856-1905'. In *Far-Flung Lines: Essays on Imperial Defence in Honour of Donald Mackenzie Schurman*, edited by Greg Kennedy and Keith Neilson, 27–54. London: Routledge, 1997.

Beeler, John F. *British Naval Policy in the Gladstone-Disraeli Era, 1866-1880*. Stanford: Stanford University Press, 1997.

Behrisch, Erika. *Discovery, Innovation, and the Victorian Admiralty: Paper Navigators*. Basingstoke: Palgrave Macmillan, 2022.

Bell, Christopher M. 'Strategy: British Naval Policy, Imperial Defence, and the Development of Dominion Navies, 1911–14'. *The International History Review* 37, no. 2 (2015): 262–81. https://doi.org/10.1080/07075332.2014.900817.

Benbow, Tim. 'The Royal Navy and Sea Power in British Strategy, 1945–55'. *Historical Research* 91, no. 252 (2018): 375–98. https://doi.org/10.1111/1468-2281.12216.

Ben-Dror, Avishai. 'Cartographic Knowledge, Colonialized-Colonizer Spaces: Egyptian Maps of Harar, 1875–1885'. *Journal of Historical Geography* 77 (2022): 85–100. https://doi.org/10.1016/j.jhg.2022.03.004.

Bennet, Zachary. '"Canoes of Great Swiftness": Rivercraft and War in the Northeast.' *Early American Studies, An Interdisciplinary Journal* 21, no. 2 (2023): 205–32. https://doi.org/10.1353/eam.2023.0008.

Bennett, G. H. *The Royal Navy in the Age of Austerity 1919-22: Naval and Foreign Policy under Lloyd George*. London: Bloomsbury Academic, 2018.

Benton, Lauren A. *A Search for Sovereignty: Law and Geography in European Empires, 1400--1900*. New York: Cambridge University Press, 2010.

Bickers, Robert A., and Jonathan J. Howlett, eds. *Britain and China, 1840-1970: Empire, Finance and War*. London: Routledge, 2017.

Biggar, Nigel. *Colonialism: A Moral Reckoning*. London: William Collins, 2023.

Bishara, Fahad, and Hollian Wint. 'Into the Bazaar: Indian Ocean Vernaculars in the Age of Global Capitalism'. *Journal of Global History* 16, no. 1 (2021): 44–64. https://doi.org/10.1017/S174002282000011X.

Blakemore, Richard. 'British Imperial Expansion and the Transformation of Violence at Sea, 1600–1850: Introduction'. *International Journal of Maritime History* 25, no. 2 (2013): 143–45. https://doi.org/10.1177/084387141302500211.

Blewitt, Mary. *Survey of the Seas*. London: Macgibbon & Kee, 1957.

Blok, Anders, Ignacio Farias, and Celia Roberts, eds. *The Routledge Companion to Actor-Network Theory*. Basingstoke: Routledge, 2023.

Blok, Anders, and Torben Elgaard Jensen. *Bruno Latour: Hybrid Thoughts in a Hybrid World*. London: Routledge, 2011.

Boghossian, Paul Artin. *Fear of Knowledge: Against Relativism and Constructivism*. Oxford: Clarendon Press, 2013.

Bond, Andrew, Frank Cowin, and Andrew D. Lambert. *Favourite of Fortune: Captain John Quilliam, Trafalgar Hero*. Barnsley: Seaforth Publishing, 2021.

Bond, Barbara. 'Strategic Considerations for International Hydrography in the 21st Century'. *International Hydrographic Review* 1, no. 2 (1996).

Bonner. 'History and IS – Broadening Our View and Understanding: Actor–Network Theory as a Methodology'. *Journal of Information Technology* 23 (2013).

Boot, Max. 'Pirates, Then and Now: How Piracy Was Defeated in the Past and Can Be Again'. *Foreign Affairs* 88, no. 4 (2009): 94–107.

Booth, Ken. *Navies and Foreign Policy*. Abingdon: Routledge, 2015.

———. 'Roles, Objectives and Tasks: An Inventory of the Functions of Navies'. *Naval War College Review* 30, no. 1 (1977): 83–97.

Bose, Sugata. *A Hundred Horizons: The Indian Ocean in the Age of Global Empire*. Cambridge: Harvard University Press, 2009.

Bowen, H. V. *The Business of Empire: The East India Company and Imperial Britain, 1756–1833*. Cambridge: Cambridge University Press, 2005. https://doi.org/10.1017/CBO9780511495724.

Boycott, A. *The Elements of Imperial Defence*. Aldershot: Gale & Polden Ltd, 1931.

Boyd, Andrew. *The Royal Navy in Eastern Waters: Linchpin of Victory 1935-1942*. Barnsley: Seaforth Publishing, 2017.

Branch, Jordan. '"Colonial Reflection" and Territoriality: The Peripheral Origins of Sovereign Statehood'. *European Journal of International Relations* 18, no. 2 (2012): 277–97. https://doi.org/10.1177/1354066110383997.

———. 'Mapping the Sovereign State: Technology, Authority, and Systemic Change'. *International Organization* 65, no. 1 (2011): 1–36. https://doi.org/10.1017/S0020818310000299.

Braudel, Fernand. *The Mediterranean and the Mediterranean World in the Age of Philip II*. Berkeley: University of California Press, 1995.

Bremner, Lindsay. 'Thinking Architecture with an Indian Ocean Aquapelago'. *GeoHumanities* 2, no. 2 (2016): 284–310. https://doi.org/10.1080/2373566X.2016.1234353.

Bridge, Gary. 'On Pragmatism, Assemblage and ANT: Assembling Reason'. *Progress in Human Geography* 45, no. 3 (2021): 417–35. https://doi.org/10.1177/0309132520924710.

Brinkman, Anna. *Balancing Strategy: Seapower, Neutrality, and Prize Law in the Seven Years' War*. Cambridge: Cambridge University Press, 2024.

Brooks, Richard. 'March Into India: The Relief of Lucknow 1857-59'. In *Seapower Ashore: 200 Years of Royal Navy Operations on Land*, edited by Peter Hore, 130–45. London: Chatham Publishing, 2000.

———. *The Long Arm of Empire: Naval Brigades from the Crimea to the Boxer Rebellion*. London: Constable, 1999.

Bueger, Christian, and Timothy Edmunds. 'Blue Crime: Conceptualising Transnational Organised Crime at Sea'. *Marine Policy* 119 (2020): 104067. https://doi.org/10.1016/j.marpol.2020.104067.

Burnett, David. *Masters Of All They Surveyed*. Chicago: University of Chicago Press, 2000.

———. 'Matthew Fontaine Maury's "Sea of Fire": Hydrography, Biogeography, and Providence in the Tropics'. In *Tropical Visions in an Age of Empire*, edited by Felix Driver and Luciana de Lima Martins, 113–36. Chicago: University of Chicago Press, 2005.

Burnett, Graham. 'Hydrographic Discipline among Navigators: Charting an "Empire of Commerce and Science" in the Nineteenth-Century Pacific'. edited by John Akerman, 185–259. London: University of Chicago, 2009.

Cable, James. *Gunboat Diplomacy 1919 - 1979: Political Applications of Limited Naval Force*. 2nd ed. 16. London: Macmillan, 1986.

Cadag, Jake Rom. 'Problems and Promises of Postmodernism in (Re)Liberating Disaster Studies'. *Disaster Prevention and Management: An International Journal* 33, no. 3 (2024): 167–80. https://doi.org/10.1108/DPM-06-2023-0153.

Cain, P, and A Hopkins. *British Imperialism: 1688-2015*. 3rd ed. New York: Routledge, 2015.

Cain, P J, and A G Hopkins. 'Gentlemanly Capitalism and British Expansion Overseas I The Old Colonial System'. *Economic History Review* 2, no. 4 (1986): 501–25.

———. 'Gentlemanly Capitalism and British Expansion Overseas II: New Imperialism'. *Economic History Review* 2, no. 1 (1987): 1–26.

Cannadine, David, ed. *Empire, the Sea and Global History: Britain's Maritime World, c. 1760-c. 1840*. Basingstoke: Palgrave Macmillan, 2007.

Caputo, Sara. 'From Surveying to Surveillance: Maritime Cartography and Naval (Self-) Tracking in the Long Nineteenth Century'. *Past & Present*, 2024. https://doi.org/10.1093/pastj/gtad023.

Carter, Christopher Ray. *Magnetic Fever: Global Imperialism and Empiricism in the Nineteenth Century*. Philadelphia: American Philosophical Society, 2009.

Castex, Raoul, and Eugenia C. Kiesling. *Strategic Theories*. Annapolis: Naval Institute Press, 2017.

Castree, Noel. 'David Harvey: Marxism, Capitalism and the Geographical Imagination'. *New Political Economy* 12, no. 1 (2007): 97–115. https://doi.org/10.1080/13563460601068859.

Cavanagh, Edward, and Lorenzo Veracini, eds. *The Routledge Handbook of the History of Settler Colonialism*. London: Routledge, 2020.

Caverley, Jonathan D., and Peter Dombrowski. 'Cruising for a Bruising: Maritime Competition in an Anti-Access Age'. *Security Studies* 29, no. 4 (2020): 671–700. https://doi.org/10.1080/09636412.2020.1811460.

Chandra, S, B Arunachalam, and V Suryanarayan. *The Indian Ocean and Its Islands: Strategic, Scientific and Historical Perspectives*. New Delhi: Sage Publications, 1993.

Chaudhuri, Kirti. *Trade and Civilisation in the Indian Ocean: An Economic History from the Rise of Islam to 1750*. Cambridge: Cambridge University Press, 1985.

Chen, Song-Chuan. *Merchants of War and Peace*. Hong Kong: Hong Kong University Press, 2017.

Christie, David. *India's Naval Strategy and the Role of the Andaman and Nicobar Islands*. 291. Canberra: Australian National University Press, 1995.

Clarence-Smith, William Gervase. 'The Economics of the Indian Ocean and Red Sea Slave Trades in the 19th Century: An Overview'. *Slavery & Abolition* 9, no. 3 (1988): 1–20. https://doi.org/10.1080/01440398808574959.

Clayton, Daniel. *Islands of Truth: The Imperial Fashioning of Vancouver Island*. Vancouver: UBC Press, 2000.

———. 'The Creation of Imperial Space in the Pacific Northwest'. *Journal of Historical Geography* 26, no. 3 (2000): 327–50. https://doi.org/10.1006/jhge.2000.0233.

Clements, William H. *Britain's Island Fortresses: Defence of the Empire 1756-1956*. Barnsley: Pen & Sword Military, 2019.

Clendinnen, Inga. *Dancing with Strangers: Europeans and Australians at First Contact*. Cambridge: Cambridge University Press, 2005.

Clout, Hugh, and Cyril Gosme. 'The Naval Intelligence Handbooks: A Monument in Geographical Writing'. *Progress in Human Geography* 27, no. 2 (2003): 153–73. https://doi.org/10.1191/0309132503ph420oa.

Cock, Randolph. "Scientific Serviceman' in the Royal Navy and the Professionalism of Science, 1816-55'. edited by David Knight and Matthew Eddy, 95–112. London: Routledge, 2005.

Cocker, Maurice P. *Coastal Forces Vessels of the Royal Navy from 1865*. Stroud: Tempus Publishing, 2006.

Cole, D. *Imperial Military Geography*. London: Sifton Praed & Co Ltd, 1929.

Colledge, J J, Ben Warlow, and Steve Bush. *Ships of the Royal Navy: The Complete Record of All Fighting Ships of the Royal Navy from The15th Century to the Present*. 5th ed. Barnsley: Seaforth Publishing, 2020.

Cook, Andrew. 'Establishing Sea Routes to India and China: Stages in the Development of Hydrographical Knowledge'. In *The Worlds of the East India Company*, edited by H. V. Bowen, Margarette Lincoln, and Nigel Rigby, 119–36. Woodbridge: Boydell & Brewer Ltd, 2002.

Corbett, Julian. *21st Century Corbett: Maritime Strategy and Naval Policy for the Modern Era*. Edited by Andrew Lambert. Annapolis, Maryland: Naval Institute Press, 2017.

Corbett, Julian Stafford. *Some Principles of Maritime Strategy*. Annapolis: Naval Institute Press, 1988.

Cornish, Vaughan. *Naval and Military Geography of the British Empire*. London: Hugh Rees Limited, 1916.

Cresswell, Tim. 'Mobilities I: Catching Up'. *Progress in Human Geography* 35, no. 4 (2011): 550–58. https://doi.org/10.1177/0309132510383348.

———. 'Mobilities II: Still'. *Progress in Human Geography* 36, no. 5 (2012): 645–53. https://doi.org/10.1177/0309132511423349.

———. 'Mobilities III: Moving On'. *Progress in Human Geography* 38, no. 5 (2014): 712–21. https://doi.org/10.1177/0309132514530316.

———. 'Towards a Politics of Mobility'. *Environment and Planning D: Society and Space* 28, no. 1 (2010): 17–31. https://doi.org/10.1068/d11407.

Dalby, Simon. *Anthropocene Geopolitics: Globalization, Security, Sustainability*: University of Ottawa Press, 2020. https://doi.org/10.2307/j.ctvx5w8dk.

———. 'Political Space: Autonomy, Liberalism, and Empire'. *Alternatives: Global, Local, Political* 30, no. 4 (2005): 415–41.

———. 'Security, Modernity, Ecology: The Dilemmas of Post-Cold War Security Discourse'. *Alternatives: Global, Local, Political* 17, no. 1 (1992): 95–134.

Dalby, Simon, and Gearóid Ó Tuathail. *Rethinking Geopolitics*. London: Taylor and Francis, 2002.

Dalrymple, William. *The Anarchy: The Relentless Rise of the East India Company*. London: Bloomsbury Publishing, 2019.

Darvall, Joseph. *The Wreck on the Andamans*. London: Pelham Richardson, 1845.

Darwin, John. *Unfinished Empire: The Global Expansion of Britain*. London: Penguin Books, 2013.

Dasgupta, Jayant. *Japanese in Andaman and Nicobar Islands: Red Sun Over Black Water*. New Delhi: Manas Publications, 2002.

Daunton, Martin, and Rick Halpern, eds. *Empire and Others: British Encounters with Indigenous Peoples, 1600 - 1850*. London: Routledge, 2003.

Davey, James. 'The Advancement of Nautical Knowledge: The Hydrographical Office, the Royal Navy and the Charting of the Baltic Sea, 1795-1815'. *Journal for Maritime Research* 13, no. 2 (2011): 81–103. https://doi.org/10.1080/21533369.2011.622869.

David, Saul. *The Indian Mutiny: 1857*. London: Viking, 2002.

———. *Victoria's Wars: The Rise of Empire*. London: Viking, 2006.

Bibliography

Davies, Stephen Nicholas Guy. *Transport to Another World: HMS Tamar and the Sinews of Empire*. Hong Kong: City University of Hong Kong Press, 2022.

Day, Archibald. *The Admiralty Hydrographic Service 1795-1919*. London: Her Majesty's Stationary Office, 1967.

De Souza, Philip. *Seafaring and Civilization: Maritime Perspectives on World History*. London: Profile Books, 2002.

Deloughrey, Elizabeth. '"The Litany of Islands, The Rosary of Archipelagoes": Caribbean and Pacific Achipelagraphy'. *Ariel* 32, no. 2 (2001): 21.

Derrida, Jacques. *Jacques Derrida: Basic Writings*. Edited by Barry Stocker. London: Routledge, 2020.

Dickinson, H. W. *Educating the Royal Navy: Eighteenth- and Nineteenth-Century Education for Officers*. London: Routledge, 2012.

Din, Gilbert C. 'Mississippi River Gunboats on the Gulf Coast: The Spanish Naval Fight against William Augustus Bowles, 1799-1803'. *Louisiana History: The Journal of the Louisiana Historical Association* 47, no. 3 (2006): 277–308.

Dittmer, Jason. 'Captain America's Empire: Reflections on Identity, Popular Culture, and Post-9/11 Geopolitics'. *Annals of the Association of American Geographers* 95, no. 3 (2005): 626–43.

———. 'Grounding the Nation-State'. In *Captain America and the Nationalist Superhero*, 102–22. Philadelphia: Temple University Press, 2013. http://www.jstor.org/stable/j.ctt14bstb0.9.

Dodds, Klaus. *Border Wars: The Conflicts That Will Define Our Future*. London: Ebury Press, 2021.

———. 'Popular Geopolitics and Audience Dispositions: James Bond and the Internet Movie Database (IMDb)'. *Transactions of the Institute of British Geographers* 31, no. 2 (2006): 116–30.

Dodds, Klaus, and James D. Sidaway. 'Halford Mackinder and the "Geographical Pivot of History": A Centennial Retrospective'. *The Geographical Journal* 170, no. 4 (2004): 292–97.

Dodds, Klauss. 'Eugenics, Fantasies of Empire and Inverted Whiggism'. *Political Geography* 13, no. 1 (1994): 85–99.

Doel, Ronald E., Tanya J. Levin, and Mason K. Marker. 'Extending Modern Cartography to the Ocean Depths: Military Patronage, Cold War Priorities, and the Heezen–Tharp Mapping Project, 1952–1959'. *Journal of Historical Geography* 32, no. 3 (2006): 605–26. https://doi.org/10.1016/j.jhg.2005.10.011.

Dolwick, Jim S. '"The Social" and Beyond: Introducing Actor-Network Theory'. *Journal of Maritime Archaeology* 4, no. 1 (2009): 21–49. https://doi.org/10.1007/s11457-009-9044-3.

Doyle, Arthur Conan. *The Sign of Four*. London: Penguin, 2001.

Driver, Felix. 'Distance and Disturbance: Travel, Exploration and Knowledge in the Nineteenth Century'. *Transactions of the Royal Historical Society* 14, no. 14 (2004): 73–92. https://doi.org/10.1017/S0080440104000088.

———. 'Exploration as Knowledge Transfer: Exhibiting Hidden Histories'. In *Mobilities of Knowledge*, edited by Heike Jons, Peter Meusburger, and Michael Heffernan, 85–104. New York: Springer Berlin Heidelberg, 2017.

———. *Geography Militant: Cultures of Exploration and Empire*. Oxford: Blackwell, 2006.

Driver, Felix, and Luciana Martins. 'Shipwreck and Salvage in the Tropics: The Case of HMS Thetis, 1830–1854'. *Journal of Historical Geography* 32, no. 3 (2006): 539–62. https://doi.org/10.1016/j.jhg.2005.10.010.

———, eds. *Tropical Visions in an Age of Empire*. Chicago: University of Chicago Press, 2005.

Dull, Paul S. *A Battle History of the Imperial Japanese Navy (1941 - 1945)*. Annapolis: Naval Institute Press, 2007.

Dunley, Richard. 'The "Problem of Asia" and Imperial Competition before World War 1'. In *The New Age of Naval Power in the Indo-Pacific: Strategy, Order, and Regional Security*, edited by Catherine L. Grant, Alessio Patalano, and James A. Russell. Washington, DC: Georgetown University Press, 2023.

Edgell, John. *Sea Surveys: Britain's Contribution to Hydrography*. London: Longmans, Green & Co, 1949.

Ehrlich, Joshua. *The East India Company and the Politics of Knowledge*. Cambridge: Cambridge University Press, 2023.

Elden, Stuart. *The Birth of Territory*. London: University of Chicago Press, 2013.

Eldridge, Colin. *Victorian Imperialism*. London: Hodder & Stoughton, 1978.

Elkins, Caroline. *Legacy of Violence: A History of the British Empire*. London: Vintage, 2023.

Elleman, Bruce A., and S. C. M. Paine, eds. *Naval Blockades and Seapower: Strategies and Counter-Strategies, 1805-2005*. 34. London: Routledge, 2006.

Epple, Angelika. 'Calling For A Practice Turn in Global History: Practices As Drivers of Globalization'. *History and Theory* 57, no. 3 (2018): 390–407. https://doi.org/10.1111/hith.12071.

Epple, Angelika, and K Kramer. 'Globalization, Imagination, Social Space. The Making of Geopolitical Imaginaries'. *Fiar Forum for Inter-American Research* 9, no. 1 (2016): 41–63.

Eriksson, Cunilla. 'Introduction', Edinburgh: Edinburgh University Press, 2016. https://doi.org/10.3366/j.ctt1g050sq.5.

Evans, David. *Building the Steam Navy: Dockyards, Technology, and the Creation of the Victorian Battle Fleet, 1830-1906*. Annapolis: Naval Institute Press, 2004.

Faulkner, Marcus, and Alessio Patalano, eds. *The Sea and the Second World War: Maritime Aspects of a Global Conflict*. Lexington: University Press of Kentucky, 2020.

Field, Andrew. *Royal Navy Strategy in the Far East: 1919 - 1939; Preparing for War against Japan*. 22. London: Cass, 2004.

Finamore, Daniel, ed. *Maritime History as World History*. Gainesville: University Press of Florida, 2008.

Finnegan, Diarmid. 'The Spatial Turn: Geographical Approaches in the History of Science'. *Journal of the History of Biology* 41, no. 2 (2008): 369–88. https://doi.org/10.1007/s10739-007-9136-6.

Fisher, Robin. *Contact and Conflict: Indian-European Relations in British Columbia, 1774-1890*. 2nd ed. Vancouver: UBC Press, 1992.

Bibliography

Fitzgerald Lee, J. *Imperial Military Geography*. 2nd ed. London: William Clowes and Sons Ltd, 1922.

Fogg, G. E. 'The Royal Society and the South Seas'. *Notes and Records of the Royal Society of London* 55, no. 1 (2001): 81–103. https://doi.org/10.1098/rsnr.2001.0127.

Foucault, Michel. *Discipline and Punish: The Birth of the Prison*. New York: Pantheon Books, 1977.

Freedman, Lawrence. *Strategy: A History*. Oxford: Oxford University Press, 2015.

———. *The Future of War: A History*. London: Allen Lane, 2017.

Friedman, Norman. *Fighting the Great War at Sea: Strategy, Tactics, and Technology*. Barnsley: Seaforth Publishing, 2014.

Friend, Jayne. 'Destroyer Flag-Flying Visits, Civic Ceremony, Empire and Identity in Interwar Britain'. *British Journal for Military History* 7, no. 2 (2021): 102–21. https://doi.org/10.25602/GOLD.bjmh.v7i2.1557.

Friendly, Alfred. *Beaufort of the Admiralty: The Life of Sir Francis Beaufort, 1774-1857*. New York: Random House, 1977.

Frost, Alan. *The Global Reach of Empire: Britain's Maritime Expansion in the Indian and Pacific Oceans, 1764-1815*. Carlton: Miegunyah Press, 2003.

Fuller, Howard. *Empire, Technology and Seapower: Royal Navy Crisis in the Age of Palmerston*. Basingstoke: Palgrave, 2013.

Fuller, Howard J. '"Had We Used the Navy's Bare Fist Instead of Its Gloved Hand..." - The Absence of Coastal Assault Vessels in the Royal Navy by 1914'. *British Journal for Military History* 3, no. 3 (2017).

Germond, Basil. *Seapower in the Post-Modern World*. Montreal: McGill-Queen's University Press, 2024.

———. *The Maritime Dimension of European Security: Seapower and the European Union*. Basingstoke: Palgrave Macmillan, 2015.

Gerth, H.H., and C. Wright Mills, eds. *From Max Weber: Essays in Sociology*. Abingdon: Routledge, 2014. https://doi.org/10.4324/9780203759240.

Goldman, Charles Sydney, ed. *The Empire and the Century: A Series of Essays on Imperial Problems and Possibilities by Various Writers*. London: John Murray, 1905.

Gommans, Jos. 'Trade and Civilization around the Bay of Bengal, c. 1650–1800'. *Itinerario* 19, no. 3 (1995): 82–108. https://doi.org/10.1017/S0165115300021331.

Goodman, Jordan. 'Making Imperial Space: Settlement, Surveying and Trade in Northern Australia in the Nineteenth Century'. In *Maritime Empires: British Imperial Maritime Trade in the Nineteenth Century*. Woodbridge: Boydell and Brewer, 2004.

Goodman, Matthew. 'Follow the Data: Administering Science at Edward Sabine's Magnetic Department, Woolwich, 1841–57'. *Notes and Records: The Royal Society Journal of the History of Science* 73, no. 2 (2019): 187–202. https://doi.org/10.1098/rsnr.2018.0036.

Gopal, Priyamvada. *Insurgent Empire: Anticolonial Resistance and British Dissent*. London: Verso, 2019.

Gorshkov, Sergei. *The Sea Power of the State*. Annapolis: Naval Institute Press, 1979.

Gough, Barry. *Gunboat Frontier: British Maritime Authority and Northwest Coast Indians, 1846-90*. Vancouver: University of British Columbia Press, 1984.

———. *Pax Britannica: Ruling the Waves and Keeping the Peace before Armageddon*. Basingstoke: Palgrave Macmillan, 2014.

Graeber, David. *Pirate Enlightenment, or The Real Libertalia*. London: Allan Lane, 2023.

Graham, Gerald. *Great Britain in the Indian Ocean: A Study of Maritime Enterprise 1810-1850*. Oxford: Clarendon, 1967.

Graham-Yooll, Andrew. *Imperial Skirmishes: War and Gunboat Diplomacy in Latin America*. Oxford: Signal Books, 2002.

Grainger, John. *The British Navy in Eastern Waters: The Indian and Pacific Oceans*. Woodbridge: The Boydell Press, 2022.

Grant, Catherine L., Alessio Patalano, and James A. Russell, eds. *The New Age of Naval Power in the Indo-Pacific: Strategy, Order, and Regional Security*. Washington, DC: Georgetown University Press, 2023.

Gray, Colin. *The Leverage of Sea Power: The Strategic Advantage of Navies in War*. New York: Free Press, 1992.

Gray, Colin, ed. *Seapower and Strategy*. London: Tri-Service Press, 1989.

Gray, Steven. 'Fuelling Mobility: Coal and Britain's Naval Power, c. 1870-1914 | Elsevier Enhanced Reader'. *Journal of Historical Geography* 58 (2017): 92–103. https://doi.org/10.1016/j.jhg.2017.06.013.

———. *Steam Power and Sea Power: Coal, the Royal Navy, and the British Empire, c. 1870-1914*. London: Palgrave Macmillan, 2018.

Greenhill, Basil, and Ann Giffard. *Steam, Politics and Patronage: The Transformation of the Royal Navy, 1815-54*. London: Conway Maritime Press, 1994.

Gregory, Derek. *Geographical Imaginations*. Cambridge: Blackwell, 1998.

Gribble, Henry. 'An Appeal And Suggestion for Lights in the Red and Indian Seas'. Pamphlet, 1862. P 28 6 Red and Indian Seas.

Grimes, Shawn. *Strategy and War Planning in the British Navy, 1887-1918*. Woodbridge: Boydell Press, 2012.

Grove, Eric. *Fleet to Fleet Encounters: Tsushima, Jutland, Philippine Sea*. London: Arms and Armour, 1991.

———. *The Future of Sea Power*. Annapolis: Naval Institute Press, 1990.

———. *The Royal Navy since 1815: A New Short History*. New York: Palgrave Macmillan, 2005.

Grydehøj, Adam. 'A Future of Island Studies'. *Island Studies Journal* 12, no. 1 (2017): 3–16.

———. 'Critical Approaches to Island Geography'. *Area* 52, no. 1 (2020): 2–5. https://doi.org/10.1111/area.12546.

Grydehøj, Adam, and Marco Casagrande. 'Islands of Connectivity: Archipelago Relationality and Transport Infrastructure in Venice Lagoon'. *Area* 52, no. 1 (2020): 56–64. https://doi.org/10.1111/area.12529.

Gupta, Shishir. 'Why Are Andaman and Nicobar Islands a Key Indian Military Asset?' *The Hindustan Times*, 2023. https://www.hindustantimes.com/india-news/why-are-andaman-and-nicobar-islands-a-key-indian-military-asset-101674528554860.html.

Hall, Richard. *Empires of the Monsoon: A History of the Indian Ocean and Its Invaders.* London: HarperCollins, 1996.

Hamilton, C. I. *The Making of the Modern Admiralty: British Naval Policy-Making, 1805–1927.* Cambridge: Cambridge University Press, 2011. https://doi.org/10.1017/CBO9780511974472.

Harman, Graham. *Bruno Latour: Reassembling the Political.* London: Pluto Press, 2014.

Harris, Steven J. 'Long-Distance Corporations, Big Sciences, and the Geography of Knowledge'. *Configurations* 6, no. 2 (1998): 269–304. https://doi.org/10.1353/con.1998.0018.

Harrison, Mark. 'Health, Sovereignty and Imperialism: The Royal Navy and Infectious Disease in Japan's Treaty Ports'. *Social Science Diliman* 14, no. 2 (2018): 49–75.

Hastings, D. J., ed. *The Royal Indian Navy, 1612-1950.* Jefferson: McFarland, 1988.

Hasty, William. 'Piracy and the Production of Knowledge in the Travels of William Dampier, c.1679–1688'. *Journal of Historical Geography* 37, no. 1 (2011): 40–54. https://doi.org/10.1016/j.jhg.2010.08.017.

Hasty, William, and Kimberley Peters. 'The Ship in Geography and the Geographies of Ships'. *Geography Compass* 6, no. 11 (2012): 660–76. https://doi.org/10.1111/gec3.12005.

Hayes, Gerald. 'How the British Admiralty Charts Are Produced'. The Admiralty Chart Agency, 1927.

Heaslip, Matthew. '21st Century Maritime Britain in Context-100 Years On'. In *Maritime Britain in the 21st Century*, edited by Katie Jamieson, Kevin Rowlands, and Andrew Young, 32–50. Dartmouth: Britannia Publishing, 2024.

———. *Gunboats, Empire and the China Station: The Royal Navy in 1920s East Asia.* London: Bloomsbury, 2022.

Heidemann, Frank, and Philipp Zehmisch, eds. *Manifestations of History: Time, Space, and Community in the Andaman Islands.* New Delhi: Primus Books, 2016.

Hernon, Ian. *Britain's Forgotten Wars: Colonial Campaigns of the 19th Century.* Stroud: Sutton, 2003.

Hevia, James. *The Imperial Security State: British Colonial Knowledge and Empire-Building in Asia.* Cambridge: Cambridge University Press, 2015.

Hodder, Jake, Michael Heffernan, and Stephen Legg. 'The Archival Geographies of Twentieth-Century Internationalism: Nation, Empire and Race'. *Journal of Historical Geography* 71 (2021): 1–11. https://doi.org/10.1016/j.jhg.2020.06.008.

Hones, Sheila, and Yasuo Endo. 'History, Distance and Text: Narratives of the 1853–1854 Perry Expedition to Japan'. *Journal of Historical Geography* 32, no. 3 (2006): 563–78. https://doi.org/10.1016/j.jhg.2005.10.008.

Hopkins, A. G. *American Empire: A Global History.* Princeton: Princeton University Press, 2018.

Horden, Peregrine, and Nicholas Purcell. *The Corrupting Sea: A Study of Mediterranean History.* Oxford: Blackwell, 2000.

Hore, Peter, ed. *Seapower Ashore: 200 Years of Royal Navy Operations on Land.* London: Chatham, 2000.

Houlberg, Kristian, Jane Wickenden, and Dennis Freshwater. 'Five Centuries of Medical Contributions from the Royal Navy'. *Clinical Medicine (London, England)* 19, no. 1 (2019): 22–25. https://doi.org/10.7861/clinmedicine.19-1-22.

Iliffe, Rob. 'Science and Voyages of Discovery', 4:618–46. Cambridge: Cambridge University Press, 2003. https://doi.org/10.1017/CHOL9780521572439.027.

Jackson, Ashley. *Distant Drums: The Role of Colonies in British Imperial Warfare*. Brighton: Sussex Academic Press, 2010.

———. *Of Islands, Ports and Sea Lanes: Africa and the Indian Ocean in the Second World War*. Warwick: Helion & Company, 2018.

———. *War and Empire in Mauritius and the Indian Ocean*. Basingstoke: Palgrave, 2001.

Jacques, Peter. *Globalization and the World Ocean*. Lanham: AltaMira Press, 2006.

James, Frank A. J. L. 'Making Money from the Royal Navy in the Late Eighteenth Century: Charles Kerr on Antigua "Breathing the True Spirit of a West India Agent"'. *The Mariner's Mirror* 107, no. 4 (2021): 402–19. https://doi.org/10.1080/00253359.2021.1978257.

James, Lawrence. *Raj: The Making and Unmaking of British India*. London: Abacus, 2009.

Jonkers, Art. *Earths Magnetism in the Age of Sail*. Baltimore: John Hopkins University Press, 2008.

Jons, Heike, Peter Meusburger, and Michael Heffernan. *Mobilities of Knowledge*. New York: Springer Berlin Heidelberg, 2017.

Keay, John. *The Honourable Company: A History of the English East India Company*. London: Harper Collins, 1993.

Keegan, John. *The Price of Admiralty: War at Sea from Man of War to Submarine*. London: Hutchinson, 1988.

Keighren, Innes, Charles Withers, and Bill Bell. *Travels into Print: Exploration, Writing, and Publishing with John Murray, 1773-1859*. London: University of Chicago Press, 2015.

Kelly, Philip. *Classical Geopolitics: A New Analytical Model*. Stanford: Stanford University Press, 2016.

Kennedy, Greg, ed. *Imperial Defence: The Old World Order 1856–1956*. London: Routledge, 2007. https://doi.org/10.4324/9780203002438.

Kennedy, Paul. *The Rise and Fall of British Naval Mastery*. London: Penguin Books, 2001.

Killingray, David, Margarette Lincoln, and Nigel Rigby, eds. *Maritime Empires: British Imperial Maritime Trade in the Nineteenth Century*. Woodbridge: Boydell Press, 2004.

Kinkel, Sarah. *Disciplining the Empire: Politics, Governance, and the Rise of the British Navy*. Cambridge: Harvard University Press, 2018.

Kloss, C. Boden. *In the Andaman and Nicobar Islands. The Narrative If a Cruise in the Schooner 'Terrapin,' With Notices of the Islands, Their Fauna, Ethnology, Etc*. London: John Murray, 1903.

Konishi, Shino, Maria Nugent, and Tiffany Shellam, eds. *Indigenous Intermediaries: New Perspectives on Exploration Archives*. Acton: Australian National University Press, 2015.

Konstam, Angus. *British Gunboats of Victoria's Empire*. Oxford: Osprey Publishing, 2022.

Korsgaard, Annika, and Martin Gibbs. 'Shipwrecks as Archaeological Signatures of a Maritime Industrial Frontier in the Solomon Islands, 1788–1942'. *International Journal of Historical Archaeology* 20, no. 1 (2016): 105–26. https://doi.org/10.1007/s10761-015-0320-7.

Kuehling, Susanne. 'The Converted War Canoe: Cannibal Raiders, Missionaries and "Pax Britannica" on Dobu Island, Papua New Guinea'. *Anthropologica* 56, no. 2 (2014): 269–84.

Kuhn, Thomas. *The Structure of Scientific Revolutions*. Chicago: Chicago University Press, 1962.

Kwan, C. Nathan. '"Barbarian Ships Sail Freely about the Seas": Qing Reactions to the British Suppression of Piracy in South China, 1841–1856'. *Asian Review of World Histories* 8, no. 1 (2020): 83–102. https://doi.org/10.1163/22879811-12340065.

———. '"Putting down a Common Enemy": Piracy and Occasional Interstate Power in South China during the Mid-Nineteenth Century'. *International Journal of Maritime History* 32, no. 3 (2020): 697–712. https://doi.org/10.1177/0843871420944629.

Lally, Jagjeet. *India and the Silk Roads: The History of a Trading World*. London: Hurst & Company, 2021.

Laloë, Anne-Flore. 'Where Is Bathybius Haeckelii? The Ship as a Scientific Instrument and a Space of Science'. edited by Don Legget and Richard Dunn, 113–30. Oxford: Routledge, 2016. https://doi.org/10.4324/9781315604657-7.

Lalvani, Kartar. *The Making of India: The Untold Story of British Enterprise*. London: Bloomsbury, 2016.

Lambert, Andrew. *Admirals: The Naval Commanders Who Made Britain Great*. London: Faber and Faber, 2008.

———. *Battleships in Transition: The Creation of the Steam Battlefleet, 1815-1860*. Annapolis: Naval Institute Press, 1984.

———. 'Economic Power, Technological Advantage, and Imperial Strength: Britain as a Unique Global Power, 1860–1890'. *International Journal of Naval History* 5, no. 2 (2006): 1–39.

———. *Franklin: Tragic Hero of Polar Navigation*. London: Faber and Faber, 2010.

———. 'Looking to the Sea - The "Art of Admiralty", and the Maintenance of Naval Power'. In *Maritime Britain in the 21st Century*, edited by Katie Jamieson, Kevin Rowlands, and Andrew Young, 53–61. Dartmouth: Britannia Publishing, 2024.

———. *Nelson: Britannia's God of War*. London: Faber and Faber, 2004.

———. *Seapower States: Maritime Culture, Continental Empires and the Conflict That Made the Modern World*. New Haven: Yale University Press, 2018.

———. 'Strategy, Policy and Shipbuilding: The Bombay Dockyard, the Indian Navy and Imperial Security in the Eastern Seas, 1784-1869'. In *The Worlds of the East India Company*, edited by H. V. Bowen, Margarette Lincoln, and Nigel Rigby, 137–52. Woodbridge: Boydell & Brewer Ltd, 2002.

———. *The British Way of War: Julian Corbett and the Battle for a National Strategy*. New Haven: Yale University Press, 2021.

———. *The Challenge: America, Britain and the War of 1812*. London: Faber and Faber, 2012.

———. *The Crimean War: British Grand Strategy against Russia, 1853-56*. 2nd ed. Abingdon: Routledge, 2011.

———. 'The Royal Navy, 1856-1914: Deterrence and the Strategy of World Power'. In *Navies and Global Defense: Theories and Strategy*, edited by Keith Neilson and Elizabeth Errington. London: Praeger, 1995.

———. 'The Royal Navy's White Sea Campaign of 1854'. In *Naval Power and Expeditionary Warfare: Peripheral Campaigns and New Theatres of Naval Warfare*, edited by Bruce A. Elleman and S. C. M. Paine, 29–44. London: Routledge, 2011.

———. *Trincomalee: The Last of Nelson's Frigates*. London: Chatham, 2002.

———. 'Under the Heel of Britannia. The Bombardment of Sweaborg 9-11 August 1855'. In *Seapower Ashore: 200 Years of Royal Navy Operations on Land*, edited by Peter Hore, 96–129. London: Chatham Publishing, 2000.

Lambert, Andrew, Jan Rüger, and Robert Blyth, eds. *The Dreadnought and the Edwardian Age*. Farnham: Ashgate, 2011.

Lambert, David. '"Taken Captive by the Mystery of the Great River": Towards an Historical Geography of British Geography and Atlantic Slavery'. *Journal of Historical Geography* 35, no. 1 (2009): 44–65. https://doi.org/10.1016/j.jhg.2008.05.017.

Lambert, Nicholas. *Neptune Factor: Alfred Thayer Mahan and the Concept of Sea Power*. Annapolis: Naval Institute Press, 2024.

Latour, Bruno. *An Inquiry into Modes of Existence: An Anthropology of the Moderns*. London: Harvard University Press, 2018.

———. *Pasteurization of France*. Cambridge: Harvard University Press, 1993. https://www.vlebooks.com/vleweb/product/openreader?id=none&isbn=9780674265301.

———. *Reassembling The Social: An Introduction to Actor-Network Theory*. Oxford: Oxford University Press, 2007.

———. *Science in Action: How to Follow Scientists and Engineers Through Society*. Cambridge: Harvard University Press, 1988.

Latour, Bruno, and Steve Woolgar. *Laboratory Life: The Construction of Scientific Facts*. 2nd ed. Princeton: Princeton University Press, 1986.

Law, John. 'Actor Network Theory and Material Semiotics'. In *The New Blackwell Companion to Social Theory*, edited by Bryan S. Turner, 141–58. Oxford: Wiley-Blackwell, 2009. https://doi.org/10.1002/9781444304992.ch7.

———. *After Method*. Routledge, 2004. https://doi.org/10.4324/9780203481141.

———. 'Notes on the Theory of the Actor-Network: Ordering, Strategy, and Heterogeneity'. *Systems Practice* 5, no. 4 (1992): 379–93. https://doi.org/10.1007/BF01059830.

———. 'On the Methods of Long-Distance Control: Vessels, Navigation and the Portuguese Route to India'. In *Power, Action and Belief: A New Sociology of Knowledge*, edited by John Law, 234–63. 32. London: Routledge and Kegan Paul, 1986.

———. 'On the Social Explanation of Technical Change: The Case of the Portuguese Maritime Expansion'. *Technology and Culture* 28, no. 2 (1987): 227–52. https://doi.org/10.2307/3105566.

———. 'Technology and Heterogeneous Engineering: The Case of Portuguese Expansion.' In *The Social Construction of Technological Systems: New Directions in the Sociology and History of Technology*, edited by Wiebe E. Bijker, Thomas Parke Hughes, and Trevor Pinch. Cambridge: MIT Press, 2012.

Law, John, and John Hassard, eds. *Actor Network Theory and After*. Oxford: Blackwell, 1999.

Lawrenson, Ross. 'Frederic John Mouat (1816–97), MD FRCS LLD of the Indian Medical Service'. *Journal of Medical Biography* 15, no. 4 (2007): 201–5. https://doi.org/10.1258/j.jmb.2007.06-45.

Levine, Philippa. *The British Empire: Sunrise to Sunset*. 3rd ed. London: Routledge Taylor & Francis Group, 2020.

Lewis, Julian. *Changing Direction: British Military Planning for Post-War Strategic Defence, 1942-1947*. London: Routledge, 2008.

Lewis, Martin, and Kären Wigen. *The Myth of Continents: A Critique of Metageography*. Berkeley: University of California Press, 1997.

Lewis, Michael. *The Navy in Transition: A Social History 1814-1864*. London: Hodder & Stoughton, 1965.

Libero, Elizabeth. 'Navigating a British South Atlantic, 1800-1815'. University of Portsmouth, 2019.

Lindberg, Michael, and Daniel Todd. *Brown-, Green-, and Blue-Water Fleets: The Influence of Geography on Naval Warfare, 1861 to the Present*. Westport: Praeger, 2002.

Livingstone, David. *Putting Science in Its Place: Geographies of Scientific Knowledge*. Chicago: University of Chicago Press, 2013.

———. *The Geographical Tradition: Episodes in a Contested Enterprise*. Oxford: Blackwell, 1994.

———. 'The Spaces of Knowledge: Contributions towards a Historical Geography of Science'. *Environment and Planning. Society and Space* 13, no. 1 (1995): 5–34. https://doi.org/10.1068/d130005.

Livingstone, David N. *Putting Science in Its Place*. Chicago: University of Chicago Press, 2003.

Livingstone, David, and Charles Withers. *Geographies of Nineteenth-Century Science*. Chicago: University of Chicago Press, 2011.

Lovell, Julia. *The Opium War: Drugs, Dreams and the Making of China*. London: Picador, 2012.

Lyon, David, and Rif Winfield. *The Sail & Steam Navy List: All the Ships of the Royal Navy, 1815-1889*. London: Chatham, 2004.

Macdougall, Doug. *Endless Novelties of Extraordinary Interest: The Voyage of H.M.S Challenger and the Birth of Modern Oceanography*. New Haven: Yale University Press, 2019.

Mack, John. *The Sea: A Cultural History*. London: Reaktion Books, 2013.

MacKenzie, John. *Propaganda and Empire: The Manipulation of British Public Opinion, 1880 - 1960*. Manchester: Manchester University Press, 2003.

Mackinder, Halford. 'The Geographical Pivot of History (1904)'. *The Geographical Journal* 170, no. 4 (2004): 298–321.

MacLeod, Christine. *Heroes of Invention: Technology, Liberalism and British Identity, 1750-1914*. Cambridge: Cambridge University Press, 2007.

Madureira, Nuno Luís. 'Oil in the Age of Steam'. *Journal of Global History* 5, no. 1 (2010): 75–94. https://doi.org/10.1017/S1740022809990349.

Mahajan, Nidhi. 'Notes on an Archipelagic Ethnography: Ships, Seas, and Islands of Relation in the Indian Ocean'. *Island Studies Journal* 16, no. 1 (2021): 9–22. https://doi.org/10.24043/isj.147.

Mahan, Alfred Thayer. *Influence of Sea Power Upon History, 1660-1783*. Great Britain: Pantianos Classics, 1890.

———. *Naval Strategy Compared and Contrasted with the Principles and Practice of Military Operations on Land*. Boston: Little, Brown and Company, 1911.

Man, Kwong Chi. '"They Are a Little Afraid of the British Admiral"'. *International Bibliography of Military History* 35, no. 2 (2015): 93–118. https://doi.org/10.1163/22115757-03502002.

Markovits, Claude. *The Global World of Indian Merchants, 1750-1947: Traders of Sind from Bukhara to Panama*. Cambridge: Cambridge University Press, 2000.

Martin, Peter. 'Indigenous Tales of the Beaufort Sea: Arctic Exploration and the Circulation of Geographical Knowledge'. *Journal of Historical Geography* 67 (2020): 24–35. https://doi.org/10.1016/j.jhg.2019.10.012.

Mathur, L. *History of the Andaman and Nicobar Islands (1756-1966)*. Delhi: Sterling Publishers, 1968.

Matzke, Rebecca Berens. *Deterrence through Strength: British Naval Power and Foreign Policy under Pax Britannica*. Nebraska: University of Nebraska Press, 2011.

Mawani, Renisa. 'Law, Settler Colonialism, and "the Forgotten Space" of Maritime Worlds'. *Annual Review of Law and Social Science* 12, no. 1 (2016): 107–31. https://doi.org/10.1146/annurev-lawsocsci-102612-134005.

McBain, Gordon Connor. 'Debt and the Gunboat: Mapping Intervention in Victorian International Legal Thought, 1848-1912'. University of Glasgow, 2023. http://theses.gla.ac.uk/id/eprint/83499.

McBeth, Barry. *Gunboats, Corruption, and Claims: Foreign Intervention in Venezuela, 1899-1908*. Westport: Greenwood Press, 2001.

McCabe, Constance, ed. 'Maurice Vidal Portman and the Platinotype in India'. In *Platinum and Palladium Photographs: Technical History, Connoisseurship and Preservation*, 318–31. Washington, DC: American Institute for Conservation of Historic and Artistic Works, 2017.

McCarthy, William J. 'Gambling on Empire: The Economic Role of Shipwreck in the Age of Discovery'. *International Journal of Maritime History* 23, no. 2 (2011): 69–84. https://doi.org/10.1177/084387141102300205.

McIntyre, David. *The Rise and Fall of the Singapore Naval Base, 1919-1942*. Hamden: Archon Books, 1979.

McLaughlin, Stephen. 'Battlelines and Fast Wings: Battlefleet Tactics in the Royal Navy, 1900–1914'. *Journal of Strategic Studies* 38, no. 7 (2015): 985–1005. https://doi.org/10.1080/01402390.2015.1005444.

McLean, David. 'Famine on the Coast: The Royal Navy and the Relief of Ireland, 1846–1847'. *The English Historical Review* 134, no. 566 (2019): 92–120. https://doi.org/10.1093/ehr/cez004.

McPherson, Kenneth. *The Indian Ocean: A History of People and the Sea*. Delhi: Oxford University Press, 1993.

Mentz, Steve. An Introduction to the Blue Humanities. London: Routledge, 2024.

Merriman, Peter, and Kimberley Peters. 'Military Mobilities in an Age of Global War, 1870–1945'. *Journal of Historical Geography* 58 (2017): 53–60. https://doi.org/10.1016/j.jhg.2017.07.005.

Metcalf, Thomas. *Imperial Connections: India in the Indian Ocean Arena, 1860 - 1920*. Berkeley: University of California Press, 2008.

Michael, Mike. *Actor-Network Theory: Trials, Trails and Translations*. 1 Oliver's Yard, 55 City Road London EC1Y 1SP: SAGE, 2017. https://doi.org/10.4135/9781473983045.

Miller, David. *Special Forces Operations in South-East Asia, 1941-1945: Minerva, Baldhead and Longshanks/Creek*. Barnsley: Pen & Sword Military, 2015.

Mohanan, Kalesh. *The Royal Indian Navy: Trajectories, Transformations and the Transfer of Power*. London: Routledge, 2021.

Moloney, Michael J. 'Re-Imagining Shipboard Societies: A Spatial Approach to Analysing Ships of the British Royal Navy during the Eighteenth and Nineteenth Centuries'. *International Journal of Maritime History* 30, no. 2 (2018): 315–42. https://doi.org/10.1177/0843871418766766.

Monahan, David, Horst Hecht, Dave Wells, Maureen R Kenny, and Aldino Campos. 'Challenges and Opportunities for Hydrography in The New Century'. *International Hydrography Review* 2, no. 3 (2001).

Moore, Grace. 'Piracy and the Ends of Romantic Commercialism: Victorian Businessmen Meet Malay Pirates'. In *Pirates and Mutineers of the Nineteenth Century: Swashbucklers and Swindlers*, edited by Grace Moore, 256–74. London: Routledge, 2016.

Morgan, Kenneth. 'Sir Joseph Banks as Patron of the Investigator Expedition: Natural History, Geographical Knowledge and Australian Exploration'. *International Journal of Maritime History* 26, no. 2 (2014): 235–64. https://doi.org/10.1177/0843871413514002.

Morgan-Owen, David. '"History Is a Record of Exploded Ideas": Sir John Fisher and Home Defence, 1904–10'. *The International History Review* 36, no. 3 (2014): 550–72. https://doi.org/10.1080/07075332.2013.828645.

Morris, Jan. *Farewell the Trumpets: An Imperial Retreat*. London: Faber, 2012.

———. *Heaven's Command: An Imperial Progress*. London: Faber, 2012.

———. *Pax Britannica: The Climax of an Empire*. London: Faber, 2012.

Morris, R. 'The Royal Naval Hydrographic Service 1795-1995'. *International Hydrographic Review* LXXII, no. 2 (1995): 7–21.

Morris, Roger, ed. *The Foundations of British Maritime Ascendancy: Resources, Logistics and the State, 1755-1815*. Cambridge: Cambridge University Press, 2013.

Mort, Maggie. *Building the Trident Network: A Study of the Enrolment of People, Knowledge, and Machines*. Cambridge: MIT Press, 2002.

Mountz, Alison. 'Political Geography II: Islands and Archipelagos'. *Progress in Human Geography* 39, no. 5 (2015): 636–46. https://doi.org/10.1177/0309132514560958.

Mukherjee, Proshanto K., and Mark Brownrigg. 'Nationality and Registration of Ships: Concept and Practice'. In *Farthing on International Shipping*, 199–222. Berlin: Springer Berlin Heidelberg, 2013. https://doi.org/10.1007/978-3-642-34598-2_11.

Mullins, Robert, and John Beeler. *Transformation of British and American Naval Policy in the Pre-Dreadnought Era*. Basingstoke: Palgrave Macmillan, 2018.

Mullins, Robert E., and John Beeler. 'The Royal Navy and the 1889 Naval Defence Act: History and Historiography'. In *The Transformation of British and American Naval Policy in the Pre-Dreadnought Era*, edited by Robert E. Mullins and John Beeler, 43–81. Cham: Springer International Publishing, 2016. https://doi.org/10.1007/978-3-319-32037-3_3.

Murthy, R. *Andaman and Nicobar Islands: A Saga of Freedom Struggle*. Delhi: Kalpaz Publications, 2011.

Musgrave, Toby. *The Multifarious Mr. Banks: From Botany Bay to Kew, the Natural Historian Who Shaped the World*. New Haven: Yale University Press, 2020.

Naylor, Simon. '"Log Books and the Law of Storms": Maritime Meteorology and the British Admiralty in the Nineteenth Century'. *Isis* 106, no. 4 (2015): 771–97. https://doi.org/10.1086/684641.

Newman, Benjamin. 'Authorising Geographical Knowledge: The Development of Peer Review in The Journal of the Royal Geographical Society, 1830–c.1880'. *Journal of Historical Geography* 64 (2019): 85–97. https://doi.org/10.1016/j.jhg.2019.03.006.

Norrgård, Stefan. 'Royal Navy Logbooks as Secondary Sources and Their Use in Climatic Investigations: Introducing the Log-Board'. *International Journal of Climatology* 37, no. 4 (2017): 2027–36. https://doi.org/10.1002/joc.4832.

Norrie, J. 'Chart of the Andaman and Nicobar Islands, with the Adjacent Continent'. London: Navigation Warehouse and Naval Academy, 1856.

Nunn, Wilfrid. *Tigris Gunboats: The Forgotten War in Iraq 1914 - 1917*. London: Chatham Publications, 2007.

Ó Tuathail, Gearóid. *Critical Geopolitics: The Politics of Writing Global Space*. London: Routledge, 1996.

———. 'The Frustrations of Geopolitics and the Pleasures of War'. In *Cinema and Popular Geopolitics*, edited by Marcus Power and Andrew Crampton. Abingdon: Routledge, 2013.

O'Connell, Callum. '"A Place of Infinite National Importance": The Military Geography of the Andaman Islands, 1777-1796'. Unpublished MA Book, Kings College London, 2018.

O'Connell, Daniel. *The Influence of Law on Sea Power*. Manchester: Manchester University Press, 1975.

O'Hara, Glen. *Britain and the Sea: Since 1600*. Basingstoke: Palgrave Macmillan, 2010.

Ong-Webb, Graham Gerard, ed. *Piracy, Maritime Terrorism and Securing the Malacca Straits*. Singapore: ISEAS Publishing, 2006.

Ong-Webb, Graham Gerard, and Xu Ke, eds. 'Piracy, Seaborne Trade and the Rivalries of Foreign Sea Powers in East and Southeast Asia, 1511 to 1839: A Chinese Perspective'. In *Piracy, Maritime Terrorism and Securing the Malacca Straits*, 221–40. Singapore: ISEAS Publishing, 2006.

Otter, Sandra den. 'Law, Authority, and Colonial Rule'. In *India and the British Empire*, by Douglas Peers and Nandini Gooptu, 168–90, 3rd ed. Oxford: Oxford University Press, 2012.

Paine, Lincoln. *The Sea and Civilization: A Maritime History of the World*. London: Atlantic Books, 2015.

Pandit, Triloki Nath, and Anthropological Survey of India, eds. *Andaman and Nicobar Islands*. Calcutta: Anthropological Survey of India, 1994.

Pandya, Vishvajit. *In the Forest: Visual and Material Worlds of Andamanese History*. Lanham: University Press of America, 2009.

Parker, Katherine. 'London's Geographic Knowledge Network and the Anson Account (1748)'. In *The Global Histories of Books*, edited by Elleke Boehmer, Rouven Kunstmann, Priyasha Mukhopadhyay, and Asha Rogers, 23–46. New Directions in Book History. Cham: Springer International Publishing, 2017. https://doi.org/10.1007/978-3-319-51334-8_2.

———. 'The Savant and the Engineer: Exploration Personnel in the Narbrough and Anson Voyage Accounts'. *Terrae Incognitae* 49, no. 1 (2017): 6–20. https://doi.org/10.1080/00822884.2017.1295594.

Parkinson, Jonathan. *The China Station, Royal Navy: A History as Seen through the Careers of the Commanders in Chief, 1864 - 1941*. Kibworth Beauchamp: Matador, 2018.

Parkinson, Roger. *The Late Victorian Navy: The Pre-Dreadnought Era and the Origins of the First World War*. Woodbridge: Boydell Press, 2008.

Patalano, Alessio. *Maritime Strategy and National Security in Japan and Britain: From the First Alliance to Post-9/11*. Folkestone: Global Oriental, 2012.

———. *Post-War Japan as a Sea Power: Imperial Legacy, Wartime Experience and the Making of a Navy*. London: Bloomsbury Academic, 2016.

Paterson, Lawrence. *Hitler's Gray Wolves: U-Boats in the Indian Ocean*. New York: Carrel Books, 2017.

Patki, Ashutosh. 'The Andaman and Nicobar Islands: New Delhi's Bulwark in the Indian Ocean', 2021. https://thediplomat.com/2021/12/the-andaman-and-nicobar-islands-new-delhis-bulwark-in-the-indian-ocean/.

Paton, George. *The 24th Regiment of Foot: From the War of Spanish Succession to the Zulu War*. Lanarkshire: Leonaur, 2017.

Pearce, Cathryn. *Cornish Wrecking, 1700-1860: Reality and Popular Myth*. Woodbridge: Boydell Press, 2010.

———. 'Gallant Officers and Benevolent Men: Royal Navy Officers, Voluntarism and the Launch of the Shipwrecked Mariners Society in the Early Victorian Era'. *The Mariner's Mirror* 110, no. 1 (2024): 5–21. https://doi.org/10.1080/00253359.2024.2291949.

———. 'What Do You Do with a Shipwrecked Sailor? Extreme Weather, Shipwreck, and Civic Responsibility in Nineteenth-Century Liverpool'. *Victorian Review* 47, no. 1 (2021): 19–24. https://doi.org/10.1353/vcr.2021.0007.

Pearson, Michael. *The Indian Ocean*. London: Routledge, 2003.

Peers, Douglas M., and Nandini Gooptu, eds. *India and the British Empire*. Oxford: Oxford University Press, 2016.

Peters, Kimberley, Philip E. Steinberg, and Elaine Stratford, eds. *Territory beyond Terra*. London: Rowman & Littlefield International, 2018.

Pietsch, Tamson. 'A British Sea: Making Sense of Global Space in the Late Nineteenth Century'. *Journal of Global History* 5, no. 3 (2010): 423–46. https://doi.org/10.1017/S1740022810000215.

Po, Ronald. *The Blue Frontier: Maritime Vision and Power in the Qing Empire*. Cambridge: Cambridge University Press, 2018.

———. 'Mapping Maritime Power and Control: A Study of the Late Eighteenth Century Qisheng Yanhai Tu (A Coastal Map of the Seven Provinces)'. *Late Imperial China* 37, no. 2 (2016): 93–136. https://doi.org/10.1353/late.2016.0012.

———. 'Tea, Porcelain, and Silk: Chinese Exports to the West in the Early Modern Period'. In *Oxford Research Encyclopaedia of Asian History*, by Ronald C. Po. Oxford: Oxford University Press, 2018. https://doi.org/10.1093/acrefore/9780190277727.013.156.

Policante, Amedeo. *The Pirate Myth: Genealogies of an Imperial Concept*. Abingdon: Routledge, 2015.

Polo, Marco, and Ralph Latham. *The Travels of Marco Polo*. Harmondsworth: Penguin, 1978.

Ponce, R. 'Multidimensional Marine Data: The next Frontier for Hydrographic Offices'. *The International Hydrographic Review* 22 (2019). https://ihr.iho.int/articles/multidimensional-marine-data-the-next-frontier-for-hydrographic-offices/.

Porter, Bernard. *The Absent-Minded Imperialists: Empire, Society, and Culture in Britain*. Oxford: Oxford University Press, 2007.

Prange, Sebastian. 'Scholars and the Sea: A Historiography of the Indian Ocean'. *History Compass* 6, no. 5 (2008): 1382–93. https://doi.org/10.1111/j.1478-0542.2008.00538.x.

Pratt, Mary Louise. *Imperial Eyes: Travel Writing and Transculturation*. London: Routledge, 1992.

Preston, Antony, and Preston Major. *Send a Gun Boat! A Study of the British Gunboat*. London: Conway, 2007.

Presutti, Kelly. '"A Better Idea than the Best Constructed Charts": Watercolor Views in Early British Hydrography'. *Grey Room*, no. 85 (2021): 70–99. https://doi.org/10.1162/grey_a_00333.

Prince, Stephen. 'The Post-Imperial Relationship with the Royal Navy: On the Beach?' *Canadian Military History* 23, no. 4 (2014): 296–310.

Pugh, Jonathan. 'Island Movements: Thinking with the Archipelago'. *Island Studies Journal* 8, no. 1 (2013): 9–24.

———. 'Relationality and Island Studies in the Anthropocene'. *Island Studies Journal* 13, no. 2 (2018): 93–110. https://doi.org/10.24043/isj.48.

———. 'The Relational Turn in Island Geographies: Bringing Together Island, Sea and Ship Relations and the Case of the Landship'. *Social & Cultural Geography* 17, no. 8 (2016): 1040–59. https://doi.org/10.1080/14649365.2016.1147064.

Ranft, Bryan, ed. *Technical Change and British Naval Policy, 1860-1939*. London: Hodder and Stoughton, 1977.

Rech, Matthew, Daniel Bos, K. Neil Jenkings, Alison Williams, and Rachel Woodward. 'Geography, Military Geography, and Critical Military Studies'. *Critical Military Studies* 1, no. 1 (2015): 47–60. https://doi.org/10.1080/23337486.2014.963416.

Redford, Duncan. 'Indifference to the Navy? Security, Identity and Naval Power 1870–84'. *Historical Research* 92, no. 256 (2019): 386–409. https://doi.org/10.1111/1468-2281.12270.

Reidy, Michael. *The Tides of History*. Chicago: University of Chicago Press, 2008.

Reidy, Michael, and Helen Rozwadowski. 'The Spaces In Between: Science, Ocean, Empire'. *Isis* 105, no. 2 (2014): 338–51. https://doi.org/10.1086/676571.

Reilly, Thomas H. *The Taiping Heavenly Kingdom: Rebellion and the Blasphemy of Empire*. Seattle: University of Washington Press, 2004.

Richmond, Herbert. *Imperial Defence and Capture at Sea in War*. London: Hutchinson, 1932.

Riemann, Malte, and Norma Rossi, eds. *Security Studies: An Applied Introduction*. Thousand Oaks: Sage, 2024.

Rigby, Nigel, Pieter van der Merwe, and Glyndwr Williams. *Pacific Exploration: Voyages of Discovery from Captain Cook's Endeavour to the Beagle*. London: Bloomsbury Publishing, 2018.

Ritchie, G. S. *The Admiralty Chart: British Naval Hydrography in the Nineteenth Century*. Edinburgh: Pentland Press, 1995.

Rodger, N.A.M. *A Naval History of Britain. 660-1649,*. London: Harper Collins, 1997.

———. *The Admiralty*. Lavenham: T. Dalton, 1979.

———. *The Command of the Ocean: 1649 - 1815*. 2. London: Allen Lane, 2004.

———. *The Wooden World: An Anatomy of the Georgian Navy*. Annapolis: Naval Institute Press, 1986.

Ronzitti, Natalino, ed. *The Law of Naval Warfare: A Collection of Agreements and Documents with Commentaries*. Boston: Kluwer Academic Publishers, 1988.

Roskill, Stephen. *The Navy at War 1939-1945*. Herts: Wordsworth Editions Ltd., 1998.

———. *The Strategy of Sea Power*. London: Collins, 1962.

———. *The Period of Reluctant Rearmament 1930-1939*. Barnsley: Seaforth Publishing, 2016.

Roskill, Stephen, and Correlli Barnett. *The Period of Anglo-American Antagonism 1919-1929*. Barnsley: Seaforth Publishing, 2016.

Rowlands, Kevin. 'Riverine Warfare'. *Naval War College Review* 71, no. 1 (2018): 53–70.

Roy, Kaushik. 'The Hybrid Military Establishment of the East India Company in South Asia: 1750–1849'. *Journal of Global History* 6, no. 2 (2011): 195–218. https://doi.org/10.1017/S1740022811000222.

Roy, P, and N Aspi Cawasji. *Strategic Vision-2030: Security and Development of Andaman & Nicobar Islands*. New Delhi: Vij Books India Pvt Ltd, 2017.

Rüger, Jan. *Heligoland: Britain, Germany, and the Struggle for the North Sea*. Oxford: Oxford University Press, 2017.

Ryan, Simon. *The Cartographic Eye: How Explorers Saw Australia*. Cambridge: Cambridge University Press, 1996.

Said, Edward. *Orientalism*. 1st ed. New York: Pantheon Books, 1978.

———. *Orientalism*. London: Penguin, 2003.

Saini, Ajay. 'How a Bloody Incident of Piracy Changed the Lives of the Nicobarese Forever'. *The Hindu*, 2018. https://www.thehindu.com/society/how-a-bloody-incident-of-piracy-changed-the-lives-of-the-nicobarese-forever/article22375511.ece.

Sanghera, Sathnam. *Empireland: How Imperialism Has Shaped Modern Britain*. London: Viking, 2021.

———. *Empireworld: How British Imperialism Has Shaped the Globe*. London: Viking, 2024.

Schaffer, Simon. 'Easily Cracked: Scientific Instruments in States of Disrepair'. *Isis* 102, no. 4 (2011): 706–17. https://doi.org/10.1086/663608.

———. 'The Bombay Case: Astronomers, Instrument Makers and the East India Company'. *Journal for the History of Astronomy* 43, no. 2 (2012): 151–80. https://doi.org/10.1177/002182861204300202.

Schlee, Susan. *A History of Oceanography: The Edge of an Unfamiliar World*. 2nd ed. Marlborough: The Crowford Press, 1975.

Schurman, D. M., and John F. Beeler. *Imperial Defence, 1868-1887*. London: Frank Cass, 2000.

Sekhsaria, Pankaj. *Islands in Flux: The Andaman and Nicobar Story*. Uttar Pradesh: Harper/Litmus, 2017.

Semmel, Bernard. *Liberalism and Naval Strategy: Ideology, Interest, and Sea Power During the Pax Britannica*. Boston: Allen & Unwin, 1986.

Sen, Satadru. 'On the Beach in the Andaman Islands: Post-Mortem of a Failed Colony'. *Economic and Political Weekly* 46, no. 26/27 (2011): 177–86.

———. 'Savage Bodies, Civilized Pleasures: M. V. Portman and the Andamanese'. *American Ethnologist* 36, no. 2 (2009): 364–79.

———. *Savagery and Colonialism in the Indian Ocean: Power, Pleasure and the Andaman Islanders*. London: Routledge, 2010.

Sen, Uditi. 'Developing "Terra Nullius": Colonialism, Nationalism, and Indigeneity in the Andaman Islands'. *Comparative Studies in Society and History* 59, no. 4 (2017): 944–73. https://doi.org/10.1017/S0010417517000330.

Sexton, Jay. 'The British Empire after A.G. Hopkins's "American Empire"'. *The Journal of Imperial and Commonwealth History* 49, no. 3 (2021): 459–80. https://doi.org/10.1080/03086534.2021.1920808.

Shapin, Steven. *A Social History of Truth*. Chicago: University of Chicago Press, 1994.

———. 'The House of Experiment in Seventeenth-Century England'. *Isis* 79, no. 3 (1988): 373–404. https://doi.org/10.1086/354773.

Shellam, Tiffany, Maria Nugent, Shino Konishi, and Allison Cadzow, eds. *Brokers and Boundaries: Colonial Exploration in Indigenous Territory*. Acton: Australian National University Press, 2016.

Shivram, Shakuntala. *Andamans: A Journey Through History*. Translated by Jayant Dasgupta. New Delhi: Confluence International, 2019.

Singh, Vipul. 'Cyclones, Shipwrecks and Environmental Anxiety: British Rule and Ecological Change in the Andaman Islands, 1780s To 1900s'. *Global Environment* 13, no. 1 (2020): 165–93. https://doi.org/10.3197/ge.2020.130106.

Sircar, Pronub. *History of the Andaman Islands: Unsung Heroes and Untold Stories*. New Delhi: Notion Press, 2021.

Sivasundaram, Sujit. 'The Indian Ocean'. In *Oceanic Histories*, edited by David Armitage, Alison Bashford, and Sujit Sivasundaram, 31–61. Cambridge: Cambridge University Press, 2017. https://doi.org/10.1017/9781108399722.002.

———. *Waves across the South: A New History of Revolution and Empire*. London: William Collins, 2020.

Skurnik, Johanna. 'Authorizing Geographical Knowledge: John Arrowsmith, Mapmaking and the Mid Nineteenth-Century British Empire'. *Journal of Historical Geography* 69 (2020): 18–31. https://doi.org/10.1016/j.jhg.2020.04.003.

Smith, Jeff. 'Andaman And Nicobar Islands: India's Strategic Outpost'. *The Diplomat*, 2014. https://www.afpc.org/publications/articles/andaman-and-nicobar-islands-indias-strategic-outpost.

Solari, Amara. 'The Relación Geográfica Map of Tabasco: Hybrid Cartography and Integrative Knowledge Systems in Sixteenth-Century New Spain'. *Terrae Incognitae* 41, no. 1 (2009): 38–58. https://doi.org/10.1179/tin.2009.41.1.38.

Sondhaus, Lawrence. *Naval Warfare, 1815-1914*. London: Routledge, 2001.

Sorrenson, Richard. 'Did the Royal Society Matter in the Eighteenth Century?' *The British Journal for the History of Science* 32 (1999).

———. 'The Ship as a Scientific Instrument in the Eighteenth Century'. *Osiris* 11 (1996): 221–36. https://doi.org/10.1086/368761.

Speller, Ian, ed. *The Royal Navy and Maritime Power in the Twentieth Century*. London: Frank Cass, 2005.

———. *Understanding Naval Warfare*. 2nd ed. London: Routledge, 2019.

Spence, Daniel Owen. *A History of the Royal Navy: Empire and Imperialism*. London: I.B. Tauris, 2015.

Stafford, Jonathan. 'A Sea View: Perceptions of Maritime Space and Landscape in Accounts of Nineteenth-Century Colonial Steamship Travel'. *Journal of Historical Geography* 55 (2017): 69–81. https://doi.org/10.1016/j.jhg.2016.09.006.

Steinberg, Philip. *The Social Construction of the Ocean*. Cambridge: Cambridge University Press, 2001.

———. 'Of Other Seas: Metaphors and Materialities in Maritime Regions'. *Atlantic Studies* 10, no. 2 (2013): 156–69. https://doi.org/10.1080/14788810.2013.785192.

Stephenson, Charles. *The Eastern Fleet and the Indian Ocean, 1942-1944: The Fleet That Had to Hide*. Barnsley: Pen & Sword Military, 2020.

Stern, Philip J. *Empire, Incorporated: The Corporations That Built British Colonialism*. Cambridge: The Belknap Press of Harvard University Press, 2023.

Stewart, Larry. 'Other Centres of Calculation, or, Where the Royal Society Didn't Count: Commerce, Coffee-Houses and Natural Philosophy in Early Modern London'. *The British Journal for the History of Science* 32, no. 2 (1999): 133–53.

Stow, Randolph. 'Denmark in the Indian Ocean, 1616-1845 An Introduction'. *Kunapipi* 1, no. 1 (1979): 11–26.

Subramanian, Lakshmi. *The Sovereign and the Pirate: Ordering Maritime Subjects in India's Western Littoral*. New Delhi: Oxford University Press, 2016.

Sumida, Jon Tetsuro. *In Defence of Naval Supremacy: Finance, Technology, and British Naval Policy 1889-1914*. Annapolis: Naval Institute Press, 2014.

Tarling, Nicholas. *Imperial Britain in South-East Asia*. Kuala Lumpur: Oxford University Press, 1975.

———. *Piracy and Politics in the Malay World*. Canberra: F.W. Cheshire Pty Ltd, 1963.

Taylor, Jeremy, and David Baillargeon, eds. *Spatial Histories of Occupation: Colonialism, Conquest and Foreign Control in Asia*. London: Bloomsbury Academic, 2022.

Taylor, Miles, ed. *The Victorian Empire and Britain's Maritime World, 1837-1901: The Sea and Global History*. Basingstoke: Palgrave Macmillan, 2013.

The Indian Express. 'PM Modi Names 21 Andaman Islands after Param Vir Chakra Recipients'. *The Indian Express*, 2023. https://indianexpress.com/article/explained/pm-modi-names-21-andaman-islands-after-param-vir-chakra-recipients-8399814/.

Thomas, David Arthur. *Japan's War at Sea: Pearl Harbor to the Coral Sea*. London: Andre Deutsch, 1978.

Thomas, Martin. *Expedition into Empire: Exploratory Journeys and the Making of the Modern World*. Basingstoke: Routledge, 2019.

Till, Geoffrey. *How to Grow a Navy: The Development of Maritime Power*. London: Routledge, 2022. https://doi.org/10.4324/9781003100553.

———. *Seapower: A Guide for the Twenty-First Century*. 2nd ed. London: Routledge, 2009.

———, ed. *Seapower: Theory and Practice*. London: F. Cass, 1994.

———. *Understanding Victory: Naval Operations from Trafalgar to the Falklands*. Santa Barbara: Praeger, 2014.

Tracy, Nicholas, ed. *The Collective Naval Defence of the Empire, 1900-1940*. Aldershot: Ashgate for the Navy Records Society, 1997.

Urry, John. 'Making Space for Space'. *Economy and Society* 15, no. 2 (1986): 273–80. https://doi.org/10.1080/03085148600000011.

———. 'Mobility and Proximity'. *Sociology* 36, no. 2 (2002): 255–74.

Vaidik, Aparna. *Imperial Andamans: Colonial Encounter and Island History*. Basingstoke: Palgrave Macmillan, 2010.

Wagner Bozzolo, Nikolas. 'Voices from the Periphery: A Critique of Postcolonial Theories and Development Practice'. *Third World Quarterly* 43, no. 7 (2022): 1765–82. https://doi.org/10.1080/01436597.2022.2067039.

Walshe, Rory A. '"Who Could Have Expected Such a Disaster?" How Responses to the 1892 Cyclone Determined Institutional Trajectories of Vulnerability in Mauritius'. *Journal of Historical Geography* 75 (2022): 55–64. https://doi.org/10.1016/j.jhg.2021.11.002.

Waring, Sophie. 'The Board of Longitude and the Funding of Scientific Work: Negotiating Authority and Expertise in the Early Nineteenth Century'. *Journal for Maritime Research* 16, no. 1 (2014): 55–71. https://doi.org/10.1080/21533369.2014.906143.

Webb, Adrian. 'More than Just Charts: Hydrographic Expertise within the Admiralty, 1795–1829'. *Journal for Maritime Research* 16, no. 1 (2014): 43–54. https://doi.org/10.1080/21533369.2014.906178.

Wess, Jane, and Charles Withers. 'Instrument Provision and Geographical Science: The Work of the Royal Geographical Society, 1830- ca 1930'. *Notes and Records of the Royal Society of London* 73, no. 2 (2019): 223–41. https://doi.org/10.1098/rsnr.2018.0034.

White, Colin. 'The Long Arm of Seapower: The Anglo-Japanese War of 1863-1864'. In *Seapower Ashore: 200 Years of Royal Navy Operations on Land*, edited by Peter Hore, 146–80. London: Chatham Publishing, 2000.

Williams, Alison J. 'Aircraft Carriers and the Capacity to Mobilise US Power across the Pacific, 1919–1929'. *Journal of Historical Geography* 58 (2017): 71–81. https://doi.org/10.1016/j.jhg.2017.07.008.

Williams, Glyndwr. *Naturalists at Sea: Scientific Travellers from Dampier to Darwin*. New Haven: Yale University Press, 2015.

Williamson, Fiona. 'Weathering the Empire: Meteorological Research in the Early British Straits Settlements'. *The British Journal for the History of Science* 48, no. 178 (2015): 475.

Wilson, Ben. *Empire of the Deep: The Rise and Fall of the British Navy*. London: Phoenix, 2013.

Wilson, Michael. *A Submariners' War: The Indian Ocean 1939-45*. Stroud: Spellmount Ltd., 2000.

Winter, Cameron. 'War-Canoes and Poisoned Arrows: Great Jolof and Imperial Mali Against the Fifteenth Century Portuguese Slave Raids'. *Journal of African Military History*, 2023, 1–31. https://doi.org/10.1163/24680966-bja10016.

Wintle, Claire. *Colonial Collecting and Display: Encounters with Material Culture from the Andaman and Nicobar Islands*. New York: Berghahn Books, 2013.

Withers, Charles. 'Place and the "Spatial Turn" in Geography and in History'. *Journal of the History of Ideas* 70, no. 4 (2009): 637–58. https://doi.org/10.1353/jhi.0.0054.

———. *Placing the Enlightenment: Thinking Geographically about the Age of Reason*. Chicago: University of Chicago Press, 2007. http://gateway.proquest.com/openurl?ctx_ver=Z39.88-2003&xri:pqil:res_ver=0.2&res_id=xri:ilcs-us&rft_id=xri:ilcs:rec:abell:R04006140.

Withers, Charles W J, and Innes M Keighren. 'Travels into Print: Authoring, Editing and Narratives of Travel and Exploration, c.1815-c.1857: Travels into Print'. *Transactions of the Institute of British Geographers* 36, no. 4 (2011): 560–73. https://doi.org/10.1111/j.1475-5661.2011.00437.x.

Woodward, Rachel. 'From Military Geography to Militarism's Geographies: Disciplinary Engagements with the Geographies of Militarism and Military Activities'. *Progress in Human Geography* 29, no. 6 (2005): 718–40.

Ziegler, Garrett. 'The Perils of Empire: Dickens, Collins and the Indian Mutiny'. In *Pirates and Mutineers of the Nineteenth Century: Swashbucklers and Swindlers*, edited by Grace Moore, 150–66. London: Routledge, 2016.

NOTES

1. This narrative is based on contemporary accounts of the flag-raising ceremony in: Maurice Vidal Portman, *A History of Our Relations with the Andamanese, Vol.I* (Calcutta: Office of the Superintendent of Government Printing, 1899), 248–53.

2. P Cain and A Hopkins, *British Imperialism: 1688-2015*, 3rd ed. (New York: Routledge, 2015).

3. 'Secret Letter and Enclosures, Feb 1858' (India Office Records, 1858), L PS 6 461, British Library.

4. P. C. Bandopadhyay and A. Carter, 'Introduction to the Geography and Geomorphology of the Andaman–Nicobar Islands', *Geological Society, London, Memoirs* 47, no. 1 (2017): 9–18, https://doi.org/10.1144/M47.2.

5. Jayant Dasgupta, *Japanese in Andaman and Nicobar Islands: Red Sun Over Black Water* (New Delhi: Manas Publications, 2002).

6. Julia Lovell, *The Opium War: Drugs, Dreams and the Making of China* (London: Picador, 2012).

7. Satadru Sen, *Savagery and Colonialism in the Indian Ocean: Power, Pleasure and the Andaman Islanders* (London: Routledge, 2010).

8. D. M. Schurman and John F. Beeler, *Imperial Defence, 1868-1887* (London: Frank Cass, 2000), 24–26.

9. Alfred Thayer Mahan, *Influence of Sea Power Upon History, 1660-1783* (Great Britain: Pantianos Classics, 1890); Julian Stafford Corbett, *Some Principles of Maritime Strategy* (Annapolis: Naval Institute Press, 1988).

10. Seapower encompasses not only the military and commercial control of the seas but also the broader social, cultural, and political influence exerted by maritime nations, while sea power is more narrowly focused on naval strength and maritime commerce. Geoffrey Till, *Seapower: A Guide for the Twenty-First Century*, 2nd ed. (London: Routledge, 2009).

11. Andrew Lambert, *Seapower States: Maritime Culture, Continental Empires and the Conflict That Made the Modern World* (New Haven: Yale University Press, 2018), 266.

12. Andrew Lambert, 'Looking to the Sea - The "Art of Admiralty", and the Maintenance of Naval Power', in *Maritime Britain in the 21st Century*, ed. Katie Jamieson, Kevin Rowlands, and Andrew Young (Dartmouth: Britannia Publishing, 2024), 53–61.

13. Lambert, *Seapower States: Maritime Culture, Continental Empires and the Conflict That Made the Modern World*.

14. Eric Grove, *The Future of Sea Power* (Annapolis: Naval Institute Press, 1990).

15. Ken Booth, *Navies and Foreign Policy* (Abingdon: Routledge, 2015).

16. Basil Germond, *Seapower in the Post-Modern World* (Montreal: McGill-Queen's University Press, 2024), 13–30.

17. Michel Foucault, *Discipline and Punish: The Birth of the Prison* (New York: Pantheon Books, 1977).

18. Barbara Adam, *Theorizing Culture: An Interdisciplinary Critique After Postmodernism* (New York: Routledge, 2019); Nikolas Wagner Bozzolo, 'Voices from the Periphery: A Critique of Postcolonial Theories and Development Practice', *Third World Quarterly* 43, no. 7 (2022): 1765–82, https://doi.org/10.1080/01436597.2022.2067039; Jake Rom Cadag, 'Problems and Promises of Postmodernism in (Re)Liberating Disaster Studies', *Disaster Prevention and Management: An International Journal* 33, no. 3 (2024): 167–80, https://doi.org/10.1108/DPM-06-2023-0153.

19. Basil Germond, *Seapower in the Post-Modern World* (Montreal: McGill-Queen's University Press, 2024), 54.

20. David Armitage, Alison Bashford, and Sujit Sivasundaram, *Oceanic Histories* (Cambridge: University of Cambridge Press, 2017), https://doi.org/10.1017/9781108399722.

21. While littoral and coastal spaces are similar in meaning, this thesis will use littoral. It is the area of land from which activity at sea can influenced. This is a common definition used within seapower studies, see: Geoffrey Till, *Seapower: A Guide for the Twenty-First Century*, 2nd ed. (London: Routledge, 2009).

22. Sociocultural refers to the interplay of social and cultural factors that shape human behaviour, identity, and institutions. According to Bruno Latour, these are always in flux and negotiated. This is a vast field, so this thesis does not engage with the philosophical debates behind this term but instead uses Latour's definition to align with ANT. Bruno Latour, *Science in Action: How to Follow Scientists and Engineers Through Society* (Cambridge: Harvard University Press, 1988), 62.

23. Arthur Conan Doyle, *The Sign of Four* (London: Penguin, 2001), 30.

24. Postcolonial treats the Andaman Islands as deeply intertwined with the penal colony set up in 1858: Satadru Sen, 'Savage Bodies, Civilized Pleasures: M. V. Portman and the Andamanese', *American Ethnologist* 36, no. 2 (2009): 364–79; Sen, *Savagery and Colonialism in the Indian Ocean: Power, Pleasure and the Andaman Islanders*; Clare Anderson, 'Colonization, Kidnap and Confinement in the Andamans Penal Colony, 1771–1864', *Journal of Historical Geography* 37, no. 1 (2011): 68–81, https://doi.org/10.1016/j.jhg.2010.07.001; Clare Anderson, *The Indian Uprising of 1857-8: Prisons, Prisoners, and Rebellion* (London: Anthem Press, 2007); R Murthy, *Andaman and Nicobar Islands: A Saga of Freedom Struggle* (Delhi: Kalpaz Publications, 2011); Pronub Sircar, *History of the Andaman Islands: Unsung Heroes and Untold Stories.* (New Delhi: Notion Press,

Notes

2021); Aparna Vaidik, *Imperial Andamans: Colonial Encounter and Island History*. (Basingstoke: Palgrave Macmillan, 2010).

25. Many islands within the Andaman and Nicobar chain have recently been renamed after Indian nationalist figures: The Indian Express, 'PM Modi Names 21 Andaman Islands after Param Vir Chakra Recipients', *The Indian Express*, 2023, https://indianexpress.com/article/explained/pm-modi-names-21-andaman-islands-after-param-vir-chakra-recipients-8399814/; Shishir Gupta, 'Why Are Andaman and Nicobar Islands a Key Indian Military Asset?', *The Hindustan Times*, 2023, https://www.hindustantimes.com/india-news/why-are-andaman-and-nicobar-islands-a-key-indian-military-asset-101674528554860.html.

26. Jeff Smith, 'Andaman And Nicobar Islands: India's Strategic Outpost', *The Diplomat*, 2014, https://www.afpc.org/publications/articles/andaman-and-nicobar-islands-indias-strategic-outpost; P Roy and N Aspi Cawasji, *Strategic Vision-2030: Security and Development of Andaman & Nicobar Islands* (New Delhi: Vij Books India Pvt Ltd, 2017).

27. David Christie, *India's Naval Strategy and the Role of the Andaman and Nicobar Islands*, 291 (Canberra: Australian National University Press, 1995); Itty Abraham, 'India's Unsinkable Aircraft Carrier', *Economic and Political Weekly* 50, no. 39 (2015): 10–13; Gupta, 'Why Are Andaman and Nicobar Islands a Key Indian Military Asset?'

28. Callum O'Connell, '"A Place of Infinite National Importance": The Military Geography of the Andaman Islands, 1777-1796' (Unpublished MA Thesis, London, Kings College London, 2018).

29. Herbert Richmond, *Imperial Defence and Capture at Sea in War* (London: Hutchinson, 1932).

30. Mahan, *Influence of Sea Power Upon History, 1660-1783*.

31. Stephen Roskill, *The Strategy of Sea Power* (London: Collins, 1962); Till, *Seapower: A Guide for the Twenty-First Century*.

Chapter 1

32. Michael describes 'messy' as antipodal to the want to find structure and order by historians. Mike Michael, *Actor-Network Theory: Trials, Trails and Translations* (1 Oliver's Yard, 55 City Road London EC1Y 1SP: SAGE, 2017), 58, https://doi.org/10.4135/9781473983045.

33. 'Despatches to India and Bengal Oct 1856' (India Office Records, 1856), E 4 839, British Library.

34. This narrative is based on the meeting record and secondary accounts of Fort William. 'Despatches to India and Bengal Oct 1856'; Dalrymple, *The Anarchy: The Relentless Rise of the East India Company*.

35. Morris, *Pax Britannica: The Climax of an Empire*.

36. Matzke, *Deterrence through Strength: British Naval Power and Foreign Policy under Pax Britannica*; Spence, *A History of the Royal Navy: Empire and Imperialism*.

37. Semmel, *Liberalism and Naval Strategy: Ideology, Interest, and Sea Power During the Pax Britannica*; Parkinson, *The Late Victorian Navy: The Pre-Dreadnought Era and the Origins of the First World War*, 243–44.

38. Cannadine, *Empire, the Sea and Global History: Britain's Maritime World, c. 1760-c. 1840*; Edward A. Alpers, *The Indian Ocean in World History* (Oxford: Oxford University Press, 2014).

39. Ó Tuathail, *Critical Geopolitics: The Politics of Writing Global Space*; Dittmer, 'Captain America's Empire: Reflections on Identity, Popular Culture, and Post-9/11 Geopolitics'.

40. Both colonial officials and contemporary literature has seen the Bay of Bengal as a British space, with a 'British Sea' being the most commonly used phrase. 'Despatches to India and Bengal Oct 1856'; Tamson Pietsch, 'A British Sea: Making Sense of Global Space in the Late Nineteenth Century', *Journal of Global History* 5, no. 3 (2010): 423–46, https://doi.org/10.1017/S1740022810000215; Alpers, 'On Becoming a British Lake: Piracy, Slaving, and British Imperialism in the Indian Ocean during the First Half of the Nineteenth Century'; Grainger, *The British Navy in Eastern Waters: The Indian and Pacific Oceans*.

41. Gough, *Pax Britannica: Ruling the Waves and Keeping the Peace before Armageddon*, 117–19; Grainger, *The British Navy in Eastern Waters: The Indian and Pacific Oceans*, 252–53.

42. Lovell, *The Opium War: Drugs, Dreams and the Making of China*; Darwin, *Unfinished Empire: The Global Expansion of Britain*, 132–33; Metcalf, *Imperial Connections: India in the Indian Ocean Arena, 1860 - 1920*.

43. David, *Victoria's Wars: The Rise of Empire*, 158–59.

44. Cain and Hopkins, *British Imperialism: 1688-2015*, 394–95.

45. McPherson, *The Indian Ocean: A History of People and the Sea*; Metcalf, *Imperial Connections: India in the Indian Ocean Arena, 1860 - 1920*; Prange, 'Scholars and the Sea'; Alpers, 'On Becoming a British Lake: Piracy, Slaving, and British Imperialism in the Indian Ocean during the First Half of the Nineteenth Century'.

46. Dittmer, 'Captain America's Empire: Reflections on Identity, Popular Culture, and Post-9/11 Geopolitics'; Dodds, 'Popular Geopolitics and Audience Dispositions: James Bond and the Internet Movie Database (IMDb)'; Ó Tuathail, 'The Frustrations of Geopolitics and the Pleasures of War'; Dalby, *Anthropocene Geopolitics: Globalization, Security, Sustainability*.

47. Corbett, *Some Principles of Maritime Strategy*; Corbett, *21st Century Corbett: Maritime Strategy and Naval Policy for the Modern Era*; Lambert, *The British Way of War: Julian Corbett and the Battle for a National Strategy*.

48. Although Corbett's work since publication has come under frequent critique, this has been focused on whether the principles are valuable to understanding the role of navies. This chapter instead uses 'critique' to refer to an epistemological challenge. For a history of previous challenges of Corbett's work, see: Andrew Lambert, *The British Way of War: Julian Corbett and the Battle for a National Strategy* (New Haven: Yale University Press, 2021); Kevin D. McCranie, *Mahan, Corbett, and the Foundations of Naval Strategic Thought* (Annapolis: Naval Institute Press, 2021).as a lawyer, civilian, and Liberal, Julian Corbett (1854-1922

49. The John Charles Mason Collection is in the John Rylands Research Institute and Library, Manchester. 'Papers Relating to the Transport of Troops and Stores' (John Charles Mason Collection of East India Company Papers, 1857), MS155, John Rylands Research Institute and Library; 'Her Majesty's Indian Navy List, July 6th 1859' (John

Notes

Charles Mason Collection of East India Company Papers, 1859), MS158, John Rylands Research Institute and Library; 'Miscellaneous Papers Relating to the Creation of Marine Department 1859' (John Charles Mason Collection of East India Company Papers, 1859), MS154, John Rylands Research Institute and Library; 'Miscellaneous Papers Naval and Maritime Services in India 1860-1862' (John Charles Mason Collection of East India Company Papers, 1862), MS154, John Rylands Research Institute and Library; 'Military Forces in India' (John Charles Mason Collection of East India Company Papers, 1863), MS144, John Rylands Research Institute and Library; 'Papers Relating to Bengal Pilot Service 1869-1871' (John Charles Mason Collection of East India Company Papers, 1871), MS143, John Rylands Research Institute and Library.

50. Portman, *A History of Our Relations with the Andamanese, Vol.I*, 56.

51. O'Connell, '"A Place of Infinite National Importance": The Military Geography of the Andaman Islands, 1777-1796'.

52. Lord Charles Cornwallis, 'Letters to Admiral William Cornwallis, 27 June 1789' (Cornwallis Letters and Papers, 1789), COR/58, National Maritime Museum, Greenwich.

53. Randolph Stow, 'Denmark in the Indian Ocean, 1616-1845 An Introduction', *Kunapipi* 1, no. 1 (1979): 20; See also for a historical perspective: Rev. C. I. Latrobe, 'Letters on the Nicobar Islands, Their Natural Productions, and the Manner, Customs, and Superstitions of the Natives; With an Account of an Attempt Made by the Church of United Brethren to Convert Them To Christianity' (Pamphlets and Manuscripts, 1812), P 62 1, Naval Historical Branch.

54. Mouat, *Adventures and Researches Among The Andaman Islanders*, 19; William Cornwallis, '1790 June. Andamans; to Lord Hood.' (Cornwallis Letters and Papers, 1790), COR 100 3 1, National Maritime Museum, Greenwich; William Cornwallis, '1791 Andaman Islands. Cornwallis to His Brother.' (Cornwallis Letters and Papers, 1791), COR 100 3 1, National Maritime Museum, Greenwich.

55. Vaidik, *Imperial Andamans: Colonial Encounter and Island History.*, 38.

56. 'Letter from A. Kyd to Governor General In Council, 02 August 1795' (India Office Records, 1795), G 34 1, British Library.

57. 'Report of Capt. Kyd, 20 August 1795' (India Office Records, 1795), G 34 1, British Library.

58. Mathur, *History of the Andaman and Nicobar Islands (1756-1966)*, 50.

59. See the UKHO Miscellaneous Papers (Remarks Books) for 1820-1840, reference Andaman Islands.

60. Joseph Moore, *The Harbour of Port Cornwallis. Island of Great Andaman With the Fleet Getting Under Weigh for Rangoon.*, 1824, Watercolour on Paper, 1824, British Library.

61. A. Achbari, 'Building Networks for Science: Conflict and Cooperation in Nineteenth-Century Global Marine Studies', *Isis* 106, no. 2 (2015): 257–82, https://doi.org/10.1086/682020.

62. Killingray, Lincoln, and Rigby, *Maritime Empires: British Imperial Maritime Trade in the Nineteenth Century*.

63. Alan Frost, *The Global Reach of Empire: Britain's Maritime Expansion in the Indian and Pacific Oceans, 1764-1815* (Carlton: Miegunyah Press, 2003).

64. Lovell, *The Opium War: Drugs, Dreams and the Making of China*; Robert A. Bickers and Jonathan J. Howlett, eds., *Britain and China, 1840-1970: Empire, Finance and War* (London: Routledge, 2017).

65. Gommans, 'Trade and Civilization around the Bay of Bengal, c. 1650–1800'; Alpers, 'On Becoming a British Lake: Piracy, Slaving, and British Imperialism in the Indian Ocean during the First Half of the Nineteenth Century'; Metcalf, *Imperial Connections: India in the Indian Ocean Arena, 1860 - 1920*.

66. Stow, 'Denmark in the Indian Ocean, 1616-1845 An Introduction'; Alpers, *The Indian Ocean in World History*; Wagner Bozzolo, 'Voices from the Periphery'; Abraham, 'The Andamans as a "Sea of Islands": Reconnecting Old Geographies through Poaching'.

67. 'Despatches to India and Bengal Oct 1856'; Pietsch, 'A British Sea'; Alpers, 'On Becoming a British Lake: Piracy, Slaving, and British Imperialism in the Indian Ocean during the First Half of the Nineteenth Century'; Grainger, *The British Navy in Eastern Waters: The Indian and Pacific Oceans*.

68. Po, *The Blue Frontier: Maritime Vision and Power in the Qing Empire*, 17.

69. Lovell, *The Opium War: Drugs, Dreams and the Making of China*, 242.

70. David, *Victoria's Wars: The Rise of Empire*, 168–70; Cain and Hopkins, *British Imperialism: 1688-2015*; Charles Sydney Goldman, ed., *The Empire and the Century: A Series of Essays on Imperial Problems and Possibilities by Various Writers* (London: John Murray, 1905), 740–41.

71. Corbett, *Some Principles of Maritime Strategy*, 16.

72. Mohanan, *The Royal Indian Navy: Trajectories, Transformations and the Transfer of Power*; Grainger, *The British Navy in Eastern Waters: The Indian and Pacific Oceans*.

73. James, *Raj: The Making and Unmaking of British India*, 180.

74. Grainger, *The British Navy in Eastern Waters: The Indian and Pacific Oceans*, 204.

75. Gommans, 'Trade and Civilization around the Bay of Bengal, c. 1650–1800'; Chaudhuri, *Trade and Civilisation in the Indian Ocean: An Economic History from the Rise of Islam to 1750*.

76. Corbett, *Some Principles of Maritime Strategy*, 93.

77. Grainger, *The British Navy in Eastern Waters: The Indian and Pacific Oceans*, 215.

78. Grainger, 182.

79. Wilson, *Empire of the Deep: The Rise and Fall of the British Navy*, 486.

80. Low, *History of the Indian Navy (1613-1863)*; Low.

81. Steinberg, *The Social Construction of the Ocean*.

82. Grainger, *The British Navy in Eastern Waters: The Indian and Pacific Oceans*, 241.

83. Tarling, *Piracy and Politics in the Malay World*, 13–14.

84. Gough, *Pax Britannica: Ruling the Waves and Keeping the Peace before Armageddon*, 118.

85. Fuller, *Empire, Technology and Seapower: Royal Navy Crisis in the Age of Palmerston*, 128.

Notes

86. Cain and Hopkins, 'Gentlemanly Capitalism and British Expansion Overseas II: New Imperialism'.

87. 'Despatches to India and Bengal Oct 1856'; 'General Orders By The Commander In Chief, 24 January 1856' (Military, 1856), National Archives of India; Alpers, 'On Becoming a British Lake: Piracy, Slaving, and British Imperialism in the Indian Ocean during the First Half of the Nineteenth Century'.

88. John Beeler, 'Steam, Strategy and Schurman: Imperial Defence in the Post-Crimean Era, 1856-1905', in *Far-Flung Lines: Essays on Imperial Defence in Honour of Donald Mackenzie Schurman*, ed. Greg Kennedy and Keith Neilson (London: Routledge, 1997), 27.

89. Rodger, *The Admiralty*, 93.

90. Darwin, *Unfinished Empire: The Global Expansion of Britain*.

91. Driver and Martins, *Tropical Visions in an Age of Empire*; David Arnold, '"Illusory Riches": Representations of the Tropical World, 1840-1950', *Singapore Journal of Tropical Geography* 21, no. 1 (2000): 6–18, https://doi.org/10.1111/1467-9493.00060; David Arnold, *The Tropics and the Travelling Gaze: India, Landscape, and Science 1800-1856* (Seattle: University of Washington Press, 2006).

92. Edward Said, *Orientalism*, 1st ed. (New York: Pantheon Books, 1978).

93. Bishara and Wint, 'Into the Bazaar', 48.

94. Derek Gregory, *Geographical Imaginations* (Cambridge: Blackwell, 1998).

95. Spence, *A History of the Royal Navy: Empire and Imperialism*, 45.

96. Frost, *The Global Reach of Empire: Britain's Maritime Expansion in the Indian and Pacific Oceans, 1764-1815*.

97. Jordan Goodman, 'Making Imperial Space: Settlement, Surveying and Trade in Northern Australia in the Nineteenth Century', in *Maritime Empires: British Imperial Maritime Trade in the Nineteenth Century* (Woodbridge: Boydell and Brewer, 2004), http://www.jstor.org/stable/10.7722/j.ctt9qdht8.14.

98. 'Despatches to India and Bengal Oct 1856'.

99. 'Despatches to India and Bengal Oct 1856', 349.

100. Colin Eldridge, *Victorian Imperialism* (London: Hodder & Stoughton, 1978); Frost, *The Global Reach of Empire: Britain's Maritime Expansion in the Indian and Pacific Oceans, 1764-1815*; James Hevia, *The Imperial Security State* (Cambridge: Cambridge University Press, 2012), https://doi.org/10.1017/CBO9781139047296; Darwin, *Unfinished Empire: The Global Expansion of Britain*.

101. 'Melbourne Papers, 15 January 1840' (1840), 859 Box 9. f.43., Royal Archive, Windsor.

102. 'Public Department Collection 26' (India Office Records, 1837), F 4 1766 72 400, British Library; 'Melbourne Papers, 15 January 1840'.

103. 'Public Department Collection 26'.

104. 'Public Department Collection 26', 1.

105. 'Military Forces in India'.

106. 'Despatches to India and Bengal Jan-Mar 1848, Marine' (India Office Records, 1848), E 4 795, British Library.

107. Jordan Branch, '"Colonial Reflection" and Territoriality: The Peripheral Origins of Sovereign Statehood', *European Journal of International Relations* 18, no. 2 (2012): 285, https://doi.org/10.1177/1354066110383997.

108. Hernon, *Britain's Forgotten Wars: Colonial Campaigns of the 19th Century*.

109. Lambert, 'Under the Heel of Britannia. The Bombardment of Sweaborg 9-11 August 1855', 96.

110. Lovell, *The Opium War: Drugs, Dreams and the Making of China*; Song-Chuan Chen, *Merchants of War and Peace* (Hong Kong: Hong Kong University Press, 2017).

111. Sondhaus, *Naval Warfare, 1815-1914*, 65.

112. Chen, *Merchants of War and Peace*.

113. Cain and Hopkins, *British Imperialism: 1688-2015*, 315.

114. Tarling, *Imperial Britain in South-East Asia*, 234.

115. 'Piracy in the Nicobars', 1852, The National Archives.

116. Gough, *Pax Britannica: Ruling the Waves and Keeping the Peace before Armageddon*, 122.

117. Gough, 122; Spence, *A History of the Royal Navy: Empire and Imperialism*, 75.

118. Vaidik, *Imperial Andamans: Colonial Encounter and Island History.*, 48.

119. Abraham, 'The Andamans as a "Sea of Islands": Reconnecting Old Geographies through Poaching', 29; Alpers, *The Indian Ocean in World History*.

120. Sen, 'Developing *Terra Nullius*', 946.

121. Sen, *Savagery and Colonialism in the Indian Ocean: Power, Pleasure and the Andaman Islanders*.

122. Alpers, *The Indian Ocean in World History*.

123. Arnold, '"Illusory Riches": Representations of the Tropical World, 1840-1950', 13.

124. Sen, 'Developing *Terra Nullius*'; Goodman, 'Making Imperial Space: Settlement, Surveying and Trade in Northern Australia in the Nineteenth Century'.

125. Pratt, *Imperial Eyes: Travel Writing and Transculturation*.

126. Arnold, '"Illusory Riches": Representations of the Tropical World, 1840-1950', 8.

127. Mouat, *Adventures and Researches Among The Andaman Islanders*; Portman, *A History of Our Relations with the Andamanese, Vol.I*, 1–20.

128. 'Despatches to India and Bengal Jul-Aug 1855, Marine' (India Office Records, 1855), 1208, E 4 831, British Library.

129. Corbett, *Some Principles of Maritime Strategy*, 94.

130. Grainger, *The British Navy in Eastern Waters: The Indian and Pacific Oceans*.

131. Grainger, 224.

132. Sondhaus, *Naval Warfare, 1815-1914*.

133. Thomas H. Reilly, *The Taiping Heavenly Kingdom: Rebellion and the Blasphemy of Empire* (Seattle: University of Washington Press, 2004).

134. Stephen Nicholas Guy Davies, *Transport to Another World: HMS Tamar and the Sinews of Empire* (Hong Kong: City University of Hong Kong Press, 2022).

135. Grainger, *The British Navy in Eastern Waters: The Indian and Pacific Oceans*, 216.

136. Cain and Hopkins, 'Gentlemanly Capitalism and British Expansion Overseas I The Old Colonial System'; Cain and Hopkins, 'Gentlemanly Capitalism and British Expansion Overseas II: New Imperialism'; Darwin, *Unfinished Empire: The Global Expansion of Britain*; Peers and Gooptu, *India and the British Empire*.

137. This work falls under the 'rise' and 'fall' narrative discussed in detailing the literature review. Kennedy, *The Rise and Fall of British Naval Mastery*; Jackson, *War and Empire in Mauritius and the Indian Ocean*; Jackson, *Distant Drums: The Role of Colonies in British Imperial Warfare*; Wilson, *Empire of the Deep: The Rise and Fall of the British Navy*; Fuller, *Empire, Technology and Seapower: Royal Navy Crisis in the Age of Palmerston*.

138. Kennedy, *The Rise and Fall of British Naval Mastery*, 178.

139. Spence, *A History of the Royal Navy: Empire and Imperialism*, 45–60.

140. Gough, *Pax Britannica: Ruling the Waves and Keeping the Peace before Armageddon*, 129.

141. Schurman and Beeler, *Imperial Defence, 1868-1887*, 1.

142. Gough, *Pax Britannica: Ruling the Waves and Keeping the Peace before Armageddon*, 38.

143. David Lyon and Rif Winfield, *The Sail & Steam Navy List: All the Ships of the Royal Navy, 1815-1889* (London: Chatham, 2004); J J Colledge, Ben Warlow, and Steve Bush, *Ships of the Royal Navy: The Complete Record of All Fighting Ships of the Royal Navy from The15th Century to the Present*, 5th ed. (Barnsley: Seaforth Publishing, 2020).

144. Preston and Major, *Send a Gun Boat! A Study of the British Gunboat*, 17.

145. Tarling, *Piracy and Politics in the Malay World*, 228.

146. Ian J. Barrow, *The East India Company, 1600-1858: A Short History with Documents* (Indianapolis: Hackett Publishing Company, Inc, 2017), 86.

147. Low, *History of the Indian Navy (1613-1863)*; Low; Mohanan, *The Royal Indian Navy: Trajectories, Transformations and the Transfer of Power*.

148. 'Her Majesty's Indian Navy List, July 6th 1859'.

149. 'Her Majesty's Indian Navy List, July 6th 1859'; 'Memorandum on Her Majesty's Indian Navy' (General Reference Collection, 1861), 08806 k.7, British Library.

150. Grainger, *The British Navy in Eastern Waters: The Indian and Pacific Oceans*, 231–32.

151. Grainger, 232.

152. Hastings, *The Royal Indian Navy, 1612-1950*, 22–25.

153. 'Miscellaneous Papers Naval and Maritime Services in India 1860-1862'.

154. Grainger, *The British Navy in Eastern Waters: The Indian and Pacific Oceans*, 231–32.

155. Booth, *Navies and Foreign Policy*.

156. 'Miscellaneous Papers Naval and Maritime Services in India 1860-1862'.

157. John Keay, *The Honourable Company: A History of the English East India Company* (London: Harper Collins, 1993), 442.

158. 'Miscellaneous Papers Relating to the Creation of Marine Department 1859'.

159. 'Miscellaneous Papers Naval and Maritime Services in India 1860-1862'.

160. 'Military Forces in India'.

161. Fuller, *Empire, Technology and Seapower: Royal Navy Crisis in the Age of Palmerston*, 248.

162. Lambert, 'The Royal Navy, 1856-1914: Deterrence and the Strategy of World Power', 72.

163. Grainger, *The British Navy in Eastern Waters: The Indian and Pacific Oceans*.

164. Cook, 'Establishing Sea Routes to India and China: Stages in the Development of Hydrographical Knowledge'.

165. Andrew Lambert's work is one of the only papers which address the role if the East India Company as supporting British seapower through infrastructure: Andrew Lambert, 'Strategy, Policy and Shipbuilding: The Bombay Dockyard, the Indian Navy and Imperial Security in the Eastern Seas, 1784-1869', in *The Worlds of the East India Company*, ed. H. V. Bowen, Margarette Lincoln, and Nigel Rigby (Woodbridge: Boydell & Brewer Ltd, 2002), 137–52.

166. Smith, 'Andaman And Nicobar Islands: India's Strategic Outpost'; Gupta, 'Why Are Andaman and Nicobar Islands a Key Indian Military Asset?'

167. Abraham, 'India's Unsinkable Aircraft Carrier'.

168. Pietsch, 'A British Sea'.

169. Darwin, *Unfinished Empire: The Global Expansion of Britain*.

170. Corbett, *Some Principles of Maritime Strategy*; Corbett, *21st Century Corbett: Maritime Strategy and Naval Policy for the Modern Era*; Lambert, *The British Way of War: Julian Corbett and the Battle for a National Strategy*.

171. 'Despatches to India and Bengal Oct 1856'.

172. Dittmer, 'Captain America's Empire: Reflections on Identity, Popular Culture, and Post-9/11 Geopolitics'.

173. Pietsch, 'A British Sea'; Alpers, 'On Becoming a British Lake: Piracy, Slaving, and British Imperialism in the Indian Ocean during the First Half of the Nineteenth Century'; Grainger, *The British Navy in Eastern Waters: The Indian and Pacific Oceans*.

174. Preston and Major, *Send a Gun Boat! A Study of the British Gunboat*, 17.

175. Grainger, *The British Navy in Eastern Waters: The Indian and Pacific Oceans*, 205.

176. Mohanan, *The Royal Indian Navy: Trajectories, Transformations and the Transfer of Power.*

177. Vaidik, *Imperial Andamans: Colonial Encounter and Island History.*, 43.

Chapter 2

178. Joseph Darvall, *The Wreck on the Andamans* (London: Pelham Richardson, 1845).

179. Chaudhuri, *Trade and Civilisation in the Indian Ocean: An Economic History from the Rise of Islam to 1750*; Lovell, *The Opium War: Drugs, Dreams and the Making of China*; Alpers, *The Indian Ocean in World History.*

180. Anyaa Anim-Addo, 'Steaming between the Islands: Nineteenth-Century Maritime Networks and the Caribbean Archipelago', *Island Studies Journal* 8, no. 1 (2013): 30, https://doi.org/10.24043/isj.274.

181. Baldacchino, 'Islands, Island Studies, Island Studies Journal'; Pugh, 'Island Movements: Thinking with the Archipelago'; Grydehøj, 'A Future of Island Studies'.

182. For savagery, see: Sen, 'Savage Bodies, Civilized Pleasures'; Sen, *Savagery and Colonialism in the Indian Ocean: Power, Pleasure and the Andaman Islanders*; For servitude, see: Murthy, *Andaman and Nicobar Islands: A Saga of Freedom Struggle*; Anderson, 'Colonization, Kidnap and Confinement in the Andamans Penal Colony, 1771–1864'; Anderson, 'The Andaman Islands Penal Colony: Race, Class, Criminality, and the British Empire'; Anderson, Mazumdar, and Pandya, *New Histories of the Andaman Islands Landscape, Place and Identity in the Bay of Bengal, 1790-2012.*

183. Richmond, *Imperial Defence and Capture at Sea in War*, 57.

184. Lambert, 'The Royal Navy, 1856-1914: Deterrence and the Strategy of World Power'.

185. Schurman and Beeler, *Imperial Defence, 1868-1887*, 22; Hamilton, *The Making of the Modern Admiralty: British Naval Policy-Making, 1805–1927*; Gray, 'Fuelling Mobility'.

186. Rüger, *Heligoland: Britain, Germany, and the Struggle for the North Sea*; Clements, *Britain's Island Fortresses: Defence of the Empire 1756-1956.*

187. Saul David, *The Indian Mutiny: 1857* (London: Viking, 2002); Anderson, *The Indian Uprising of 1857-8: Prisons, Prisoners, and Rebellion*; Gopal, *Insurgent Empire: Anticolonial Resistance and British Dissent*, 41.

188. Mouat, 'Narrative of an Expedition to the Andaman Islands in 1857'; Mouat, *Adventures and Researches Among The Andaman Islanders*; Portman, *A History of Our Relations with the Andamanese, Vol.I.*

189. Anderson, *The Indian Uprising of 1857-8: Prisons, Prisoners, and Rebellion*; James, *Raj: The Making and Unmaking of British India*; Peers and Gooptu, *India and the British Empire.*

190. Dasgupta, *Japanese in Andaman and Nicobar Islands: Red Sun Over Black Water*; Murthy, *Andaman and Nicobar Islands: A Saga of Freedom Struggle*; Bandopadhyay and Carter, 'Introduction to the Geography and Geomorphology of the Andaman–Nicobar Islands'.

191. Nidhi Mahajan, 'Notes on an Archipelagic Ethnography: Ships, Seas, and Islands of Relation in the Indian Ocean', *Island Studies Journal* 16, no. 1 (2021): 20, https://doi.org/10.24043/isj.147.

192. Stow, 'Denmark in the Indian Ocean, 1616-1845 An Introduction'.

193. Tarling, *Piracy and Politics in the Malay World*; Graham Gerard Ong-Webb and Xu Ke, eds., 'Piracy, Seaborne Trade and the Rivalries of Foreign Sea Powers in East and Southeast Asia, 1511 to 1839: A Chinese Perspective', in *Piracy, Maritime Terrorism and Securing the Malacca Straits* (Singapore: ISEAS Publishing, 2006), 221–40; William Hasty, 'Piracy and the Production of Knowledge in the Travels of William Dampier, c.1679–1688', *Journal of Historical Geography* 37, no. 1 (2011): 40–54, https://doi.org/10.1016/j.jhg.2010.08.017; Moore, 'Piracy and the Ends of Romantic Commercialism: Victorian Businessmen Meet Malay Pirates'; C. Nathan Kwan, '"Putting down a Common Enemy": Piracy and Occasional Interstate Power in South China during the Mid-Nineteenth Century', *International Journal of Maritime History* 32, no. 3 (2020): 697–712, https://doi.org/10.1177/0843871420944629.

194. Boot, 'Pirates, Then and Now: How Piracy Was Defeated in the Past and Can Be Again'.

195. Hasty, 'Piracy and the Production of Knowledge in the Travels of William Dampier, c.1679–1688'.

196. 'Piracy at Nicobar Islands' (Admiralty, 1852), The National Archives.

197. 'Marine, Sep 1855' (Military, 1855), National Archives of India.

198. Tarling, *Imperial Britain in South-East Asia*, 235.

199. 'Despatches to India and Bengal Jul-Sep 1841, Marine' (India Office Records, 1841), E 4 767, British Library.

200. 'Despatches to India and Bengal Apr-Jul 1841, Marine' (India Office Records, 1842), E 4770, British Library.

201. Heaslip, *Gunboats, Empire and the China Station: The Royal Navy in 1920s East Asia*, 105–6; Hore, *Seapower Ashore: 200 Years of Royal Navy Operations on Land*; Hernon, *Britain's Forgotten Wars: Colonial Campaigns of the 19th Century*.

202. Tarling, *Imperial Britain in South-East Asia*, 241.

203. Boot, 'Pirates, Then and Now: How Piracy Was Defeated in the Past and Can Be Again'.

204. 'Despatches to India and Bengal Jul-Sep 1841, Marine'.

205. 'Marine, Sep 1844' (Military, 1844), National Archives of India.

206. 'Despatches to India and Bengal Jul-Sep 1841, Marine'.

207. 'Despatches to India and Bengal Aug-Sep 1846, Marine' (India Office Records, 1846), E 4 789, British Library.

208. 'Despatches to India and Bengal Sep-Nov 1845, Marine' (General Correspondence, 1845), 523–24, E 4 785, British Library.

209. 'Despatches to India and Bengal Jul-Sep 1841, Marine'.

210. 'Miscellaneous Papers Relating to the Creation of Marine Department 1859'.

211. Grainger, *The British Navy in Eastern Waters: The Indian and Pacific Oceans*.

212. Sen, 'Savage Bodies, Civilized Pleasures'.

213. Grainger, *The British Navy in Eastern Waters: The Indian and Pacific Oceans*, 203.

214. Colledge, Warlow, and Bush, *Ships of the Royal Navy: The Complete Record of All Fighting Ships of the Royal Navy from The15th Century to the Present*, 408 and 161.

215. 'Despatches to India and Bengal Aug-Sep 1846, Marine'.

216. 'Despatches to India and Bengal Aug-Sep 1847, Marine' (India Office Records, 1847), E 4 791, British Library.

217. Tarling, *Piracy and Politics in the Malay World*.

218. Tarling, 27.

219. Tarling, *Imperial Britain in South-East Asia*, 242.

220. Tarling, *Piracy and Politics in the Malay World*.

221. Maurice Vidal Portman is by far the most studied British official in the historiography of the Andaman Islands. Portman, *A History of Our Relations with the Andamanese, Vol.I*; Portman, *A History of Our Relations with the Andamanese, Vol.II*; Sen, 'Savage Bodies, Civilized Pleasures'; Constance McCabe, ed., 'Maurice Vidal Portman and the Platinotype in India', in *Platinum and Palladium Photographs: Technical History, Connoisseurship and Preservation*, by John Falconer (Washington, DC: American Institute for Conservation of Historic and Artistic Works, 2017), 318–31.

222. Portman, *A History of Our Relations with the Andamanese, Vol.I*.

223. 'Despatches to India and Bengal Oct 1856'.

224. 'Despatches to India and Bengal Oct 1856'.

225. Cain and Hopkins, 'Gentlemanly Capitalism and British Expansion Overseas I The Old Colonial System'.

226. Semmel, *Liberalism and Naval Strategy: Ideology, Interest, and Sea Power During the Pax Britannica*.

227. Alpers, 'On Becoming a British Lake: Piracy, Slaving, and British Imperialism in the Indian Ocean during the First Half of the Nineteenth Century'; Anderson, 'Colonization, Kidnap and Confinement in the Andamans Penal Colony, 1771–1864'.

228. Sarah Kinkel, *Disciplining the Empire: Politics, Governance, and the Rise of the British Navy* (Cambridge: Harvard University Press, 2018).

229. Lambert, *Battleships in Transition: The Creation of the Steam Battlefleet, 1815-1860*; Greenhill and Giffard, *Steam, Politics and Patronage: The Transformation of the Royal Navy, 1815-54*.

230. Grainger, *The British Navy in Eastern Waters: The Indian and Pacific Oceans*, 188.

231. Henry Gribble, 'An Appeal And Suggestion for Lights in the Red and Indian Seas' (Pamphlet, 1862), P 28 6 Red and Indian Seas.

232. William J. McCarthy, 'Gambling on Empire: The Economic Role of Shipwreck in the Age of Discovery', *International Journal of Maritime History* 23, no. 2 (2011): 69–84, https://doi.org/10.1177/084387141102300205; Felix Driver and Luciana

Martins, 'Shipwreck and Salvage in the Tropics: The Case of HMS Thetis, 1830–1854', *Journal of Historical Geography* 32, no. 3 (2006): 539–62, https://doi.org/10.1016/j.jhg.2005.10.010; Annika Korsgaard and Martin Gibbs, 'Shipwrecks as Archaeological Signatures of a Maritime Industrial Frontier in the Solomon Islands, 1788–1942', *International Journal of Historical Archaeology* 20, no. 1 (2016): 105–26, https://doi.org/10.1007/s10761-015-0320-7; Cathryn Pearce, *Cornish Wrecking, 1700-1860: Reality and Popular Myth* (Woodbridge: Boydell Press, 2010); Cathryn Pearce, 'What Do You Do with a Shipwrecked Sailor? Extreme Weather, Shipwreck, and Civic Responsibility in Nineteenth-Century Liverpool', *Victorian Review* 47, no. 1 (2021): 19–24, https://doi.org/10.1353/vcr.2021.0007; Cathryn Pearce, 'Gallant Officers and Benevolent Men: Royal Navy Officers, Voluntarism and the Launch of the Shipwrecked Mariners Society in the Early Victorian Era', *The Mariner's Mirror* 110, no. 1 (2024): 5–21, https://doi.org/10.1080/00253359.2024.2291949.

233. Sircar, *History of the Andaman Islands: Unsung Heroes and Untold Stories.*, 34.

234. 'Despatches to India and Bengal May-Jun 1853, Marine' (India Office Records, 1853), E 4 820, British Library.

235. Preston and Major, *Send a Gun Boat! A Study of the British Gunboat*.

236. 'Letter from Maurice Vidal Portman to Rev William Alexander Ayton, 22 January 1886' (Ayton Collection, 1886), GBR 1991 GD 2/5/4/1, Museum of Freemasonry.

237. Portman, *A History of Our Relations with the Andamanese, Vol.I*. See Chapter 4.

238. Henry Piddington, *Twelfth Memoir With Reference to Storms in India* (Calcutta: Journal of the Asiatic Society of Bengal, 1840), 23.

239. Piddington, *Twelfth Memoir With Reference to Storms in India*.

240. Vipul Singh, 'Cyclones, Shipwrecks and Environmental Anxiety: British Rule and Ecological Change in the Andaman Islands, 1780s To 1900s', *Global Environment* 13, no. 1 (2020): 165–93, https://doi.org/10.3197/ge.2020.130106.

241. Simon Schaffer, 'Easily Cracked: Scientific Instruments in States of Disrepair', *Isis* 102, no. 4 (2011): 706–17, https://doi.org/10.1086/663608; Simon Schaffer, 'The Bombay Case: Astronomers, Instrument Makers and the East India Company', *Journal for the History of Astronomy* 43, no. 2 (2012): 151–80, https://doi.org/10.1177/002182861204300202; Simon Naylor, '"Log Books and the Law of Storms": Maritime Meteorology and the British Admiralty in the Nineteenth Century', *Isis* 106, no. 4 (2015): 771–97, https://doi.org/10.1086/684641.

242. Darvall, *The Wreck on the Andamans*.

243. Portman, *A History of Our Relations with the Andamanese, Vol.I*, 132–35.

244. Driver and Martins, 'Shipwreck and Salvage in the Tropics'.

245. Stafford, 'A Sea View'.

246. 'Letter from Commissioner of Tavoy, to Commissioner of Tenasserim and Martaban, 29 May 1857' (Foreign, 1857), National Archives of India.

247. John MacKenzie, *Propaganda and Empire: The Manipulation of British Public Opinion, 1880 - 1960* (Manchester: Manchester University Press, 2003).

248. 'Letter from Commissioner of Tavoy, to Commissioner of Tenasserim and Martaban, 29 May 1857'.

Notes

249. The Standard, 'Murder and Piracy, 20 September 1841', *The Standard*, 1841, British Library Newspapers.

250. MacKenzie, *Propaganda and Empire: The Manipulation of British Public Opinion, 1880 - 1960*; Driver and Martins, 'Shipwreck and Salvage in the Tropics'; Singh, 'Cyclones, Shipwrecks and Environmental Anxiety'.

251. 'Foreign Intelligence, 13 August 1852', *Liverpool Mercury*, 1852, British Library Newspapers.

252. 'Massacre of British Subjects and Piracy at Nancowry Harbour, 11 August 1852', *Daily News*, 1852, British Library Newspapers.

253. Pearce, *Cornish Wrecking, 1700-1860: Reality and Popular Myth*; Pearce, 'What Do You Do with a Shipwrecked Sailor?'

254. 'Dreadful Shipwrecks in the Indian Ocean, 14 March 1845', *Glasgow Herald*, 1845, British Library Newspapers.

255. 'Loss of Runnymede and Briton, 15 March 1845', *York Herald*, 1845, British Library Newspapers.

256. 'Fury and Piracy, 23 March 1852', *Bengal Gazette*, 1852, British Library Newspapers; 'The Andamans, 22 April 1852', *Bengal Gazette*, 1852, British Library Newspapers.

257. 'Despatches to India and Bengal Jul-Sep 1841, Marine', 316.

258. Tarling, *Imperial Britain in South-East Asia*, 238.

259. Gerald Graham, *Great Britain in the Indian Ocean: A Study of Maritime Enterprise 1810-1850* (Oxford: Clarendon, 1967).

260. MacKenzie, *Propaganda and Empire: The Manipulation of British Public Opinion, 1880 - 1960*.

261. Driver, *Geography Militant: Cultures of Exploration and Empire*.

262. Bernard Porter, *The Absent-Minded Imperialists: Empire, Society, and Culture in Britain* (Oxford: Oxford University Press, 2007); Jeffrey A. Auerbach, *Imperial Boredom: Monotony and the British Empire* (Oxford: Oxford University Press, 2018); Stern, *Empire, Incorporated: The Corporations That Built British Colonialism*.

263. Porter, *The Absent-Minded Imperialists: Empire, Society, and Culture in Britain*.

264. Cain and Hopkins, *British Imperialism: 1688-2015*.

265. 'Public, 7 Dec 1836' (Home, 1836), National Archives of India.

266. Tarling, *Imperial Britain in South-East Asia*, 236–37.

267. 'Despatches to India and Bengal Aug-Oct 1849, Marine' (India Office Records, 1849), 178–79, E 4 801, British Library.

268. 'Despatches to India and Bengal Jun-Jul 1851, Marine' (India Office Records, 1851), E 4 795, British Library.

269. 'Despatches to India and Bengal May-Jun 1853, Marine'.

270. 'Piracy at Nicobar Islands'.

271. Preston and Major, *Send a Gun Boat! A Study of the British Gunboat*, 62.

272. Mahajan, 'Notes on an Archipelagic Ethnography'.

273. Tarling, *Piracy and Politics in the Malay World*.

274. 'Despatches to India and Bengal Sep-Oct 1855, Marine' (India Office Records, 1855), E 4 832, British Library.

275. Portman, *A History of Our Relations with the Andamanese, Vol.I*, 185.

276. Portman, 185.

277. Vaidik, *Imperial Andamans: Colonial Encounter and Island History*., 48.

278. 'Despatches to India and Bengal Oct 1856'.

279. 'Despatches to India and Bengal Sep-Oct 1855, Marine'.

280. Vaidik, *Imperial Andamans: Colonial Encounter and Island History*., 53.

281. Vaidik, 51.

282. 'Despatches to India and Bengal Oct 1856'.

283. Eldridge, *Victorian Imperialism*.

284. Portman, *A History of Our Relations with the Andamanese, Vol.I*, 190–96.

285. 'Public, 6 Aug 1858' (Home, 1858), National Archives of India.

286. 'Marine, 27 March 1857, No19' (Home, 1857), National Archives of India.

287. Anderson, *The Indian Uprising of 1857-8: Prisons, Prisoners, and Rebellion*; den Otter, 'Law, Authority, and Colonial Rule'; Dalrymple, *The Anarchy: The Relentless Rise of the East India Company*.

288. Murthy, *Andaman and Nicobar Islands: A Saga of Freedom Struggle*; Anderson, Mazumdar, and Pandya, *New Histories of the Andaman Islands Landscape, Place and Identity in the Bay of Bengal, 1790-2012*; Anderson, 'The Andaman Islands Penal Colony: Race, Class, Criminality, and the British Empire'; Anderson, 'Colonization, Kidnap and Confinement in the Andamans Penal Colony, 1771–1864'.

289. Brooks, 'March Into India: The Relief of Lucknow 1857 59'; Spence, *A History of the Royal Navy: Empire and Imperialism*, 75–76.

290. Spence, *A History of the Royal Navy: Empire and Imperialism*, 75.

291. Brooks, 'March Into India: The Relief of Lucknow 1857-59'.

292. Spence, *A History of the Royal Navy: Empire and Imperialism*, 73.

293. James, *Raj: The Making and Unmaking of British India*, 329.

294. Eldridge, *Victorian Imperialism*.

295. Anderson, *The Indian Uprising of 1857-8: Prisons, Prisoners, and Rebellion*.

296. Low, *History of the Indian Navy (1613-1863)*.

297. 'Marine, 11 Nov 1857' (Military, 1857).

298. Vaidik, *Imperial Andamans: Colonial Encounter and Island History*., 35.

299. Portman, *A History of Our Relations with the Andamanese, Vol.I*, 242. (Letter from Secretary to the Government of India, to Captain H. Man, 15 January 1858).

Notes

300. 'Despatches to India and Bengal Sep 1858, Marine'.

301. Kinkel, *Disciplining the Empire: Politics, Governance, and the Rise of the British Navy*.

302. Alpers, 'On Becoming a British Lake: Piracy, Slaving, and British Imperialism in the Indian Ocean during the First Half of the Nineteenth Century'.

303. Grainger, *The British Navy in Eastern Waters: The Indian and Pacific Oceans*, 241.

304. James, *Raj: The Making and Unmaking of British India*, 290–98.

305. 'Mason's Index Book RE East India Company Affairs 1841-1870' (Papers of John Charles Mason (1798-1881) mainly to the East India Company's Interests in Poplar, 1870), P/MAS/1/2/5, Tower Hamlets Local Library and Archive.

306. 'Military Forces in India'; 'Payments to Surgeons' (Papers of John Charles Mason (1798-1881) mainly to the East India Company's Interests in Poplar, 1870), P/MAS/1/2/1, Tower Hamlets Local Library and Archive; 'Papers Relating to the Transport of Troops and Stores'; 'Miscellaneous Papers Relating to the Creation of Marine Department 1859'; 'Miscellaneous Papers Naval and Maritime Services in India 1860-1862'; 'Papers Relating to Bengal Pilot Service 1869-1871'.

307. 'Military Forces in India'.

308. 'Miscellaneous Papers Relating to the Creation of Marine Department 1859'.

309. Beeler, 'Steam, Strategy and Schurman: Imperial Defence in the Post-Crimean Era, 1856-1905'; Lambert, 'The Royal Navy, 1856-1914: Deterrence and the Strategy of World Power'; Kennedy, *Imperial Defence: The Old World Order 1856–1956*.

310. Grainger, *The British Navy in Eastern Waters: The Indian and Pacific Oceans*, 232; 'Miscellaneous Papers Relating to the Creation of Marine Department 1859'.

311. Grainger, *The British Navy in Eastern Waters: The Indian and Pacific Oceans*, 232.

312. 'Miscellaneous Papers Relating to the Creation of Marine Department 1859'.

313. 'Military Forces in India'.

314. Jackson, *Distant Drums: The Role of Colonies in British Imperial Warfare*; Jackson, *Of Islands, Ports and Sea Lanes: Africa and the Indian Ocean in the Second World War*.

315. 'Miscellaneous Papers Relating to the Creation of Marine Department 1859'; 'Miscellaneous Papers Naval and Maritime Services in India 1860-1862'.

316. 'Despatches to India and Bengal Apr-May 1858, Marine' (India Office Records, 1858), E 4 1858, British Library; 'Public, 6 Aug 1858'.

317. James, *Raj: The Making and Unmaking of British India*, 329.

318. Grainger, *The British Navy in Eastern Waters: The Indian and Pacific Oceans*, 241.

319. Clements, *Britain's Island Fortresses: Defence of the Empire 1756-1956*.

320. Singh, 'Cyclones, Shipwrecks and Environmental Anxiety'.

321. Grainger, *The British Navy in Eastern Waters: The Indian and Pacific Oceans*, 241.

322. Lambert, 'The Royal Navy, 1856-1914: Deterrence and the Strategy of World Power'; Beeler, 'Steam, Strategy and Schurman: Imperial Defence in the Post-Crimean Era, 1856-1905'; Kennedy, *Imperial Defence: The Old World Order 1856–1956*.

Chapter 3

323. 'Despatches to India and Bengal Sep 1858, Marine'; 'The Andamans Survey' (Monographs, 1858), rgs303761, Royal Geographical Society.

324. Sen, *Savagery and Colonialism in the Indian Ocean: Power, Pleasure and the Andaman Islanders*; Murthy, *Andaman and Nicobar Islands: A Saga of Freedom Struggle*.

325. Joshua Ehrlich, *The East India Company and the Politics of Knowledge* (Cambridge: Cambridge University Press, 2023).

326. Mahan, *Influence of Sea Power Upon History, 1660-1783*, 18; Mahan, *Naval Strategy Compared and Contrasted with the Principles and Practice of Military Operations on Land*; Armstrong and Mahan, *21st Century Mahan: Sound Military Conclusions for the Modern Era*; Lambert, *Neptune Factor: Alfred Thayer Mahan and the Concept of Sea Power*.

327. Mahan, *Influence of Sea Power Upon History, 1660-1783*, 17.

328. This literature often focuses on the 'leader' as the lens through which to explore the survey work, which results in an individual centric gaze. Cook, 'Establishing Sea Routes to India and China: Stages in the Development of Hydrographical Knowledge'; Rigby, Merwe, and Williams, *Pacific Exploration: Voyages of Discovery from Captain Cook's Endeavour to the Beagle*; Lambert, *Franklin: Tragic Hero of Polar Navigation*; Iliffe, 'Science and Voyages of Discovery'; Glyndwr Williams, *Naturalists at Sea: Scientific Travellers from Dampier to Darwin* (New Haven: Yale University Press, 2015).

329. Edward Armston-Sheret, 'Diversifying the Historical Geography of Exploration: Subaltern Body Work on British-Led Expeditions c.1850–1914', *Journal of Historical Geography* 80 (2023): 58–68, https://doi.org/10.1016/j.jhg.2023.02.004.

330. Livingstone, *The Geographical Tradition: Episodes in a Contested Enterprise*; Livingstone, 'The Spaces of Knowledge: Contributions towards a Historical Geography of Science'; Livingstone, *Putting Science in Its Place*; Arnold, '"Illusory Riches": Representations of the Tropical World, 1840-1950'; Arnold, *The Tropics and the Travelling Gaze: India, Landscape, and Science 1800-1856*; Withers, *Placing the Enlightenment: Thinking Geographically about the Age of Reason*; Withers, 'Place and the "Spatial Turn" in Geography and in History'; Wess and Withers, 'Instrument Provision and Geographical Science: The Work of the Royal Geographical Society, 1830- ca 1930'; Driver, 'Distance and Disturbance: Travel, Exploration and Knowledge in the Nineteenth Century'; Driver and Martins, *Tropical Visions in an Age of Empire*; Driver, *Geography Militant: Cultures of Exploration and Empire*.

331. Gregory, *Geographical Imaginations*; Noel Castree, 'David Harvey: Marxism, Capitalism and the Geographical Imagination', *New Political Economy* 12, no. 1 (2007): 97–115, https://doi.org/10.1080/13563460601068859.

332. Hastings, *The Royal Indian Navy, 1612-1950*, 61–71.

333. Sen, 'Developing *Terra Nullius*'; Peters, Steinberg, and Stratford, *Territory beyond Terra*.

334. Mackinder, 'The Geographical Pivot of History (1904)'; Cornish, *Naval and Military Geography of the British Empire*.

335. Dodds and Sidaway, 'Halford Mackinder and the "Geographical Pivot of History": A Centennial Retrospective'; Dodds, 'Eugenics, Fantasies of Empire and Inverted Whiggism'; Lambert, *Neptune Factor: Alfred Thayer Mahan and the Concept of Sea Power*.

336. Even since its publication, Mahan's work has been challenged and critiqued. However, a critical reflection is taken here as one that challenges the epistemological foundations of his work, such as that conducted on the work of Halford Mackinder discussed in the literature review. For an overview of the debates, see: McCranie, *Mahan, Corbett, and the Foundations of Naval Strategic Thought*; Nicholas Lambert, *Neptune Factor: Alfred Thayer Mahan and the Concept of Sea Power* (Annapolis: Naval Institute Press, 2024).

337. Mahan, *Influence of Sea Power Upon History, 1660-1783*, 18–24.

338. Withers, *Placing the Enlightenment: Thinking Geographically about the Age of Reason*; Withers, 'Place and the "Spatial Turn" in Geography and in History'.

339. Withers, 'Place and the "Spatial Turn" in Geography and in History'.

340. Livingstone, *The Geographical Tradition: Episodes in a Contested Enterprise*; Livingstone; Livingstone, 'The Spaces of Knowledge: Contributions towards a Historical Geography of Science'; Livingstone, *Putting Science in Its Place*.

341. Arnold, '"Illusory Riches": Representations of the Tropical World, 1840-1950'; Arnold, *The Tropics and the Travelling Gaze: India, Landscape, and Science 1800-1856*; Withers, *Placing the Enlightenment: Thinking Geographically about the Age of Reason*; Withers, 'Place and the "Spatial Turn" in Geography and in History'; Driver, 'Distance and Disturbance: Travel, Exploration and Knowledge in the Nineteenth Century'; Driver and Martins, *Tropical Visions in an Age of Empire*; Driver, *Geography Militant: Cultures of Exploration and Empire*.

342. Driver, *Geography Militant: Cultures of Exploration and Empire*, 9.

343. Goodman, 'Making Imperial Space: Settlement, Surveying and Trade in Northern Australia in the Nineteenth Century', 130.

344. Goodman, 128.

345. Driver, 'Distance and Disturbance: Travel, Exploration and Knowledge in the Nineteenth Century', 76.

346. Thomas Tizard, *Chronological List of the Officers Conducting British Maritime Discoveries and Surveys* (London: H.M. Stationary Office, 1900).

347. Cock, '"Scientific Serviceman' in the Royal Navy and the Professionalism of Science, 1816-55'.

348. Morgan, 'Sir Joseph Banks as Patron of the Investigator Expedition: Natural History, Geographical Knowledge and Australian Exploration'.

349. Driver, 'Distance and Disturbance: Travel, Exploration and Knowledge in the Nineteenth Century', 91.

350. Low, *History of the Indian Navy (1613-1863)*, 1:398–99; Hastings, *The Royal Indian Navy, 1612-1950*, 61–63.

351. Low, *History of the Indian Navy (1613-1863)*, 1:416–17.

352. Behrisch, *Discovery, Innovation, and the Victorian Admiralty: Paper Navigators*, 8.

353. Law, 'On the Social Explanation of Technical Change: The Case of the Portuguese Maritime Expansion'; Latour, *Pasteurization of France*.

354. Amara Solari, 'The Relación Geográfica Map of Tabasco: Hybrid Cartography and Integrative Knowledge Systems in Sixteenth-Century New Spain', *Terrae Incognitae* 41, no. 1 (2009): 38–58, https://doi.org/10.1179/tin.2009.41.1.38; Livingstone, *Putting Science in Its Place*, 171.

355. The focus has been the output over the process. Williams, *Naturalists at Sea: Scientific Travellers from Dampier to Darwin*; Friendly, *Beaufort of the Admiralty: The Life of Sir Francis Beaufort, 1774-1857*; Christine MacLeod, *Heroes of Invention: Technology, Liberalism and British Identity, 1750-1914* (Cambridge: Cambridge University Press, 2007), 212–49; Behrisch, *Discovery, Innovation, and the Victorian Admiralty: Paper Navigators*.

356. Cook, 'Establishing Sea Routes to India and China: Stages in the Development of Hydrographical Knowledge'; Burnett, 'Hydrographic Discipline among Navigators: Charting an "Empire of Commerce and Science" in the Nineteenth-Century Pacific'; Achbari, 'Building Networks for Science: Conflict and Cooperation in Nineteenth-Century Global Marine Studies'; Anderson, 'The Hydrographer's Narrative: Writing Global Knowledge in the 1830s'; Ehrlich, *The East India Company and the Politics of Knowledge*.

357. Mahan, *Influence of Sea Power Upon History, 1660-1783*, 18.

358. Mahan, 18–30.

359. Alpers, 'On Becoming a British Lake: Piracy, Slaving, and British Imperialism in the Indian Ocean during the First Half of the Nineteenth Century'; Anderson, 'The Age of Revolution in the Indian Ocean, Bay of Bengal and South China Sea: A Maritime Perspective'.

360. Iliffe, 'Science and Voyages of Discovery'.

361. Thomas Kuhn, *The Structure of Scientific Revolutions* (Chicago: Chicago University Press, 1962).

362. Shapin, 'The House of Experiment in Seventeenth-Century England'; Steven Shapin, *A Social History of Truth* (Chicago: University of Chicago Press, 1994), https://doi.org/10.7208/9780226148847-007.

363. Agnew and Livingstone, *The SAGE Handbook of Geographical Knowledge*.

364. Daniel Clayton, 'The Creation of Imperial Space in the Pacific Northwest', *Journal of Historical Geography* 26, no. 3 (2000): 327–50, https://doi.org/10.1006/jhge.2000.0233; Hevia, *The Imperial Security State*; Branch, '"Colonial Reflection" and Territoriality: The Peripheral Origins of Sovereign Statehood'.

365. David Arnold's work is the seminal text, and his methodology has since been used throughout historical geography. Arnold, '"Illusory Riches": Representations of the Tropical World, 1840-1950'; Driver, 'Distance and Disturbance: Travel, Exploration and Knowledge in the Nineteenth Century'; Driver and Martins, *Tropical Visions in an Age of Empire*; David Burnett, 'Matthew Fontaine Maury's "Sea of Fire": Hydrography, Biogeography, and Providence in the Tropics', in *Tropical Visions in an Age of Empire*,

ed. Felix Driver and Luciana de Lima Martins (Chicago: University of Chicago Press, 2005), 113–36.

366. James, *Raj: The Making and Unmaking of British India*; Stern, *Empire, Incorporated: The Corporations That Built British Colonialism*; Sanghera, *Empireworld: How British Imperialism Has Shaped the Globe*.

367. Pratt, *Imperial Eyes: Travel Writing and Transculturation*.

368. G. E. Fogg, 'The Royal Society and the South Seas', *Notes and Records of the Royal Society of London* 55, no. 1 (2001): 81–103, https://doi.org/10.1098/rsnr.2001.0127; Wess and Withers, 'Instrument Provision and Geographical Science: The Work of the Royal Geographical Society, 1830- ca 1930'; Benjamin Newman, 'Authorising Geographical Knowledge: The Development of Peer Review in The Journal of the Royal Geographical Society, 1830–c.1880', *Journal of Historical Geography* 64 (2019): 85–97, https://doi.org/10.1016/j.jhg.2019.03.006.

369. MacLeod, *Heroes of Invention: Technology, Liberalism and British Identity, 1750-1914*, 227.

370. Latour, *Science in Action: How to Follow Scientists and Engineers Through Society*, 272.

371. 'Despatches to India and Bengal Jul-Aug 1852, Marine' (India Office Records, 1852), E 4 816, British Library.

372. Low, *History of the Indian Navy (1613-1863)*, 1:429.

373. 'Marine, Mar 1857, No19' (Home, 1857), National Archives of India.

374. Portman, *A History of Our Relations with the Andamanese, Vol.I*, 208.

375. 'The Andamans Survey'.

376. Clayton, 'The Creation of Imperial Space in the Pacific Northwest'; Goodman, 'Making Imperial Space: Settlement, Surveying and Trade in Northern Australia in the Nineteenth Century'; Driver, 'Distance and Disturbance: Travel, Exploration and Knowledge in the Nineteenth Century'; James R. Akerman, ed., *The Imperial Map: Cartography and the Mastery of Empire* (Chicago: University of Chicago Press, 2009); Keighren, Withers, and Bell, *Travels into Print: Exploration, Writing, and Publishing with John Murray, 1773-1859*.

377. Pratt, *Imperial Eyes: Travel Writing and Transculturation*.

378. Hones and Endo, 'History, Distance and Text: Narratives of the 1853–1854 Perry Expedition to Japan'; Burnett, 'Hydrographic Discipline among Navigators: Charting an "Empire of Commerce and Science" in the Nineteenth-Century Pacific'; Reidy and Rozwadowski, 'The Spaces In Between: Science, Ocean, Empire'.

379. Clayton, *Islands of Truth: The Imperial Fashioning of Vancouver Island*; Branch, '"Colonial Reflection" and Territoriality: The Peripheral Origins of Sovereign Statehood'.

380. Mahan, *Influence of Sea Power Upon History, 1660-1783*, 20.

381. 'Marine, Nov 1857, No38' (Military, 1857), National Archives of India.

382. Keighren, Withers, and Bell, *Travels into Print: Exploration, Writing, and Publishing with John Murray, 1773-1859*.

383. Shapin, 'The House of Experiment in Seventeenth-Century England', 134.

384. Rigby, Merwe, and Williams, *Pacific Exploration: Voyages of Discovery from Captain Cook's Endeavour to the Beagle*.

385. Grainger, *The British Navy in Eastern Waters: The Indian and Pacific Oceans*, 232.

386. Hastings, *The Royal Indian Navy, 1612-1950*, 61–62; Newman, 'Authorising Geographical Knowledge: The Development of Peer Review in The Journal of the Royal Geographical Society, 1830–c.1880'.

387. Latour, *Reassembling The Social: An Introduction to Actor-Network Theory*, 257.

388. Shapin, *A Social History of Truth*, 81.

389. Shapin, *A Social History of Truth*.

390. Portman, *A History of Our Relations with the Andamanese, Vol.I*, 214.

391. 'General Orders By The Commander In Chief, 17 March 1858' (Military, 1858), National Archives of India.

392. Both secondary and primary sources acknowledge the experimentation of prison life on the Andamans. Ross Lawrenson, 'Frederic John Mouat (1816–97), MD FRCS LLD of the Indian Medical Service', *Journal of Medical Biography* 15, no. 4 (2007): 201–5, https://doi.org/10.1258/j.jmb.2007.06-45; 'General Orders By The Commander In Chief, 24 January 1856'.

393. 'Marine, Nov 1857, No38'.

394. 'Public, Dec 1857, No83' (Home, 1857), National Archives of India; 'Public, Dec 1857 No84' (Home, 1857), National Archives of India; 'Marine, Mar 1858' (Military, 1858), National Archives of India.

395. Cock, "Scientific Serviceman' in the Royal Navy and the Professionalism of Science, 1816-55'.

396. Ehrlich, *The East India Company and the Politics of Knowledge*.

397. Achbari, 'Building Networks for Science: Conflict and Cooperation in Nineteenth-Century Global Marine Studies', 259.

398. Friendly, *Beaufort of the Admiralty: The Life of Sir Francis Beaufort, 1774-1857*, 277.

399. John Herschel, *Manual of Scientific Inquiry. Prepared for the Use of Officers in Her Majesty's Navy*, 5th ed. (London: Eyre and Spottiswode, 1886).

400. Behrisch, *Discovery, Innovation, and the Victorian Admiralty: Paper Navigators*, 147.

401. Schaffer, 'The Bombay Case: Astronomers, Instrument Makers and the East India Company', 175.

402. 'Marine, 27 March 1857, No20' (Home, 1857), National Archives of India.

403. 'Dalrymple Maps, Charts and Plans' (India Office Records, 1790), Maps C.21-C.22, British Library.

404. Driver, 'Distance and Disturbance: Travel, Exploration and Knowledge in the Nineteenth Century', 81.

405. Lambert, '"Taken Captive by the Mystery of the Great River": Towards an Historical Geography of British Geography and Atlantic Slavery'; Driver and Martins, *Tropical Visions in an Age of Empire*; Keighren, Withers, and Bell, *Travels into Print: Exploration, Writing, and Publishing with John Murray, 1773-1859*.

406. Iliffe, 'Science and Voyages of Discovery'; Achbari, 'Building Networks for Science: Conflict and Cooperation in Nineteenth-Century Global Marine Studies'.

407. Iliffe, 'Science and Voyages of Discovery', 644.

408. 'Public, Dec 1857, No83'.

409. 'Public, Dec 1857 No84'.

410. Edgell, *Sea Surveys: Britain's Contribution to Hydrography*, 10.

411. Richard Sorrenson, 'The Ship as a Scientific Instrument in the Eighteenth Century', *Osiris* 11 (1996): 221–36, https://doi.org/10.1086/368761; Sorrenson, 'Did the Royal Society Matter in the Eighteenth Century?'

412. Hastings, *The Royal Indian Navy, 1612-1950*, 63.

413. Day, *The Admiralty Hydrographic Service 1795-1919*, 68–69.

414. 'Despatches to India and Bengal May-Jun 1855, Marine' (India Office Records, 1855), E 4 830, British Library.

415. *Plan of Port Meadows of the Andaman Islands*, 1812, India Office Records, 1812, G 251 410, British Library; Hydrographic Office, 'Andaman Islands, Port Chatham or Port Blair' (Old Copy Book, 1789), OCB 836 A4, UK Hydrographic Office; Hydrographic Office, 'Gulf of Bengal, South Andaman West Coast, Port Campbell' (Old Copy Book, 1789), OCB 836 B1, UK Hydrographic Office; Hydrographic Office, 'Old Port Cornwallis on the Andaman Islands' (Old Copy Book, 1789), OCB 836 A1-4, UK Hydrographic Office; Hydrographic Office, 'Gulf of Bengal XII Andaman Isles' (Old Copy Book, 1790), OCB 835 A1-5, UK Hydrographic Office; Hydrographic Office, 'Andaman Islands, Port Chatham or Port Blair'.

416. Livingstone, *Putting Science in Its Place*, 137.

417. 'Marine, Mar 1858'.

418. 'Marine, Nov 1857, No38'.

419. Mouat, 'Narrative of an Expedition to the Andaman Islands in 1857'; Mouat, *Adventures and Researches Among The Andaman Islanders*.

420. Portman, *A History of Our Relations with the Andamanese, Vol.I*, 209.

421. Mouat, 'Narrative of an Expedition to the Andaman Islands in 1857'.

422. 'The Andamans Survey'.

423. 'The Andamans Survey'.

424. Christopher Ray Carter, *Magnetic Fever: Global Imperialism and Empiricism in the Nineteenth Century* (Philadelphia: American Philosophical Society, 2009), 24.

425. Sen, 'Developing *Terra Nullius*'.

426. Mouat, 'Narrative of an Expedition to the Andaman Islands in 1857'.

427. Naylor, '"Log Books and the Law of Storms": Maritime Meteorology and the British Admiralty in the Nineteenth Century'.

428. Mouat, 'Narrative of an Expedition to the Andaman Islands in 1857'.

429. Arnold, '"Illusory Riches": Representations of the Tropical World, 1840-1950', 7.

430. Sen, *Savagery and Colonialism in the Indian Ocean: Power, Pleasure and the Andaman Islanders*; Sen, 'On the Beach in the Andaman Islands'; Anderson, 'Writing Indigenous Women's Lives in the Bay of Bengal: Cultures of Empire in the Andaman Islands, 1789-1906'; Murthy, *Andaman and Nicobar Islands: A Saga of Freedom Struggle*.

431. Sen, 'On the Beach in the Andaman Islands'; Anderson, 'Colonization, Kidnap and Confinement in the Andamans Penal Colony, 1771–1864'.

432. Harrison, 'Health, Sovereignty and Imperialism'.

433. 'The Andamans Survey'.

434. Mouat, 'Narrative of an Expedition to the Andaman Islands in 1857', 277.

435. Mouat, 278.

436. Portman, *A History of Our Relations with the Andamanese, Vol.I*, 217–41.

437. 'The Andamans Survey'.

438. 'Public, Oct 1858, No17' (Home, 1858), National Archives of India.

439. 'Public, Jun 1859, No14' (Home, 1859), National Archives of India.

440. Mouat, 'Narrative of an Expedition to the Andaman Islands in 1857'; Mouat, *Adventures and Researches Among The Andaman Islanders*.

441. MacLeod, *Heroes of Invention: Technology, Liberalism and British Identity, 1750-1914*, 7.

442. 'Public, May 1858, No74' (Home, 1858), National Archives of India.

443. 'Public, Jul 1859, No17' (Home, 1859), National Archives of India.

444. 'Public, Mar 1858, No81' (Home, 1858), National Archives of India; 'Public, Mar 1858, No83' (Home, 1858), National Archives of India; 'Public, Mar 1858, No84' (Home, 1858), National Archives of India.

445. Murthy, *Andaman and Nicobar Islands: A Saga of Freedom Struggle*.

446. 'Public, Jul 1859, No17'.

447. Clayton, 'The Creation of Imperial Space in the Pacific Northwest'.

448. 'Public, Jun 1859, No15' (Home, 1859), National Archives of India.

449. Avishai Ben-Dror, 'Cartographic Knowledge, Colonialized-Colonizer Spaces: Egyptian Maps of Harar, 1875–1885', *Journal of Historical Geography* 77 (2022): 85–100, https://doi.org/10.1016/j.jhg.2022.03.004.

450. Wess and Withers, 'Instrument Provision and Geographical Science: The Work of the Royal Geographical Society, 1830- ca 1930', 229.

Notes

451. Jordan Branch, 'Mapping the Sovereign State: Technology, Authority, and Systemic Change', *International Organization* 65, no. 1 (2011): 2, https://doi.org/10.1017/S0020818310000299.

452. 'Public, Apr 1858, No99' (Home, 1858), National Archives of India; 'Public, Apr 1858, No29' (Home, 1858), National Archives of India; 'Public, Jun 1858, No22' (Home, 1858), National Archives of India; 'Public, Apr 1858, No100' (Home, 1858), National Archives of India.

453. Mouat, 'Narrative of an Expedition to the Andaman Islands in 1857'.

454. Mouat, *Adventures and Researches Among The Andaman Islanders*.

455. Fogg, 'The Royal Society and the South Seas', 84.

456. Newman, 'Authorising Geographical Knowledge: The Development of Peer Review in The Journal of the Royal Geographical Society, 1830–c.1880'.

457. Charles W J Withers and Innes M Keighren, 'Travels into Print: Authoring, Editing and Narratives of Travel and Exploration, c.1815-c.1857: Travels into Print', *Transactions of the Institute of British Geographers* 36, no. 4 (2011): 560–73, https://doi.org/10.1111/j.1475-5661.2011.00437.x; Heike Jons, Peter Meusburger, and Michael Heffernan, *Mobilities of Knowledge* (New York: Springer Berlin Heidelberg, 2017).

458. Williams, *Naturalists at Sea: Scientific Travellers from Dampier to Darwin*, 263.

459. 'Military General Orders, Feb 1861, No113' (Military, 1861), National Archives of India; 'Military General Orders, Mar 1861, No287' (Military, 1861), National Archives of India.

460. 'No. 56 Private Secretary's Correspondence', Nos. 5501 to 5550, May 1859-Jul 1859' (India Office Records, 1859), MSS F699/1/2/2/156, British Library.

461. Low, *History of the Indian Navy (1613-1863)*; Low.

462. James, *Raj: The Making and Unmaking of British India*.

463. Day, *The Admiralty Hydrographic Service 1795-1919*, 68–69.

464. 'Papers Relating to the Transport of Troops and Stores'; 'Marine, Jun 1860, No4' (Military, 1860), National Archives of India; 'Marine, Sept 1860, No30' (Military, 1860), National Archives of India.

465. Colledge, Warlow, and Bush, *Ships of the Royal Navy: The Complete Record of All Fighting Ships of the Royal Navy from The15th Century to the Present*, 154.

466. T.M. Philbrick, 'Notes on the Andamans: The Transactions of the Bombay Geographical Society. From May 1858 to May 1860. (Edited by the Secretary.) Volume XV.' (India Office Records, 1860), ST 393, vol 15, Qatar National Library.

467. A.D. Taylor, 'On the Present State and Requirement for Surveys in the Indian Ocean: The Transactions of the Bombay Geographical Society. From May 1858 to May 1860. (Edited by the Secretary.) Volume XV.' (India Office Records, 1860), ST 393, vol 15, Qatar National Library; Philbrick, 'Notes on the Andamans: The Transactions of the Bombay Geographical Society. From May 1858 to May 1860. (Edited by the Secretary.) Volume XV.'

468. Lambert, *Seapower States: Maritime Culture, Continental Empires and the Conflict That Made the Modern World*, 323.

469. Kelly Presutti, '"A Better Idea than the Best Constructed Charts": Watercolor Views in Early British Hydrography', *Grey Room*, no. 85 (2021): 70–99, https://doi.org/10.1162/grey_a_00333.

470. Burnett, 'Hydrographic Discipline among Navigators: Charting an "Empire of Commerce and Science" in the Nineteenth-Century Pacific'.

471. Mahan, *Naval Strategy Compared and Contrasted with the Principles and Practice of Military Operations on Land.*

472. Chaudhuri, *Trade and Civilisation in the Indian Ocean: An Economic History from the Rise of Islam to 1750*; Alpers, 'On Becoming a British Lake: Piracy, Slaving, and British Imperialism in the Indian Ocean during the First Half of the Nineteenth Century'.

473. Burnett, 'Matthew Fontaine Maury's "Sea of Fire": Hydrography, Biogeography, and Providence in the Tropics'.

474. Newman, 'Authorising Geographical Knowledge: The Development of Peer Review in The Journal of the Royal Geographical Society, 1830–c.1880'.

475. Ehrlich, *The East India Company and the Politics of Knowledge.*

476. Pratt, *Imperial Eyes: Travel Writing and Transculturation.*

477. Withers and Keighren, 'Travels into Print'.

478. Auerbach, *Imperial Boredom: Monotony and the British Empire.*

479. Auerbach, 37.

480. Auerbach, 26–28.

481. Auerbach, 25.

482. 'Papers Relating to the Transport of Troops and Stores'.

483. Sen, 'Developing *Terra Nullius*'.

484. Mouat, *Adventures and Researches Among The Andaman Islanders.*

485. Grainger, *The British Navy in Eastern Waters: The Indian and Pacific Oceans*, 232.

486. Sen, *Savagery and Colonialism in the Indian Ocean: Power, Pleasure and the Andaman Islanders.*

487. Sen, 'Developing *Terra Nullius*'.

488. Ritchie, *The Admiralty Chart: British Naval Hydrography in the Nineteenth Century.*

Chapter 4

489. Indian naval officers were well aware of the dangers of crossing the Bay of Bengal at the latter stages of the 1850s: Taylor, 'On the Present State and Requirement for Surveys in the Indian Ocean: The Transactions of the Bombay Geographical Society. From May 1858 to May 1860. (Edited by the Secretary.) Volume XV.'

490. Mary Blewitt, *Survey of the Seas* (London: Macgibbon & Kee, 1957); Law, 'On the Social Explanation of Technical Change: The Case of the Portuguese Maritime Expansion'; Burnett, *Masters Of All They Surveyed*; Burnett, 'Hydrographic Discipline among

Navigators: Charting an "Empire of Commerce and Science" in the Nineteenth-Century Pacific'; Carter, *Magnetic Fever: Global Imperialism and Empiricism in the Nineteenth Century*; Ballantyne and Burton, *Empires and the Reach of the Global, 1870-1945*; Rory A. Walshe, "'Who Could Have Expected Such a Disaster?" How Responses to the 1892 Cyclone Determined Institutional Trajectories of Vulnerability in Mauritius', *Journal of Historical Geography* 75 (2022): 55–64, https://doi.org/10.1016/j.jhg.2021.11.002.

491. Matthew Goodman, 'Follow the Data: Administering Science at Edward Sabine's Magnetic Department, Woolwich, 1841–57', *Notes and Records: The Royal Society Journal of the History of Science* 73, no. 2 (2019): 187–202, https://doi.org/10.1098/rsnr.2018.0036.

492. Reidy, *The Tides of History*; Davey, 'The Advancement of Nautical Knowledge: The Hydrographical Office, the Royal Navy and the Charting of the Baltic Sea, 1795-1815'; Ritchie, *The Admiralty Chart: British Naval Hydrography in the Nineteenth Century*.

493. Williams, *Naturalists at Sea: Scientific Travellers from Dampier to Darwin*; Driver, 'Distance and Disturbance: Travel, Exploration and Knowledge in the Nineteenth Century'; Driver, *Geography Militant: Cultures of Exploration and Empire*; Cock, "Scientific Serviceman' in the Royal Navy and the Professionalism of Science, 1816-55'.

494. Parker, 'The Savant and the Engineer'; Parker, 'London's Geographic Knowledge Network and the Anson Account (1748)'; Cook, 'Establishing Sea Routes to India and China: Stages in the Development of Hydrographical Knowledge'; Rigby, Merwe, and Williams, *Pacific Exploration: Voyages of Discovery from Captain Cook's Endeavour to the Beagle*; Toby Musgrave, *The Multifarious Mr. Banks: From Botany Bay to Kew, the Natural Historian Who Shaped the World* (New Haven: Yale University Press, 2020).

495. Sara Caputo, 'From Surveying to Surveillance: Maritime Cartography and Naval (Self-)Tracking in the Long Nineteenth Century', *Past & Present*, 2024, gtad023, https://doi.org/10.1093/pastj/gtad023.

496. Harrison, 'Health, Sovereignty and Imperialism'; Clout and Gosme, 'The Naval Intelligence Handbooks: A Monument in Geographical Writing'; Boyd, *The Royal Navy in Eastern Waters: Linchpin of Victory 1935-1942*.

497. Networks of knowledge in the maritime have long been a focus of ANT scholars. Law, 'On the Methods of Long-Distance Control: Vessels, Navigation and the Portuguese Route to India'; Law, 'On the Social Explanation of Technical Change: The Case of the Portuguese Maritime Expansion'; John Law, 'Technology and Heterogeneous Engineering: The Case of Portuguese Expansion.', in *The Social Construction of Technological Systems: New Directions in the Sociology and History of Technology*, ed. Wiebe E. Bijker, Thomas Parke Hughes, and Trevor Pinch (Cambridge: MIT Press, 2012); Solari, 'The Relación Geográfica Map of Tabasco: Hybrid Cartography and Integrative Knowledge Systems in Sixteenth-Century New Spain'.

498. Edgell, *Sea Surveys: Britain's Contribution to Hydrography*, 3.

499. Colledge, Warlow, and Bush, *Ships of the Royal Navy: The Complete Record of All Fighting Ships of the Royal Navy from The15th Century to the Present*, 89.

500. Hydrographic Office, 'Gulf of Bengal, South Andaman I, East Coast, Port Blair'.

501. Booth, *Navies and Foreign Policy*, 7–19; Booth, 'Roles, Objectives and Tasks: An Inventory of the Functions of Navies'.

502. Behrisch, *Discovery, Innovation, and the Victorian Admiralty: Paper Navigators*, 8; Caputo, 'From Surveying to Surveillance'.

503. Michael Barritt, *Nelson's Pathfinders: A Forgotten Story in the Triumph of British Sea Power* (New Haven: Yale University Press, 2024).

504. Barbara Bond, 'Strategic Considerations for International Hydrography in the 21st Century', *International Hydrographic Review* 1, no. 2 (1996); David Monahan et al., 'Challenges and Opportunities for Hydrography in The New Century', *International Hydrography Review* 2, no. 3 (2001); Doel, Levin, and Marker, 'Extending Modern Cartography to the Ocean Depths: Military Patronage, Cold War Priorities, and the Heezen–Tharp Mapping Project, 1952–1959'; R. Ponce, 'Multidimensional Marine Data: The next Frontier for Hydrographic Offices', *The International Hydrographic Review* 22 (2019), https://ihr.iho.int/articles/multidimensional-marine-data-the-next-frontier-for-hydrographic-offices/.

505. Agnew and Livingstone, *The SAGE Handbook of Geographical Knowledge*.

506. Agnew and Livingstone.

507. R Morris, 'The Royal Naval Hydrographic Service 1795-1995', *International Hydrographic Review* LXXII, no. 2 (1995): 7–21.

508. Edgell, *Sea Surveys: Britain's Contribution to Hydrography*.

509. Burnett, 'Hydrographic Discipline among Navigators: Charting an "Empire of Commerce and Science" in the Nineteenth-Century Pacific'.

510. Herschel, *Manual of Scientific Inquiry. Prepared for the Use of Officers in Her Majesty's Navy*; Ritchie, *The Admiralty Chart: British Naval Hydrography in the Nineteenth Century*.

511. Burnett, *Masters Of All They Surveyed*.

512. Finnegan, 'The Spatial Turn: Geographical Approaches in the History of Science', 370.

513. Latour and Woolgar, *Laboratory Life: The Construction of Scientific Facts*.

514. Latour, *Reassembling The Social: An Introduction to Actor-Network Theory*.

515. Lambert, '"Taken Captive by the Mystery of the Great River": Towards an Historical Geography of British Geography and Atlantic Slavery'.

516. Doel, Levin, and Marker, 'Extending Modern Cartography to the Ocean Depths: Military Patronage, Cold War Priorities, and the Heezen–Tharp Mapping Project, 1952–1959'; Davey, 'The Advancement of Nautical Knowledge: The Hydrographical Office, the Royal Navy and the Charting of the Baltic Sea, 1795-1815'; Behrisch, *Discovery, Innovation, and the Victorian Admiralty: Paper Navigators*.

517. Taylor, 'On the Present State and Requirement for Surveys in the Indian Ocean: The Transactions of the Bombay Geographical Society. From May 1858 to May 1860. (Edited by the Secretary.) Volume XV.'

518. 'Marine, Mar 1858, No14' (Military, 1858), National Archives of India.

519. Goodman, 'Follow the Data'.

520. Sorrenson, 'The Ship as a Scientific Instrument in the Eighteenth Century', 236.

Notes

521. Hasty, 'Piracy and the Production of Knowledge in the Travels of William Dampier, c.1679–1688'; William Hasty and Kimberley Peters, 'The Ship in Geography and the Geographies of Ships', *Geography Compass* 6, no. 11 (2012): 660–76, https://doi.org/10.1111/gec3.12005; Antony Adler, 'The Ship as Laboratory: Making Space for Field Science at Sea', *Journal of the History of Biology* 47, no. 3 (2014): 333–62, https://doi.org/10.1007/s10739-013-9367-7; Anne-Flore Laloë, 'Where Is Bathybius Haeckelii? The Ship as a Scientific Instrument and a Space of Science', ed. Don Legget and Richard Dunn (Oxford: Routledge, 2016), 113–30, https://doi.org/10.4324/9781315604657-7.

522. Driver and Martins, 'Shipwreck and Salvage in the Tropics'; Macdougall, *Endless Novelties of Extraordinary Interest: The Voyage of H.M.S Challenger and the Birth of Modern Oceanography*.

523. Day, *The Admiralty Hydrographic Service 1795-1919*.

524. Naylor, '"Log Books and the Law of Storms": Maritime Meteorology and the British Admiralty in the Nineteenth Century'; Anderson, 'The Hydrographer's Narrative: Writing Global Knowledge in the 1830s'; Presutti, '"A Better Idea than the Best Constructed Charts"'; Behrisch, *Discovery, Innovation, and the Victorian Admiralty: Paper Navigators*; Herschel, *Manual of Scientific Inquiry. Prepared for the Use of Officers in Her Majesty's Navy*.

525. Herschel, *Manual of Scientific Inquiry. Prepared for the Use of Officers in Her Majesty's Navy*.

526. Law, 'On the Methods of Long-Distance Control: Vessels, Navigation and the Portuguese Route to India'; Matzke, *Deterrence through Strength: British Naval Power and Foreign Policy under Pax Britannica*.

527. Akerman, *The Imperial Map: Cartography and the Mastery of Empire*; Carter, *Magnetic Fever: Global Imperialism and Empiricism in the Nineteenth Century*.

528. Driver and Martins, 'Shipwreck and Salvage in the Tropics', 542.

529. Latour, *Reassembling The Social: An Introduction to Actor-Network Theory*, 178.

530. Driver, 'Distance and Disturbance: Travel, Exploration and Knowledge in the Nineteenth Century', 85.

531. Edgell, *Sea Surveys: Britain's Contribution to Hydrography*, 4.

532. Dawson, *Memoirs of Hydrography. Part II*; Gerald Hayes, 'How the British Admiralty Charts Are Produced' (The Admiralty Chart Agency, 1927); Edgell, *Sea Surveys: Britain's Contribution to Hydrography*; Day, *The Admiralty Hydrographic Service 1795-1919*; Friendly, *Beaufort of the Admiralty: The Life of Sir Francis Beaufort, 1774-1857*; 'Admiralty Sailing Directions: A Historical Perspective' (Andrew David Collection, 1982), AD 30, UK Hydrographic Office.

533. Portman, *A History of Our Relations with the Andamanese, Vol.I*, 64; Archibald Blair, *Plan of Port Andaman*, 1789, India Office Records, 1789, Maps K. Top. 116.32, British Library; Archibald Blair, 'Chart of Part of the Coast of the Great Andaman, 1789' (Pamphlets and Manuscripts, 1789), VZ 6 47, Naval Historical Branch; Archibald Blair, *Chart of Old Port Cornwallis on the Andaman Islands*, 1789, India Office Records, 1789, G 251 47, British Library; Archibald Blair, 'A General Chart of the Andaman Islands' (Misc Charts, 1796), 571 BA4, UK Hydrographic Office.

534. Low, *History of the Indian Navy (1613-1863)*, 1:187.

535. Low, 1:186.

536. 'Letters from Cdre Edward Vernon. Commander-in-Chief, East Indies' (Admiralty, 30 September 1779), The National Archives.

537. 'Bengal Correspondence, 27 October 1785' (India Office Records, 1785), H 555, British Library.

538. 'Dalrymple Maps, Charts and Plans'.

539. Low, *History of the Indian Navy (1613-1863)*, 1:186.

540. Driver, 'Distance and Disturbance: Travel, Exploration and Knowledge in the Nineteenth Century', 81.

541. Presutti, '"A Better Idea than the Best Constructed Charts"', 74.

542. Portman, *A History of Our Relations with the Andamanese, Vol.I*, 56.

543. Low, *History of the Indian Navy (1613-1863)*; Hastings, *The Royal Indian Navy, 1612-1950*; Ehrlich, *The East India Company and the Politics of Knowledge*.

544. Ritchie, *The Admiralty Chart: British Naval Hydrography in the Nineteenth Century*; Day, *The Admiralty Hydrographic Service 1795-1919*; Adrian Webb, 'More than Just Charts: Hydrographic Expertise within the Admiralty, 1795–1829', *Journal for Maritime Research* 16, no. 1 (2014): 43–54, https://doi.org/10.1080/21533366 9.2014.906178.

545. Behrisch, *Discovery, Innovation, and the Victorian Admiralty: Paper Navigators*.

546. Portman, *A History of Our Relations with the Andamanese, Vol.I*, 57–66.

547. Robert Colebrooke, *View of Port Cornwallis of the Andaman Islands*, 1790, Watercolour on Paper, 1790, WD 1476, British Library.

548. Robert Colebrooke, 'On the Andaman Islands', in *Transactions of the Society Instituted in Bengal for Inquiring into the History and Antiquities, the Arts, Sciences and Literature of Asia in 1799* (Calcutta: Asiatic Society of Bengal, 1799).

549. Blair, 'Plan of Port Andaman'; Blair, 'Chart of Part of the Coast of the Great Andaman, 1789'; Blair; Blair, 'Chart of Old Port Cornwallis on the Andaman Islands'; Blair, 'A General Chart of the Andaman Islands'; Hydrographic Office, 'Andaman Islands, Port Chatham or Port Blair'.

550. Presutti, '"A Better Idea than the Best Constructed Charts"', 74.

551. Latour, *Reassembling The Social: An Introduction to Actor-Network Theory*, 223.

552. Sen, 'Developing *Terra Nullius*'.

553. 'Chart of the Andamans' (1793), VZ 6 46, Naval Historical Branch; Blair, 'A General Chart of the Andaman Islands'; 'A Concise Account of Port Cornwallis, Andamans, With a Plan of Harbour' (India Office Records, 1794), H 388 4, British Library.

554. 'Journal of the Weather at Port Cornwallis During the Years 1793-4' (India Office Records, 1794), G 34.1, British Library; 'Reports of the Surgeon at Port Cornwallis for the Years 1793-4' (India Office Records, 1794), G 34 1, British Library; Archibald Blair, 'Letter from Blair to Cornwallis, Andaman Island Report' (India Office Records, 1789), MSS 344 67, British Library.

555. Shellam et al., *Brokers and Boundaries: Colonial Exploration in Indigenous Territory*, 1.

556. Konishi, Nugent, and Shellam, *Indigenous Intermediaries: New Perspectives on Exploration Archives*; Thomas, *Expedition into Empire: Exploratory Journeys and the Making of the Modern World*; Armston-Sheret, 'Diversifying the Historical Geography of Exploration: Subaltern Body Work on British-Led Expeditions c.1850–1914'.

557. Martin, 'Indigenous Tales of the Beaufort Sea: Arctic Exploration and the Circulation of Geographical Knowledge', 34.

558. Portman, *A History of Our Relations with the Andamanese, Vol.I*, 79; Clare Anderson, *Subaltern Lives: Biographies of Colonialism in the Indian Ocean World, 1790-1920* (Cambridge: Cambridge University Press, 2012); Armston-Sheret, 'Diversifying the Historical Geography of Exploration: Subaltern Body Work on British-Led Expeditions c.1850–1914'.

559. Pratt, *Imperial Eyes: Travel Writing and Transculturation*.

560. Paul Artin Boghossian, *Fear of Knowledge: Against Relativism and Constructivism* (Oxford: Clarendon Press, 2013).

561. 'Report of Capt. Kyd, 20 August 1795'; 'Letter from A. Kyd to Governor General In Council, 02 August 1795'.

562. 'Marine, Feb 1861, No14-15' (Military, 1861), National Archives of India.

563. 'Marine, Mar 1858, No14', 185.

564. Lambert, 'Economic Power, Technological Advantage, and Imperial Strength: Britain as a Unique Global Power, 1860–1890', 4.

565. Behrisch, *Discovery, Innovation, and the Victorian Admiralty: Paper Navigators*, 8.

566. Davey, 'The Advancement of Nautical Knowledge: The Hydrographical Office, the Royal Navy and the Charting of the Baltic Sea, 1795-1815'.

567. 'Marine, Feb 1860, No14-21' (1860), National Archives of India.

568. 'Marine, Feb 1860, No14-21'; 'Marine, Oct 1860, No22-23' (Military, 1860), National Archives of India.

569. 'Marine, Feb 1860, No14-21'.

570. Branch, 'Mapping the Sovereign State'; Branch, '"Colonial Reflection" and Territoriality: The Peripheral Origins of Sovereign Statehood'.

571. Ritchie, *The Admiralty Chart: British Naval Hydrography in the Nineteenth Century*, 319.

572. 'Marine, Mar 1861, No16' (Military, 1861), National Archives of India.

573. 'Marine, Feb 1861, No14-15'.

574. Hydrographic Office, 'Gulf of Bengal, South Andaman I, East Coast, Port Blair'.

575. 'Miscellaneous Papers Naval and Maritime Services in India 1860-1862'.

576. 'Miscellaneous Papers Relating to the Creation of Marine Department 1859'.

577. Day, *The Admiralty Hydrographic Service 1795-1919*, 68.

578. Unknown, 'A Rought Draught of the Nicomba Islands' (Chart, 1812), E 19 3 Shelf WS, U; French Unknown, *A View of the Nicobar Islands (Francais)*, 1824, Watercolour on Paper, 1824, ADM 344/1106, The National Archives; Duncan Weir and Archibald Blair, *Plan of Port Cornwallis, Great Andaman*, 1800, Misc Charts, 1800, C 139, UK Hydrographic Office.

579. 'HMS Lyra Observations' (Miscellaneous Papers (Remarks Books), 1817), MP69 26, UK Hydrographic Office; 'HMS Crocodile Observations' (Miscellaneous Papers (Remarks Books), 1830), MP108 7, UK Hydrographic Office; 'HMS Challenger Observations' (Miscellaneous Papers (Remarks Books), March 1832), MP107 14; 'HMS Wolf Observations' (Miscellaneous Papers (Remarks Books), 1833), MP108 33, UK Hydrographic Office.

580. Davey, 'The Advancement of Nautical Knowledge: The Hydrographical Office, the Royal Navy and the Charting of the Baltic Sea, 1795-1815', 86.

581. Behrisch, *Discovery, Innovation, and the Victorian Admiralty: Paper Navigators*, 10.

582. Friendly, *Beaufort of the Admiralty: The Life of Sir Francis Beaufort, 1774-1857*, 261–65.

583. 'Marine, Apr 1859' (Military, 1859), National Archives of India.

584. 'Marine, Feb 1859, No33/35' (Military, 1859), National Archives of India; 'Judicial, Jan 1860, No2' (Home, 1860), National Archives of India.

585. 'Marine, Jun 1860, No44' (Military, 1860), National Archives of India.

586. 'Marine, Jul 1860, No27-28' (Military, 1860), 27, National Archives of India; 'Marine, Jun 1860, No44', 34.

587. Ehrlich, *The East India Company and the Politics of Knowledge*.

588. 'Marine, Feb 1861, No14-15'.

589. 'Judicial, Aug 1860, No3' (Home, 1860), National Archives of India.

590. 'Miscellaneous Papers Naval and Maritime Services in India 1860-1862'.

591. 'Marine, May 1860, No02' (Military, 1860), National Archives of India.

592. 'Her Majesty's Indian Navy List, July 6th 1859'.

593. Hasty and Peters, 'The Ship in Geography and the Geographies of Ships'.

594. Low, *History of the Indian Navy (1613-1863)*, 1:418.

595. Preston and Major, *Send a Gun Boat! A Study of the British Gunboat*.

596. Cock, '"Scientific Serviceman' in the Royal Navy and the Professionalism of Science, 1816-55'.

597. 'Miscellaneous Papers Relating to the Creation of Marine Department 1859'.

598. Hastings, *The Royal Indian Navy, 1612-1950*, 61–70.

599. 'Military General Orders, Mar 1861, No287'.

600. J Norrie, *Chart of the Andaman and Nicobar Islands, with the Adjacent Continent* (London: Navigation Warehouse and Naval Academy, 1856).

Notes

601. Davey, 'The Advancement of Nautical Knowledge: The Hydrographical Office, the Royal Navy and the Charting of the Baltic Sea, 1795-1815', 97.

602. Lambert, *Battleships in Transition: The Creation of the Steam Battlefleet, 1815-1860*; Greenhill and Giffard, *Steam, Politics and Patronage: The Transformation of the Royal Navy, 1815-54*; Evans, *Building the Steam Navy: Dockyards, Technology, and the Creation of the Victorian Battle Fleet, 1830-1906*; Gray, 'Fuelling Mobility'.

603. Behrisch, *Discovery, Innovation, and the Victorian Admiralty: Paper Navigators*, 10.

604. Anderson, 'The Hydrographer's Narrative: Writing Global Knowledge in the 1830s', 51–53.

605. 'Admiralty Sailing Directions: A Historical Perspective'.

606. Caputo, 'From Surveying to Surveillance'.

607. Presutti, '"A Better Idea than the Best Constructed Charts"'.

608. Naylor, '"Log Books and the Law of Storms": Maritime Meteorology and the British Admiralty in the Nineteenth Century'.

609. Behrisch, *Discovery, Innovation, and the Victorian Admiralty: Paper Navigators*, 37–39.

610. Anderson, 'The Hydrographer's Narrative: Writing Global Knowledge in the 1830s', 52.

611. 'Judicial, Mar 1860, No15' (Home, 1860), National Archives of India; 'Judicial, Mar 1860, No17-18' (Home, 1860), National Archives of India; 'Judicial, May 1860, No9-12' (Home, 1860), National Archives of India.

612. Portman, *A History of Our Relations with the Andamanese, Vol.I*, 310.

613. Behrisch, *Discovery, Innovation, and the Victorian Admiralty: Paper Navigators*, 66.

614. Day, *The Admiralty Hydrographic Service 1795-1919*, 306–7.

615. Day, 25–26.

616. Presutti, '"A Better Idea than the Best Constructed Charts"'.

617. Anderson, 'The Hydrographer's Narrative: Writing Global Knowledge in the 1830s'.

618. Day, *The Admiralty Hydrographic Service 1795-1919*, 74.

619. Behrisch, *Discovery, Innovation, and the Victorian Admiralty: Paper Navigators*, 42–43.

620. Taylor, 'On the Present State and Requirement for Surveys in the Indian Ocean: The Transactions of the Bombay Geographical Society. From May 1858 to May 1860. (Edited by the Secretary.) Volume XV.'; Philbrick, 'Notes on the Andamans: The Transactions of the Bombay Geographical Society. From May 1858 to May 1860. (Edited by the Secretary.) Volume XV.'

621. 'Marine, Mar 1861, No16'.

622. Edgell, *Sea Surveys: Britain's Contribution to Hydrography*.

623. Day, *The Admiralty Hydrographic Service 1795-1919*, 64–66.

624. Ritchie, *The Admiralty Chart: British Naval Hydrography in the Nineteenth Century*, 198.

625. 'Miscellaneous Papers Relating to the Creation of Marine Department 1859'.

626. Law, 'On the Methods of Long-Distance Control: Vessels, Navigation and the Portuguese Route to India', 251.

627. Day, *The Admiralty Hydrographic Service 1795-1919*, 69.

628. Ehrlich, *The East India Company and the Politics of Knowledge*.

629. Day, *The Admiralty Hydrographic Service 1795-1919*, 74; Hayes, 'How the British Admiralty Charts Are Produced'.

630. Driver, 'Distance and Disturbance: Travel, Exploration and Knowledge in the Nineteenth Century'.

631. Achbari, 'Building Networks for Science: Conflict and Cooperation in Nineteenth-Century Global Marine Studies', 260.

632. Iliffe, 'Science and Voyages of Discovery'; Davey, 'The Advancement of Nautical Knowledge: The Hydrographical Office, the Royal Navy and the Charting of the Baltic Sea, 1795-1815'; McCarthy, 'Gambling on Empire'; Sophie Waring, 'The Board of Longitude and the Funding of Scientific Work: Negotiating Authority and Expertise in the Early Nineteenth Century', *Journal for Maritime Research* 16, no. 1 (2014): 55–71, https://doi.org/10.1080/21533369.2014.906143; Rigby, Merwe, and Williams, *Pacific Exploration: Voyages of Discovery from Captain Cook's Endeavour to the Beagle*.

633. Friendly, *Beaufort of the Admiralty: The Life of Sir Francis Beaufort, 1774-1857*.

634. Johanna Skurnik, 'Authorizing Geographical Knowledge: John Arrowsmith, Mapmaking and the Mid Nineteenth-Century British Empire', *Journal of Historical Geography* 69 (2020): 21, https://doi.org/10.1016/j.jhg.2020.04.003.

635. Day, *The Admiralty Hydrographic Service 1795-1919*, 76.

636. Law, 'On the Methods of Long-Distance Control: Vessels, Navigation and the Portuguese Route to India', 256.

637. Simon Ryan, *The Cartographic Eye: How Explorers Saw Australia* (Cambridge: Cambridge University Press, 1996).

638. Low, *History of the Indian Navy (1613-1863)*, 1:571.

639. Tizard lists the surveys conducted by British naval officers, and from 1863 until 1866 by the Royal Navy. Tizard, *Chronological List of the Officers Conducting British Maritime Discoveries and Surveys*.

640. Hydrographic Office, 'Gulf of Bengal, Andaman Islands' (Old Copy Book, 1867), OCB 835 B1A, UK Hydrographic Office; Hydrographic Office, 'Bay of Bengal, Nicobar Group, Nancowry Harbour'; Hydrographic Office, 'Gulf of Bengal, Andaman Islands' (Old Copy Book, 1881), OCB 835 B5, UK Hydrographic Office; Hydrographic Office, 'Chart of Part of the Coast of Great Andaman, 1789' (Misc Charts, 1885), D989, UK Hydrographic Office; Hydrographic Office, 'Bay of Bengal, South Andaman I. East Coast, Port Blair.' (Old Copy Book, 1888), OCB 514 C1-8, UK Hydrographic Office; Hydrographic Office, 'Bay of Bengal, Andaman Islands' (Old Copy Book, 1891), OCB 825 C1, UK Hydrographic Office.

Notes

641. 'Public, Apr 1863, No24' (Home, 1863), National Archives of India.

642. 'Marine, Mar 1871, No38-40' (Military, 1871), National Archives of India.

643. Notice to Mariners were published in newspapers, and also as a printed publication. 'Admiralty Sailing Directions: A Historical Perspective'.

644. Hydrographic Office, 'Bay of Bengal, South Andaman I. East Coast, Port Blair.'

645. Ritchie, *The Admiralty Chart: British Naval Hydrography in the Nineteenth Century*.

646. Driver and Martins, 'Shipwreck and Salvage in the Tropics'; Davey, 'The Advancement of Nautical Knowledge: The Hydrographical Office, the Royal Navy and the Charting of the Baltic Sea, 1795-1815'; Auerbach, *Imperial Boredom: Monotony and the British Empire*, 31–35.

647. Spence, *A History of the Royal Navy: Empire and Imperialism*, 27.

648. Hydrographic Office, 'Bay of Bengal, South Andaman I. East Coast, Port Blair.'

649. 'Miscellaneous Papers Naval and Maritime Services in India 1860-1862'.

650. Low, *History of the Indian Navy (1613-1863)*, 1:548.

651. Booth, *Navies and Foreign Policy*; Michael Lewis, *The Navy in Transition: A Social History 1814-1864* (London: Hodder & Stoughton, 1965); Dickinson, *Educating the Royal Navy: Eighteenth- and Nineteenth-Century Education for Officers*.

652. Latour, *Reassembling The Social: An Introduction to Actor-Network Theory*, 257.

653. Shapin, *A Social History of Truth*, 81.

654. Driver, 'Distance and Disturbance: Travel, Exploration and Knowledge in the Nineteenth Century'.

655. Davey, 'The Advancement of Nautical Knowledge: The Hydrographical Office, the Royal Navy and the Charting of the Baltic Sea, 1795-1815', 97.

656. Sen, 'Developing *Terra Nullius*'.

657. Booth, 'Roles, Objectives and Tasks: An Inventory of the Functions of Navies', 96–97.

658. Anderson, 'The Hydrographer's Narrative: Writing Global Knowledge in the 1830s'.

659. Booth, *Navies and Foreign Policy*.

660. Hydrographic Office, 'Gulf of Bengal, South Andaman I, East Coast, Port Blair'; Hydrographic Office, 'Bay of Bengal, Nicobar Group, Nancowry Harbour'; Hydrographic Office, 'Gulf of Bengal, Andaman Islands', 1867.

Chapter 5

661. 'Letter from Commander E. Brooker of HMS Sylvia, to Secretary of the Admiralty, 6 May 1867.' (Admiralty, 1867), ADM 125/12, The National Archives.

662. 'Letter from Major H.N. Davies, Secretary to Chief Commission British Burmah, to Superintendent Port Blair, 12 April 1867' (Admiralty, 1867), ADM 125/12, The National Archives.

663. Cable, *Gunboat Diplomacy 1919 - 1979: Political Applications of Limited Naval Force*; Preston and Major, *Send a Gun Boat! A Study of the British Gunboat.*

664. Brooks, *The Long Arm of Empire: Naval Brigades from the Crimea to the Boxer Rebellion*, 101–5; John F. Beeler, *British Naval Policy in the Gladstone-Disraeli Era, 1866-1880* (Stanford: Stanford University Press, 1997), 351; White, 'The Long Arm of Seapower: The Anglo-Japanese War of 1863-1864'.

665. 'Letter from Lieutenant-Colonel B. Ford, Superintendent to Port Blair, to Commander HMS Sylvia, 15 April 1867' (Admiralty, 1867), ADM 125/12, The National Archives; 'Letter from Commander E. Brooker of HMS Sylvia, to Secretary of the Admiralty, 6 May 1867.'; 'Letter from Commander E. Brooker of HMS Sylvia, to Superintendent Port Blair, 19 April 1867.' (Admiralty, 1867), ADM 125/12, The National Archives; 'Letter from Major H.N. Davies, Secretary to Chief Commission British Burmah, to Superintendent Port Blair, 12 April 1867'.

666. 'Victoria Cross Details: Little Andaman Campaign' (War Office, 1867), WO 98/4 17-21, The National Archives; Hernon, *Britain's Forgotten Wars: Colonial Campaigns of the 19th Century*, 101–7.

667. Spence, *A History of the Royal Navy: Empire and Imperialism*, 58.

668. Preston and Major, *Send a Gun Boat! A Study of the British Gunboat*, 8–9.

669. Evans, *Building the Steam Navy: Dockyards, Technology, and the Creation of the Victorian Battle Fleet, 1830-1906*; Cocker, *Coastal Forces Vessels of the Royal Navy from 1865*; Howard J. Fuller, '"Had We Used the Navy's Bare Fist Instead of Its Gloved Hand..." - The Absence of Coastal Assault Vessels in the Royal Navy by 1914', *British Journal for Military History* 3, no. 3 (2017); Davies, *Transport to Another World: HMS Tamar and the Sinews of Empire*.

670. Barry Gough, *Gunboat Frontier: British Maritime Authority and Northwest Coast Indians, 1846-90* (Vancouver: University of British Columbia Press, 1984); Barry McBeth, *Gunboats, Corruption, and Claims: Foreign Intervention in Venezuela, 1899-1908* (Westport: Greenwood Press, 2001); Gilbert C. Din, 'Mississippi River Gunboats on the Gulf Coast: The Spanish Naval Fight against William Augustus Bowles, 1799-1803', *Louisiana History: The Journal of the Louisiana Historical Association* 47, no. 3 (2006): 277–308; Wilfrid Nunn, *Tigris Gunboats: The Forgotten War in Iraq 1914 - 1917* (London: Chatham Publications, 2007); Kevin Rowlands, 'Riverine Warfare', *Naval War College Review* 71, no. 1 (2018): 53–70; Gordon Connor McBain, 'Debt and the Gunboat: Mapping Intervention in Victorian International Legal Thought, 1848-1912' (University of Glasgow, 2023), http://theses.gla.ac.uk/id/eprint/83499.

671. Merriman and Peters, 'Military Mobilities in an Age of Global War, 1870–1945'; Merriman et al., 'Mobility'; Cresswell, 'Towards a Politics of Mobility'.

672. Preston and Major, *Send a Gun Boat! A Study of the British Gunboat*, 57.

673. For the strategic role of gunboats, see: Beeler, 'Steam, Strategy and Schurman: Imperial Defence in the Post-Crimean Era, 1856-1905'; For tactical considerations, see: Preston and Major, *Send a Gun Boat! A Study of the British Gunboat*; For a study of gunboats as platforms, see: Cocker, *Coastal Forces Vessels of the Royal Navy from 1865*.

674. Portman, *A History of Our Relations with the Andamanese, Vol.I*; Pandit and Anthropological Survey of India, *Andaman and Nicobar Islands*.

675. Evans, *Building the Steam Navy: Dockyards, Technology, and the Creation of the Victorian Battle Fleet, 1830-1906*.

676. 'Military Forces in India'.

677. James, *Raj: The Making and Unmaking of British India*.

678. David, *Victoria's Wars: The Rise of Empire*.

679. 'Instructions in Landing Men to Quell Disturbances' (Admiralty, 1866), ADM 127/1, The National Archives.

680. Graham-Yooll, *Imperial Skirmishes: War and Gunboat Diplomacy in Latin America*; Nunn, *Tigris Gunboats: The Forgotten War in Iraq 1914 - 1917*; McBain, 'Debt and the Gunboat'.

681. Heaslip, *Gunboats, Empire and the China Station: The Royal Navy in 1920s East Asia*, 273.

682. Beeler, 'Steam, Strategy and Schurman: Imperial Defence in the Post-Crimean Era, 1856-1905', 6–8.

683. Brooks, *The Long Arm of Empire: Naval Brigades from the Crimea to the Boxer Rebellion*, 77.

684. Portman, *A History of Our Relations with the Andamanese, Vol.I*, 278.

685. 'Letter from Lieutenant-Colonel B. Ford, Superintendent to Port Blair, to Commander HMS Sylvia, 15 April 1867'.

686. Hernon, *Britain's Forgotten Wars: Colonial Campaigns of the 19th Century*, 495–500.

687. Daunton and Halpern, *Empire and Others: British Encounters with Indigenous Peoples, 1600 - 1850*; Anderson, *Subaltern Lives: Biographies of Colonialism in the Indian Ocean World, 1790-1920*.

688. David, *Victoria's Wars: The Rise of Empire*; Gopal, *Insurgent Empire: Anticolonial Resistance and British Dissent*; Zachary Bennet, '"Canoes of Great Swiftness": Rivercraft and War in the Northeast.', *Early American Studies, An Interdisciplinary Journal* 21, no. 2 (2023): 205–32, https://doi.org/10.1353/eam.2023.0008; Cameron Winter, 'War-Canoes and Poisoned Arrows: Great Jolof and Imperial Mali Against the Fifteenth Century Portuguese Slave Raids', *Journal of African Military History*, 2023, 1–31, https://doi.org/10.1163/24680966-bja10016.

689. Grainger, *The British Navy in Eastern Waters: The Indian and Pacific Oceans*, 241.

690. Beeler, *British Naval Policy in the Gladstone-Disraeli Era, 1866-1880*, 6–8.

691. Beeler, 'Steam, Strategy and Schurman: Imperial Defence in the Post-Crimean Era, 1856-1905', 28.

692. Beeler, *British Naval Policy in the Gladstone-Disraeli Era, 1866-1880*, 28–29.

693. Low, *History of the Indian Navy (1613-1863)*.

694. Bickers and Howlett, *Britain and China, 1840-1970: Empire, Finance and War*.

695. 'Political and Secret, November 1864' (India Office Records, 1864), L PS 6 456, British Library.

696. Grainger, *The British Navy in Eastern Waters: The Indian and Pacific Oceans*; Mohanan, *The Royal Indian Navy: Trajectories, Transformations and the Transfer of Power*.

697. 'Letter from Major H.N. Davies, Secretary to Chief Commission British Burmah, to Superintendent Port Blair, 12 April 1867'.

698. Portman, *A History of Our Relations with the Andamanese, Vol.II*, 546–48.

699. 'Abstract of Letters from India, Expedition to North Sentinel, February 1868' (India Office Records and Private Papers, 1868), IOR/L/PS/20/CA8, Qatar National Library; Portman, *A History of Our Relations with the Andamanese, Vol.II*, 547.

700. 'Military, Sep 1867, No862-3' (India Office Records, 1867), L PS 6 554, British Library.

701. Markovits, *The Global World of Indian Merchants, 1750-1947: Traders of Sind from Bukhara to Panama*; Amrith, *Crossing the Bay of Bengal: The Furies of Nature and the Fortunes of Migrants*.

702. 'Letter from Major H.N. Davies, Secretary to Chief Commission British Burmah, to Superintendent Port Blair, 12 April 1867'.

703. Hernon, *Britain's Forgotten Wars: Colonial Campaigns of the 19th Century*, 104.

704. 'Letter from Lieutenant-Colonel B. Ford, Superintendent to Port Blair, to Commander HMS Arracan, 15 May 1867' (Admiralty, 1867), ADM 125/12, The National Archives.

705. 'Abstract of Letters from India, Expedition to the Little Andaman Islands, 1867' (India Office Records and Private Papers, 1867), IOR/L/PS/20/CA8, Qatar National Library.

706. Lyon and Winfield, *The Sail & Steam Navy List: All the Ships of the Royal Navy, 1815-1889*, 138.

707. 'Letter from Commander E. Brooker of HMS Sylvia, to Secretary of the Admiralty, 6 May 1867.'

708. 'Letter from Commander E. Brooker of HMS Sylvia, to Superintendent Port Blair, 19 April 1867.'

709. Preston and Major, *Send a Gun Boat! A Study of the British Gunboat*, 17.

710. Hernon, *Britain's Forgotten Wars: Colonial Campaigns of the 19th Century*.

711. 'Letter from Commander E. Brooker of HMS Sylvia, to Superintendent Port Blair, 19 April 1867.'

712. 'Letter from Commander E. Brooker of HMS Sylvia, to Secretary of the Admiralty, 6 May 1867.'

713. Hernon, *Britain's Forgotten Wars: Colonial Campaigns of the 19th Century*, 102.

714. 'Military, Sep 1867, No862-3'.

715. Low, *History of the Indian Navy (1613-1863)*.

716. 'Military, Sep 1867, No253' (India Office Records, 1867), L PS 5 553 214, British Library.

717. Her Majesty's Indian Marine Ship (HMIMS) replaced HMINS as of 1863. Hastings, *The Royal Indian Navy, 1612-1950*.

718. Low, *History of the Indian Navy (1613-1863)*, 1:558.

719. 'Letter from Lieutenant-Colonel B. Ford, Superintendent to Port Blair, to Commander HMS Sylvia, 15 April 1867'.

720. 'Letter from Major B. Ford, Superintendent of Port Blair, to the Secretary to the Government of India, 6 June 1864' (India Office Records, 1864), L PS 5 553 No20, British Library.

721. 'Letter from Lieutenant-Colonel B. Ford, Superintendent to Port Blair, to Commander HMS Arracan, 15 May 1867'; 'Letter from Lieutenant-Colonel B. Ford, Superintendent to Port Blair, to Commander HMS Arracan, 5 May 1867' (India Office Records, 1867), L PS 6 554, British Library.

722. 'Letter from Lieutenant-Colonel B. Ford, Superintendent to Port Blair, to Commander HMS Arracan, 15 May 1867'.

723. George Paton, *The 24th Regiment of Foot: From the War of Spanish Succession to the Zulu War* (Lanarkshire: Leonaur, 2017).

724. Hore, *Seapower Ashore: 200 Years of Royal Navy Operations on Land*.

725. 'Military, Sep 1867, No862-3'.

726. Graham-Yooll, *Imperial Skirmishes: War and Gunboat Diplomacy in Latin America*, 90.

727. Preston and Major, *Send a Gun Boat! A Study of the British Gunboat*, 17.

728. Cable, *Gunboat Diplomacy 1919 - 1979: Political Applications of Limited Naval Force*, 194.

729. 'Letter from Commander E. Brooker of HMS Sylvia, to Secretary of the Admiralty, 6 May 1867.'; 'Letter from Commander E. Brooker of HMS Sylvia, to Superintendent Port Blair, 19 April 1867.'

730. 'Letter from Military Department to Commodore Commanding East India Station, 25 September 1867' (Admiralty, 1867), ADM 125/12, The National Archives.

731. Tarling, *Imperial Britain in South-East Asia*.

732. Hore, *Seapower Ashore: 200 Years of Royal Navy Operations on Land*.

733. Preston and Major, *Send a Gun Boat! A Study of the British Gunboat*, 44–45.

734. Pandit and Anthropological Survey of India, *Andaman and Nicobar Islands*.

735. 'Letter from Lieutenant W. L. Much, 2-24th Regiment Commanding Troops on the Little Andaman Expedition, to Officer Commanding 2-24th Regiment, Port Blair 10 May 1867' (Admiralty, 1867), ADM 125/12, The National Archives; 'Letter from Captain H. Barrow Commander of HMS Arracan to Superintendent of Port Blair, 8 May 1867' (Admiralty, 1867), ADM 125/12, The National Archives; Hernon, *Britain's Forgotten Wars: Colonial Campaigns of the 19th Century*.

736. Hernon, *Britain's Forgotten Wars: Colonial Campaigns of the 19th Century*, 103–4.

737. Brooks, *The Long Arm of Empire: Naval Brigades from the Crimea to the Boxer Rebellion*.

738. 'Letters from Vice Admiral Henry Keppel, Commodore in Chief China Station, to Governor General of India, 21 Sep 1867' (Admiralty, 1867), ADM 125/147, The National Archives.

739. 'Letter from Lieutenant W. L. Much, 2-24th Regiment Commanding Troops on the Little Andaman Expedition, to Officer Commanding 2-24th Regiment, Port Blair 10 May 1867'.

740. 'Letter from Lieutenant W. L. Much, 2-24th Regiment Commanding Troops on the Little Andaman Expedition, to Officer Commanding 2-24th Regiment, Port Blair 10 May 1867'.

741. 'Victoria Cross Details: Little Andaman Campaign'.

742. 'Letters from Vice Admiral Henry Keppel, Commodore in Chief China Station, to Governor General of India, 21 Sep 1867'; 'Letter from Commodore Charles T. Hillyar, Commanding East Indies Station, to Viceroy and Governor General, 13 June 1867' (India Office Records, 1867), L PS 5 553 214, British Library.

743. 'Abstract of Letters from India, Expedition to the Little Andaman Islands, 1867'; 'Marine, Mar 1868, No09' (Military, 1868), National Archives of India.

744. Grainger, *The British Navy in Eastern Waters: The Indian and Pacific Oceans*, 217–18.

745. 'Marine, Dec 1867, No19' (India Office Records and Private Papers, 1867), IOR/L/PS/20/CA8, Qatar National Library.

746. Beeler, 'Steam, Strategy and Schurman: Imperial Defence in the Post-Crimean Era, 1856-1905'; Beeler, *British Naval Policy in the Gladstone-Disraeli Era, 1866-1880*; Gough, *Pax Britannica: Ruling the Waves and Keeping the Peace before Armageddon*; Lambert, 'The Royal Navy, 1856-1914: Deterrence and the Strategy of World Power'; Cook, 'Establishing Sea Routes to India and China: Stages in the Development of Hydrographical Knowledge'.

747. Cable, *Gunboat Diplomacy 1919 - 1979: Political Applications of Limited Naval Force*.

748. For an account of the campaigns in Borneo, see. Hernon, *Britain's Forgotten Wars: Colonial Campaigns of the 19th Century*, 495; Tarling explores the role of auxiliary naval vessels in campaigns against littoral states in the Cocos-Keeling and Malaya through the 1840s to 1860s: Tarling, *Piracy and Politics in the Malay World*, 258.

749. David, *Victoria's Wars: The Rise of Empire*, 3.

750. Latour, *Reassembling The Social: An Introduction to Actor-Network Theory*, 217.

Chapter 6

751. 'Letter from Secretary to the Government of India, Foreign Department, to the Secretary of State for India, 23 July 1867' (India Office Records, 1867), L PS 5 553 214, British Library.

752. Roskill, *The Strategy of Sea Power*; Roskill, *The Navy at War 1939-1945*; Till, *Seapower: Theory and Practice*; Till, *Seapower: A Guide for the Twenty-First Century*; Till, *Understanding Victory: Naval Operations from Trafalgar to the Falklands*.

753. For other accounts of blockade, see: Gray, *Seapower and Strategy*, 20–21; Grove, *The Future of Sea Power*, 15–16; Hedley Paul Willmott, *The Last Century of Sea Power* (Bloomington: Indiana University Press, 2009), 31–44; Hamilton, *The Making of the Modern Admiralty: British Naval Policy-Making, 1805–1927*, 82; Morris, *The Foundations of British Maritime Ascendancy: Resources, Logistics and the State, 1755-1815*, 48–53.

754. This is a similar perspective through seapower studies: Gray, *Seapower and Strategy*, 20–21.

755. Brooks, *The Long Arm of Empire: Naval Brigades from the Crimea to the Boxer Rebellion*, 75.

756. For Pearl River, see: Lovell, *The Opium War: Drugs, Dreams and the Making of China*, 141–67; For Rangoon, see: Brooks, *The Long Arm of Empire: Naval Brigades from the Crimea to the Boxer Rebellion*, 101–5; For Kagoshima, see: White, 'The Long Arm of Seapower: The Anglo-Japanese War of 1863-1864', 1461–62.

757. Brooks, *The Long Arm of Empire: Naval Brigades from the Crimea to the Boxer Rebellion*, 74–76.

758. Grainger, *The British Navy in Eastern Waters: The Indian and Pacific Oceans*, 241.

759. Grainger, *The British Navy in Eastern Waters: The Indian and Pacific Oceans*, 241.

760. Alpers, 'On Becoming a British Lake: Piracy, Slaving, and British Imperialism in the Indian Ocean during the First Half of the Nineteenth Century'; Stefan Amirell, *Piracy in World History* (Amsterdam: Amsterdam University Press, 2022); Subramanian, *The Sovereign and the Pirate: Ordering Maritime Subjects in India's Western Littoral*.

761. Tarling, *Piracy and Politics in the Malay World*; Subramanian, *The Sovereign and the Pirate: Ordering Maritime Subjects in India's Western Littoral*; Policante, *The Pirate Myth: Genealogies of an Imperial Concept*.

762. Roskill, *The Strategy of Sea Power*, 48–49.

763. Natalino Ronzitti, ed., *The Law of Naval Warfare: A Collection of Agreements and Documents with Commentaries* (Boston: Kluwer Academic Publishers, 1988), 64–65.

764. 'Letter from Commodore Charles T. Hillyar, Commanding East Indies Station, to Viceroy and Governor General, 30 July 1867' (India Office Records, 1867), L PS 5 553 214, British Library.

765. Bruce A. Elleman and S. C. M. Paine, eds., *Naval Blockades and Seapower: Strategies and Counter-Strategies, 1805-2005*, 34 (London: Routledge, 2006).

766. Roskill, *The Strategy of Sea Power*, 46–49; Andrew Lambert, 'The Royal Navy's White Sea Campaign of 1854', in *Naval Power and Expeditionary Warfare: Peripheral Campaigns and New Theatres of Naval Warfare*, ed. Bruce A. Elleman and S. C. M. Paine (London: Routledge, 2011), 29–32.

767. Brooks, *The Long Arm of Empire: Naval Brigades from the Crimea to the Boxer Rebellion*, 102.

768. Tarling, *Piracy and Politics in the Malay World*.

769. Cable, *Gunboat Diplomacy 1919 - 1979: Political Applications of Limited Naval Force*; Preston and Major, *Send a Gun Boat! A Study of the British Gunboat*; Kwan, '"Barbarian Ships Sail Freely about the Seas"'; Amirell, *Piracy in World History*.

770. 'Letter from Captain Arthur Kinloch, H.M. 36th Regt., to the Secretary of State for India, 8 Nov 1868' (Pamphlets and Manuscripts, 1868), P Mil 32, Naval Historical Branch; 'Letter from Captain Arthur Kinloch, H.M. 36th Regt., to the Secretary of State for India, 13 December 1868' (Pamphlets and Manuscripts, 1868), P Mil 32, Naval Historical Branch.

771. Brinkman, *Balancing Strategy: Seapower, Neutrality, and Prize Law in the Seven Years' War*.

772. Ong-Webb and Ke, 'Piracy, Seaborne Trade and the Rivalries of Foreign Sea Powers in East and Southeast Asia, 1511 to 1839: A Chinese Perspective'.

773. Chaudhuri, *Trade and Civilisation in the Indian Ocean: An Economic History from the Rise of Islam to 1750*.

774. Spence, *A History of the Royal Navy: Empire and Imperialism*, 45.

775. Garrett Ziegler, 'The Perils of Empire: Dickens, Collins and the Indian Mutiny', in *Pirates and Mutineers of the Nineteenth Century: Swashbucklers and Swindlers*, ed. Grace Moore (London: Routledge, 2016), 150–66; Moore, 'Piracy and the Ends of Romantic Commercialism: Victorian Businessmen Meet Malay Pirates'; Ong-Webb and Ke, 'Piracy, Seaborne Trade and the Rivalries of Foreign Sea Powers in East and Southeast Asia, 1511 to 1839: A Chinese Perspective'.

776. 'Marine, Mar 1868, N009'.

777. 'Letter from Captain Norman B. Bedingfield, HMS Wasp, to Commodore East Indies Station, 6 July 1867' (India Office Records, 1867), L PS 5 553 214, British Library.

778. Ziegler, 'The Perils of Empire: Dickens, Collins and the Indian Mutiny'.

779. Brooks, *The Long Arm of Empire: Naval Brigades from the Crimea to the Boxer Rebellion*; Subramanian, *The Sovereign and the Pirate: Ordering Maritime Subjects in India's Western Littoral*; David McLean, 'Famine on the Coast: The Royal Navy and the Relief of Ireland, 1846–1847', *The English Historical Review* 134, no. 566 (2019): 92–120, https://doi.org/10.1093/ehr/cez004.

780. Anderson, 'The Age of Revolution in the Indian Ocean, Bay of Bengal and South China Sea: A Maritime Perspective'.

781. Subramanian, *The Sovereign and the Pirate: Ordering Maritime Subjects in India's Western Littoral*, 23.

782. Lambert, 'The Royal Navy, 1856-1914: Deterrence and the Strategy of World Power'.

783. 'Letter from Secretary to the Government of India to the Chief Commissioner of British Burmah, December 1867' (India Office Records and Private Papers, 1867), IOR/L/PS/20/CA8, Qatar National Library.

784. Grainger, *The British Navy in Eastern Waters: The Indian and Pacific Oceans*, 233.

785. Beeler, *British Naval Policy in the Gladstone-Disraeli Era, 1866-1880*, 24–27.

786. Beeler, 26.

787. Grainger, *The British Navy in Eastern Waters: The Indian and Pacific Oceans*, 239.

788. Spence, *A History of the Royal Navy: Empire and Imperialism*, 49.

789. 'Letter from Vice Admiral Henry Keppel, Commodore in Chief China Station, to Secretary of the Admiralty, 18 December 1867' (Admiralty, 1867), ADM 125/12, The National Archives.

790. Ajay Saini, 'How a Bloody Incident of Piracy Changed the Lives of the Nicobarese Forever', *The Hindu*, 2018, https://www.thehindu.com/society/how-a-bloody-incident-of-piracy-changed-the-lives-of-the-nicobarese-forever/article22375511.ece.

791. 'Letters from Vice Admiral Henry Keppel, Commodore in Chief China Station, to Secretary of the Admiralty, 13 January 1868' (Admiralty, 1868), ADM 125/147, The National Archives.

792. 'Letter from Commander E. Brooker of HMS Sylvia, to Secretary of the Admiralty, 6 May 1867.'

793. Saini, 'How a Bloody Incident of Piracy Changed the Lives of the Nicobarese Forever'.

794. 'Letter from Commodore Charles T. Hillyar, Commanding East Indies Station, to Viceroy and Governor General, 13 June 1867'.

795. Tarling, *Imperial Britain in South-East Asia*, 254.

796. 'Letter from Commodore Charles T. Hillyar, Commanding East Indies Station, to Viceroy and Governor General, 30 July 1867'.

797. 'Letter from Secretary to the Government of India, Foreign Department, to the Secretary of State for India, 23 July 1867'.

798. 'Letter from Sir A.E.H. Anson, Lieutenant Governor of Penang, to Captain of HMS Wasp, 28 June 1867' (India Office Records, 1867), L PS 5 553 214, British Library.

799. 'Letter from Captain Norman B. Bedingfield, HMS Wasp, to Commodore East Indies Station, 6 July 1867'.

800. 'Letter from Captain Norman B. Bedingfield, HMS Wasp, to Commodore East Indies Station, 6 July 1867'.

801. Killingray, Lincoln, and Rigby, *Maritime Empires: British Imperial Maritime Trade in the Nineteenth Century*.

802. 'Letter from Secretary of State for India to Governor General of India, 16 July 1867' (Admiralty, 1867), ADM 125/12, The National Archives.

803. 'Letter from Commodore Charles T. Hillyar, Commanding East Indies Station, to Viceroy and Governor General, 13 June 1867'.

804. 'Letter from Commodore Charles T. Hillyar, Commanding East Indies Station, to Viceroy and Governor General, 13 June 1867'.

805. 'Letter from Sir A.H.E Anson, Lieutenant Governor of Penang, to Foreign Secretary, Indian Government, 22 August 1867' (India Office Records, 1867), L PS 6 554, British Library.

806. 'Letter from Commodore Charles T. Hillyar, Commanding East Indies Station, to Viceroy and Governor General, 13 June 1867'.

807. Gough, *Pax Britannica: Ruling the Waves and Keeping the Peace before Armageddon*.

808. 'Letter from Secretary to the Government of India, Foreign Department, to the Secretary of State for India, 23 July 1867'.

809. 'Letter from Secretary to the Government of India, Foreign Department, to the Secretary of State for India, 23 July 1867'.

810. Subramanian, *The Sovereign and the Pirate: Ordering Maritime Subjects in India's Western Littoral*, 22.

811. 'Letter from Secretary to the Government of India to the Chief Commissioner of British Burmah, December 1867'.

812. 'Letter from Lieutenant Colonel H.K. Burne, Military Department to the Chief Commissioner of British Burmah, 5 September 1867' (India Office Records, 1867), L PS 6 554, British Library.

813. 'Letter from Commodore Charles T. Hillyar, Commanding East Indies Station, to Viceroy and Governor General, 30 July 1867'.

814. 'Letter from Commodore Charles T. Hillyar, Commanding East Indies Station, to Viceroy and Governor General, 30 July 1867'.

815. 'Letter from Commodore Charles T. Hillyar, Commanding East Indies Station, to Viceroy and Governor General, 30 July 1867'.

816. 'Letter from Lieutenant Colonel H.K. Burne, Military Department to the Commodore Commanding East India Station, 25 September 1867' (India Office Records, 1867), L PS 6 554, British Library; 'Letter from Lieutenant Colonel H.K. Burne, Military Department to the Chief Commissioner of British Burmah, 5 September 1867'.

817. Tarling, *Piracy and Politics in the Malay World*; 'Letter from Sir A.E.H. Anson, Lieutenant Governor of Penang, to Captain of HMS Wasp, 28 June 1867'.

818. 'Letter from Commodore Leopold G. Heath, Commanding East Indies Station, to Captain HMS Wasp, 26 July 1867' (India Office Records, 1867), L PS 5 553 214, British Library.

819. 'Letter from Secretary of State for India to Governor General of India, 16 July 1867', 18676.

820. 'Notes from a Conversation on the Nicobars with Colonel H. Man, Officiating Superintendent Port Blair, by Secretary to the Government of India, 12 March 1869' (India Office Records, 1869), L PS 6 564 163, British Library.

821. 'Letter from Commodore Leopold G. Heath, Commanding East Indies Station, to Captain HMS Wasp, 26 July 1867'.

822. 'Letter from Captain Norman B. Bedingfield, HMS Wasp, to Commodore East Indies Station, 6 July 1867'.

823. 'Letter from Captain Norman B. Bedingfield, HMS Wasp, to Lieutenant Governor of Penang, 28 June 1867' (India Office Records, 1867), L PS 5 553 214, British Library.

824. 'Letter from Captain Norman B. Bedingfield, HMS Wasp, to Commodore East Indies Station, 6 July 1867'.

825. 'Marine, Aug 1867, No13' (Military, 1867), National Archives of India.

826. Colledge, Warlow, and Bush, *Ships of the Royal Navy: The Complete Record of All Fighting Ships of the Royal Navy from The15th Century to the Present*, 385.

Notes

827. 'Letter from Commodore Leopold G. Heath, Commanding East Indies Station, to Captain HMS Wasp, 26 July 1867'.

828. 'Letter from Commodore Leopold G. Heath, Commanding East India Station, to Viceroy and Governor General, 30 September 1867' (India Office Records, 1867), L PS 6 554, British Library.

829. 'Letter from Commodore Leopold G. Heath, Commanding East Indies Station, to Viceroy and Governor General, 5 August 1867' (India Office Records, 1867), L PS 5 553 214, British Library.

830. 'Letter from Commander E. Brooker of HMS Sylvia, to Superintendent Port Blair, 19 April 1867.'; 'Letter from Lieutenant-Colonel B. Ford, Superintendent to Port Blair, to Commander HMS Sylvia, 15 April 1867'.

831. Kloss was one of the first to publish images of the Nicobarese and Andamanese canoes, although did not record the warfighting elements. C. Boden Kloss, *In the Andaman and Nicobar Islands. The Narrative If a Cruise in the Schooner 'Terrapin,' With Notices of the Islands, Their Fauna, Ethnology, Etc.* (London: John Murray, 1903); For other postcolonial analysis of canoes, see: Susanne Kuehling, 'The Converted War Canoe: Cannibal Raiders, Missionaries and "Pax Britannica" on Dobu Island, Papua New Guinea', *Anthropologica* 56, no. 2 (2014): 274; Robin Fisher, *Contact and Conflict: Indian-European Relations in British Columbia, 1774-1890*, 2nd ed. (Vancouver: UBC Press, 1992); Bennet, '"Canoes of Great Swiftness": Rivercraft and War in the Northeast.'; Winter, 'War-Canoes and Poisoned Arrows'.

832. 'Marine, Sep 1867, No9' (India Office Records and Private Papers, 1867), IOR/L/PS/20/CA7, Qatar National Library; 'Marine, Dec 1867, No19'.

833. 'Letters from Vice Admiral Henry Keppel, Commodore in Chief China Station, to Governor General of India, 21 Sep 1867'.

834. 'Marine, Dec 1867, No25' (Military, 1867), National Archives of India.

835. 'Letter from Commodore Leopold G. Heath, Commanding East Indies Station, to Viceroy and Governor General, 5 August 1867'.

836. 'Marine, Feb 1868, No27' (India Office Records and Private Papers, 1868), IOR/L/PS/20/CA8, Qatar National Library.

837. 'Letter from Commodore Leopold G. Heath, Commanding East Indies Station, to Captain HMS Wasp, 26 July 1867'.

838. 'Letter from Commodore Leopold G. Heath, Commanding East Indies Station, to Viceroy and Governor General, 4 March 1869' (India Office Records, 1869), L PS 6 564, British Library.

839. 'Letters from Vice Admiral Henry Keppel, Commodore in Chief China Station, to Governor General of India, 21 Sep 1867'.

840. 'Letters from Vice Admiral Henry Keppel, Commodore in Chief China Station, to Governor General of India, 13 Aug 1867' (Admiralty, 1867), ADM 125/147, The National Archives.

841. Colledge, Warlow, and Bush, *Ships of the Royal Navy: The Complete Record of All Fighting Ships of the Royal Navy from The15th Century to the Present*, 326.

842. 'Letter from Lieutenant Colonel H.K. Burne, Military Department to the Chief Commissioner of British Burmah, 5 September 1867'; 'Letter from Colonel Henry Man, to the Military Secretary to the Government of India, 27 September 1867', 27.

843. Subramanian, *The Sovereign and the Pirate: Ordering Maritime Subjects in India's Western Littoral.*

844. 'Letter from Commodore Leopold G. Heath, Commanding East India Station, to Viceroy and Governor General, 30 September 1867'.

845. 'Journal of Proceedings and Intercourse Between HMS Perseus and the Nicobar Islanders between the 22 December 1867 and 23 January 1868' (Admiralty, 1868), ADM 125/147, The National Archives.

846. Pandit and Anthropological Survey of India, *Andaman and Nicobar Islands.*

847. 'Notes from a Conversation on the Nicobars with Colonel H. Man, Officiating Superintendent Port Blair, by Secretary to the Government of India, 12 March 1869'.

848. 'Letter from the Marine Department, to the Secretary of State for India, 7 Dec 1867' (India Office Records, 1867), L PS 6 554, British Library; 'Letter from Secretary to the Government of India, Foreign Department, to the Secretary of State for India, 23 July 1867'.

849. 'Letter from Foreign Department, Government of India, to Secretary of State for India, 13 February 1868' (India Office Records, 1868), L PS 560, British Library.

850. 'Letter from Colonel Henry Man, to the Military Secretary to the Government of India, 23 September 1867' (India Office Records, 1867), L PS 6 554, British Library; 'Letter from Colonel Henry Man, to the Military Secretary to the Government of India, 27 September 1867'.

851. 'Letter from Secretary of State for India to Foreign Department, Government of India, 23 December 1867' (India Office Records, 1867), L PS 560, British Library.

852. 'Letter from Foreign Department, Government of India, to Secretary of State for India, 8 March 1869' (India Office Records, 1869), L PS 6 564 163, British Library.

853. 'Note on the Subject of the Nicobars by Colonel H. Man, Officiating Superintendent Port Blair, 12 March 1869' (India Office Records, 1869), L PS 6 564 163, British Library.

854. 'Letter from Captain H. Lewis, Master Attendant, to Secretary to Chief Commissioner, British Burmah, 9 January 1868' (India Office Records, 1868), L PS 560, British Library.

855. 'Letter from the Duke of Argyll, Secretary of State for India, to Viceroy and Governor General of India, 20 January 1869' (India Office Records, 1869), L PS 6 564, British Library.

856. 'Letter from Foreign Department, Government of India, to Secretary of State for India, 8 March 1869'.

857. Colledge, Warlow, and Bush, *Ships of the Royal Navy: The Complete Record of All Fighting Ships of the Royal Navy from The15th Century to the Present*, 408.

858. 'Letter from E.C. Bayley, Secretary to the Government of India, to Commander of HMS Spiteful, 22 May 1869' (India Office Records, 1869), L PS 6 564, British Library.

859. 'Abstract of Letters from India, Annexation of the Nicobar Islands, 1869' (India Office Records and Private Papers, 1869), IOR/L/PS/20/CA9, Qatar National Library.

Notes

860. 'Letter from Foreign Department, Government of India, to Secretary of State for India, 12 April 1869' (India Office Records, 1869), L PS 6 564 163, British Library.

861. 'Letter from Commander A. Morrell of HMS Spiteful, to Governor General and Viceroy of India, 24 April 1869' (India Office Records, 1869), L PS 6 564, British Library.

862. 'Note on the Subject of the Nicobars by Colonel H. Man, Officiating Superintendent Port Blair, 12 March 1869'.

863. 'Notes from a Conversation on the Nicobars with Colonel H. Man, Officiating Superintendent Port Blair, by Secretary to the Government of India, 12 March 1869'.

864. 'Abstract of Letters from India, Administration of the Nicobar Islands, 1869' (India Office Records and Private Papers, 1869), IOR/L/PS/20/CA9, Qatar National Library.

865. 'Letter from Commodore Leopold G. Heath, Commanding East Indies Station, to Viceroy and Governor-General, 4 March 1869'.

866. 'Letter from Lieutenant Colonel H.K. Burne, Military Department to the Commodore Commanding East India Station, 25 September 1867'.

867. 'Letter from Commander A. Morrell of HMS Spiteful, to Governor General and Viceroy of India, 24 April 1869'.

868. 'Letter from W.S. Seton-Karr, Secretary to Govt of India, Foreign Department, to Commodore East India Station, 25 February 1869' (India Office Records, 1869), L PS 6 564, British Library.

869. 'Letter from E.C. Bayley, Secretary to the Government of India, to Commanding Officer of HMS Spiteful, 14 March 1869' (India Office Records, 1869), LPS 6 564 163, British Library.

870. 'Abstract of Letters from India, Occupation of the Nicobar Islands, 22 May 1869' (India Office Records and Private Papers, 1869), IOR/L/PS/20/CA9, Qatar National Library.

871. Pratt, *Imperial Eyes: Travel Writing and Transculturation*.

872. Edward W. Said, *Orientalism* (London: Penguin, 2003).

873. 'Letter from E.C. Bayley, Secretary to the Government of India, to Commander of HMS Spiteful, 22 May 1869'.

874. Arnold, '"Illusory Riches": Representations of the Tropical World, 1840-1950'.

875. 'Letter from Home Department, Government of India, to Secretary of State for India, 22 May 1869' (India Office Records, 1869), L PS 6 564, British Library.

876. Lambert, 'The Royal Navy's White Sea Campaign of 1854'; Subramanian, *The Sovereign and the Pirate: Ordering Maritime Subjects in India's Western Littoral*.

877. 'Telegraphic Communication with the Andamans, 21 May 1874'; 'Report on the Administration of the Andaman and Nicobar Islands, and the Penal Settlements of Port Blair and the Nicobars for the Years 1872-1873' (India Office Records, 1873), V 10 680, British Library.

878. 'Marine, Apr 1872, No66-67' (Military, 1872), National Archives of India; 'Marine, Jul 1872, No21' (Military, 1872), IOR/L/PS/20/CA12, Qatar National Library.

879. 'Letter from the Office of the Defence Committee, to Secretary to the Indian Government, Military Department, 24 June 1886' (Admiralty, 1886), ADM 127 13, The National Archives; Anim-Adoo, 'Steaming Between The Islands. Nineteenth Century Maritime Networks and the Caribbean Archipelago'.

880. 'Telegraphic Communication with the Andamans, 21 May 1874'.

881. 'Report on the Administration of the Andaman and Nicobar Islands, and the Penal Settlements of Port Blair and the Nicobars for the Years 1872-1873'.

882. Brinkman, *Balancing Strategy: Seapower, Neutrality, and Prize Law in the Seven Years' War*.

883. 'Note on the Subject of the Nicobars by Colonel H. Man, Officiating Superintendent Port Blair, 12 March 1869'.

884. Steven Gray, *Steam Power and Sea Power: Coal, the Royal Navy, and the British Empire, c. 1870-1914* (London: Palgrave Macmillan, 2018).

885. Kuehling, 'The Converted War Canoe: Cannibal Raiders, Missionaries and "Pax Britannica" on Dobu Island, Papua New Guinea'; Bennet, '"Canoes of Great Swiftness": Rivercraft and War in the Northeast.'; Winter, 'War-Canoes and Poisoned Arrows'.

886. Preston and Major, *Send a Gun Boat! A Study of the British Gunboat*.

887. Daunton and Halpern, *Empire and Others: British Encounters with Indigenous Peoples, 1600 - 1850*; Vaidik, *Imperial Andamans: Colonial Encounter and Island History*.

888. Saini, 'How a Bloody Incident of Piracy Changed the Lives of the Nicobarese Forever'.

889. Subramanian, *The Sovereign and the Pirate: Ordering Maritime Subjects in India's Western Littoral*, 20.

890. For definitions of piracy, see: Policante, *The Pirate Myth: Genealogies of an Imperial Concept*.

891. Latour, *An Inquiry into Modes of Existence: An Anthropology of the Moderns*, 66.

892. 'Letter from Lieutenant Colonel H. K. Burne, Military Department to the Chief Commissioner of British Burmah, 5 September 1867'.

893. 'Marine, Sep 1867, No9'.

894. 'Marine, Dec 1867, No19'.

895. Proshanto K. Mukherjee and Mark Brownrigg, 'Nationality and Registration of Ships: Concept and Practice', in *Farthing on International Shipping* (Berlin: Springer Berlin Heidelberg, 2013), 199–222, https://doi.org/10.1007/978-3-642-34598-2_11.

896. Tarling, *Imperial Britain in South-East Asia*, 233–34.

897. 'Letter from Lord Mayo, Viceroy and Governor General of India, to the Secretary of State for India, 8 March 1869' (India Office Records, 1869), L PS 6 564, British Library.

898. 'Letter from the Duke of Argyll, Secretary of State for India, to Viceroy and Governor General of India, 20 January 1869', 1; 'Letter from the Secretary of State for India, to the Governor-General of India in Council, 16 July 1867' (India Office Records, 1867), L PS 6 554, British Library.

899. 'Letter from Vice Admiral Henry Keppel, Commodore in Chief China Station, to Secretary of the Admiralty, 18 December 1867'.

900. Portman, *A History of Our Relations with the Andamanese, Vol.II*, 550–52.

901. Sen, 'Savage Bodies, Civilized Pleasures'.

902. Lambert, 'The Royal Navy's White Sea Campaign of 1854'.

Conclusion

903. Mahan, *Influence of Sea Power Upon History, 1660-1783*; Alfred Thayer Mahan, *Naval Strategy Compared and Contrasted with the Principles and Practice of Military Operations on Land* (Boston: Little, Brown and Company, 1911); Corbett, *Some Principles of Maritime Strategy*; Raoul Castex and Eugenia C. Kiesling, *Strategic Theories* (Annapolis: Naval Institute Press, 2017); Sergei Gorshkov, *The Sea Power of the State* (Annapolis: Naval Institute Press, 1979).

904. Benjamin Armstrong and A Mahan, *21st Century Mahan: Sound Military Conclusions for the Modern Era* (Annapolis: Naval Institute Press, 2013); Nicholas Lambert, *Neptune Factor: Alfred Thayer Mahan and the Concept of Sea Power* (Annapolis: Naval Institute Press, 2024); Julian Corbett, *21st Century Corbett: Maritime Strategy and Naval Policy for the Modern Era*, ed. Andrew Lambert (Annapolis, Maryland: Naval Institute Press, 2017); Andrew Lambert, *The British Way of War: Julian Corbett and the Battle for a National Strategy* (New Haven: Yale University Press, 2021).

905. Lawrence Sondhaus, *Naval Warfare, 1815-1914* (London: Routledge, 2001); Howard Fuller, *Empire, Technology and Seapower: Royal Navy Crisis in the Age of Palmerston* (Basingstoke: Palgrave, 2013); Daniel Owen Spence, *A History of the Royal Navy: Empire and Imperialism* (London: I.B. Tauris, 2015).

906. Basil Greenhill and Ann Giffard, *Steam, Politics and Patronage: The Transformation of the Royal Navy, 1815-54* (London: Conway Maritime Press, 1994); David Evans, *Building the Steam Navy: Dockyards, Technology, and the Creation of the Victorian Battle Fleet, 1830-1906* (Annapolis: Naval Institute Press, 2004); Norman Friedman, *Fighting the Great War at Sea: Strategy, Tactics, and Technology* (Barnsley: Seaforth Publishing, 2014); Eric Grove, *The Royal Navy since 1815: A New Short History* (New York: Palgrave Macmillan, 2005); Grove, *The Future of Sea Power*.

907. Eric Grove was very influential in this field and contributed to the development of the rise and fall paradigm through his lectureship at Brittania Royal Naval College. Eric Grove, *Fleet to Fleet Encounters: Tsushima, Jutland, Philippine Sea* (London: Arms and Armour, 1991); Stephen McLaughlin, 'Battlelines and Fast Wings: Battlefleet Tactics in the Royal Navy, 1900–1914', *Journal of Strategic Studies* 38, no. 7 (2015): 985–1005, https://doi.org/10.1080/01402390.2015.1005444; Evans, *Building the Steam Navy: Dockyards, Technology, and the Creation of the Victorian Battle Fleet, 1830-1906*; Paul Kennedy, *The Rise and Fall of British Naval Mastery* (London: Penguin Books, 2001); Roger Morris, ed., *The Foundations of British Maritime Ascendancy: Resources, Logistics and the State, 1755-1815* (Cambridge: Cambridge University Press, 2013); Ben Wilson, *Empire of the Deep: The Rise and Fall of the British Navy* (London: Phoenix, 2013).

908. Andrew Lambert's work is exceptional in rigour, but very much follows a classical focus on the 'grand' over the 'everyday'. For great men, see: Andrew Lambert, *Nelson: Britannia's God of War* (London: Faber and Faber, 2004); Andrew Lambert, *Admirals: The Naval Commanders Who Made Britain Great* (London: Faber and Faber, 2008); Andrew

Lambert, *Franklin: Tragic Hero of Polar Navigation* (London: Faber and Faber, 2010); Andrew Bond, Frank Cowin, and Andrew D. Lambert, *Favourite of Fortune: Captain John Quilliam, Trafalgar Hero* (Barnsley: Seaforth Publishing, 2021); For great battles, see: Andrew Lambert, 'Under the Heel of Britannia. The Bombardment of Sweaborg 9-11 August 1855', in *Seapower Ashore: 200 Years of Royal Navy Operations on Land*, ed. Peter Hore (London: Chatham Publishing, 2000), 96–129; Andrew Lambert, *The Crimean War: British Grand Strategy against Russia, 1853-56*, 2nd ed. (Abingdon: Routledge, 2011); Andrew Lambert, *The Challenge: America, Britain and the War of 1812* (London: Faber and Faber, 2012); For work on great ships, see: Andrew Lambert, *Battleships in Transition: The Creation of the Steam Battlefleet, 1815-1860* (Annapolis: Naval Institute Press, 1984); Andrew Lambert, *Trincomalee: The Last of Nelson's Frigates* (London: Chatham, 2002); Andrew Lambert, Jan Rüger, and Robert Blyth, eds., *The Dreadnought and the Edwardian Age* (Farnham: Ashgate, 2011).

909. Vaidik, *Imperial Andamans: Colonial Encounter and Island History.*, 43.

910. Frederick Mouat, *Adventures and Researches Among The Andaman Islanders* (London: Hurst and Blackett, 1863).

911. Hydrographic Office, 'Gulf of Bengal, South Andaman I, East Coast, Port Blair' (Old Copy Book, 1861), OCB 514 B1-4, UK Hydrographic Office; Hydrographic Office, 'Bay of Bengal, Nicobar Group, Nancowry Harbour' (Old Copy Book, 1869), OCB 841 A2-5, UK Hydrographic Office.

912. Evans, *Building the Steam Navy: Dockyards, Technology, and the Creation of the Victorian Battle Fleet, 1830-1906*; Nuno Luís Madureira, 'Oil in the Age of Steam', *Journal of Global History* 5, no. 1 (2010): 75–94, https://doi.org/10.1017/S1740022809990349; Gray, 'Fuelling Mobility'; Rüger, *Heligoland: Britain, Germany, and the Struggle for the North Sea*; William H. Clements, *Britain's Island Fortresses: Defence of the Empire 1756-1956* (Barnsley: Pen & Sword Military, 2019); Frank A. J. L. James, 'Making Money from the Royal Navy in the Late Eighteenth Century: Charles Kerr on Antigua "Breathing the True Spirit of a West India Agent"', *The Mariner's Mirror* 107, no. 4 (2021): 402–19, https://doi.org/10.1080/00253359.2021.1978257.

913. Felix Driver, 'Distance and Disturbance: Travel, Exploration and Knowledge in the Nineteenth Century', *Transactions of the Royal Historical Society* 14, no. 14 (2004): 73–92, https://doi.org/10.1017/S0080440104000088.

914. Michael Lindberg and Daniel Todd, *Brown-, Green-, and Blue-Water Fleets: The Influence of Geography on Naval Warfare, 1861 to the Present* (Westport: Praeger, 2002); Gartzke and Lindsay, 'The Influence of Sea Power on Politics'.

915. Hydrography and surveying is another vast literature body, however the focus is on the practice as a 'science' and technical endeavour, rather than a tool of military utility. Llewellyn Dawson, *Memoirs of Hydrography. Part II* (Eastbourne: The Imperial Library, 1885); John Edgell, *Sea Surveys: Britain's Contribution to Hydrography* (London: Longmans, Green & Co, 1949); Archibald Day, *The Admiralty Hydrographic Service 1795-1919* (London: Her Majesty's Stationary Office, 1967); Alfred Friendly, *Beaufort of the Admiralty: The Life of Sir Francis Beaufort, 1774-1857* (New York: Random House, 1977); G. S. Ritchie, *The Admiralty Chart: British Naval Hydrography in the Nineteenth Century* (Edinburgh: Pentland Press, 1995); Michael Reidy, *The Tides of History* (Chicago: University of Chicago Press, 2008); Burnett, 'Hydrographic Discipline among Navigators: Charting an "Empire of Commerce and Science" in the Nineteenth-Century Pacific'; James Davey, 'The Advancement of Nautical Knowledge: The Hydrographical Office, the Royal Navy and the Charting of the Baltic Sea, 1795-1815', *Journal for Maritime Research* 13,

no. 2 (2011): 81–103, https://doi.org/10.1080/21533369.2011.622869; Anderson, 'The Hydrographer's Narrative: Writing Global Knowledge in the 1830s'; Doug Macdougall, *Endless Novelties of Extraordinary Interest: The Voyage of H.M.S Challenger and the Birth of Modern Oceanography* (New Haven: Yale University Press, 2019); Peter Martin, 'Indigenous Tales of the Beaufort Sea: Arctic Exploration and the Circulation of Geographical Knowledge', *Journal of Historical Geography* 67 (2020): 24–35, https://doi.org/10.1016/j.jhg.2019.10.012; Behrisch, *Discovery, Innovation, and the Victorian Admiralty: Paper Navigators*.

916. Uditi Sen, 'Developing "Terra Nullius": Colonialism, Nationalism, and Indigeneity in the Andaman Islands', *Comparative Studies in Society and History* 59, no. 4 (2017): 944–73, https://doi.org/10.1017/S0010417517000330.

917. These campaigns are, however, often viewed independently. Spence, *A History of the Royal Navy: Empire and Imperialism*; Richard Brooks, 'March Into India: The Relief of Lucknow 1857-59', in *Seapower Ashore: 200 Years of Royal Navy Operations on Land*, ed. Peter Hore (London: Chatham Publishing, 2000), 130–45; Peter Hore, ed., *Seapower Ashore: 200 Years of Royal Navy Operations on Land* (London: Chatham, 2000); Colin White, 'The Long Arm of Seapower: The Anglo-Japanese War of 1863-1864', in *Seapower Ashore: 200 Years of Royal Navy Operations on Land*, ed. Peter Hore (London: Chatham Publishing, 2000), 146–80; Richard Brooks, *The Long Arm of Empire: Naval Brigades from the Crimea to the Boxer Rebellion* (London: Constable, 1999); Preston and Major, *Send a Gun Boat! A Study of the British Gunboat*; Hastings, *The Royal Indian Navy, 1612-1950*; Caroline Elkins, *Legacy of Violence: A History of the British Empire* (London: Vintage, 2023); Saul David, *Victoria's Wars: The Rise of Empire* (London: Viking, 2006).

918. Dalrymple, *The Anarchy: The Relentless Rise of the East India Company*.

919. Mohanan, *The Royal Indian Navy: Trajectories, Transformations and the Transfer of Power*, 1.

920. Low, *History of the Indian Navy (1613-1863)*; Low; Hastings, *The Royal Indian Navy, 1612-1950*; Cook, 'Establishing Sea Routes to India and China: Stages in the Development of Hydrographical Knowledge'; Mohanan, *The Royal Indian Navy: Trajectories, Transformations and the Transfer of Power*.

921. Mohanan, *The Royal Indian Navy: Trajectories, Transformations and the Transfer of Power*.

922. Marco Polo and Ralph Latham, *The Travels of Marco Polo* (Harmondsworth: Penguin, 1978); Arthur Conan Doyle, *The Sign of Four* (London: Penguin, 2001); Portman, *A History of Our Relations with the Andamanese, Vol.I*; Portman; Portman, *A History of Our Relations with the Andamanese, Vol.II*.

923. Roskill, *The Strategy of Sea Power*; Till, *Seapower: A Guide for the Twenty-First Century*.

924. 'Memoranda and Papers Laid Before the Council of India 17 January 1874- 11 January 1875' (India Office Records, 1875), C 137, British Library.

925. 'Marine, Sep 1876, No135-9' (Military, 1876), National Archives of India.

926. 'Memorandum by the Colonial Defence Committee for Local Preparations to Be Made in the Event of War, 18 November 1886' (Admiralty, 1886), ADM 127/13, The National Archives.

927. 'Report by Captain Shone, R.E., on Defensive Measures for Port Blair Harbour' (Admiralty, 1886), ADM 127 13, The National Archives; See also the Report on Admiralty Surveys for areas perceived to be vulnerable. 'Report on Admiralty Surveys For The Year 1888' (1888), Houses of Commons Parliamentary Papers Online.

928. 'Letter from Military Department, Government of India, to the Secretary Defence Committee, 25 January 1887' (Admiralty, 1887), ADM 127/13, The National Archives; 'Report of the Committee Appointed to Consider Questions Connected with the Annual Subsidy Paid by the Indian Government to the Admiralty for the Maintenance of a Naval Force in Indian Waters' (Admiralty, 1887), ADM 127/5, The National Archives; 'Correspondence in India While Commander-in-Chief in India, 1885-1888' (Collection Gen Sir Ian Standish Monteith Hamilton (1853-1947), 1890), HAMILTON, ISM 1/3/5, Liddell Hart Centre for Military Archives.

929. For the perspective of the Indian Government, see: 'Memoranda and Papers Laid Before the Council of India 17 January 1874- 11 January 1875'; 'Memoranda and Papers Laid Before the Council of India, 1 October 1877- 1 October 1878' (India Office Records, 1878), C 141 8, British Library; Dougherty provides a 'crew' perspective on how Port Blair was a place for the Royal Navy to stop, refuel, and enjoy 'civilised' activities like cricket and church. Rev. John Anderson Dougherty, *The East Indies Station: The Cruise of H.M.S 'Garnet'* (Malta: Muscat Printing Office, 1890).

930. The Department of Finance of the Indian Government requested a reduction in troops, but increase in guardships as a cost effective means to protect Port Blair. 'Letter from Department of Finance and Commerce, Indian Government, to the Secretary of State for India, 6 December 1880' (India Office Records, 1881), L PJ 6 34, File 350, British Library.

931. Richard Dunley, 'The "Problem of Asia" and Imperial Competition before World War 1', in *The New Age of Naval Power in the Indo-Pacific: Strategy, Order, and Regional Security*, ed. Catherine L. Grant, Alessio Patalano, and James A. Russell (Washington, DC: Georgetown University Press, 2023), 157–58.

932. Kennedy, *The Rise and Fall of British Naval Mastery*, 262.

933. Vaidik, *Imperial Andamans: Colonial Encounter and Island History.*, 178.

934. Vaidik, 179.

935. Jackson, *War and Empire in Mauritius and the Indian Ocean*; Jackson, *Distant Drums: The Role of Colonies in British Imperial Warfare*; Jackson, *Of Islands, Ports and Sea Lanes: Africa and the Indian Ocean in the Second World War*.

936. Glen O'Hara, *Britain and the Sea: Since 1600* (Basingstoke: Palgrave Macmillan, 2010), 134; Wilson, *Empire of the Deep: The Rise and Fall of the British Navy*, 557.

937. Field, *Royal Navy Strategy in the Far East: 1919 - 1939; Preparing for War against Japan*; Prince, 'The Post-Imperial Relationship with the Royal Navy: On the Beach?'

938. Patalano, *Post-War Japan as a Sea Power: Imperial Legacy, Wartime Experience and the Making of a Navy*.

939. David McIntyre, *The Rise and Fall of the Singapore Naval Base, 1919-1942* (Hamden: Archon Books, 1979); Parkinson, *The China Station, Royal Navy: A History as Seen through the Careers of the Commanders in Chief, 1864 - 1941*.

940. Sircar, *History of the Andaman Islands: Unsung Heroes and Untold Stories.*, 176.

941. Boyd, *The Royal Navy in Eastern Waters: Linchpin of Victory 1935-1942*; Stephenson, *The Eastern Fleet and the Indian Ocean, 1942-1944: The Fleet That Had to Hide*.

942. David Arthur Thomas, *Japan's War at Sea: Pearl Harbor to the Coral Sea* (London: Andre Deutsch, 1978); Paul S. Dull, *A Battle History of the Imperial Japanese Navy (1941 - 1945)* (Annapolis: Naval Institute Press, 2007); Michael Wilson, *A Submariners' War: The Indian Ocean 1939-45* (Stroud: Spellmount Ltd., 2000); Lawrence Paterson, *Hitler's Gray Wolves: U-Boats in the Indian Ocean* (New York: Carrel Books, 2017); Roskill, *The Navy at War 1939-1945*; Faulkner and Patalano, *The Sea and the Second World War: Maritime Aspects of a Global Conflict*.

943. Dasgupta, *Japanese in Andaman and Nicobar Islands: Red Sun Over Black Water*.

944. Sircar, *History of the Andaman Islands: Unsung Heroes and Untold Stories.*, 175–210.

945. David Miller, *Special Forces Operations in South-East Asia, 1941-1945: Minerva, Baldhead and Longshanks/Creek* (Barnsley: Pen & Sword Military, 2015), 46–88.

946. Abraham, 'India's Unsinkable Aircraft Carrier'.

947. Julian Lewis, *Changing Direction: British Military Planning for Post-War Strategic Defence, 1942-1947* (London: Routledge, 2008).

948. Morris, *Farewell the Trumpets: An Imperial Retreat*.

949. 'File Containing the Official Viceregal Correspondence of Louis Mountbatten, First Viscount Mountbatten, and Copy Minutes of Meetings of the Viceregal Staff and Conference, Concerning the Proposed Exclusion of the Andaman and Nicobar Islands from the Jurisdiction of the Government of India, 4 April 1947 - 11 March 1948' (Mountbatten Papers, 1948), MS62/MB/1/D/91, University of Southampton.

950. Matthew Heaslip, '21st Century Maritime Britain in Context-100 Years On', in *Maritime Britain in the 21st Century*, ed. Katie Jamieson, Kevin Rowlands, and Andrew Young (Dartmouth: Britannia Publishing, 2024), 47.

951. Basil Germond provides a deep analysis into the future potential role of seapower and climate change, emphasising how navies can and should be used in a changing environment. Germond, *Seapower in the Post-Modern World*.

INDEX

Symbols
24th (the 2nd Warwickshire) Regiment of Foot 245, 315
80th Regiment of the Foot 45, 58

A
Accidental imperialist 62
Anchorage 117, 126
Andaman Committee 75, 76, 77, 81, 82, 83, 84, 86, 88, 89, 90, 91, 92, 93, 94, 95, 96, 97, 98, 99, 100, 101, 103, 104, 105, 106, 109, 112, 115, 122, 209
Andamanese (tribes) 7, 25, 32, 48, 53, 56, 61, 82, 93, 94, 104, 118, 123, 142, 144, 145, 149, 150, 153, 157, 210, 223, 224, 226, 245, 248, 277, 278, 281, 284, 287, 289, 290, 292, 297, 298, 299, 300, 305, 306, 307, 309, 312, 313, 314, 321, 325, 327
Anglo-Burmese War (1852–1853) 84, 140, 205
Anglo-Japanese War (1863–1864) 140, 206
Annex, annexation 2, 11, 21, 49, 96, 190, 191, 193, 194, 198, 200, 201
Arakan Yoma range 2
Arnold, James 75, 84, 124
Arrow, ship 24, 28
Assam Valley, ship 139, 140, 147, 148, 149, 150, 154, 155, 157, 163, 164, 165, 169
Assistant Superintendent, Port Blair 146

B
Barren Island 91, 100
Barrow, Henry 148, 156, 157, 228, 285, 315
Battle of Aberdeen 144
Beaufort, Francis 109, 121, 235, 296, 298, 305, 308, 310, 326

Bedingfield, Norman 175, 184
Bengal Army 1, 26, 68, 84, 95, 98, 103, 151, 152, 174, 190
Bengal Chamber of Commerce 52, 61
Bengal Civil Service 25
Bengal Gazette 59, 61, 226, 291
Bengal Marine 71, 118, 141, 206
Bengal Presidency 13, 19
Blackmore, Henry 52, 53
Blair, Archibald 90, 92, 109, 115, 305, 306, 308
Blockades 11, 170, 171, 173, 177, 195, 200, 211
Bombardments 142
Bombay Geographical Society 83, 99, 127, 301, 302, 304, 309
Bombay Marine 19, 35, 71, 90, 109, 115, 131, 140, 142, 143, 144, 145, 146, 150, 151, 152, 153, 154, 156, 158, 161, 165, 166, 193, 206, 211, 214
Borneo pirates 145
Britishness 61, 194, 198
Briton, ship 45, 57, 58, 59, 60, 61, 291
Brooke, George 55
Brooker, Edward 149
Burma 2, 15, 20, 21, 29, 32, 34, 36, 41, 65, 80, 140, 147, 149, 154, 163, 183, 188, 191, 215

C
Calcutta 13, 20, 28, 34, 37, 45, 48, 52, 60, 61, 66, 75, 76, 87, 89, 90, 94, 95, 122, 128, 145, 151, 177, 183, 195, 204, 210, 226, 245, 277, 290, 306
cannibalism 2, 9, 31, 87, 101, 104, 207
Canning, Charlotte 94
Canning, Viscount 65, 67
Canoes 50, 55, 64, 145, 160, 169, 171, 175, 183, 184, 185, 186, 188, 192, 196, 201, 321
Car Nicobar 27
Categorisation of piracy 176
Ceremony 1, 2, 95, 96, 190, 277

Chennai 20
Chief Commissioner in Port Blair 170
Chief Commissioner of Burma 154
China Station 29, 33, 34, 35, 40, 50, 51, 52, 63, 64, 67, 74, 145, 148, 156, 158, 165, 173, 177, 183, 187, 189, 200, 201, 225, 237, 245, 288, 313, 316, 319, 321, 325, 329
Chokepoints 7
Climate change 216, 217, 329
Cochin 37
Colebrooke, Robert Hyde 116, 117, 118, 226, 306
Colombo 34
Commander-in-Chief of East Indies Station 18
Commander-in-Chief of the China Station 177, 187
Command of the sea 16, 21, 25, 33, 37, 38, 40, 42, 43, 54, 81, 212
Commercial navigation 131
Commissioner of Arakan 26, 53, 65
Commissioner of Tavoy 59, 290
Communications 21, 22, 33, 40, 41, 43, 46, 48, 58, 100, 120, 136, 194, 195, 217
Convicts 18, 68, 89, 97, 122
Corbett, Julian 3, 6, 7, 16, 21, 22, 23, 38, 43, 203, 212, 232, 239, 277, 280, 282, 284, 286, 295, 325
Cornwallis, Commodore William 18, 224, 281
Cornwallis, Earl Charles 18
Council of India 67, 224, 327, 328
Court of Directors 63
Credibility, credible 79, 86, 134, 147
Crimean War (1853–1856) 27, 33, 47, 90, 104, 141, 173, 177, 240, 326
Critical Geopolitics 244, 280
Crown rule 1, 8, 67, 98, 113, 143
Cyclone, cyclones 45, 57

D

Dalrymple, Alexander 89, 90, 109, 114, 115, 116, 232, 279, 292, 298, 306, 327
Danish 18, 27, 28, 49, 51, 52, 53, 62, 63, 115, 178, 182, 191. *See also* Denmark
Denmark 18, 27, 51, 178, 191, 249, 281, 282, 288
Depth sounding 126
Dickson, William Burnie 125, 136
Disraeli, Benjamin 2

Doutty, William Clement 45
Draughtsmen 127

E

East India Company 2, 3, 5, 8, 9, 10, 14, 21, 23, 29, 35, 36, 37, 45, 48, 67, 71, 74, 85, 90, 92, 103, 115, 116, 117, 118, 124, 129, 132, 206, 209, 224, 225, 228, 229, 232, 234, 238, 239, 247, 248, 279, 280, 281, 285, 286, 290, 292, 293, 294, 296, 298, 302, 306, 308, 310, 327
East Indies and China Station 29, 33, 34, 35, 40, 50, 51, 52, 63, 64, 67, 74, 173, 201
East Indies Station 18, 27, 34, 36, 37, 145, 146, 150, 151, 154, 158, 169, 173, 176, 177, 180, 182, 183, 192, 193, 200, 226, 316, 317, 318, 319, 320, 321, 323, 328
Edgell, John 108, 326
Emily, ship 55
Escalation 151, 170, 185
European naval power 144
European seamen 89, 157

F

Ferozeshah, ship 147
First Burmese War (1824–1826) 19
First Opium War (1839–1842) 14, 20, 21, 46, 207
First World War (1914-1918) 13, 212, 213, 214, 245, 279
Flag 1, 63, 95, 190, 192, 194, 198, 277
Fleet 5, 13, 19, 27, 34, 35, 133, 142, 144, 145, 146, 161, 166, 170, 171, 173, 200, 202, 204, 211, 216
Flying Fish, ship 55
Ford, Barret 148, 151
Foreign Office 27, 28, 51, 52, 85
Fort William 13, 31, 59, 62, 65, 67, 73, 118, 279
France 27, 240, 296
French 27, 63, 308. *See also* France
Futteh Islam, ship 169, 174, 175, 176, 177, 178, 179, 181, 183, 184, 185, 186, 198, 201
Fyze Buksh, ship 64

G

Geographical imagination 24, 31, 77, 82, 104, 126, 137, 171
Giffard, Henry 50

308

Gorshkov, Sergey 203
Government of India Act 1858 48, 67, 77, 98
Government of India Act of 1833 21
Governor-General of India 21, 65, 325
Grant, John Peter 13, 25
Guardship 122, 185
Gunboat diplomacy 140, 153, 162
Gunboats 11, 56, 139, 140, 141, 142, 143, 144, 152, 153, 159, 161, 162, 163, 165, 211, 233, 237, 238, 242, 244, 288, 312, 313

H

Hall, Alexander 45
Halstead, Edward 51
Havelock Island 107
HCS *Dalhousie* 97
HCS *Fire Queen* 99, 122
HCS *Pluto* 1, 75, 89, 94, 104, 237
HCS *Ranger* 115
HCS *Semiramis* 89
HCS *Sesostris* 97, 122
HCS *Tenasserim* 55
HCS *Tubal Cain* 97, 122
HCS *Viper* 115
Heathcote, James Arnold 84, 124
Hillyar, Charles 154
HMIMS *Arracan* 148, 151
HMIMS *Kwan Tung* 151
HMINS *Clive* 122
HMINS *Clyde* 107, 122
HMINS *Fire Queen* 99, 122
HMINS *Sesostris* 122
HMINS *Tubal Cain* 97, 122
HMS *Calcutta* 28
HMS *Challenger* 112, 308
HMS *Charlotte* 144
HMS *Childers* 51
HMS *Cruiser* 50
HMS *Fox* 52
HMS *Ganges* 51
HMS *Pearl* 66, 180
HMS *Prince of Wales* 215
HMS *Proserpine* 55
HMS *Repulse* 215
HMS *Satellite* 170, 185, 187
HMS *Shannon* 66
HMS *Spiteful* 52, 191, 192, 193, 201, 322, 323
HMS *Sylvia* 148, 149, 153, 160, 165, 185, 311, 312, 313, 314, 315, 319, 321

HMS *Wasp* 169, 175, 180, 182, 184, 187, 189, 318, 319, 320, 321
Ho-Ho harbour 50
Holmes, Sherlock 8
Home Department 95, 96, 224, 323
Hong Kong 15, 66, 72, 99, 231, 233, 284, 285
Hopkinson, Henry 26, 53, 65
House of Commons Select Committee 47
Hydrographic Office 37, 90, 93, 102, 108, 109, 111, 113, 114, 115, 116, 117, 121, 126, 127, 128, 129, 130, 131, 135, 136, 137, 138, 204, 210, 221, 223, 225, 299, 303, 305, 306, 307, 308, 310, 311, 326
Hydrography 93, 106, 108, 110, 111, 112, 113, 125, 132, 133, 134, 135, 205, 210

I

Imperial defence 10, 47, 67, 69, 70, 71, 72, 74, 144, 207, 209, 211, 212, 213, 214
Imperial folklore 157
Imperial maritime network 14, 17, 38, 46, 49, 52, 57, 58, 62, 71, 72, 80, 84, 89, 98, 99, 100, 117, 120, 137, 138, 180, 197, 213
Imperial policing 11, 40, 50, 66, 140, 141, 142, 145, 152, 153, 154, 155, 156, 159, 161, 162, 163, 165, 166, 211
imperial state 2, 58, 80, 81, 117, 138, 140, 166, 169, 170, 186, 187, 201, 202
Indian Navy 10, 13, 16, 17, 19, 21, 22, 23, 25, 28, 33, 35, 36, 37, 38, 40, 42, 43, 48, 52, 53, 54, 64, 66, 67, 70, 71, 73, 74, 75, 76, 77, 80, 83, 84, 86, 87, 88, 89, 90, 91, 94, 95, 96, 97, 98, 99, 100, 101, 102, 103, 104, 105, 106, 107, 109, 112, 113, 114, 119, 120, 121, 122, 123, 124, 125, 129, 130, 131, 132, 133, 134, 135, 136, 137, 138, 141, 146, 148, 156, 204, 206, 209, 210, 224, 226, 237, 239, 243, 280, 282, 285, 286, 287, 292, 294, 295, 296, 297, 298, 299, 301, 305, 306, 308, 310, 311, 313, 314, 315, 327
Indian Ocean 1, 8, 14, 24, 25, 28, 32, 36, 37, 40, 61, 71, 133, 145, 146, 148, 150, 200, 213, 214, 215, 227,

229, 230, 231, 236, 237, 238, 242, 243, 245, 246, 248, 249, 251, 277, 278, 280, 281, 282, 283, 284, 285, 286, 287, 288, 289, 291, 293, 294, 296, 300, 301, 302, 304, 307, 309, 313, 317, 318, 328, 329
Indian Rebellion 48, 66, 68, 73, 76, 84, 151, 205, 209
Indigenous population 35, 59, 91, 118, 126, 138, 140, 145, 153, 155, 156, 161, 176, 181, 189, 202, 224
Indonesian Archipelago 2
Insurance 29, 57, 147
Intelligence 51, 52, 62, 108, 151, 152, 153, 183, 213, 214

J

Japan 214, 234, 237, 245, 250, 297, 328, 329
Japanese 2, 140, 206, 213, 214, 215, 232, 234, 250, 277, 287, 312, 317, 327, 329. *See also* Japan
Japanese Navy 213, 214, 215, 234, 329
John Lawrence Island 45, 57
Journal of Asiatic Society of Bengal 116, 226, 290, 306

K

Keppel, Henry 156, 177, 187, 316, 319, 321, 325
Kinloch, Arthur 174, 318

L

Little Andaman 139, 140, 141, 142, 147, 148, 149, 150, 151, 152, 153, 155, 156, 158, 159, 160, 161, 162, 163, 164, 165, 166, 169, 172, 181, 182, 183, 189, 197, 201, 206, 210, 312, 314, 315, 316
Little Andaman Campaign 139, 141, 142, 147, 151, 156, 159, 161, 162, 165, 166, 172, 182, 197, 206, 312, 316
Littoral 7, 28, 38, 41, 47, 49, 54, 55, 62, 65, 68, 69, 73, 104, 108, 112, 123, 130, 135, 144, 170, 171, 173, 174, 181, 183, 202, 210, 278, 316
Local expertise 104

M

Mackinder, Halford 78, 233, 295
Madras Native Infantry 185, 186, 193
Mahan, Alfred Thayer 3, 10, 76, 203, 212, 240, 277, 294, 295, 325
Man, Henry 1, 68, 95, 190, 322
Marine Secretary 70, 124
Marshall, William 107, 136
Mary, ship 51
Mason, John Charles 17, 70, 124, 224, 225, 280, 281, 293
Mayo, Viceroy Lord 198
Merchant marine 5
Military Department 95, 150, 151, 183, 188, 191, 224, 315, 320, 322, 323, 324, 328
Military mobility 141
Missionaries 239, 321, 324
Morrell, Arthur 323
Morris, Thomas 99
Mouat, Frederic 75
Mountbatten, Louis 215, 329
Much, William 156

N

Nancowry 28, 60, 166, 169, 172, 175, 176, 177, 178, 179, 180, 181, 182, 183, 184, 185, 186, 187, 188, 190, 192, 193, 197, 198, 200, 201, 202, 291, 310, 311, 326
Nancowry Harbour 28, 60, 166, 169, 172, 175, 176, 177, 178, 180, 182, 183, 185, 186, 192, 193, 197, 198, 201, 202, 291, 310, 311, 326
Native infantry 185, 186, 193
Natives 46, 50, 60, 150
Naval assistants 127, 129
Naval brigadesman 157
Naval supremacy 249
Nicobarese (tribes) 25, 32, 53, 56, 166, 169, 170, 171, 175, 176, 178, 179, 180, 182, 183, 184, 185, 186, 188, 189, 190, 191, 192, 194, 196, 197, 198, 199, 201, 202, 211, 223, 224, 247, 319, 321, 324
Nineveh, ship 147
Notice to Mariners 160

O

Observation 81, 82, 118
Oligopticons 114
Onge 139, 147, 150, 153, 155, 157, 159, 160, 163, 164, 166
Operation Baldhead 215

Index

Opium 2, 14, 20, 21, 23, 26, 27, 28, 29, 46, 140, 146, 205, 207, 241, 277, 280, 282, 284, 287, 317

Orientalism 60, 150, 176, 194, 201. See also Orientalist

Orientalist 24, 201, 224

Othering 20, 194

P

Paris Declaration Respecting Maritime Law, 1856 173, 177, 182

Pax Britannica 13, 14, 16, 25, 66, 110, 236, 239, 242, 243, 248, 279, 280, 282, 284, 285, 289, 305, 316, 319, 321, 324

Penal colony 8, 49, 65, 103, 206, 208, 210, 278

Permanent presence 103, 153, 173, 178, 182, 188, 189, 191, 193

Pilot, ship 50, 51

Piracy 50, 53, 169, 172, 173, 195, 227, 229, 237, 239, 243, 244, 247, 249, 280, 282, 283, 284, 285, 286, 288, 289, 291, 292, 293, 296, 302, 305, 316, 317, 318, 319, 320, 324

Playfair, George 84

Porcelain 246

Port Blair 2, 8, 19, 46, 49, 67, 82, 92, 94, 96, 97, 99, 100, 105, 107, 109, 110, 113, 115, 116, 118, 119, 120, 122, 123, 124, 126, 130, 131, 133, 135, 136, 138, 140, 143, 144, 146, 147, 148, 150, 151, 152, 158, 160, 163, 164, 170, 172, 174, 175, 178, 185, 187, 188, 190, 192, 193, 194, 195, 198, 199, 202, 207, 210, 212, 213, 214, 226, 299, 303, 306, 307, 310, 311, 312, 313, 314, 315, 316, 320, 321, 322, 323, 324, 326, 328

Port Blair Administration 120, 131, 147, 158, 178, 192

Port Cornwallis 18, 19, 67, 75, 90, 92, 114, 118, 119, 281, 299, 305, 306, 308

Portman, Maurice Vidal 53, 56, 86, 147, 242, 277, 289, 290

Postcolonial 9, 47, 72, 155, 206, 209, 321

Postmodern 6

Postmodernism 6, 227, 230, 278

Postmodernists 6

President in Council 13, 25

Prince of Wales Island (Penang) 19

Public discourse 31

R

Race (racial) 86

Rangoon 139

Remarks Books 121, 126, 225, 281, 308

Richmond, Herbert 10, 47, 74, 212, 279

Riverine 52, 71

Royal Geographical Society 83, 91, 95, 97, 101, 109, 204, 223, 225, 244, 250, 294, 297, 298, 300, 301, 302

Royal Navy 3, 9, 10, 13, 17, 19, 21, 22, 23, 24, 25, 28, 33, 34, 35, 36, 37, 38, 40, 42, 43, 47, 48, 52, 53, 54, 64, 66, 70, 71, 73, 74, 76, 80, 81, 83, 86, 88, 89, 90, 98, 101, 103, 104, 109, 112, 113, 115, 117, 120, 121, 122, 129, 131, 133, 134, 136, 140, 141, 143, 144, 145, 146, 149, 150, 151, 154, 158, 161, 165, 166, 169, 171, 172, 173, 175, 176, 178, 180, 187, 188, 189, 193, 194, 196, 197, 201, 205, 206, 209, 210, 211, 214, 215, 223, 228, 229, 230, 231, 232, 233, 234, 235, 236, 237, 238, 240, 241, 242, 243, 244, 245, 246, 249, 250, 279, 282, 283, 284, 285, 286, 287, 288, 289, 290, 292, 293, 294, 295, 298, 301, 303, 304, 307, 308, 309, 310, 311, 312, 313, 314, 315, 316, 317, 318, 320, 321, 322, 323, 324, 325, 326, 327, 328, 329

Royal Salute 194

Royal Society 83, 89, 97, 113, 235, 249, 250, 297, 299, 301, 303

Runnymede, ship 45, 57, 58, 59, 60, 291

S

Sarawak 34, 72

Scientific method 88, 96, 97, 99, 116, 118, 129, 130

Scientific servicemen 79, 108, 127

Second Anglo-Burmese War (1852–1856), 21, 29, 84, 140. *See also* Anglo-Burmese War (1852–1853)

Second Opium War (1856–1860) 14, 21, 23, 146

Second World War (1939-1945) 71, 213, 215, 234, 238, 293, 328, 329

Sesampore 51

Sextants 116, 126

Shipping routes 6, 147, 174

311

Shipwrecking 56, 234, 242, 245, 289, 290, 291, 305, 311
Singapore 13, 34, 52, 64, 66, 67, 72, 99, 177, 178, 184, 187, 214, 215, 228, 242, 244, 283, 288, 329
Slavery 25, 33, 34, 37, 176, 177
SLOC 14, 15, 16, 17, 18, 20, 21, 27, 31, 34, 41, 42, 43, 46, 72, 74, 80, 104, 112, 119, 136, 143, 159, 176, 178, 184, 191, 195, 209, 210, 214
Small science 108
South China Sea 29, 33, 34, 35, 158, 227, 296, 318
Sovereignty 15, 26, 28, 63, 67, 85, 86, 92, 100, 119, 120, 134, 135, 147, 163, 165, 192, 193, 194, 195, 198
Standardisation 127, 137
Steam frigates 35
Steam-powered 35, 58, 196
Steamships 19, 24, 123, 124
Straits of Malacca 8, 14, 20, 34, 35, 38, 148, 178, 180, 187, 214
Straits Settlements 20, 147, 180, 183, 184, 190, 251
Strategic interests 40, 176
Superintendent of Port Blair 148, 151, 152, 158, 160, 175, 188, 193, 198, 315. *See also* Port Blair
Surveying 10, 37, 39, 40, 52, 53, 66, 77, 79, 80, 84, 87, 88, 90, 96, 98, 99, 104, 106, 108, 109, 110, 111, 113, 115, 116, 119, 121, 123, 124, 125, 126, 129, 131, 134, 137, 205, 208, 326

T

Taylor, Alfred Dundas 99
Tea 14, 20, 35, 175, 203
Terra Nullius 79, 248, 284, 294, 299, 302, 306, 311, 327
Trade bodies 61
Trade routes 2, 3, 8, 9, 15, 26, 40, 84, 107, 148, 193, 198, 217
Treaty of Nanjing (1842) 15, 21, 24, 46
Treaty of Yandabo 29
Trigonometry Survey of India 109, 131
Trincomalee 20, 34, 187, 240, 326
Troopship 23, 71, 151, 152, 154, 162, 166
Tropicality 24, 31, 32, 41, 62, 82, 101, 171

U

UNCLOS 172

V

Vernon, Edward 115, 306
Viceroy 94, 96, 103, 182, 190, 192, 198, 215, 316, 317, 319, 320, 321, 322, 323, 324
Viceroy of India 94, 103, 190, 215, 323. *See also* Viceroy
Victoria Cross, Victoria Crosses 157, 225, 312, 316

W

War Office 85, 225, 312
Washington, John 129
Weather 4, 19, 46, 55, 57, 58, 59, 73, 75, 93, 117, 118, 124, 125, 187
Westphalian framework 31, 53
Whitehall 121
Workboats 1